The German Polity

Seventh Edition

David P. Conradt

East Carolina University

New York   San Francisco   Boston
London   Toronto   Sydney   Tokyo   Singapore   Madrid
Mexico City   Munich   Paris   Capetown   Hong Kong   Montreal

Editor-in-Chief: Priscilla McGeehon
Senior Acquisitions Editor: Eric Stano
Associate Editor: Anita Castro
Marketing Manager: Megan Galvin-Fak
Production Manager: Patti Brecht
Project Coordination, Text Design, and Electronic Page Makeup: Pre-Press Company, Inc.
Cover Designer/Senior Manager: Nancy Danahy
Cover Photo: PhotoDisc, Inc.
Senior Manufacturing Buyer: Dennis J. Para
Printer and Binder: Courier Stoughton
Cover Printer: Phoenix Color Corp.

Library of Congress Cataloging-in-Publication Data

Conradt, David P.
    The German polity / David P. Conradt.— 7th ed.
        p. cm.
    Includes bibliographical references and index.
    ISBN 0-8013-1917-X
    1. Germany—Politics and government—1990– 2. Germany (East)—Politics and
government—1989-1990. I. Title.

    JN3971.A2 C63 2001
    320.943—dc21

                                                                            00-020242

Please visit our website at http://www.awlonline.com

ISBN 0-8013-1917-X

1 2 3 4 5 6 7 8 9 10—CRS—03 02 01 00

To Phillip, Thomas, and Elisabeth

Contents

CHAPTER 6   **ELECTIONS AND VOTING BEHAVIOR   145**

CHAPTER 7   **POLICYMAKING INSTITUTIONS I: PARLIAMENT AND EXECUTIVE   171**

Tables and Figures

TABLES

FIGURES

Preface

The end of the Kohl era, the return to power of the Social Democrats, the Greens' assumption of national political responsibility for the first time in their history, the quickening pace of European integration as seen above all in the introduction of a common European currency, German military participation in the NATO Serbian conflict over Kosovo, and the return of the national government to Berlin—these are some of the major developments that necessitate this new edition. These and other topics have been the subject of important research by social scientists on both sides of the Atlantic, which this edition attempts to incorporate.

This edition also gives us the opportunity to consider the first half-century of the Federal Republic—the most extensive and successful democratic political experience that has ever taken place on German soil. The events of the past fifty years—and indeed developments since the first edition in 1978—have confirmed the validity of *The German Polity*'s fundamental thesis: The Federal Republic has become an established liberal democracy with all of the problems and potential of other advanced industrial democracies. The success of the unification process thus far has been in part the result of the transformation of West German politics since 1949. Would Germany's neighbors, including those in Eastern Europe and the former Soviet Union, have consented to unification if West Germany had not shown its commitment to democratic values, the peaceful resolution of conflict, and European unity during the past five decades?

During the past decade, unification—the complex and difficult process of putting Germany back together again—has placed an added burden on the political, economic, and social systems. Initial hopes that the forty-year (1949–1989) division could be quickly overcome have been replaced by the sober realization that it will take at least a generation to achieve economic and cultural unification. Such a difficult process—the aftermath of unification—is examined in this new edition, especially in a greatly expanded Chapter 2. I have also attempted in Chapter 10 to explore in greater detail the question of Germany's new international role in the post-unification period. Sections on the 1998 federal election, the second since the 1990 unification; changes in the party system; and expanded treatments of major policy problems have also been added to this edition. The rest of the work has been updated and the findings of recent research incorporated in the text and cited in the expanded bibliography.

This edition also differs from its predecessors in the emphasis given to the role of international—and above all European—factors as important determinants of German politics and policy. Many of the trends and problems discussed in this new edition, such as high unemployment, slow economic growth, and soaring public deficits, are the result of Germany's poor adjustment to the demands of globalization. The fabled "social market economy" is now in crisis.

This study has benefited greatly from the stimulation and research support provided by institutions and colleagues on both sides of the Atlantic. The generous support of the Press and Information Office of the Federal Republic enabled the author to observe the 1998 campaign and election. Included in this trip were numerous interviews with leading candidates. The German-American *Arbeitskreis,* ably led by Wolfgang-Uwe Friedrich, provided generous support, which enabled me to conduct research in Germany on the aftermath of unification. In Germany, I am indebted to Jürgen W. Falter, Helmut Hoffmann, Max Kaase, Jürgen Kalkbrenner, Werner Kaltefleiter, Hans-Dieter Klingemann, Peter Müller, Ferdinand Müller-Rommel, Franz-Urban Pappi, Walter Picard, Lutz Reuter, Erwin K. Scheuch, Dieter Roth, Hans-Joachim Veen, and the late Rudolf Wildenmann. Special mention must go to the founder and director of the Institut für Demoskopie, Elisabeth Noelle-Neumann, who, over the years, has generously shared her invaluable archive of public opinion surveys. In the United States, Hannelore Köhler of the German Information Center in New York was willing to fax answers to my sometimes arcane queries about fast-breaking developments. All or parts of this and earlier editions were carefully read by Henry S. Albinski, M. Donald Hancock, David Klein, Hermann M. Kurthen, Peter Merkl, Charles A. Miller, Joyce Mushaben, Goldie Shabad, and James H. Wolfe. Their comments saved me from many embarrassing mistakes. Mark S. Wheeler also rendered major assistance in the preparation of this edition. I am also grateful to the following individuals who reviewed the manuscript for the seventh edition of this text: David Patton, Connecticut College; Henry S. Albinski, Pennsylvania State University; Arthur M. Hanhardt, Jr., University of Oregon; and Gebhard Schweigler, Georgetown University. I am, of course, solely responsible for any remaining errors of fact or judgment.

Introduction

This book seeks to provide an introduction to the modern German polity that will enable the student of comparative politics to acquire a detailed knowledge of this particular system and to compare it meaningfully with others.

This study departs from earlier treatments of the Federal Republic in its emphasis on the institutionalized character of the postwar system and the multiplicity of policy changes and conflicts that are now taking place within the Republic. In short, the key question is no longer whether Germany will remain a liberal democratic society, but what kind of democracy the Federal Republic has been and will be in the future. This approach does not deny the influence of the past on current institutions and processes; throughout the work, and especially in the treatment of national identity in Chapter 4, I have attempted to relate historical factors—particularly the Third Reich and World War II—to the current politics of the Republic. But this approach does suggest that a portrayal of the Republic as provisional or as one in which the leadership is insecure or anxious about its abilities to maintain the liberal democratic order is misleading. Indeed, as Josef Joffe has pointed out, the intensive and extensive examination of Germany's tragic past and, of course, above all the responsiblity of Germans for the Holocaust, has been and continues to be a vital part of the Federal Republic's identity and a major reason for Germany's half-century of peaceful and positive relationships with its neighbors in Europe and the larger world community.[1] The capacity of postwar Germans to undertake this painful confrontation with their past is an important factor in the Republic's international status. Entering the twenty-first century, the Federal Republic, in stark contrast to the position of earlier regimes, is surrounded by friends. For American and British students whose image of Germany derives largely from movies and television programs dealing with the Third Reich, this approach may provide a surprising but more realistic portrait of how Germans today conduct their politics.

THE STUDY OF GERMAN POLITICS

To the student of comparative politics, knowledge and understanding of the German polity is important for several reasons. First, Germany offers an excellent example of the complexities, difficulties, and tragedies of political development. In contrast to the experiences of the United States or Great Britain, political stability—much less democratic political stability—has been a rarity in the German political experience. Throughout its history, Germany frequently has faced the same basic problem confronting many less-developed countries: establishing a political order that achieves a balance of conflict and consensus, liberty and order, individualism and community, unity and diversity.

Second, German politics offers the student a laboratory in which to study political change. Within the last century not only specific governments but also the entire regime or form of government have been subject to frequent and sudden change. The empire proclaimed in 1871 collapsed with Germany's defeat in World War I and was followed by the formation of a democratic republic in 1919. This first attempt at political democracy lasted only fourteen years and was replaced in 1933 by the Nazi dictatorship. The Nazis' Thousand-Year Reich lasted only twelve years, with catastrophic consequences for Germany and the world. The destruction of the Nazi regime in 1945 brought a system of military occupation to Germany, which was followed in 1949 by the creation of two German states: a Federal Republic of Germany, composed of the American, British, and French zones of occupation; and a communist state, the German Democratic Republic (GDR) in the Soviet zone. In 1989–1990 the communist regime in the GDR collapsed. In East Germany's first free election in 1990, voters left little doubt that they wanted unification with West Germany as soon as possible. On October 3, 1990, East Germany ceased to exist as an independent state and joined the Federal Republic. Europe once again has a single German state. Thus in less than a century Germany has had two republics, one empire, one fascist dictatorship, one period of foreign military occupation, and one communist dictatorship. Few countries present the student with a better opportunity to examine the causes and consequences of such political change.

Third, German politics illustrates the effects of the international political system on domestic politics. As discussed in Chapters 1 and 2, the current political organization of the German people is the by-product of the postwar struggle between East and West and the end of that struggle in the early 1990s. The basic decisions from 1945 to 1949 that established the two German states and ceded large portions of the prewar *Reich* (literally, "kingdom") to the Soviet Union and Poland were not made by German political leaders. Similarly, the breaching of the Berlin Wall in 1989, the end of the East German state, and formal unification in 1990 were in part the consequences of Soviet president Gorbachev's reform policies. The politics of Germany, more than that of any other Western European country, have been affected by decisions made in Washington, Moscow, and elsewhere.

Fourth, the study of German politics gives the student an opportunity to examine one of the most important capitalist or market economies in the world today, and particularly the relationship between the policies of government and this economic system. For most of the past half-century Germany has dealt with the problems of inflation, unemployment, and economic growth more successfully than most of her neighbors and economic competitors. In fact, economic performance has been cited as a prime factor in the postwar growth of popular support for the values and institutions of liberal democracy. Yet in recent years the German economy has been slow to respond to the challenges of globalization. Unemployment is among the highest in Europe and economic growth now lags behind that of many of Germany's neighbors. What effect will economic "hard times" have on the political system?

Finally, Germany is a very important country in the international political system. It is the strongest member of the fifteen-nation European Union, accounting for over 30 percent of its total economic output. Germany has become the most powerful ally of the United States and will play a key role in the development of postcommunist societies in Eastern Europe and the former Soviet Union. Indeed, a knowledge and understanding of German politics offer the student insights into a key actor in the future of Europe and the international political system.

THE PLAN OF THE BOOK

A knowledge of the major historical developments preceding the establishment of the Federal Republic is essential background for the later chapters. This information is provided in Chapter 1. Chapter 2 examines the rise and fall of the communist regime in East Germany from 1949 to 1989, the unification process that culminated in October 1990 with the accession of the former East German territories into the Federal Republic, and the difficult challenge of putting Germany back together again. The social and economic structure of the Federal Republic is surveyed in Chapter 3. Emphasis in this chapter is placed on postwar changes and their impact on political attitudes and behavior. German political culture and participation, as well as the role and status of minority groups, are discussed in Chapter 4. The postwar party system, the key role of the three established parties (Social Democrats, Christian Democrats, and Free Democrats), and the emergence of the Greens, along with the activity of the major postwar interest groups, are the topics of Chapter 5. Postwar elections and electoral politics are analyzed in Chapter 6. The major national policymaking institutions—the parliament, executive, bureaucracy, courts, and an array of semipublic institutions—are the subjects of Chapters 7 and 8. Germany's subnational governmental units—the states and local communities—are examined in Chapter 9. The work concludes in Chapter 10 with an examination of several current and future policy problems confronting the Federal Republic, including a discussion of Germany's future international political role.

The book attempts to develop two major themes. First, since 1949, the Federal Republic has achieved a degree of legitimacy and consensus unmatched by any other German regime in this century; Germany and the Germans have changed.

1 The Historical Setting

Established in 1949, the Federal Republic of Germany is certainly one of Europe's younger states. Yet the people within its borders belong to one of Europe's oldest linguistic, ethnic, and cultural units—the German nation. This nation dates back at least to A.D. 843, when Charlemagne's empire was partitioned following his death into the West Frankish (much of modern France), Central Frankish (the modern Netherlands, Belgium, Alsace, and Lorraine), and East Frankish (modern Germany) empires. The East Frankish empire under Otto the Great (936–973) was later proclaimed the Holy Roman Empire. But neither this first empire, or *Reich,* nor any of its successors has ever united all of Europe's German-speaking peoples into a single state with a strong central government.

THE FIRST REICH

The medieval Reich was, in fact, a loose-knit collection of many different regions, each with distinct dialects and varying degrees of economic and military strength. Although this empire held together formally and was not finally abolished until the time of Napoleon, it had in fact ceased to exist as a viable political entity by the end of the seventeenth century. The first German Reich then became little more than a fragmented collection of hundreds of principalities and free cities.[1] While the process of building a unified nation-state continued in Britain and France, the German peoples of Central Europe were deeply divided. This decentralization of political authority, characteristic of feudalism, meant that many separate political institutions and processes took root within the German nation.

Through Luther's translation of the Bible into High German, the Reformation of the sixteenth century brought a uniform style of written German, but it did little else to facilitate unity and integration. Indeed, it divided Central Europe still further into Protestant and Catholic territories. The Thirty Years War (1618–1648) that followed the Reformation was fought largely on German soil, with the different German states

FIGURE 1.1   The Federal Republic of Germany today

- - - Former East-West Border

allied with various foreign powers, fighting one another. The war severely weakened the states, both individually and collectively. On the eve of Europe's transformation from an agrarian-feudal to a capitalist-urban society, much of Germany—unlike Britain or France—remained backward and divided, lacking

1. a strong central state with established administrative, legislative, and legal institutions;

2. a middle class growing in political importance; and

3. an emerging secular culture.

THE RISE OF PRUSSIA

The second major effort at unifying Germany began in a distant eastern territory on the Baltic sea: the province of Brandenburg in 1701 proclaimed itself the Kingdom of Prussia. Ruled by the Hohenzollern dynasty, Prussia undertook a territorial expansion at the expense of its Slavic neighbors while other German states served as the helpless pawns of the far stronger nation-states of France, Sweden, England, and Spain. Although it was a relatively poor and backward area, Prussia under the Hohenzollerns did have a series of skillful monarchs, from Frederick William (1640–1786), through Frederick the Great (1744–1786), who through wars, diplomatic coups, and a strong and efficient administration transformed Prussia into one of Europe's great powers. Lacking wealth or natural resources, the Hohenzollerns demanded discipline, hard work, and sacrifice from their subjects. It was the first German state with a bureaucracy and army comparable to those of the major powers of Western Europe.

This style of politics worked, but there was little room in the Prussian system for the values of political liberalism, which together with nationalism had begun to sweep Western Europe in the wake of the French Revolution. Moreover, the Prussian approach to politics was also disliked and feared by many smaller German states and free cities, which admired Prussian successes but were less enthusiastic about the emphasis on authoritarian discipline and territorial expansion through military conquest.

The misgivings of the various German states regarding Prussia soon gave way, however, to a far greater concern with revolutionary France under Napoleon. Beginning in 1806, Napoleon invaded and dissolved most of the small German principalities, consolidating them into larger units and, in effect, preparing the way for the third major effort at unification. By invading Germany, the French also brought the ideologies of nationalism and liberalism, which found considerable support among the small but growing urban middle classes, especially in the western German states.

Following Napoleon's defeat, under the settlement reached at the Congress of Vienna in 1815, the number of German political units was reduced to thirty-nine. Only two of them—Prussia under the Hohenzollerns and Austria under the Hapsburgs—had the size and resources needed to create a single unified German nation-state. Between 1815 and 1866, these states formed a confederation within which the struggle for supremacy between Prussia and Austria took place.

With its multinational empire, Austria felt far less enthusiastic about German nationalism and unity than did Prussia or the liberals in the other states. The Hapsburgs preferred a weak confederation and defended the autonomy of the constituent units. Most liberals, although still distrustful of Prussia, were also committed to national unity.

In 1848 liberal uprisings in Berlin, Vienna, Frankfurt, and elsewhere culminated in the convening of a parliament in Frankfurt to draft a liberal constitution for a unified state that was to include a constitutional monarch. However, the German liberals of 1848, predominantly middle-class intellectuals and professionals, were at least a generation behind their British counterparts in political finesse and expertise. They were unable to agree whether a Prussian or an Austrian should become emperor, and their own disunity allowed the various rulers in the constituent states to regain power. When the parliament finally offered the crown to the Prussian king, he scornfully rejected it, and the Revolution of 1848 was soon crushed by Prussian and Austrian troops loyal to the monarchs. If Germany was to have a second Reich, it would not be acquired through political liberalism.

After 1848 the Prussian and Austrian rivalry continued within the confederation, but the combination of Prussian military superiority and the skillful diplomacy and leadership of the Prussian prime minister, Otto von Bismarck, overwhelmed the larger but internally divided Austria. Prussia under Bismarck fought successfully against Denmark (1864), Austria (1866), and France (1870), thereby establishing its hegemony in most of the northern German states. These military successes dazzled the political liberals and won most of them over to the rather illiberal empire. In 1871, after some last-minute bargaining with the reluctant southern Germans, Bismarck was able to inform the Prussian king that all the German princes and free cities such as Hamburg, Bremen, and Lübeck wanted him to accept the imperial crown. Thus at Versailles, the temporary headquarters of the army after the victorious war against France, Wilhelm I became the Kaiser (emperor) of the Second Reich.

THE EMPIRE (1871–1918)

The second Reich was largely Bismarck's creation, and he dominated German and European politics for almost the next two decades. His constitution for the empire, a complex structure, ensured Prussian hegemony behind a liberal and federal facade. The emperor, who was also the Prussian king, appointed the chancellor (head of government), who was responsible to him and not to the parliament. The chancellor then appointed his cabinet ministers. Moreover, the key policy areas of defense and foreign affairs were largely the domains of the emperor and chancellor. Parliament had only indirect control over these matters through its power of appropriations. But in the event of a deadlock between chancellor and parliament, the constitution gave sweeping emergency powers to the emperor.

The imperial parliament was bicameral. A lower house (*Reichstag*) was directly elected on the basis of universal male suffrage, but important legislation also required approval by the upper house (*Bundesrat,* or federal council), which was dominated by Prussia. This upper house was composed of delegates sent by the governments of the constituent states; its members were thus not directly elected by the people. Prussia, as the largest state, controlled 17 of the chamber's 58 votes and could in fact veto most legislation. The Prussian government, which sent and instructed these delegates, was led by the omnipresent Bismarck, who was both Premier of Prussia and chancellor of the Reich. To complete the picture, Bismarck headed the Prussian delegation to the Bundesrat and, as leader of the largest state, served as president of the upper house. Bismarck's power within Prussia was based not only on his relationship to the king, but also on a voting system for elections to the Prussian parliament that was heavily weighted in favor of conservative, nationalist, and upper-status groups. Thus Bismarck, who brought the empire into being, also dominated its politics.

Although it was strongly biased in favor of Prussian executive power, this complex system was nonetheless far from being a totalitarian or even a dictatorial state. The lower house was directly elected and did exercise considerable authority over appropriations. There were also some genuine federal elements in the system. The states had major responsibilities for education, domestic order and security (police), and cultural affairs.

Bismarck's success in creating this empire, his resultant prestige and heroic stature, and his unquestioned political skill enabled him, for the most part, to control both parliament and the states. In addition to the conservatives, the middle-class liberals were especially fascinated by his foreign policy successes. In retrospect, they should have known better and worked to increase the power of parliament instead of generally supporting the continued dominance of traditional Prussian elites—the nationalistic nobility and military.

WORLD WAR I AND THE COLLAPSE OF THE SECOND REICH

As long as Bismarck led the Prussian and Reich governments, the complex system could survive and, indeed, prosper. After 1871 the new Reich was unquestionably the strongest military power in continental Europe and was rivaled in the world only by Great Britain with its still superior fleet. A period of rapid industrialization and urbanization after 1871 brought relative economic prosperity as well. Forging the Second Reich, Bismarck and the Prussians made many enemies in Europe—chiefly France, humiliated in the 1870 Franco-Prussian War and deprived of the regions of Alsace and Lorraine. Russia was also fearful of further German expansion. Bismarck was able to prevent a French-Russian alliance, although his successors were not.

Neither were they able to contain the further growth of imperialist sentiment, which was manifested in the German effort at the turn of the century to expand its fleet in order to match or exceed that of Great Britain and to acquire, like Britain and France, an extensive overseas empire. Indeed, one of the most romantic nationalists in Germany at this time was Kaiser Wilhelm II.

As the political power of the middle classes in Britain and France grew and generally exerted a moderating influence on policy, in the Prussian-dominated Second Reich the old feudal classes—nobility, military, large landowners—maintained and expanded their domestic hegemony while pursuing defense and foreign policies designed to unify a divided society and maintain their own position of power.

Between 1871 and 1914 Germany was a society that was rapidly modernizing yet was still ruled by traditional elites. The middle class, expanding in size because of this modernization, did not assume and—for the most part—did not seek political power and influence commensurate with its socioeconomic importance.

This faulted social and political order could not survive a lengthy war. Indeed, World War I exposed its fatal weaknesses. After the failure of the initial German offensive in the West, designed to produce a quick victory, the prospect of a protracted conflict began to make manifest the latent tensions and contradictions in the social and political structure of the Second Reich. The Liberal, Socialist, and Catholic political parties in the parliament became less enthusiastic about supporting a war against countries such as Britain and the United States, whose level of constitutional democracy they hoped some day to achieve in Germany. Indeed, victory would strengthen the authoritarian regime. Food and raw materials became ever more scarce as imports, which had accounted for one-third of prewar supplies, dwindled under the pressure of the Allied blockade. Officially forbidden strikes broke out in various industries as workers reacted to mounting casualty lists and severe wartime rationing. A virtual military dictatorship emerged by 1917 as the army, intent on achieving maximum production and mobilization, began to make key political, social, and economic decisions. However, when the army could not deliver victory, the generals, chief among them Erich Ludendorff, advised the Kaiser to call for a cease fire and abdicate. The parliamentary leadership then proclaimed a republic and attempted to negotiate a peace with the Western powers.

THE WEIMAR REPUBLIC (1919–1933)

The departure of the Kaiser, and the proclamation of a republic in the wake of Germany's surrender, took place in an atmosphere of increasing revolutionary fervor. Mindful of the Bolshevik success in Russia, several German Marxists split from the moderate Social Democratic party (SPD) and formed the Spartakus League, which later became the Communist party (KPD). Workers' and soldiers' councils based on the Bolshevik model were formed in major cities. In Bavaria, a short-lived Soviet socialist republic was proclaimed. Germany seemed for a time to be on the verge of a communist revolution.

Conservatives and middle-class liberals combined with the Social Democrats to crush the communist uprising with military and paramilitary units. Many conservatives and nationalists, shocked at the prospect of a communist revolution, were willing to accept, at least in the short run, a parliamentary republic. In the small town of Weimar in 1919, a constitution was prepared and later ratified by a constituent assembly. Germany's first attempt at liberal democracy had begun.

The Weimar Constitution, drafted by learned constitutional and legal scholars, was widely acclaimed as one of the most democratic in the world. It featured universal adult suffrage; proportional representation; extensive provisions for popular referenda, petition, and recall; and an extensive catalogue of civil liberties. The constitution created a dual executive: a chancellor as head of government appointed by the president but enjoying the confidence of the lower house, and a directly elected president as chief of state. The president under Article 48 also had the power to issue decrees in lieu of legislation in case of a state of emergency. Many historians and political scientists cite this latter provision as a major defect of the document.

The Weimar Republic could hardly have been started under less favorable circumstances. Defeat and national humiliation following the world war, widespread political violence, severe economic and social dislocation, and a political leadership with no real executive policymaking experience were major "birth defects" that the new state never entirely surmounted. The World War I peace settlement saddled Germany with a huge war debt; deprived it of 15 percent of its arable land and 10 percent of its population; and ensured the loss of all its foreign colonies and investments, much of its military and merchant fleet, and its railway stock. Conservatives and nationalists, soon forgetting the help of liberals and socialists in defeating the communists, openly opposed the new system. The military, whose antirepublican officer corps was never purged, fostered the myth that Germany in World War I had been stabbed in the back by liberal, socialist, and Marxist civilian politicians. For some, the entire Weimar Republic was a Jewish, liberal conspiracy—a system devised by criminals. The bureaucracy and especially the judiciary harbored many avowed opponents of democracy who were never removed from their positions. Likewise, on the left, communists and some socialists viewed Weimar only as a brief prelude to the socialist revolution that, in their view, had been only delayed by the failure of the radical revolutionaries in 1918.

Shortly after its inauspicious beginning, the Republic had to confront an attempted military coup (the Kapp *Putsch* of 1920), a disastrous wave of inflation that virtually wiped out the savings of the middle class (1922–1923), an attempted communist revolution in the state of Saxony (1923), Hitler's unsuccessful Putsch in Munich (1923), and the French occupation of the Rhineland due to Weimar's inability to pay the huge war debts imposed by the victorious Allies at Versailles.

For an all-too-brief period in the mid-1920s Weimar nonetheless appeared to have stabilized itself. Long-term loans from the United States and less stringent payment plans eased the war debt problem and aided the state's economic recovery. Conservatives appeared to be slowly accepting the system as legitimate, and the election in 1925 of the World War I hero Paul von Hindenburg as president brought still more conservatives and nationalists into a position of at least tacit acceptance of the Weimar Republic.

But the worldwide depression sparked by the collapse of the U.S. stock market in 1929 dealt a new blow from which Weimar never rallied. By 1931 roughly half of all German families were directly affected by unemployment. Voters began to desert the republican parties. Between 1919 and 1932 the proportion of the electorate supporting the Social Democrats, the Liberals, and the Catholic centrists declined from 64 percent to only 30 percent. The big gainers were the Nazis on the right and the Communists on the left. Between 1930 and 1933 no government could secure majority support in the lower house of parliament (the Reichstag). Indeed, by 1932 the two antisystem parties, the Nazis and Communists—who both in their own way were determined to overthrow the institution to which they belonged—had a majority of seats. The president, a now aging von Hindenburg, ambivalent toward parliamentary democracy, in fact governed by the decree-granting powers given him in Article 48 of the constitution.

The Nazi Seizure of Power

By 1932 the Nazis had legally become the strongest party in the Reichstag. Conservatives and nationalists wanted them in a right-wing government but refused to accept the demand of their leader, Adolf Hitler, that he lead such a government. Support for the liberal, prodemocratic parties had dwindled to such a point that they had little influence. German politics were polarized between a growing antisystem right, headed by the Nazis, and an increasingly radical left, composed of

Communists and splinter socialist groups. Caught between these extremes and plagued by internal divisions, the democratic middle was unable to act decisively to save the Republic. After extensive behind-the-scenes intrigue, some conservatives persuaded the now almost senile von Hindenburg that Hitler and the Nazis could be handled by traditional authoritarian conservatives and asked him to make Hitler the chancellor of a new conservative-nationalist government. Von Hindenburg agreed, and on January 30, 1933, Hitler became chancellor. By March 1933, Hitler had eliminated all significant opposition in parliament after the Nazis pushed through an Enabling Act that essentially granted him dictatorial powers. The Third Reich, which was to have lasted a thousand years, had begun.

Why did the Weimar Republic fail? What happened to make a highly developed modern society turn to the primitive racist and nationalist appeals of the Nazis? Certainly there is no more important question confronting the student of modern German history. Some historians view Hitler's triumph as an abnormal, unique event unrelated to previous German historical and political development. They emphasize (1) the specific set of circumstances facing interwar Germany and Europe, coupled with (2) defects in the Weimar Constitution, especially proportional representation, which worked to the benefit of small splinter parties and increased the difficulty of forming stable majorities in parliament. Thus with at times only 3 percent of the vote, the Nazis were still represented in the Reichstag as a very noisy minority. The dual executive of the Weimar system, which created a strong president independent of parliament, has also been cited by numerous analysts. The mediocre leadership of the democratic parties, the absence of any strong commitment to the system among some of its supporters, the behavior of key personalities such as von Hindenburg, and the effects of the foreign policies of the victorious Western powers are cited as other factors that contributed to the Nazi dictatorship.[2]

Had one or more of these factors been lacking, the Nazi seizure of power could have been avoided. According to this view, there was nothing inevitable about Nazism; it represented a clear break from Germany's course of political development.

Many non-German historians, especially those from the United States and Britain, have taken a different approach to the origins of the Third Reich. They see Nazism more as the logical, if not predictable, outcome of German historical development and political culture.[3] They point to the absence of a liberal middle-class revolution, which did occur elsewhere, as in France and Britain; and the later unification of the Reich, which occurred not on the basis of constitutional procedures but through the "blood and iron" policies of Bismarck. The cultural emphasis on authoritarian values—deference and obedience to superiors, reverence for order and discipline—and the hierarchical character of child rearing in the family and school are also cited. In addition, the German tradition of political philosophy (with its particular stress on *statism,* the treatment of the state as an organization superior to other social organizations), collectivism, intolerance toward minorities, especially Jews, and the absence of a strong tradition of liberal individualism in political theory have also been singled out as precursors of Nazism.[4]

Other scholars emphasize the disunity and internal contradictions within the German middle class as a major factor in the collapse of the Weimar system. According to this perspective, the capitalist class was divided among heavy industry, export industry, and the *Mittelstand* (lower-middle class of shopkeepers, artisans, and some salaried employees). Each of these groups had a somewhat different view of what kind of Republic it wanted and, above all, of the extent to which it was willing to cooperate with Germany's manual workers and their major political party—the Social Democrats. Internal disunity plagued the capitalist camp throughout the Republic and left it with no viable alternative to the Nazis after 1930, when further cooperation with the Social Democrats became impossible for all capitalist groups; that is, when none was willing to support or finance the social welfare programs that were an indispensable condition of any continuation of a coalition with the Social Democrats. According to this view, Nazism or fascism was not the inevitable result of the capitalist system but, rather the consequence of the German middle class's inability to develop an alternative solution (e.g., a presidential dictatorship or a corporatist system) to the post-1930 economic and political crisis.[5]

A fourth category of explanation stresses the relationship between socioeconomic structure and National Socialism. Specifically, the success of the Nazis is explained by the support of the German upper and middle classes who, fearing a socialist revolution and their loss of status more than incipient fascism, gave Hitler and the Nazis key political and financial support. Other analysts have argued that fascism is a phase in the development of late capitalist societies and the Nazis simply exploited this conservative aversion to the democratization of German political, social, and economic life, something the Weimar Republic might eventually have achieved had it not been for the conservative counterrevolution. As we discuss in Chapter 3, some critics of the Federal Republic have argued that it represents a restoration following the Nazi defeat, of the same capitalist institutions and processes that produced fascism in 1933.

THE NAZI THIRD REICH AND WORLD WAR II

The Nazi or National Socialist German Workers party (NSDAP), was only one of numerous radical nationalist and *völkisch* (racialist) parties and movements that sprang up in the chaotic atmosphere of postwar Germany. Founded in 1919 in Munich, the party probably would have remained insignificant and eventually have disappeared had it not been for the extraordinary leadership ability of Adolf Hitler. The son of a low-level Austrian civil servant, Hitler had fought in World War I as a volunteer for the German army. Before the war he was a sometime art student in Vienna, where he absorbed the pan-German nationalism, anti-Semitism, and anti-Marxism characteristic of right-wing circles in the Austrian capital. A powerful orator, Hitler quickly assumed leadership of the National Socialists, and by the early 1920s the party had become the most prominent of the radical right-wing groups in Munich. In 1923 the Nazis, allied with other nationalist groups including one led by World War I hero Ludendorff, made an amateurish attempt to overthrow the Bavarian government and trigger a revolution throughout Germany. The *Putsch* (coup) failed, and Hitler was arrested and tried for treason; although convicted, he was treated very leniently by sympathetic Bavarian authorities.

Imprisoned—or, rather, detained for two years, Hitler used the time to outline his future political plans in his book *Mein Kampf* ("My Struggle"), which appeared in 1928 and became the oft-cited but seldom read "bible" of the Nazi movement. The Munich fiasco convinced Hitler that in order to succeed, the party would have to come to power legally. A legal seizure of power would ensure the Nazis the support of most of the bureaucracy, the judiciary, and the army. Thus with a program that promised a national renewal, rearmament, revision of the hated Versailles Treaty, and social and economic reform for the working classes, the Nazis attempted to appeal to all members of the "racialist community" (*Volksgemeinschaft*). The party was particularly attractive for the marginal groups in German society: the small shopkeepers and artisans caught between big labor and big business, the small farmers losing out to larger enterprises and middlemen, the unemployed university graduates or university dropouts blaming the system for their condition. Yet in spite of its program and well-developed propaganda apparatus, the party remained a negligible factor until the Great Depression. Not until the economic crisis of 1929 could the Nazis break through and become the strongest force in the antirepublican camp.

After the appointment of Hitler as chancellor and the March 1933 Enabling Act, which suspended the parliament and constitution and essentially gave the Nazis carte blanche, the process of consolidating totalitarian one-party rule began in earnest. What Hitler and the Nazis sought was the *Gleichschaltung,* or coordination, of all areas of German life to the Nazi pattern. By the end of 1934 this objective was largely accomplished; all major social, economic, and political institutions were brought under the control of the party and were subjected to reorganizations corresponding to the party's hierarchic, centralized structure. The leadership principle—unquestioning obedience and acceptance of the *Führer's* (leader's) will as the highest law and authority—became the overriding organizational criterion.

Most Nazi coordination efforts took place under the pretext of legality. The burning of the Reichstag in February 1933 was used to secure a presidential emergency decree outlawing the Communist party and simultaneously allowing the Nazis to destroy the independence of the Reich's constituent states. Even the murder of hundreds of counterrevolutionary SA (storm troop) leaders and other "enemies" in June 1934 was later legalized by the puppet parliament.

This pattern of lawlessness or flagrant manipulation of the law lasted until the collapse of the regime through military defeat in 1945. Indeed, there was little qualitative difference between the June 1934 murders, the elimination of other political and racial enemies in the concentration camps, and the later extermination of six million Jews.

Rule by a racially "superior" elite, manipulation of the racially acceptable but "stupid" masses, and the extermination of Jews and other "inferior" peoples was, according to one authority, "the only genuine kernel of Hitler's ideology."[6] The socialist aspect of National Socialism and Hitler's professed opposition to plutocracy were designed to generate mass support for the leader.

Regardless of the party's rhetoric or the views of its "left" wing, whose leaders were liquidated or had fled by 1934, "a strong state and the leadership principle, not economic and social reform, were the ideas guiding Hitler's policies on capitalism and socialism, organizations and group interests, reform and revolution."[7]

As Hitler promised in *Mein Kampf,* the elimination of the Jews as the greatest threat to the German *Volk* (race) began shortly after the seizure of power. On April 1, 1933, the Nazis initiated a boycott of Jewish shops in Berlin. Over succeeding months Jews were dismissed from political positions and limited in their economic activities. In 1935 the Nuremberg Race Laws deprived Germany's half-million Jews of all political and civil liberties. Terror and violence were used on a mass scale beginning in November 1938 when the Nazis used the assassination of a German diplomat in Paris by a young Jew as an excuse to loot and burn Jewish shops and synagogues throughout the Reich. Moreover, the remaining Jews were forced to pay for the damages caused by the Nazi mobs. By 1939 about 400,000 German and Austrian Jews had emigrated. Most of the remaining 300,000 were eventually to suffer the same fate as the rest of European Jewry, namely mass extermination.

There can be little doubt that the Nazi regime, at least until the onset of World War II, enjoyed considerable mass support. Even in 1951, 42 percent of adult West Germans and 53 percent of those over 35 still stated that the prewar years of the Third Reich (1933–1939) were the "best" that Germany had experienced in this century. Those were years of economic growth and at least a surface prosperity. Unemployment was virtually eliminated; inflation was checked; and the economy, fueled by expenditures for rearmament and public works, boomed. The fact during these "good years" thousands of Germans were imprisoned, tortured, and murdered in concentration camps, and hundreds of thousands of German Jews systematically persecuted, was apparently of minor importance to most citizens in comparison with the economic and policy successes of the regime. In fact, the suppression of civil liberties and all political opposition—along with the *Gleichschaltung* of the churches, schools, universities, the press, and trade unions—was accepted with little overt opposition. In a sense most Germans (at least between 1933 and 1939) were willing to give up the democratic political order and the liberal society and accept the regime's racism and persecution of political opponents in exchange for economic prosperity, social stability, and a resurgence of national pride.

Yet sizable segments of German society remained relatively immune to the Nazis even after Hitler became chancellor in January 1933. For example, the Nazis never received an absolute majority of votes in any free election during the Weimar Republic. Even in the last election in March 1933 (approximately five weeks after Hitler took power), which was less free than preceding polls because of Nazi agitation and terror tactics against opposing parties, the party received only 44 percent of the vote; in some electoral districts its support was as low as 10 or 20 percent. Catholics and Socialists with strong ties to the highly developed secondary organizations of the church and party, such as youth, labor, and women's groups, were especially resistant to Nazi appeals.

From the beginning, the Nazi system was directed at the total mobilization of Germany for the purpose of conducting an aggressive war. Military expansion was intended not only to secure *Lebensraum* (living space) for the superior German race but also to justify one-party dictatorship and unify the racial community. Capitalizing on the internal weaknesses and division among the major European democracies (Britain and France), the isolationist United States, and a suspicious Soviet Union, Hitler marched from success to success beginning with the 1938 annexation of Austria and the Sudetenland, until late 1942 when Soviet troops finally turned the tide at Stalingrad. Each military and foreign political success strengthened the Nazi system at home, while at the same time rendering the small and scattered opposition groups unable to mount any serious challenge to the regime.

It was not until July 1944, less than a year before the end of the war, that a group of military officers and civilian opponents made a desperate attempt at a coup d'état. But the key element in the plan, the assassination of Hitler, failed—with the result that the entire opposition movement was soon crushed by large scale arrests and executions.

In territories conquered by the German armies, the full horror of Nazism was experienced. To establish Hitler's "New Order," millions of European civilians and prisoners of war—men, women, and children—were systematically murdered by special Nazi extermination units and even regular German army personnel. In the name of the German people, "useless human material"—the mentally retarded in hospitals and asylums and Europe's gypsies—were murdered. Also marked for extermination were actual or potential political opponents—the Polish intelligentsia, the political commissars in the Soviet army, and the resistance fighters. Finally, military conquest meant the "final solution" of the "Jewish problem." At large camps serviced by special railway lines and selected Nazi personnel, six million European Jews were murdered.

Although the SS (elite guard) mobile killing squads and extermination camps were officially a top secret, there is little doubt that millions of ordinary Germans knew something of the Jews' fate and that very few made any effort to find out more about what the Nazis and the German army were doing in the occupied territories, much less to try and stop it.[8] Caught up in the demands of war, subjected to incessant propaganda, and fearful of the regime's extensive domestic terror apparatus, which included the secret police (*Gestapo*) and informers among the civilian population, most Germans remained passive until the end.

But many ordinary Germans also remained passive because they profited from the Holocaust by acquiring the stolen assets of murdered Jews. In Hamburg alone between March 1942 and July 1943 at least 100,000 households were the recipients of property (furniture, clothing, jewelry) stolen primarily from Dutch and French Jews.[9] The bank accounts, stocks, real estate, insurance policies, and social security contributions of murdered Jews enriched the Reich's treasury. From these stolen Jewish assets Germany bought "iron ore from Sweden, butter and machines from Switzerland, grain, cooking oil and aluminum from Hungary. In the final analysis every German had something on his or her table that came from the assets of murdered Jews."[10] Finally, there is increasing evidence that many Germans embraced the Nazis' anti-Semitic message—that is, they supported the elimination of the Jews from German society.[11]

The Third Reich finally collapsed in May 1945 as American, Soviet, British, French, and their Allied forces totally defeated the German armies and occupied the Reich. Unlike 1918, there could be no stab-in-the-back legend following this defeat. The defeat and destruction of the Nazi system brought military occupation and massive uncertainty about the future of Germany as a national community, much less a political system. Point Zero, the absolute bottom, had been reached.

FOREIGN OCCUPATION AND NATIONAL DIVISION

Between 1945 and 1949, Germany's conquerors reduced the size of its territory, divided the remainder into four zones of military occupation, and established two new states out of these zones: the Federal Republic of Germany (British, French, and American zones) and the German Democratic Republic (Soviet zone). All territories annexed by the Nazis between 1938 and 1941 were returned to their former Austrian, Czechoslovakian (the Sudetenland), Yugoslavian (Slovenia), or French (Alsace-Lorraine) owners. Consistent with the Allied agreements at Yalta, those German areas east of the Oder and Neisse rivers (the Oder-Neisse line), including East Prussia and Silesia, were put under "temporary" Soviet or Polish administration. The ultimate fate of these eastern territories was to be decided by a final peace treaty between Germany and the wartime Allies. However, such a treaty was never signed because of the Cold War. In 1970 and again in 1991, following the accession of East Germany into the Federal Republic, treaties with the Soviet Union and Poland recognized their losses as permanent. Most Germans living in these regions had been expelled by Soviet and Polish forces after 1945 and resettled in the remaining German territory. Many expellees died or were murdered en route to the West. Deprived of their property without compensation, the surviving expellees had to build new lives in what remained of a war-ravaged country. The integration of some ten million refugees into postwar German society was but one major task confronting the new Federal Republic in 1949.

The rest of the prewar Reich was divided into British, French, American, and Soviet zones of occupation. The former capital, Berlin, lying within the Soviet zone, was given special status and was also divided into four sectors. Each military commander exercised authority in his respective zone; and an Allied Control Council, composed of the four commanders, was jointly and unanimously to make decisions affecting Germany as a whole.

During the war the Allies had determined the general lines of postwar policy toward Germany:

1. Germany was to be *denazified;* all vestiges of the Nazi system were to be removed, its top Nazi and government officials tried as war criminals, and lesser party activists punished by fines and imprisonment.

2. The country was to be *demilitarized,* with its capability to wage aggressive war permanently removed.

3. Postwar Germany was to become a *democratic* society. To this end, extensive programs of political education were to be designed and implemented in the postwar period. A complete reform of the education system was included under this democratization program.

4. The former Reich was to be *decentralized,* with important political responsibilities delegated to states (*Länder*) and local governments under a system of constitutional federalism.

THE FORMATION OF
THE FEDERAL REPUBLIC

The wartime consensus that produced these policy plans quickly disintegrated after 1945, as differences between the three Western powers and the Soviet Union made any common occupation policy impossible. In the Soviet occupation zone, local governments controlled by Communist party officials or pro-Soviet elements were quickly established. Entire plants were dismantled and shipped to the Soviet Union; the remaining industry was eventually nationalized and agriculture collectivized.

These actions, basically designed to turn the Soviet zone into a communist state and society, were politically and ideologically unacceptable to the Western powers already alarmed by similar Soviet moves in Poland and Hungary. By 1948 it was apparent that no all-German political or economic cooperation was possible. In the face of what was perceived by Western policymakers to be a growing Soviet threat, the Western Allies began to envision a postwar German state excluding the Soviet zone of occupation—a West German entity composed of the American, British, and French zones. The French were reluctant at first to agree to the establishment of even a centralized West German state, which might become a power rivaling France on the European continent. By 1948, however, French fear of the Soviet Union exceeded its fear of Germany, enabling the three Western Allies to announce a common economic policy and issue a common currency in their zones. The Soviet Union responded with an attempt to deny the Western powers access to Berlin (the Berlin Blockade, June 1948 to May 1949) and undertook the construction of another separate German state in its zone, the German Democratic Republic (GDR) with its capital in East Berlin (see Figure 1.1).

By the late 1940s it was thus clear that neither the United States nor the Soviet Union were prepared to allow "their" Germans to pursue policies that they could not control and that could possibly be directed against their interests. Each superpower wanted a single German state only on its own terms: a liberal, pluralistic democratic state for the United States; a communist, worker-and-peasant state for the Soviet Union. Unable to achieve such a unified state without military conflict, the two superpowers settled for two states, each having the social, economic, and political characteristics of its respective protector. Ironically, the division of Germany enabled both states within a relatively short time to achieve a status within their respective power bloc that a single German state could never have attained.

These fateful developments, which sealed the division and dismemberment of the prewar Reich, took place with little direct German participation, even though German governments had existed at the local and state levels since 1946. The initial intent of Western and especially American occupiers was to democratize Germany in stages, beginning at the local level, where a stronger tradition of democratic self-government existed. Thus the establishment of local and state institutions *preceded* the creation of central institutions for West Germany.

Most Germans were not concerned with the future of the nation nor with their own responsibility or guilt relative to Nazism, much less with politics. Their immediate problem was physical survival: food, clothing, and shelter. According to surveys, six out of every ten Germans stated that they "suffered greatly" from hunger in the postwar years. The average caloric intake during the period 1945–1947 was less than 70 percent of that deemed adequate.[12] Almost half of all families suffered partial or total loss of their households through bombing raids. After physical survival came the problem of putting their personal lives back together again: returning to school, resuming a career, starting the business again, finding a job, or raising a fatherless family. Thus the events and decisions between 1945 and 1949 so crucial to the birth of the Federal Republic were made within a context of mass indifference to politics. Germans in the immediate postwar years had reduced their sphere of social concern to the most basic level: the self and the immediate family.

On July 1, 1948, the three Western Allied military governors met in Frankfurt with the *Ministerpräsidenten,* or premiers, of the various states and "recommended" (i.e., ordered) the calling of a constituent assembly by September 1, 1948, which was to draft a constitution for the three Western zones. This constitution was then to be placed before the electorate for approval. None of the state premiers was enthusiastic about establishing a separate West German state, fearing that the constituent assembly and the resultant constitution would seal the division of Germany. Meeting before the assembly with the leaders of the two major political parties, the state executives decided to term the document they were to draft a "Basic Law" rather than a constitution and to stress in it the provisional character of the new state. After a long delay, the states finally convened an assembly to draft the document. Nine months later, in May 1949, their work was completed. Again, wanting to avoid the appearance of permanence, they asked for ratification through the state parliaments rather than through popular referendum. This proved acceptable to the Allied authorities. Thus the West German constitution was never directly approved by the citizens of West Germany.

The declaration of ratification hardly evoked any celebration. One influential news magazine termed the document a "bastard of a constitution" produced in nine months through pressure by the military occupation.[13] In one national survey conducted at the time, 40 percent of the adult population stated that they were indifferent to the constitution, 33 percent were "moderately interested," and only 21 percent were "very interested." Only 51 percent, in another 1949 survey, favored the creation of the Federal Republic; the remainder of the sample were either against it (23 percent), indifferent (13 percent), or undecided (13 percent).[14] Like it or not, however, Germans in the Western-occupied zones of the former Reich had a new constitution and political system that took effect on May 23, 1949.

As we discuss throughout the remainder of this book, according to standards used to judge political systems and especially in comparison to past regimes, the institutions of the Federal Republic have performed well. The reluctant drafters of the constitution produced a document that, unlike the constitution of the Weimar Republic, has survived to structure meaningfully the behavior of Germans and their political decision makers. Moreover, the success of the West German political order served as a powerful model and magnet for East Germans living under a one-party communist system.

On October 7, 1949, the thirty-second anniversary of the Communist revolution in Russia, a second postwar German state, the German Democratic Republic (GDR), was proclaimed in East Berlin. The boundaries of this state corresponded to the Soviet zone of military occupation. The rise and fall of the GDR, the chain of events that rapidly led to the unification of Germany in October 1990, and the difficult post-unification period that has followed are the subjects of Chapter 2, "Putting Germany Back Together Again: Unification and Its Aftermath."

Notes

1. Donald S. Detweiler, *Germany: A Short History* (Carbondale: Southern Illinois University Press, 1976), pp. 46ff.
2. Karl Dietrich Bracher, *The German Dictatorship* (New York: Praeger, 1970).
3. Bertram Schaffner, *Fatherland: A Study of Authoritarianism in the German Family* (New York: Columbia University Press, 1948); Leonard Krieger, *The German Idea of Freedom* (Chicago: University of Chicago Press, 1957).
4. For an excellent critique of this approach, see Richard Hamilton, "Some Difficulties with Cultural Explanations of National Socialism," in *Politics, Society and Democracy,* ed. H.E. Chehabi and Alfred Stephan (Boulder, CO: Westview Press, 1995), pp. 197–216.
5. David Abraham, "Intra-Class Conflict and the Formulation of Ruling Class Consensus in Late Weimar Germany" (Ph.D. dissertation, Department of History, University of Chicago, 1977).
6. Bracher, *The German Dictatorship,* p. 181.
7. Ibid., p. 183.
8. Daniel Jonah Goldhagen, *Hitler's Willing Executioners,* New York: Alfred A. Knopf, 1996. See also David Bankier, *The Germans and the Final Solution: Public Opinion under Nazism,* Oxford: Blackwell, 1992.
9. Frank Bajohr, *Arisierung in Hamburg,* cited in Götz Aly, "Der Holocaust," *Der Spiegel,* no. 36 (September 6, 1999).
10. Götz Aly, "Der Holocaust . . . ."
11. Bankier, *The Germans and the Final Solution . . .*
12. In some urban areas in the Rhine-Ruhr region, daily food rations in the winter of 1946–1947 dropped to 800 calories per person. By the end of 1946, per capita industrial production had declined to the level of 1865. Günter J. Trittle, "Die westlichen Besatzungsmächte und der Kampf gegen den Mangel, 1945–1949," *Aus Politik und Zeitgeschichte,* no. 22 (May 31, 1986): 20–21.
13. *Der Spiegel* commentary cited in Karl-Heinz Janßen, "Das dauerhafte Provisorium," *Die Zeit,* no. 21 (May 24, 1974), p. 10.
14. Institut für Demoskopie, *Jahrbuch der öffentlichen Meinung. 1947–1955* (Allensbach: Verlag für Demoskopie), Vol. 1, p. 161.

2

Putting Germany Back Together Again: Unification and Its Aftermath

Neither of the two German states founded on the ruins of the Third Reich in 1949 was the result of an indigenous, grass-roots movement for democracy. As we discussed in Chapter 1, the two postwar superpowers, the United States and the Soviet Union, installed models of their own political systems in their respective parts of Germany: a liberal republic in the West and eventually a communist dictatorship in the East. However, in the East, there was substantial opposition to communism. Millions of East Germans fled the country between 1949 and the building of the Berlin Wall in 1961; the remainder accommodated themselves in a variety of ways to the regime. A combination of internal police state repression, the presence of twenty-one Red Army divisions, and modest but steady improvements in the standard of living encouraged this accommodation. Thus until 1989 there had never been a successful, much less peaceful, democratic revolution on German soil. Such an extraordinary development is the subject of this chapter. But before we examine the revolution and its aftermath, the unification process, we offer a brief review of the German Democratic Republic's forty-year history in order to provide the necessary background.

The German Democratic Republic (GDR) was from the time of its birth smaller and poorer than its cousin in the West. Its area of 41,700 square miles was less than half that of West Germany; and its population, which stabilized only after the construction of the Berlin Wall in 1961, amounted to about one-fourth the size of the Federal Republic. Bounded by the Elbe River in the west, the Oder-Neisse rivers in the east, the Baltic Sea in the north, and the Czech Republic in the southern regions, the GDR was also less urbanized and industrialized than the Federal Republic. Its northern regions were largely agricultural, and the south, although industrialized, could not match the prosperous and productive Rhine-Main and Ruhr regions in the west. Unlike the Federal Republic, East Germany did not benefit from the postwar Marshall Plan, which served as an important catalyst to economic reconstruction in Western Europe. Indeed, the Soviet occupiers dismantled substantial portions of East Germany's industrial base (factories, machines, power plants) and shipped them to the Soviet Union as reparations for the destruction caused by Hitler's armies.

Following the lead of the Soviet Union, the GDR, like other satellite states in Eastern Europe after 1945, sought to greatly reduce or eliminate the private economic sector. Much property and many businesses were seized or put under the "people's"—in actuality, state—control. Farmers were forced to put their land into large collective farms, which became dependent on the state for equipment and markets.

BUILDING SOCIALISM: 1949–1961

East Germany's forty-year history can be divided into four fairly distinct periods. During the first period, from 1949 until the construction of the Berlin Wall in 1961, the regime attempted to construct a socialist state and society modeled after the Soviet Union. By 1950 most opposition had been suppressed. Any independent noncommunists had either fled to the West, accepted communist control, or found themselves in prison. In 1950 alone the GDR courts, staffed with politically reliable judges and prosecutors, meted out over 78,000 prison sentences in political trials. In some cases recalcitrant citizens were terrorized. In January 1950 Communist party "shock troops" stormed the offices of the Christian Democrats in Saxony and forced the independent-minded party chairman to resign. The country was ostensibly governed by a "National Front" composed of the Communists (officially the Socialist Unity Party, or SED, the product of a forced merger in 1946 between the Communists and the Social Democrats), several "bloc" or satellite parties (the Christian Democrats, Liberals, National Democrats, and Farmers' party), and the "mass organizations" (trade unions, youth, and women's groups).

Apart from the Communists, none of these parties and organizations exercised any independent power. Their leaders and functionaries received special privileges—housing, automobiles, luxury goods—in exchange for their cooperation. All worked in some form with either the East German (*Stasi*) or Soviet (KGB) secret police. The budgets of the bloc parties were heavily subsidized by the state. With these funds the parties maintained extensive staffs, newspapers, and even recreational facilities and hotels.

The Stasi

During this period, a crucial institution for maintenance of the regime—the Ministry for State Security or *"Stasi"*—was founded. Like its counterpart in the Soviet Union, the KGB, the Stasi considered itself the "sword and shield" of the party. With 90,000 full-time employees and up to 500,000 unofficial coworkers or "officers with special duties" (i.e., spies and informers), the Stasi sought to observe and control all areas of life. (The Nazi Gestapo, by contrast, had 65,000 full-time employees.) The central office in Berlin alone had a staff of 33,000; in the fifteen district offices the number of full-time employees ranged from 1,700 to almost 4,000. In addition, the Stasi had auxiliary units in most factories, military bases, universities, and even hospitals.[1]

The Stasi's operative principles, as summed up by one East German dissident group, presumed that (1) everyone is a potential security risk; (2) therefore everything possible must be known; and (3) security always takes precedence over the law.[2] Largely through information supplied by informants and through mail intercepts, wiretaps, and other electronic surveillance methods, the Stasi assembled files on over six million citizens—almost two-thirds of the adult population. Even children as young as 9 years of age were observed for the Stasi by their teachers and school principal if they expressed views critical of the communist system or favorable to the West. In addition, the agency was very active in West Germany and West Berlin. Following the collapse of the regime in 1989 almost two million dossiers on West Germans were discovered in Stasi offices. Other Stasi activities included the brutal interrogation and torture of prisoners, special internment camps for regime opponents, the attempted sabotage of West German nuclear power plants, the training of West German communists for paramilitary activities, and the support of international terrorists including West Germany's Red Army faction (see Chapter 4). After the Soviet army, the Stasi was probably the most important instrument for the maintenance of the party dictatorship.[3]

The June 1953 Uprising

Following Stalin's death in 1953 the East German regime began its "New Course" program. The coercive activities of the secret police were somewhat reduced, more consumer goods were made available, and prices were stabilized. In June 1953 the hardliners in the party leadership sought to push through an increase in work norms (quotas) for manual workers. The increases sparked demonstrations throughout the country, with the largest taking place in East Berlin. This was the first attempted revolt in the Soviet Union's postwar Eastern European empire; it would be followed by more extensive protests in Poland (1955), Hungary (1956), and Czechoslovakia (1968; now the Czech Republic). Soviet tanks and troops put down the uprising. Without this intervention the regime would have collapsed. The party denounced the revolt as a fascist plot; 1,400 people were arrested and sentenced to long prison terms.[4] In the aftermath of the affair, the regime dropped the increase in work norms. The Soviets also stopped the reparations program, that is, the systematic looting of the country.

Two years earlier, in 1951, the GDR embarked on its first Soviet-style five-year plan. Its goal was to double the 1936 level of production by 1955. Yet the country's economy still lagged far behind West Germany. Well into the 1950s meat, sugar, butter, and cooking oil were rationed.

The second five-year plan (1956–1960) saw some improvement in living standards and a decrease in overt police coercion. Over 20,000 political prisoners were released. Rationing was eliminated in 1958, but the forced collectivization of agriculture, completed in 1960, produced severe shortages of meat, butter, and milk.

East Germans continued to flee the country. Between 1949 and 1961 almost three million residents left, usually via West Berlin, which although located within the GDR's borders remained under Western (American, British, and French) control. A subway ride from East Berlin was all that was necessary. In 1961 the East German authorities, with the consent of the Soviet Union, did the unthinkable. They sealed off the borders between the two parts of the city, first with barbed wire and later with a large wall consisting of heavily reinforced concrete. The borders between East and West Germany were fortified with mine fields and automatic firing devices. Border guards were ordered to shoot to kill any East Germans seeking to escape. Apart from diplomatic protests, the Western powers made no attempt to stop the building of the Wall. To the dismay of many Germans, none of Bonn's Western allies were willing to risk a possible nuclear conflict with the Soviet Union over Berlin. As long as the communists did not threaten West Berlin directly, the West would take no action.

AFTER THE WALL—STABILITY AND CONSOLIDATION: 1961–1970

Shortly after the sealing of the borders, the party sought to make it easier for the East German population to reconcile itself with the system. A "New Economic System" promising more consumer goods, greater independence for individual firms, and salaries and wages more related to performance was announced. The system did lead to some improvements in living standards such as better-quality goods and improved housing, but the GDR continued to fall further behind prosperous West Germany. "The Republic needs everybody and everybody needs the Republic" summarized the new line. In 1968 a new constitution and legal code with ostensibly greater protection for civil liberties and rights was also approved. The GDR's fabled sports program, which would lead to many Olympic medals in the 1970s and 1980s, was initiated during this period.

Most East Germans who remained behind after the Wall was erected made their own private peace with the system. Many accepted the terms of the regime's social contract: (1) a generally free, personal, private sphere; (2) a tolerable standard of living and consumption, especially when compared to that of other communist societies; (3) social security (a guaranteed job, cheap housing, free health care, pensions); and (4) some social mobility. The regime, in turn, asked for (1) a readiness to work more or less diligently; and (2) formal acceptance of party and state authority, with the tacit understanding that one could talk, in private, differently about the system than in public.

After the Wall, West German efforts to normalize relations with Eastern Europe and the Soviet Union put the GDR in a difficult position. The Federal Republic concluded a treaty in 1970 with the Soviet Union, the GDR's protector. In the pact the two countries pledged to respect each other's territory and to improve their economic, cultural, and political relations. But before the treaty could take force, West Germany, supported by its Western allies, insisted that Moscow and the three occupying powers conclude an agreement over West Berlin. West Germany wanted the city's independence and Bonn's access rights guaranteed by the Soviet Union. In 1971 the Berlin Quadripartite Agreement was completed; this in fact guaranteed Western access to the city through the GDR and undercut East Germany's claim that it had to be involved in any decision affecting the city's future. The GDR leader at the time, Walter Ulbricht, had attempted to sabotage the entire process but thereby had provoked Moscow's wrath. He was forced to resign as party and state chief in May 1971.

THE HONECKER ERA: 1971–1985

Erich Honecker had been the longtime head of the party's youth organization, the Free German Youth, and chief of the security apparatus. In 1961 he had assumed primary responsibility for the building of the Berlin Wall. Improved supplies of consumer goods, the development of an extensive welfare state, and increased contacts with the West characterized this period of GDR history. Honecker stressed that economic policy and social policy should be linked. That is, increases in industrial production should lead directly to improvements in living standards, especially wages, pensions, consumer goods, and housing. To finance many of these programs the GDR began to borrow heavily from Western Europe, and above all, from the Federal Republic. Honecker quickly discovered that in exchange for liberalizing his regime and allowing more of his citizens to visit the West, the Federal Republic would respond with increased economic and humanitarian aid.[5]

In 1972 a Treaty of Basic Relations was concluded between the two states, which constituted the de facto recognition of the GDR by West Germany. Prior to this treaty Bonn had insisted that it was the only legitimate German state and had refused to recognize East Germany or any other state that did. The Basic Treaty abandoned this policy. Soon after both German states were admitted to the United Nations, and East Germany assumed diplomatic relations with over 150 states.

In 1975 the GDR participated in the Helsinki Conference on Peace and Security in Europe and became a signatory to the Helsinki Agreement on Human Rights. Over the next several years many GDR citizens, citing this document, submitted formal applications to leave the country. In certain cases involving personal or medical problems these petitions were approved.

During the Honecker era the party achieved a *modus vivendi* (workable compromise) with the Protestant Church, the only major social institution not under the complete control of the party. Under the slogan "Not the Church against, nor the Church next to, but the Church in Socialism," the regime agreed to certain concessions, including increased support for the training of pastors and the maintenance of church property. The Protestants, in turn, agreed not to challenge the fundamental assumptions of the regime: one-party rule and a planned economy. Several small dissident groups were somewhat protected by the Church, but discrimination against Christians continued. Their employment prospects and access to higher education remained limited.

Honecker's efforts to improve the living conditions of East Germans sharply increased the country's foreign debt. But the GDR had a rich cousin, and throughout the early 1980s the GDR's dependence on West German aid increased. Several multibillion-dollar credit lines were negotiated and Bonn secured favorable terms for East German exports to Western Europe. In 1984 a record 35,000 GDR residents were allowed to emigrate to the West. Visits by West Germans to the GDR also increased. The country's small opposition movement, consisting largely of Church-oriented peace and ecology activists, was closely watched by the secret police and some of its leaders were arrested and deported to the West, but the movement was not eliminated.

PERESTROIKA AND THE CRISIS OF THE REGIME: 1985–1989

During this period no Eastern European state feared the Soviet leader Mikhail Gorbachev's reform policies more than the German Democratic Republic. "Socialism" as practiced in the GDR—a one-party dictatorship with control of the economy and society—is what gave this state its identity and its reason for existence. If the GDR were to abandon this system, there could be no realistic alternative to unification with West Germany. The regime's attempts to create a separate "East" German identity had failed.[6] East Germans watched Western television daily, wore Western-style clothes if they could afford them, listened to Western music, and since the 1980s traveled to the West in increasing numbers on short trips.

At first the party elite denied that Gorbachev's reforms had any relevance for the GDR: "Just because your neighbor puts up new wallpaper does not mean that you have to do so too" was the oft-quoted response of one GDR leader. However, this obstinacy of what reformers called the "cement heads" in the East German leadership was based on a very rational and realistic calculation of their interests. Without socialism, without the Wall and the sealed borders, there would be no GDR. They were correct.

Honecker attempted to deflect criticism of his opposition to *perestroika* (restructuring) by further improving economic conditions (again largely with West German aid), increasing cultural ties with the Federal Republic, and allowing more and more East Germans to visit the West. In 1987, just two years before the collapse of his state, Honecker himself became the first GDR leader to step onto West German soil.[7] The visit, which the Kohl government after 1989 regretted, represented at the time the culmination of fifteen years of improved relations. In 1987 a million East Germans under the pension age were allowed to visit the Federal Republic— up from only 50,000 in 1985. The regime also announced a general amnesty for thousands of political and other prisoners, and East Germany became the first communist state to abolish the death penalty. In 1988 the GDR for the first time acknowledged its responsibility to Jewish victims of the Holocaust and announced a special program of reparations.

Encouraged by changes in the Soviet Union, the GDR's fledgling human rights, environmental, and peace groups increased their activity. The regime reacted at times with mass arrests; on other occasions such dissident activity was tolerated. In January 1988, demonstrators at the celebration of the seventieth anniversary of the death of the founders of the German Communist party, Rosa Luxemburg and Karl Liebknecht, were arrested, jailed, or expelled to West Germany. A few months later in a meeting with the leader of the Protestant Church, Honecker apologized for the incident, claiming that he had not been properly informed. The regime's policy of allowing its citizens to visit the Federal Republic continued, and by 1988 East Germans had made over five million trips to the West. Yet the shoot-to-kill order remained in effect for citizens attempting to flee. In February 1989 a young East German was shot and killed at the Wall. He was the last victim of the communist system.[8]

In spite of various forms of West German aid, the economy and the supply of consumer goods continued to worsen. But the party leadership rejected any dialogue with the growing opposition. Honecker defiantly declared that the Wall would stand for another fifty or one hundred years. Meanwhile, church leaders and some officials of the satellite parties began to criticize the regime publicly and call for reforms.

THE "GREAT ESCAPE" AND THE COLLAPSE OF COMMUNISM

Although changes in the Soviet Union—specifically the reforms undertaken by Soviet president Gorbachev—were fundamental to the collapse of communist regimes in Eastern Europe, the chain of immediate events that led to East Germany's revolution in 1989 started in May when Hungary began to dismantle its fortified border with Austria (see Table 2.1 for a chronology). By midsummer some East Germans ostensibly vacationing in Hungary discovered that they could cross unhindered into Austria and then, of course, on into West Germany. When in August the Hungarian authorities stopped GDR citizens from crossing, several hundred East Germans took refuge in West Germany's embassy in Budapest. A few days later they were transported to the West under the auspices of the International Red Cross.

At a pan-European festival celebrating the opening of the Austro-Hungarian border on August 19, 1989, almost 700 GDR residents crashed the party and raced over the boundary. The Great Escape had begun. By the end of the month, over 4,000 had fled through Hungary and an additional 2,000 East Germans still in the country were seeking permission to leave for the West.

Czechoslovakia (now the Czech Republic) became the next escape hatch. In early September approximately 100 East Germans "vacationing" there were allowed to leave. Then on September 10, 1989, in a critical decision, the government of Hungary suspended a 1969 treaty with the GDR under which it had agreed not to allow East Germans to cross its borders. Hungary declared its western borders open to all.[9] By the end of the month almost 25,000 East Germans had left via this route. The GDR now attempted to close this exit by suspending the issuance of travel permits to Hungary. The action prompted a renewed stream of refugees into Czechoslovakia and also Poland.

With its fortieth anniversary celebration and a visit by Gorbachev just a week away, the Honecker regime on September 30, 1989, announced that the 6,000 GDR refugees camped around West Germany's embassies in Prague and Warsaw could leave for the West after they were "expelled" from the GDR. Meanwhile, the wave of refugees from Hungary continued; and by the end of October an additional 24,000 had found their way to the West.

But they still kept coming. Just five days after 6,000 refugees left Prague, an additional 7,600 appeared at the West German embassy in the city. They, too, were allowed to leave after traveling by train briefly through East Germany so that they could be "expelled." At train stations in Leipzig and Dresden, police and secret

TABLE 2.1   The German revolution of 1989–1990: A chronology

1989

May	Hungary announces it will uphold the Geneva Accord on Refugees and opens its border to Austria.
August	East Germans occupy West German embassies in East Berlin, Prague, Warsaw, and Budapest.
August 19	At a celebration of the Pan-European Union held at the Austro-Hungarian border, about 700 vacationing East Germans flee to Austria. Since the opening of the Austro-Hungarian border in May almost 2,000 East Germans have (illegally) crossed into Austria.
September 10	Hungary decides to allow East Germans to leave for the West. By the end of the month, over 25,000 East Germans enter the Federal Republic.
October 1	Following negotiations between Bonn and Prague, 6,000 refugees leave Czechoslovakia for the West.
October 7	East Germany celebrates its fortieth anniversary. Gorbachev warns the GDR leadership that "life punishes those who arrive too late." Thousands demonstrate against the dictatorship.
October 9	"Monday Demonstration" in Leipzig. Large-scale demonstrations in other cities.
October 18	After eighteen years in power, Communist party boss Erich Honecker resigns. He is succeeded by Egon Krenz.
November 4	In East Berlin, the largest protest demonstration in the history of East Germany draws over a million people.
November 7	The East German government resigns.
November 9	The Berlin Wall and border crossings to the West are opened. Millions of East Germans visit the West.
November 28	Chancellor Kohl announces his 10-point unification plan.
December 3, 6	Communist party leader Krenz resigns from all his party and state offices.
December 19–20	Kohl holds talks in Dresden with interim East German prime minister Modrow on the future of the two states.

1990

February 10	Kohl and Foreign Minister Genscher meet with President Gorbachev in Moscow, who assures them that Germans may live together in one state.
February 14	The foreign ministers of the four World War II powers and of the two German states agree to begin formal talks on German unity ("2+4" talks).
March 18	The first free elections are held in East Germany. The Kohl-led "Alliance for Germany" emerges as the largest party; over three-fourths of East Germans vote for parties committed to speedy unification.

TABLE 2.1	*(continued)*
April 19	The new GDR Prime Minister, Lothar de Maiziére, announces that his government wants unity with West Germany as soon as possible.
June 8	Chancellor Kohl and President Bush emphasize in Washington that full membership of unified Germany in NATO is indispensable.
July 1	A monetary, economic, and social union between the two German states enters into force.
July 14–16	Kohl and Genscher visit Gorbachev and agree that united Germany will have full sovereignty, can remain in NATO, and will reduce its armed forces to 370,000. The Soviet Union agrees to withdraw all its forces from East Germany by the end of 1994. Germany agrees to large-scale economic aid for the Soviet Union.
August 23, 31	The East German parliament agrees to join the Federal Republic on October 3, 1990. The Unification Treaty is signed in Berlin.
October 1–2	All Four-Power Rights in Germany and Berlin are ended. Berlin is united.
October 3	East Germany joins the Federal Republic. Five new states are formed in the territory of the former GDR.
December 2	The first free all-German election since 1932 is held. The governing coalition led by Chancellor Kohl wins a solid majority.

Source: Ilse Spittmann and Gisela Helwig (eds.), *Chronik der Ereignisse in der DDR* (Bonn: Deutschland Archiv, 4th ed., 1990).

police agents used clubs and tear gas to stop other East Germans from jumping on the "freedom trains." In the first few days following the opening of the Czech border, over 10,000 more East Germans fled.

Emboldened by the regime's inability to stop the mass exodus, dissident groups began to organize in the GDR. In mid-September the "New Forum" became the first formal opposition group to apply to the government for official recognition; it had already set up organizations in eleven of the GDR's fifteen government districts. Soon thereafter the government declared the group to be "anti-state" and rejected its application. Ignoring the ban, the New Forum held its first congress in Leipzig on September 24.[10] It proclaimed itself the umbrella organization for all dissident groups in the country. Numerous other opposition groups and parties, including an East German version of the Social Democrats, were also founded throughout September and October.

The growing opposition movement and the Protestant Church urged East Germans to take to the streets in peaceful demonstrations. The largest center of opposition was in Leipzig, where the weekly Monday evening "peace prayer vigil" at the St. Nicholas Church was followed by marches around the center of the city. The Monday demonstrations spread to other cities, and by early October hundreds of thousands of East Germans throughout the country filled the streets chanting: "Wir sind das Volk!" ("We are the people!") and "Wir bleiben hier!" ("We're staying here!") For the first time in German history a peaceful, grass-roots democratic revolution was under way.

On October 7, 1989, the regime's fortieth anniversary celebrations were overshadowed by massive opposition demonstrations in East Berlin and other major cities. Denounced as rowdies by the party and official media, demonstrators met with violence from police and security forces in an attempt to suppress the demonstrations. Gorbachev told Honecker that the time for reform had come, citing a Russian proverb: "Life punishes those who arrive too late." His warning fell on deaf ears.

Ten days after the anniversary, Honecker resigned under heavy criticism from all sides, including his own party, the SED. His successor, Egon Krenz, was forced by the pressure of the demonstrations to retreat quickly from prior positions and grant increasing concessions to the opposition. On November 1, Krenz still defended some of the policies of the Honecker regime. One week later he placed all the blame for the upheaval on the ailing former leader. Upon taking office, Krenz emphasized that the Socialist Unity party (Communist) would not under any circumstances give up its leading role, enshrined in Article 1 of the constitution. By the end of November, he conceded that the party would have to give up its privileged constitutional position. The SED's policy on the participation of the new opposition groups (e.g., the New Forum and Democratic Breakthrough) also changed from rejection to acceptance. Opposition within the Communist party to its own leadership further weakened the regime. Many party members supported the new opposition groups; between October and December 1989, over one million members left the SED. Given this division within the party and Gorbachev's refusal to allow Soviet troops to intervene, it was impossible for party diehards to make any last stand against the revolution. Clearly on the defensive, the party leadership began seeking some credibility among the mass of the population.

The dictatorship that could only exist by walling its citizens in collapsed when its wall went down. On November 9, 1989, in a desperate attempt to save the regime, the country's borders with the West, including the Berlin Wall, were opened.[11] As the world watched, millions of East Germans flooded into West Berlin and West Germany. But it was too little, too late for the communists. The more the regime conceded, the more East Germans demanded. They wanted freedom and prosperity as soon as possible. Both appeared to be available through unification with West Germany. The demonstrators' chant of "We are the people!" began to be replaced by the slogan, "We are *one* people!"

THE UNIFICATION PROCESS

The West German Response

Bonn was ill-prepared for the collapse of the East German regime. Prior to the opening of the Wall, there was no committee or department of the government working on any plans for unification. Few believed that unification would take place quickly, especially in view of East Germany's ties to the Soviet Union. Clearly, the key to unification lay in Moscow. German leaders were also aware that the country's Western neighbors were somewhat anxious about what unification would mean for the European Community and for its neighbors in Eastern Europe. Finally, there was the (largely unspoken) fear that a unified Germany might once again seek to dominate Europe.

While not denying these problems, West Germany had to move quickly. By the end of 1989 the East German state was on the verge of collapse. Non-communist and opposition groups were brought into the government, but the flow of Germans from East to West did not abate with the opening of the borders or with the liberalization of the regime. Clearly, unification on West German soil would have been a demographic and economic disaster for both states.

In late November the Kohl government attempted to gain control over the process. In parliament, Kohl announced a ten-point program that envisaged a package of treaties between the two states, leading in four or five years to "confederal structures," then to a confederation (*Staatenbund*) and, finally, to a federation (*Bundesstaat*) between them. The entire process would take approximately ten years and the two states would remain equal partners throughout the process. The proposal drew widespread support, including that of the political opposition in the West; but some of Germany's allies thought the chancellor was moving too fast and had failed to consult them before announcing the plan.

The East German Opposition

The small, marginal groups of political activists who sparked the revolution and brought down the communist regime did not want rapid unification with West Germany. In spite of differences over policies and ideologies, this indigenous GDR opposition shared some common characteristics. First, a strong belief in *nonviolence;* the tactics of nonviolence as developed in the West European peace movement and the civil rights movement in the United States had strongly influenced their thinking. Second, they were largely antipolitical or apolitical in their thinking. According to one authority, "These groups were oriented to issues of *Kultur* (culture) and society rather than of power."[12] They had little experience in the give and take of democratic politics and were hence ill-equipped to assume political responsibility when the communist regime collapsed. Third, the opposition *lacked leadership.* There was no East German Lech Walesa (Poland) or Vaclav Havel (Czech Republic). The communist regime's practice of isolating dissidents through imprisonment or deportation had hindered the development of any significant leadership. Fourth, the opposition was fragmented by *conflicting goals and personalities.* Some groups wanted to emphasize a renewal of socialism, others concentrated on environmental problems. Fifth, most opposition figures belonged to what East Germans termed the *intelligentsia,* the relatively large number of artists, writers, dramatists, academics, and pastors whom the regime subsidized. Many of these intellectuals had built their own "self-contained" counterculture. Few if any of their ideas had ever been tested in public debate.

Despite differing characteristics, the opposition groups did have a general agenda.

1. They wanted a humane, socialist East Germany. For the opposition, socialism as an ideal had not failed because it had not been given a chance. The opposition also argued that there were aspects of East

Germany worth preserving: low rents, full employment, free health care, cheap public transportation, and extensive day care programs. The opposition thus sought a third way between capitalism and socialism, a goal other intellectuals in Eastern Europe—especially in Poland and Hungary—had sought but not found during the 1960s and 1970s.

2. The opposition agreed that the new East Germany would have to be a democratic system with direct citizen participation, a multiparty system, abolition of the secret police, the rule of law, and drastic reductions in military spending. The GDR opposition also wanted democratically controlled economic structures, although its leaders never made clear what they meant by this term. Daniel Hamilton has pointed out: "A feature common to all groups was a lack of economists, businessmen, or people with economic experience in government, which proved to be a severe handicap to the opposition once the Communist-dominated government collapsed."[13]

3. The opposition agreed on the necessity of maintaining a separate East German state as an alternative to the Federal Republic. Some actually proposed that the Wall be kept up a while longer to enable the new state to mobilize some popular support.

The great majority of East Germans, however, were not impressed by this idealistic vision of the opposition. With the breaching of the Wall and the opening of the borders, the "common people" of the GDR could see for themselves how they had been deceived by their own media, schools, and intellectuals. The decay of East German cities; the life-threatening water, air, and ground pollution; the low productivity of most businesses; the inadequate health care system; the impoverished state of many elderly people; and the cynical disregard for human rights exhibited by the hated Stasi and party *Bonzen* (bosses) convinced most East Germans that there was little if anything about the GDR worth preserving. For better or worse, the average East German in early 1990 finally wanted his or her share of the good life, West German style, as soon as possible: a Western automobile, a VCR, CD players, trips to Paris and London and Rome, Western clothes and appliances. One worker in Leipzig said to great applause: "I have worked hard for forty years, paid the rent on time, am still with my wife, I haven't seen the world, and my city is decaying. I won't allow myself to become a guinea pig again."[14]

In spite of their courage and idealism, the native East German revolutionaries had little to offer this population beyond their hopes for some third way between capitalism and socialism. They were unable to fill the vacuum that was created once the communist regime fell. Revolutionaries who had lived on the margins of East German society now had to become campaign managers and political operatives within weeks. They were not up to the task. So the vacuum was ultimately filled by the West German parties, with their well-organized campaign staffs, media-smart elites, and promises of prosperity and integration with the West. Their success, however, was based on solid support among East Germans. By early 1990 over 90 percent of the adult population in the GDR supported unification.[15] East Germany's indigenous revolutionaries were once again a small minority.

In a variety of polls conducted between November 1989 and September 1990, the great majority of West Germans (75–80 percent) also supported unification. Opposition was centered among those West Germans who were wary of the costs involved, or who felt that the whole process was going too fast and disregarded the interests and feelings of East Germans. But this high level of West German support was conditional upon the Federal Republic's remaining in the European Community and NATO. In a June 1990 survey the proportion of Germans favoring unification dropped from 77 percent to only 21 percent when the respondents were asked if they would support unity "if it meant leaving NATO and the European Community."[16]

The Soviet Factor

Following the opening of the Berlin Wall, the Soviet Union steadily backed down from its opposition to a united Germany within the Atlantic Alliance. Less than a week after the opening of the Wall, Gorbachev declared that German unification was not on the agenda in any form. A few weeks later Moscow announced that it could accept a unified, but demilitarized and neutral Germany. When this was rejected by West Germany, Gorbachev in early 1990 proposed that Germany remain in both NATO and the Warsaw Pact for a transitional period. This proposal also received no support from Bonn or its Western allies, especially the United States. The West German counteroffer, however, did attempt to deal with Moscow's major security concerns by proposing to reduce the size of the army and not to allow NATO forces or its nuclear weapons to be stationed on the territory of the former East Germany.

East Germany's fate was decided between December 19, 1989, when Kohl went to Dresden to meet with the GDR's Prime Minister, Hans Modrow (who had succeeded Egon Krenz two weeks earlier), and February 13, 1990, when Modrow returned the visit. In the interim Kohl and Foreign Minister Hans-Dietrich Genscher had met with Gorbachev in Moscow. At that meeting the Soviet leader assured them that the Soviet Union would not stand in the way of German unification.

Kohl was surprised by the hundreds of thousands of cheering East Germans who greeted him in Dresden with calls for unity. That experience, he later reported, convinced him that unification would and should come quickly.[17] The Modrow government had little legitimacy. A "Round Table" in East Berlin, composed of representatives of the various opposition groups and the old National Front, became the de facto government. Free elections, scheduled for May 1990, were moved up to March. The economy continued to deteriorate and thousands of East Germans left for the West each day. In Bonn, Modrow asked for an emergency grant of about $7 billion to shore up his regime. Kohl refused any expenditure of this magnitude, contending that the GDR's socialist economy and bloated bureaucracy would waste the money. Aid would come only after a freely elected government changed to a market economy. A disappointed Modrow returned to East Berlin empty-handed.[18]

The March 18, 1990, parliamentary election, the first and last in the GDR's history, confirmed that the great majority of the GDR's citizens wanted unification as soon as possible. The surprise winner was the "Alliance for Germany," a coalition of center-right groups, including the Christian Democrats, the one-time puppet party in the National Front. The Alliance had been hastily assembled by Chancellor Kohl as a forum for his appearances in the GDR. The Alliance, together with the Free Democrats and the Social Democrats, received over three-fourths of the vote.[19] These parties formed a Grand Coalition that governed until unification in October 1990.

The last remaining international obstacle to unification was removed when President Gorbachev announced after a two-day meeting with Chancellor Kohl in mid-July 1990 that a unified Germany would be fully sovereign and free to join whatever alliance it desired. In exchange, Germany agreed to reduce its total troop strength (to 370,000 from the then combined level of 640,000) as well as to complete a major treaty with the Soviet Union addressing all aspects of their relationship—political, military, cultural, and scientific. The Treaty, ratified in 1991, regulated the withdrawal of 385,000 Soviet troops from East Germany, a process that was completed on schedule in 1994. In addition, the Federal Republic agreed to provide over $30 billion in economic and technical aid.

Earlier that month the West German Deutsche Mark became the sole currency for both states and their economic and social welfare systems were merged. A few weeks later a second unification treaty was concluded that regulated most, but not all, of the remaining issues between the two states. East Germany, reorganized into five states (*Länder*), entered the Federal Republic according to Article 23 of the West German Constitution, which allows new states to join the federation much like new states once joined the United States.

Unification took place largely on West German terms. Few if any of the "social achievements" of the GDR, such as cheap, subsidized housing, full employment, and the extensive system of child- and day-care facilities were carried over into the enlarged Federal Republic. However, there were two issues that the two states could not resolve—the abortion question and the problem of the Stasi files. In East Germany abortion had been allowed on demand during the first trimester of pregnancy. Since 1972, in the West a woman has to prove that a "social," that is, poverty, medical, or other emergency—such as a pregnancy due to rape—exists before an abortion can be performed in the first trimester.[20] The certification of such an emergency must be obtained from a family planning service approved by the government. The abortion must be carried out by a different physician from the one certifying the emergency.

The great majority of East Germans (77 percent according to one survey) wanted to retain the former GDR's liberal law, and the issue threatened to delay the completion of the unification process. Finally, the question was resolved by passing it on to the parliament. According to the treaty, a unified law had to be passed by December 1992. In the meantime, each part of the country retained its own law, and women from the West who traveled to the former East could avail themselves of the East German law without penalty. In June 1992 the parliament passed a new law that was similar to the pro-choice East German law.

A year later, however, the Constitutional Court (see Chapter 8 for a description of this institution) declared the new law unconstitutional. In 1995 still another law was passed that allows abortions during the first trimester but requires the woman to visit a counseling center before the procedure can take place. The counseling must be oriented to the "protection of unborn life." This law has been upheld by the courts.

The question of what to do with the millions of files collected by the secret police (Stasi) also remained a source of division between the two regions. The West Germans, less affected by the files than the East Germans, wanted them transferred to the Federal Archives in Koblenz (West Germany), with limited public access. As in the case of abortion, the issue was resolved or postponed by assigning it to the all-German parliament. The documents will remain in East Berlin under the supervision of a special commissioner responsible to the parliament. East Germans wanted these materials to be the special responsibility of the five new states.

In November 1991 the parliament passed new legislation that allows citizens to examine their files and identify those individuals who were spying on them. The opening of the files yielded new information about the extent of secret police activity in the former GDR and led to further resignations of party and government officials. The president of Humboldt University in the former East Berlin, the chairman of the Party of Democratic Socialism (PDS), as well as the minister-president of Brandenburg were all under investigation because of documents found in the Stasi archives. One deputy from the former Communist party (now renamed the Party of Democratic Socialism [PDS]), apparently deeply depressed because of impending revelations about his past work for the Stasi, committed suicide in early 1992. Critics of the new law claimed it unleashed a witch hunt, which will ultimately do more harm than good to the development of democratic values in the former GDR.

As of 1999 about 1.8 million Germans have gained access to their files, and the Gauck Office, as it is termed, has conducted background checks on over 750,000 East Germans. (Joachim Gauck, a former Protestant minister and dissident leader heads the office.) But public support for the work of the Gauck Office among East Germans has waned. Between 1990 and 1995 the proportion of East Germans who want to "wrap up" the last forty years, by drawing a bottom line under communism, has increased from 23 percent to 54 percent. Only about 40 percent of East Germans now want the Office to continue its investigative work. During the same period the proportion of East Germans who want the Stasi documents destroyed has increased from 14 percent to 24 percent.[21]

Unification: A Brief Analysis

Why did this entire process proceed so rapidly, yet also so peacefully? Certainly the West German government must be given high marks for seizing the initiative and completing the process before East Germany collapsed and a mass exodus to the West could begin. The attempted coup in the Soviet Union in August 1991 and the subsequent decline of Gorbachev's influence supports the German decision to move quickly on the unification issue. Internationally, of course, the key to unification rested in Moscow and specifically in the hands of Gorbachev and his foreign minister, Eduard Shevardnadze. As Robert Gerald Livingston has observed, both men "had the sense to see that outsiders could not halt unification, the audacity to change Soviet policies totally, and the skill to gain substantial concessions for what by any measure is the greatest setback for the Soviet Union since Hitler's invasion a half century ago."[22] Moreover, Germany's Western allies, above all the United States, were generally cooperative and supportive throughout the entire operation. The initial lack of enthusiasm about unification demonstrated by British prime minister Thatcher and French president Mitterrand did not delay or hinder the course of events.

West Germany's economic wealth and power was another important factor in the unification process. International support for unification was smoothed by a steady flow of Deutsche Marks to Germany's allies and neighbors in East and West. Germany's "higher than expected" financial support for the Gulf War in 1990–1991 was in part an expression of the Kohl government's appreciation for the strong support of the Bush administration during the unification process. In return for its consent to unification and Germany's continuing membership in NATO the Soviet Union and its successors received over $44 billion from 1990 to 1995. French apprehension about unification were eased by Kohl's promise to introduce a common European currency by the end of the decade. Earlier in the process smaller players such as Hungary, which opened its borders to Austria in September 1989, received generous loan and aid packages from Bonn.[23]

Finally, through their peaceful, "gentle" revolution, the East Germans made the prospect of a unified Germany less disturbing to all of Germany's neighbors. Because so many of the East German "successes" did not find their way into the final unification treaties, and because the courageous East German opposition once again found itself on the margins of political life, many observers have asked what exactly the East Germans contributed to unity—what they "brought" into unified Germany. The answer, of course, is that they brought themselves. Without their willingness to challenge the Stasi state, to put their lives on the line when certain party hardliners were urging a "Chinese solution" to the unrest, the unification process would never have proceeded as smoothly as it did.

THE AFTERMATH OF UNIFICATION

For the rest of the world the German revolution of 1989–1990 ended on October 3, 1990, when the former German Democratic Republic ceased to exist and, reconstituted into five *Länder,* merged with the Federal Republic. For the new citizens of the unified state and indirectly the old as well, the revolution will continue well into the twenty-first century. In the East unification has meant unemployment; anxiety about possible unemployment; rising rents; restructured schools, colleges, and universities; countless new forms to be filled out; social isolation; competition; and rising crime rates.[24] It has also meant new cars (on credit); telephones; foreign vacations; VCRs; CD players; and lots of good, cheap coffee and bananas.[25] There was not a single revolution in the fall of 1989, but the beginning of 16 million individual revolutions. With West Germany supplying most of the resources, the former East Germany is being fast-forwarded through the last forty years. The West is also paying for much of this change. However, West Germans' empathy and sympathy are limited.

In this section we will briefly review the first nine years of the unification process. We will focus on the economic, environmental, and psychological dimensions of putting Germany back together again.

The Economy

By the standards prevalent in Eastern Europe and the Soviet Union, the East German economy was a model of efficiency. The GDR's industrial products were widely distributed throughout the communist world. The shipbuilding and railroad car industry produced largely for the huge Soviet market; there was never a shortage of demand. Admittedly outmoded in construction and design and often inferior in quality, the East German industrial products were affordable and did not require hard currency to purchase.

This changed suddenly after unification and the collapse of communism. Now the purchase of East German goods required hard currency, which the former communists rarely had. Moreover, even if potential East European customers had the currency, they now preferred Western goods that were of better quality and usually even less expensive than East German products. Thus the GDR's industrial economy went into an unprecedented tailspin between the currency union of July 1, 1990, and mid-1992. Approximately 60 percent of the country's industrial plants shut down. Out of a work force of over 9 million men and women, only 6.5 million still had jobs in 1992.

Nine years after unification, the economic picture in the East is mixed. Following a 30 percent decline in Gross National Product (GNP) in 1990 and 1991 the economy in the new states began to grow rapidly. As Table 2.2 shows, growth rates in the East between 1992 and 1996 were far higher than similar rates in the West. Net growth during this period in the East was almost 32 percent, as compared to roughly 5 percent in the West. Much of this growth was the result of sharp increases in construction (particularly in the public sector) and the service industries (banking, insurance, retail sales). But since 1997 the growth rate in the East has slowed and now lags behind the Western level. This means that the economic gap between the two regions has actually become larger since 1997. A decline in construction activity and a lack of export-oriented economic enterprises in the new states are the primary factors in the relative slowdown.

The amount of infrastructure investment has been staggering but little-known. By 1995 the former East Germany was the largest rail line construction site in the world. The "Germany Unity" transportation plan involves seventeen railroad, Autobahn, and

TABLE 2.2	Economic growth in East and West Germany, 1991–1999 (percentage increase in Gross Domestic Product adjusted for inflation)								
	1991	1992	1993	1994	1995	1996	1997	1998	1999*
East Germany	−16.0	8.7	6.3	8.9	4.4	3.2	1.7	2.1	2.3
West Germany	4.5	1.8	−1.9	2.3	0.9	1.1	2.3	2.9	2.3

*Estimate

Source: Federal Statistical Office; Deutsches Institut für Wirtschaft (DIW).

waterway construction projects at a total cost of over $40 billion.[26] When these are completed, the eastern region will have one of the most modern and efficient transportation systems in the world. The largest single infrastructure investment was for the telephone system. Completed in 1998 at a cost of over $27 billion, the Eastern region now has a phone system that is actually technologically superior to that of West Germany. This enormous project involved the installation of almost six million telephone lines.[27] Connecting East Germany to the European natural gas supply system has cost another $7 billion. The work was completed in June 1995, over four years ahead of schedule.

Who is paying for all this investment? The bulk of it is coming, of course, from the West German taxpayer. By early 2000 the net cost of the 1990 unification to West Germany had grown to over $700 billion. This amounts to about $11,200 for every man, woman, and child in West Germany. Every East German in the first decade of unification has received Western transfers amounting to almost $40,000.[28]

In addition to investment funds, many of these West German transfers have been grants to finance state and local governments in the East, as well as to supplement the social security system (unemployment payments, pensions, health care).[29] Approximately half of the transfers have been financed through increased taxes, and the other half has been borrowed.[30] Since 1991 the taxes have included a 7.5 percent "solidarity surtax" levied on income taxes from July 1, 1991, until June 3, 1992, and then reinstated in January 1995. Fuel oil and gasoline taxes were increased by 63 percent between 1991 and 1994. Between 1991 and 1995 taxes on insurance policies increased from 7 percent to 15 percent. Since 1991 the financial burden on West German households caused by these transfers has totaled over $230 billion. By 1999 unification was costing the average German household about $225 per month in increased taxes and social insurance contributions. Thus far the burden has been distributed proportionately across all income groups; that is, the upper income groups have not been paying more for unification than the lower income groups.[31]

The large amount of West German transfers, the generous tax breaks for investors in Eastern projects, and the pressures to produce an economic upturn as quickly as possible have led in some cases to waste and inefficiency in the expenditure of these transferred funds. Generous tax write-offs, for example, have yielded a glut of rental apartments and office buildings in the new states. In 1995 approximately $147 billion was transferred to the East, with roughly 25 percent of this amount spent on the construction of rental apartments. Some Eastern cities now have twice as much retail store space as do their Western counterparts. Investors who finance such projects may deduct from 25 to 50 percent of the construction costs from their taxable income. Thus a $240,000 investment could yield a net tax saving of almost $70,000 for those in the top (56 percent) tax bracket. Further, the fragile administrative structures in many Eastern regions have also led to poor investment decisions for projects such as waste water and sewage treatment facilities.

The massive investments and transfers have begun to pay dividends for many East Germans. By 1999 the buying power of the average Eastern resident amounts to about 75 percent of the Western level, a 50 percent gain since unification. However, substantial regional differences remain. Per capita buying power in Hamburg (Germany and Europe's richest city) is approximately 80 percent greater than in the poorest Eastern state, Mecklenburg-West Pomerania.

FIGURE 2.1   The economic catch-up process in the former East Germany, 1991–1999 (as proportion of Western level)

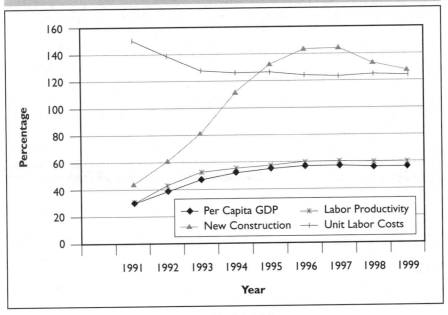

Source: Deutsches Institut für Wirtschaft; Federal Statistical Office.

As Figure 2.1 shows, worker productivity in the East has increased from only 28 percent of that in the West in 1990 to over 60 percent in 1998. Wage levels have also risen sharply. By 1998 the average East German worker was earning roughly 80 percent as much as his or her counterpart in the West.[32] In some white-collar positions such as accounting, sales, and marketing, parity in salaries has almost been achieved. Note, however, that East German wages are still much higher than East German productivity—which means that many East Germans are being paid more than they produce. While unit labor costs in the East have declined from 151 percent of the West German level in 1991 to 123 percent in 1998 (see Figure 2.1), they still are a major factor in the higher production costs for East German goods. The high production costs in turn do not help resolve the East's biggest economic problem: unemployment.

Before unification there were approximately 9.2 million jobs in East Germany. By 1992 the figure had dropped to 6.2 million, where it has since stabilized. What happened to the 3 million lost jobs and—more important—the people who filled them? Roughly 1.3 million are officially unemployed (1999 figures) and draw benefits (heavily subsidized by the West) from the unemployment insurance system or welfare. Another 850,000 have taken some form of early retirement, which was offered to workers as "young" as 50 years of age. Approximately 550,000 East Germans, or 7 percent of the work force, now commute to the West. The remaining 300,000 are in government-subsidized retraining programs, are working in part-time positions, or have moved permanently to the West. Thus through a variety of programs, usually involving government subsides, the number of officially unemployed has been kept to about 17 percent of the work force.

Jobs for these East Germans will only come when the economy is self-sustaining, that is no longer dependent on Western aid. East Germans have made some progress in this area. Western subsidies as a percentage of Eastern Gross Domestic Product (GDP) have dropped from 51 percent in 1991 to about 30 percent by 1998.[33] Thus Easterners now produce about 70 percent of what they consume as compared to less than half in 1991.

Most economists believe that this gap will be completely closed only when the technological and industrial base of the region is expanded to the point at which East German industrial products can be successfully marketed in West Germany and throughout the world. Most observers now estimate that full economic parity between the regions will take at least another ten to fifteen years. Will West Germans be willing to subsidize an East German standard of living that is in fact higher than Easterners' economic productivity for that period of time?

The Environment

The former German Democratic Republic was an environmental disaster area. Water, ground, and air pollution levels were among the highest in Europe. Since unification, the closing down of some of the worst industrial polluters, largely for economic reasons, has already produced some marginal improvement in air and water quality, but the gigantic task of cleaning up will last well into the next century.

As Table 2.3 shows, in 1991 only 3 percent of the former East Germany's rivers and streams were ecologically intact and only 1 percent of the region's lakes were free from pollution. Almost 80 percent of the rivers, streams, and lakes were either biologically dead or heavily polluted. The most important river in the East, the Elbe, which flows from Czechoslovakia through Germany before emptying into the North Sea, is still the most polluted river in Europe. Until recently, a cellulose plant south of Dresden dumped about a hundred tons of organic waste, including poisonous chlorine compounds, into the river daily.

In terms of air pollution, in the Leipzig area autumn and winter were virtually nonstop smog seasons. In the city of Bitterfeld, 30 miles north of Leipzig, children suffered from respiratory diseases at a rate two to three times greater than elsewhere in the former Eastern state. The major cause of air pollution in this area was the

TABLE 2.3   Water pollution in East Germany, 1991

Condition	Rivers, Streams (%)	Lakes (%)
Biologically dead	42	24
Heavily polluted	36	54
Moderately polluted	19	21
Ecologically intact	3	1

Source: Environmental Ministry statistics cited in *Der Bürger im Staat* 41, no. 3 (August, 1991), p. 162.

brown coal, or lignite, used in heating, power plants, and the chemical industry. When burned, lignite emits sulphur dioxide, an irritant gas that affects the nose, throat, and lungs. Used as a domestic fuel, the coal met almost 70 percent of East Germany's energy needs, as compared to only 8 percent in the West. Lignite, because of its high water content, has a much lower heat yield than anthracite or hard coal. But it was East Germany's sole indigenous energy source. Oil, natural gas, and hard coal had to be imported and paid for in scarce hard currency.

East Germany's chemical industry was also a major consumer of lignite. Fuel, lubricants, fertilizers, pesticides, medicines, and synthetic fibers were all produced from the coal in outmoded prewar plants. Even the plastic body of the Trabant, East Germany's two-stroke car, was made from lignite.

Uranium mining operations in Thuringia and Saxony have contributed to extensive environmental damage. Beginning in 1946 a joint East German–Soviet company, under tight security, supplied the Soviet Union with the uranium needed for its nuclear weapons and power plants. From 1946 until 1990 over 220,000 tons were shipped to Soviet weapons plants and power stations. As a result a 1,200-square-kilometer area is now heavily contaminated. Almost 300 mine shafts, 3,000 radioactive waste dumps, 18 processing plants, and numerous storage facilities are now being cleaned up by 4,000 specially trained workers and technicians. In addition, the mining operations caused several villages to be evacuated and destroyed, and thousands of acres of soil were polluted in the search for uranium ore. In some homes in the region, radon gas levels up to 100,000 Becquerels (Bq) per square meter have been measured; 250 Bq is considered the maximum allowable level. Cleaning up this area will take eight to ten years at a cost of about $10 billion.[34]

Since unification the major focus of the environmental cleanup has been on water and air quality. Modern water treatment facilities are being constructed in East German cities where the problem has been most acute.[35] The water quality in rivers, lakes, and streams has also improved. One recent study of the Elbe found that over two hundred species of mussels have reappeared in the past five years. The concentration of heavy metals such as lead, cadmium, zinc, and nickel in the river has dropped by over 45 percent, and the copper and chrome traces now found in the Elbe are down almost 50 percent since unification. Environmentalists, however, remain very concerned about the amount of toxic materials present in the river's sediments.[36]

The air has become cleaner, although much still remains to be done. Between 1989 and 1995 emissions of sulphur dioxide declined by about 45 percent, but the East German level remains higher than in the West. In 1992 the air in the East still contained nine times more dust particles than in the West, but this represented a substantial improvement over preunification levels. In 1989, for example, dust emissions in the East were 19 times greater than in the West.[37]

The Psychological Aftermath: The "Wall in People's Heads"

Many citizens of the former East Germany perceive West Germans as rich, arrogant know-it-alls (*Besser-Wessis*) who treat their former country like a colony. East Germans also consider them selfish, materialistic, and manipulative.[38] Many feel that their condition was an accident of history, and they have neither a sense of guilt nor a sense of responsibility for the communist regime. According to polls conducted in 1997, 80 percent of East Germans still feel they are second-class citizens.[39] Two-thirds of East Germans in another post-unification survey stated that this psychological wall had grown since unification.[40] Many in the West consider their Eastern cousins to be lazy, passive ingrates who fail to realize that prosperity only comes through hard work and sacrifice. Some West Germans now resent the stiff tax increases and large deficits needed to finance unification. They view the *Ossis* (Easterners) as "wanting it all" without sacrificing "as they did" following World War II.[41]

East Germans are twice as likely as West Germans to criticize the Trusteeship Authority, the agency charged with converting the formerly state-owned economy to the market system, as a "job-killer" that was indifferent to the human costs of unemployment. Almost half of the East German population believes that West German firms are attempting to destroy potential East German competition, rather than trying to save the East German enterprises; only 20 percent of West Germans share this view.[42] However, West Germans are far more likely to view East German workers as unable to adapt to the competitive pressures of a free economy.

East Germans still feel suppressed. They have a sense of being an irrelevant population. Particularly affected are (1) 40- to 60-year-old men who have lost their jobs and are unlikely to find new positions in the near future; (2) 25- to 35-year-olds who are optimistic about new possibilities in the market economy but are nonetheless fearful of being fired; (3) people with minor handicaps or behavioral problems; (4) the unemployed, for whom any previous job had social significance; and (5) the former *Nutznießer* (beneficiaries) of the old regime—this group receives no help or sympathy.

The wrenching economic problems in the East, above all rising unemployment; the dislocations associated with changes in the schools; the voluntary associations; the perceived second-class status; the real or imagined media "campaigns" against Easterners such as Manfred Stolpe, the chief executive of the state of Brandenburg, and sport star Katrina Krabbe; and the devaluation of native intellectuals have all led to a sharp decline in the self-image of citizens in the new states as "German."[43] Since unification the proportion of East Germans who think of themselves as citizens of the old GDR and not Germans has *increased.* Clearly, the psychological wall has grown higher.[44]

The psychological pressures of unification are stronger for residents of the former GDR than they are for West Germans. The East Germans lost their state and with it a part of their identity. Unlike West Germans they must redefine themselves; abandon their old values, beliefs, and verities; adapt to Western ways or become marginalized. Unlike West Germans they must confront and "overcome" the past forty years in order to preserve some aspects of their own identity. Even non-communists regret the quick demise of the GDR and are searching for positive elements in its history, such as anti-fascism and the ideal of socialism. East Germans are also more likely to be anxious about their economic future. These psychological pressures are differentially present among the various age groups or political generations in the East. Older generations are having more difficulty in adjusting than are younger age groups.[45]

For some analysts, the dominance of West Germans means that the social needs of East Germans are not being met. In politics, economics, and society they lack opportunities to make decisions.[46] All the power centers are controlled by Wessis. The need to create, to control is frustrated. The result: a concentration on the material-need level—individual material acquisition—or a withdrawal into the private sphere. If the economic needs cannot be fulfilled, a substantial aggressive potential is developed. This can manifest itself in aggression against foreigners.

Racism and Violence in the East

Up to one-third of the young people in the East have extreme right-wing orientations.[47] In 1997 about half of all reported acts of violence committed by right-wing groups took place in the East, even though only about 19 percent of the total German population lives in the five new states. Only 2 percent of Eastern residents are foreigners as compared to 10 percent in the West. Racist attacks are three times more likely in the East. Support for radical right parties is about twice as high in the East as in the West. Outbreaks of violence against foreign residents and especially those seeking asylum began in 1991 and flared up again in the late summer of 1992.

These can be seen to represent an extreme reaction to the psychic and economic stress of unification. Young East Germans with low levels of education have been especially susceptible to the appeals of radical right-wing organizations. One study in Saxony and Saxony-Anhalt found that approximately 20 percent of 14- to 25-year-olds considered themselves right-wing or extreme right-wing. Among the latter group, about 6 percent of the total, majorities of 75 percent and more agreed with sentiments such as "Germany for the Germans" and "National Socialism also had its good points." Between 60 percent and 75 percent of radical right-wing youth agreed with statements such as "the former Eastern territories should be returned to Germany" and "Germany should once again have a strong leader." Anti-Semitism, nationalism, and a general hostility to foreigners (*Ausländerfeindlichkeit*) were also most likely among students in grades 8 to 10 in the *Hauptschule* (general school) and apprentices. There was a substantial decline in these attitudes among students at academic secondary schools. The acceptance of violence was also much higher among East German youth with low levels of education.[48]

Yet in spite of these difficulties, the great majority of East Germans (over 80 percent) do not regret unification.[49] Approximately one-half believe they are doing better or much better than before unification, and less than one-fourth state that their condition has gotten worse or much worse. They want to live in a unified state, but they also want to be respected and appreciated by their Western cousins. Yet the Westerners believe the Ossis complain a lot in spite of an undeniably improved life. When asked when this will stop, the first and last freely elected East German prime minister, Lothar de Maizire, replied:

> Remember that Moses led his people through the desert for 40 years, and that after 20 years people began to complain. . . . They told Moses that life in the desert was too difficult, and that at least when they were slaves they had food and water and places to sleep. Moses' friends asked him how long he thought

people would be complaining like this and he replied, "Until the last person born under slavery has died." Our situation here is very similar. The psychological gap between eastern and western Germany will last for at least a generation, or perhaps until the last person born under Communism has passed away.[50]

Notes

1. For each East German there was a *Kaderakte,* a type of personnel file, that began in elementary school and followed the person throughout his or her life. The Stasi had access to all Kaderakte; the subject of each file did not.
2. Cited in Karl Wilhelm Fricke, "The Inherited Burden of the East German State Security Apparatus," *Aussenpolitik* 41, no. 4 (1990): 408.
3. The Stasi was by no means the only security institution in the country. There was 1 police officer for every 170 residents, as compared to 1 for every 385 West Germans. All police personnel were under the direct control of the national Interior Ministry, which in turn was controlled by the party.
4. For an excellent analysis of the June 17, 1953, uprising, which is based on new evidence from party and state archives, see Armin Mitter, Stefan Wolle, *Untergang auf Raten. Unbekannte Kapiteln der DDR Geschichte,* Munich: Bertelsmann Verlag, 1993, pp. 27–162. The authors contend that the uprising actually saved the Stalinist Ulbricht regime, which the Soviet Union, in the wake of Stalin's death in March, was preparing to abandon.
5. Included in West Germany's humanitarian aid was money paid to the GDR for the release of political prisoners. From 1964 to 1990 the Federal Republic paid over $2 billion for the freedom of 34,000 prisoners held in deplorable conditions in East German jails. An additional 200,000 East Germans, usually relatives of the released prisoners, were included in the ransom deal. East Germany considered the payments as reimbursement for the expenses it incurred in educating its former citizens. This top-secret ransom program was an important source of hard currency for the GDR. Indeed, it became an item in the country's annual budget. The average cost per prisoner increased from about $12,000 in the 1960s to over $50,000 by the 1980s. To reduce the chances of negative publicity, both sides agreed to use the offices of the Protestant Church to transfer the payments, which were made either in cash or commodities, from West to East. For one account of the beginnings of this program see Craig R. Whitney, *Spy Trader,* New York: Times Books, 1993, pp. 51–80. There are also reports of an "unofficial channel" that was used to bring other East Germans to the West. This involved direct payments to an East German lawyer with close ties to Stasi chief Erich Mielke and to Honecker. *Frankfurter Allgemeine Zeitung,* June 3, 1992, p. 3.
6. For an analysis of public opinion data on the question of a GDR identity, see Peter Förster and Günter Roski, *DDR Zwischen Wende und Wahl* (Berlin: LinksDruck Sachbuchverlag, 1990). Political socialization in the former GDR is examined in Christiane Lemke, *Die Ursachen des Umbruchs 1989. Politische Sozialisation in der ehemaligen DDR* (Wiesbaden: Westdeutscher Verlag, 1991).
7. Honecker had planned to visit West Germany several years earlier, but Moscow, fearing an intra-German rapprochement, forced him to cancel the trip.
8. In all, from 1961 to 1989 over 600 East Germans were killed by GDR border troops and police as they attempted to flee the country either through Berlin or at other border crossings. In several trials after 1989, former border guards and some of the East German communist leadership responsible for the shoot-to-kill order were sentenced to prison terms. Many leaders, however, including Erich Honecker, escaped prosecution for reasons of health, old age, and lack of evidence that met West German legal standards. *Frankfurter Allgemeine Zeitung,* August 13, 1993, p. 6. By late 1998 German authorities had investigated over 22,000 cases of alleged criminal activity and human rights viola-

tions during the communist regime. These investigations have yielded 211 convictions of state and party officials, border guards, judges, and prosecutors. *Süddeutsche Zeitung,* December 8, 1998.

9. Hungary's decision was, of course, enthusiastically supported by the West Germans, and Bonn's promise of substantial aid to the new democratic government in Budapest did not hurt the cause of the East Germans.

10. See Helmut Müller-Enbergs, et al. eds., *Von der Illegalität ins Parlament. Werdegang und Konzept der neuen Bürgerbewegungen* (Berlin: LinksDruck Sachbuchverlag, 1991), for a detailed examination of the various GDR opposition groups that emerged at this time.

11. The sequence of events that led to the opening of the Wall on the evening of November 9, 1989, is still not clear. Apparently the communist leadership had intended to announce only more liberal and simplified procedures for GDR citizens desiring to travel to the West; they would still have to apply for exit visas. But when the communist official making the announcement was asked by reporters to clarify his statement, he said that the borders were open. Quickly the news spread that the Wall was open. GDR border guards, faced with thousands of people waiting to cross over, made a decision not to require any visas or identity cards; they simply let people cross. See Günter Schabowski, *Das Politbüro* (Reinbek bei Hamburg: Rowohlt Verlag, 1990), pp. 134–140.

12. Daniel Hamilton, "After the Revolution: The New Political Landscape in East Germany," *German Issues,* no. 7 (Washington, D.C.: American Institute for Contemporary German Studies, 1990), p. 11. This section of the book owes much to Hamilton's excellent analysis.

13. Hamilton, "After the Revolution," p. 11.

14. Cited in Hamilton, "After the Revolution," p. 11.

15. Forschungsgruppe Wahlen survey cited in Erwin K. Scheuch, *Wie Deutsch sind die Deutschen?* (Bergisch Gladbach: Gustav Lübbe Verlag, 1991), p. 352.

16. EMNID surveys cited in *Der Spiegel,* no. 26 (June 25, 1990), p. 48.

17. Personal Interview, November 29, 1990, Bonn.

18. Peter Christ and Klaus-Peter Schmid, "Hauptsache guter Wille," *Die Zeit,* no. 8 (February 23, 1990), p. 10.

19. Not all East Germans, of course, were dissatisfied with the regime. At the March 1990 parliamentary election over 16 percent voted for the former Communist party (renamed the Party of Democratic Socialism, PDS); in East Berlin the PDS received over 30 percent of the vote. Much of this support came from the beneficiaries of the system: the hundreds of thousands of party and state bureaucrats, secret police officials, informers, artists, intellectuals, and privileged athletes.

20. Abortions are also allowed for "eugenic" reasons (hereditary physical or mental illness).

21. EMNID surveys cited in *Der Spiegel,* no. 27 (July 3, 1995), p. 49.

22. Robert Gerald Livingston, "Relinquishment of East Germany," in *East Central Europe and the USSR,* ed. Richard F. Starr (New York: St. Martin's Press, 1991), p. 83.

23. James Baker (former American Secretary of State, cited in *Der Spiegel,* no. 24, 1998 (Internet edition).

24. Detlef Landua, "Magere Zeiten," *Aus Politik und Zeitgeschichte,* nos. 29–30 (July 10, 1992): 29–43.

25. In 1991 the East Germans consumed a record 56.3 pounds of bananas per capita as compared to 32.1 pounds for each West German. Between 1991 and 1996 the proportion of Easterners with a telephone increased from 18 percent to 91 percent; VCR ownership jumped from 40 percent to 78 percent during the same period (Federal Statistical Office).

26. For a description of each of these transportation projects, see "Die Verkehrsprojekte Deutsche Einheit," *Frankfurter Allgemeine Zeitung,* December 5, 1994, pp. 8–10.

27. Stephen Economides, "Rebuilding the Telecommunications System in the New German States," unpublished manuscript, Telekom Fachhochschule Berlin, 1994, p. 5.

28. Andres Borchers, et al., "Die Bilanz—Wo ist das ganze Geld geblieben?" *Der Stern,* no. 38 (September 15, 1999).

29. From 1990 to 1993 the pensions of East Germans increased from 47 percent to 86 percent of the Western level (Federal Labor Ministry Statistics). There is also still a substantial inequality in capital resources. While 45 percent of West Germans own their own home, only 19 percent of Easterners are property owners. Federal Statistical Office, Income and Consumer Sample, September 7, 1997.

30. In the first year of unification the federal budget increased a phenomenal 31 percent with approximately one-third of the new spending coming from federal borrowing.

31. Ullrich Heilemann and Wolfgang Reinicke, *Welcome to Hard Times: The Fiscal Consequences of German Unity* (Washington, D.C.: Brookings Institution and American Institute for Contemporary German Studies, 1995), p. 48.

32. Deutsches Institut für Wirtschaft, *Wochenbericht,* no. 33, August 1998, p. 30.

33. *Ibid.*

34. Rainer Karlsch, "'Ein Staat im Staate'. Der Uranbergbau der Wismut AG in Sachsen und Thüringen." *Aus Politik und Zeitgeschichte,* nos. 49–50 (December 3, 1993), pp. 14–23.

35. *Der Spiegel,* no. 36, September 4, 1995, p. 139.

36. The findings of the Elbe River study are cited in the *Frankfurter Allgemeine Zeitung,* July 26, 1995, p. 1.

37. *Der Spiegel,* no. 36, September 4, 1995, p. 135.

38. EMNID surveys cited in *Der Spiegel,* no. 30 (July 22, 1991), p. 28. Over 90 percent of East Germans, but only 7 percent of West Germans, agree with the statement that West Germany is using the East as a new market and is less interested in developing the economic independence of the region.

39. Dieter Walz, Wolfram Brunner, "Das Sein bestimmt das Bewußtsein," *Aus Politik und Zeitgeschichte,* no. 51 (December 12, 1997): 13–19.

40. Renate Köcher, "Opfern fällt den Westdeutschen schwer," *Frankfurter Allgemeine Zeitung,* August 7, 1992, p. 5.

41. *Ibid.,* p. 5.

42. EMNID surveys, *Der Spiegel,* p. 41.

43. Stolpe, the current chief executive of the state of Brandenburg, was accused of collaborating with the Communist regime while he was a high-ranking administrator in the Protestant Church. Krabbe, a former Olympic sprinter, was suspected of informing on her fellow athletes for the Stasi.

44. Institut für Demoskopie (Allensbach) data cited in *Frankfurter Allgemeine Zeitung,* August 6, 1995, p. 3.

45. Hans-Joachim Maaz, "Psychosoziale Aspekte im deutschen Einigungsprozeß," *Aus Politik und Zeitgeschichte,* no. 19 (May 3, 1991): 3–10.

46. Ingrid Stratemann, *Psychologishe Aspekte des wirtschaftlichen Wiederaufbaus in den neuen Bundesländern* (Göttingen, 1991).

47. Peter Förster and Walter Friedrich, "Politische Einstellungen und Grundpositionen Jugendlicher in Ostdeutschland," *Aus Politik und Zeitgeschichte,* no. 38 (September 11, 1992): 9.

48. *Ibid.*

49. EMNID surveys cited in *Der Spiegel,* No. 13, March 23, 1998, p. 53.

50. Cited in Craig Whitney, "Instead of Barbed Wire, Resentment Now Divides Germans," *New York Times,* October 14, 1994, p. A6.

3 The Social and Economic Setting

N either people nor states function in a vacuum. The historical, geographical, and socioeconomic contexts influence political attitudes and behavior as well as policymaking institutions. This is especially true of the Federal Republic, where important postwar geographic, social, and economic changes have created a setting for politics quite different from that experienced by past regimes. This chapter surveys these contextual changes as they relate to modern German politics.

AREA AND POPULATION

The unified Federal Republic, with an area of approximately 138,000 square miles, about half the size of Texas, now comprises roughly 75 percent of the pre–World War II territory of the Reich. As we will discuss later, this postwar loss had several important consequences for postwar German politics. Germany has more neighbors than any other European nation. On the north it is bordered by Denmark, on the east by Poland and the Czech Republic, on the south by Austria and Switzerland, and on the west by France, Luxembourg, Belgium, and the Netherlands. The Federal Republic extends 530 miles from the Danish border in the north to the Bavarian Alps in the south (See Figure 1.1), 270 miles from the Austrian border in the southeast to the border with France in the southwest and 300 miles from the border with Poland in the northeast to the border with the Netherlands in the northwest.

Unified Germany now has a population of over 82 million, making it by far the largest state in Western and Central Europe. In the former West Germany the population has grown to almost 67 million in the postwar period through the influx of refugees from German territories annexed or occupied by Poland and the Soviet Union in 1945, from German nationals expelled from what was then Czechoslovakia (Sudetenland), and from additional refugees—almost 3 million—from the former East Germany from 1949 until the construction of the Berlin Wall in 1961. There are also at least 8 million foreign residents, mainly foreign workers and their families, in the former West Germany. The five new Eastern German states have a combined population of about 15.5 million.

The birth rate for native West Germans in the past twenty years has been among the lowest in the world. Most of the population growth in recent years has come from foreign residents. Over half of Germany's 30 million families are without children, and about half of the remaining families, or one-fourth of the total, have only one child. Less than one family in four has two or more children. Modern contraceptive techniques and the growing number of women opting for the work force instead of the traditional *Hausfrau* role are the major reasons for the low birth rate.[1]

The territory of the former GDR in 1948 had a population of 19.1 million. When the Berlin Wall was completed in 1961 the population had dropped to 17.1 million. By 1986 a low birth rate had reduced this still further to 16.6 million. The emigration that triggered the collapse of the communist regime reduced the population even more to an estimated 16 million at the time of unification.[2] Since unification interregional migration has resulted in a net loss of about 500,000 more East Germans. Finally, about 550,000 residents of the new states commute daily or weekly to jobs in the old states. Thus, on a typical work day less than 15 million people actually live in the former East Germany.

The enormous economic, social, and cultural adjustments being made by East Germans after forty years of division have had a depressing effect on such basic life decisions as marriage and childbirth. Between 1989 and 1993 the number of marriages in the East dropped from about 131,000 to 49,000 and the number of births from about 200,000 to only 80,000. Demographic changes of this magnitude are usually associated only with traumatic events such as war and economic depression.[3] They indicate the extent of fear and uncertainty felt by many East Germans. Since 1993, however, there is a slow trend toward normalization; marriages and births have increased and now are converging with those in the West. This postunification decline in population has concerned some Eastern governments. In 1994 one East German state, Brandenburg, announced that it will pay parents a $650 premium for every new child.

URBANIZATION AND INDUSTRIALIZATION

With 230 inhabitants per square kilometer, Germany is one of the most densely populated nation-states in Europe. It is also a heavily urbanized society, with half of its population living on less than 10 percent of the land. The large urban areas, however, are distributed throughout the country and make for considerable diversity. The largest of these, with 11 million residents, is the Rhine-Ruhr region between Düsseldorf and Dortmund. Seven other metropolitan areas each have a population of more than a million: Berlin, the Rhine-Main area (Frankfurt), Stuttgart, Hamburg, Munich, the Rhine-Neckar region, and Leipzig. Another seven urban areas have a population exceeding 500,000: Nuremberg, Hanover, Bremen, Dresden, the Saar, Aachen, Bielefeld, and Herford.

Much of this urbanization took place during the last quarter of the nineteenth century when, within one generation, Germany became one of the world's leading industrial powers. Today the Federal Republic is the world's third-largest industrial power (after the United States and Japan) and the largest in Europe.

An Export-Oriented Economy

Lacking self-sufficiency in food and raw materials, Germany's economic well-being, like that of Britain and Japan, is heavily dependent on successful competition in the international economic arena. In essence, Germany imports food, raw materials, and manufactured products and pays for them by exporting its own manufactured goods. Almost 90 percent of German exports are manufactured goods—automobiles, chemicals, heavy machinery—sent in 1998 to fellow European Union members (53 percent); other West European countries (19 percent); North America (10 percent); the developing countries of Asia, Africa, and Latin America (10 percent); and the former communist bloc countries (8 percent).[4] Imports of food, raw materials and semi-finished products account for about a third of Germany's imports.[5] Success in this exchange depends on the ability of German ·industry to sell its manufactured goods at a price greater than the costs of its raw materials and production. Successful production is in turn strongly related to an adequate supply of skilled, disciplined industrial labor, management expertise, and scientific know-how.

The Germans have been very successful in the business of international trade. The balance of trade, that is, the value of exports minus the costs of imports, has been positive since 1955. In 1987 it reached a record high of over $90 billion. In 1998 the export balance of about $86 billion was the highest since unification; the value of German exports at $633 billion was exceeded only by the United States. The export component of the economy is reaping the benefits of the extensive structuring of recent years, which, however, has included a downsizing of the labor force. This impressive export performance has been achieved with almost 11 percent of the work force unemployed. Overall German enterprises receive about 25 to 30 percent of their gross sales from exports. In some industries—automobiles, steel, chemicals, machine tools—almost half of total sales come from the foreign market.

Like the United States and Britain, the Federal Republic, however, has in recent years lost significant portions of its shipbuilding, electronics, and even automobile market to foreign imports, especially from Taiwan, Korea, Singapore, and other countries where labor costs are lower. To meet this challenge and reduce labor costs, German industry has turned to increased automation, which has, at least in the short run, aggravated the unemployment problem.

In spite of these difficulties, the overall performance of postwar Germany in foreign trade cannot be equaled by any other advanced industrial society during this period with the possible exception of Japan. Little wonder that *die Wirtschaft* (the economy) and its representatives are an important power factor in German politics and policymaking. German business has a record of accomplishment that ensures it respectful consideration by any government.

TABLE 3.1	Occupational composition of the work force, 1882–1998 (in percentages)					
Occupational Category	**1882**	**1925**	**1950**	**1974**	**1986**	**1998**
Agricultural and self-employed	36	33	28	14	13	11
Manual workers	57	50	51	45	39	36
Salaried nonmanual (white-collar and service)	7	17	21	41	48	53

Source: *Statistisches Jahrbuch für die Bundesrepublik Deutschland,* 1971, 1975, 1998 (Stuttgart: Kohlhammer Verlag); Emil Hübner and Horst-Hennek Rohlfs, *Jahrbuch der Bundesrepublik Deutschland* 1987–1988 (Munich: Deutscher Taschenbuch Verlag, 1988).

intensified by the demands of the two world wars, and continuing to the present day. The main characteristics of these changes are common to all advanced industrial societies:

1. A steady decline in the proportion employed in the "primary sphere" of the economy: agriculture and independent nonmanuals. At the turn of the century, 36 percent of the work force was still in these occupations, but as Table 3.1 shows, by 1998 they comprised only 11 percent of the work force.

2. A relative stagnation or even slow decline in the proportion employed in the secondary or production sphere of the economy (industrial manual occupations). Its relative position declined from 57 percent in 1882 to 36 percent by 1998.

3. Rapid growth among those in the tertiary sphere: the white-collar and service occupations. The size of this group has more than doubled since 1950. The tertiary sector overtook manual workers by the late 1970s. The United States reached this point by the mid-1950s.[8]

Such structural changes have brought increasing social mobility to Germany, although *upward* mobility is still lower than the United States. Upper-class and status occupations requiring extensive academic training still remain relatively closed to the offspring of manual and low-level white-collar workers.

THE ECONOMY

Postwar Germany has become one of the world's most prosperous societies. The sophisticated industrial economy staffed by a highly skilled work force has made the Federal Republic an affluent, mass-consumption society in a relatively short time. A

TABLE 3.2   German economic trends, 1950–1999

Period	Economic Growth %*	Inflation %	Unemployment (average)**
1950–1959	7.9	1.9	1,200,000
1960–1969	5.0	2.4	223,000
1970–1979	3.2	4.9	647,000
1980–1989	2.2	3.0	2,000,000
1990–1999***	2.4	2.3	3,700,000

* Adjusted for inflation (real growth)
** Average annual level
*** 1991–1999 figures include the former East Germany

Source: Federal Statistical Office, *Bundesbank.*

1994 study found that the average West German household had combined assets (property, savings, automobiles, insurance, stocks) of about $200,000; the average level of assets in the former East Germany, however, was only about $54,000.[9]

The country was not spared the effects of recessions in 1974, 1981, and 1992. The latter was the most severe. By early 1993 over 10 percent of the work force was unemployed, the highest level in over thirty years. In spite of record unemployment, however, the extensive system of social insurance and welfare, which links compensation to actual earnings, meant that few Germans suffered a devastating loss in their standard of living.

As Table 3.2 shows, the postwar German economy has gone through four rather distinct stages since 1950 and since unification in 1990 it entered its fifth and current stage. The first stage occurred during the 1950s, the years of reconstruction and the "economic miracle," and it paved the way for later decades. Economic growth averaged almost a phenomenal 8 percent per year during the 1950s. Inflation, which averaged less than 2 percent during the 1950s, was among the lowest in the industrialized world. During this reconstruction phase, unemployment was substantial—especially during the early 1950s. But the ten-year average of 1.2 million still represented less than 5 percent of the work force.

Heavy investment in capital equipment during reconstruction bore fruit in the second stage: the "golden 1960s." Economic growth averaged a healthy 5 percent; inflation remained nominal at only 2.4 percent, and more important, unemployment practically disappeared, dropping to less than 1 percent. In fact, Germany during the 1960s had such a labor shortage that almost 2 million foreign workers had to be brought in. This impressive performance throughout the 1960s also took place in spite of the 1966–1967 economic slump, the first in the Republic's history.

A sharp increase in oil prices and the resultant worldwide recession affected the German economy during the 1970s. These were the "difficult years." Yet the economy remained strong relative to other Western European nations and the United States. Economic growth averaged 3.2 percent annually throughout the period—a very respectable performance, especially in light of the 1974–1976 recession. However, inflation jumped sharply to almost 5 percent, a high figure by German standards. Finally, unemployment became a serious problem for the first time since the early 1950s. From the mid-1970s to the end of the decade, between 800,000 and 1 million Germans found themselves out of work. This was partly attributable to the general worldwide recession, but much of it was structural as well. Certain industries were no longer competitive: textiles, shipping, consumer electronics, and even cameras were lost to low-wage exporting countries such as Taiwan and South Korea.

From 1980 to 1989 the economy experienced slow but steady growth. Following the 1981–1983 recession real increases in the gross national product averaged 3.3 per cent per year, or 2.2 percent for the entire decade. Unemployment remained persistently high until the 1988–1989 period, when it began a slow decline. One of the few bright spots of the 1980s was the low inflation rate, which because of the strong Deutsche Mark and falling oil prices dropped to only about 2 percent in 1988. This lackluster economic performance was a major reason for the collapse of the Schmidt government in 1982. Unemployment, for example, was considered to be an important issue by 88 percent of the voters in the 1983 election.[10] The belief or hope that the Christian Democrats could do a better job than the Social Democrats was a decisive factor in the party's victory.

Since unification in 1990, unemployment has once again become without doubt Germany's major economic problem. Unemployment has averaged about 3.7 million per year in the 1990s. About a third of this total is from East Germany, but the West German economy has also been unable to produce enough new jobs to compensate for the losses due to global competition and the export of German capital to cheaper foreign labor markets.

The weak performance of the economy in recent years and especially the high unemployment level were the result of a variety of factors.

1. Many economists contend that there is too much regulation and inflexibility throughout the economy. Government monopolies in the postal and telecommunications fields, for example, have inhibited innovation or expansion in these areas, whereas in countries such as the United States the same areas have been the source of high growth rates and many new jobs.

2. A second problem contributing to low economic growth is the shortage of venture capital. The German capital market is dominated by large banks that work well with established industries but have been slow to fund innovative, high-risk projects.

3. Germany's labor laws and regulations make it difficult to lay off employees even if the companies are losing money. Even in periods of expansion, many firms increase overtime or hire temporary workers instead of adding to the regular work force.

4. Long-term subsidies to declining industries such as coal, steel, and shipbuilding as well as agriculture have had a negative impact on growth. Germany's coal mining industry, for example, receives annual subsidies amounting to about $60,000 for each of the remaining 85,000 miners. Foreign coal could be imported for about $60 per ton; German coal, thanks to the subsidies, costs about $240 a ton.[11] These funds could be better spent in funding new, high-tech projects with growth potential.

5. Finally, the service sectors of the German economy could grow at a faster rate were it not for trade-union opposition and rigid government regulations. German retail shops, for example, must close by 8:00 P.M. from Monday through Friday and at 4:00 on most Saturdays. (Until a few years ago, all retail stores had to close at 6:30 P.M. during the week and at 2:00 P.M. on Saturday.) Never on Sunday remains the rule for retailers. Economists estimate that removing these various regulations and restrictions would increase the growth rate by about 2 percent and cut unemployment by 25 percent.

The costs of labor in Germany have grown to the extent that many firms are moving to other countries. By 1999 hourly labor costs, including fringe benefits, reached almost $30 an hour in comparison to about $18 in the United States. These costs include the six weeks of paid vacation that most workers receive as well as other benefits such as holiday bonuses and generous sick-leave provisions. German employers must also contribute to their workers' unemployment insurance premiums and even long-term nursing care insurance. Little wonder that in the 1990s German firms have more than quadrupled their investments overseas, producing hundreds of thousands of jobs in Eastern Europe, Latin America, and the United States. Many marquee companies such as Daimler-Benz, Siemens, Volkswagen and BMW will, by the year 2000, have more employees outside of Germany than they do in their homeland.

The roughly 90 percent of the population, well organized into interest groups and political parties, that still benefits from high wages, short work weeks, and a comprehensive social security net has been unwilling to support any changes that would reduce these programs. No real improvement can be made in unemployment until economic growth exceeds about 4 percent. To achieve this level would require new investments that, given the present high labor costs, few German or foreign firms are willing to make.

The burden of high labor costs, taxes, and heavy government regulations has also spawned a rapidly growing underground economy. Working "off the books" means heavy losses for the tax collector and social welfare system, but for a growing number of employers it is the only way to stay in business. Economists now estimate that this underground economy, or in the German term "black" labor market, has doubled in the past twenty years and now accounts for about $350 billion or 15 percent of the country's total Gross Domestic Product.[12] Obviously, the reduction of labor costs is a major challenge facing the new Schröder government, which was elected in 1998.

The German Economy since Unification

The July 1990 currency union, which enabled East Germans to exchange their Eastern Marks for Deutsche Marks—at a rate, in most cases, of from 1 or 2 East Marks to 1 West Mark—unleashed a surge of demand from the East that propelled West Germany's economy into a boom. In 1990 the West German economy grew by almost 5 percent, the highest level since 1976. Inflation remained relatively low at 3 percent, in spite of a rise in oil prices following the Iraqi invasion of Kuwait. Unemployment dropped to less than 7 percent, the lowest level since 1981.

However, the economy of the former East Germany declined rapidly following unification. With the currency reform, East German firms had neither capital reserves nor any price advantage over Western companies. Moreover, the collapse of the Soviet Union's economy meant that East German companies had lost their best customer. Other former Socialist bloc countries, now required to pay in hard Western currency, found the quality of East German goods to be below Western levels. Finally, East Germans themselves stopped buying the products made in their own region, further accelerating the economic downturn.

But by 1992 massive West German aid and investment capital, however, were beginning to show results. Since 1994 the former East Germany has been Europe's fastest growing region. The bottom of the unemployment spiral in the East was reached in late 1994. Since then the number of new jobs created in the region has exceeded the number of jobs lost.

Income Structure

Although almost all gainfully employed West Germans enjoy a relatively high standard of living, there remain persistent and in some cases growing gaps in income and capital resources between different occupational and class groups. In addition, East Germans, regardless of occupation, lag behind their West German counterparts. Income parity between the two regions is not expected until 2005–2008. Modern Germany is still a stratified society. The average monthly net income of different occupational groups is presented in Table 3.3. At the top is the group referred to by German sociologists as "independents" or "employers" (the owners and directors of enterprises, farmers with their own land holdings, and free professionals: doctors, lawyers, small businessmen), which constitutes about 11 percent of the work force. In 1998 these individuals had average net incomes more than three times greater than those of employees (white-collar or manual workers). White-collar employees, who constitute 52 percent of the work force, had monthly take-home incomes of about $3,200 in 1998, whereas manual workers (38 percent of the work force) had net monthly incomes of approximately $2,500.

In the former East Germany, as Table 3.3 shows, there are fewer significant income differences between the various occupational groups. An independent class of small businessmen, entrepreneurs, and professionals is only in its infancy in the

TABLE 3.3   Income by occupation, 1998

	Average Monthly Income, in $*	
	West	**East**
Occupation Group		
Independents (owners and directors of enterprises, free professionals, and farmers)	9546	3354
White-collar, civil servants	3152	2403
Manual workers	2463	1900

*DM 1.5 equal $1.00

Source: Deutsches Institut für Wirtschaftsforschung; Das Institut für Angewandte Wirtschaftsforschung.

East. Few East German independents can afford to pay themselves the salaries earned by their Western counterparts. As a market economy continues to develop in the former GDR, however, the differences between East and West should become smaller.[13]

Capital Resources

In view of the pattern of income distribution in the West, we should not be surprised to find substantial differences in capital resources between the various occupations. For example, ownership of private property in the form of family homes will not be experienced by the majority of manual workers. Although they make up almost 40 percent of the work force, manual workers buy only about 20 percent of the private homes. Independents, only about one-tenth of the work force, own over 40 percent of all private homes and almost half of all common stock.

As Figure 3.1 shows, capital resources are unevenly distributed in modern Germany. At the top of the pyramid, 2.7 percent of all households owns 28 percent of all stocks, bonds, land, savings accounts, and other wealth. The top 9 percent of German households owns about 45 percent of the nation's wealth. Roughly the lower half (46 percent) of Germany's households owns less than 10 percent of the country's wealth, usually in the form of lower-interest savings accounts. There has been little change in this general pattern over the past twenty years, which indicates that German governments have not pursued policies designed to redistribute the country's wealth.

This economic inequality, which has also been reinforced by the education system, is largely the result of postwar government economic policy that gave a free hand to market forces and created a very favorable atmosphere for investment capital. The 1948 currency reforms, for example, which abolished the Reichsmark and installed the now-famous Deutsche Mark (DM), to a large extent wiped out

---

FIGURE 3.1   Distribution of capital resources

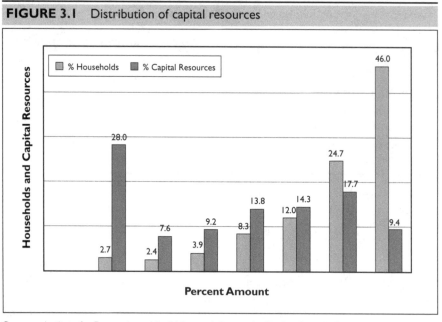

Source: Institute for Economic and Social Research figures cited in *Der Spiegel*, "Die gespaltene Gesellschaft," no. 40 (September 29, 1997), p. 90.

the savings of lower- and middle-income groups, who received only about one new Mark for every seven old Reichsmarks. Landowners and holders of stocks, securities, and capital in foreign countries lost nothing, however. Indeed, they gained. Moderate tax rates on profits and income from investments, generous subsidies for new plants and equipment, and lucrative tax write-offs also helped to prime the investment pump.

The major economic structures of prewar Germany—business, banking, and industrial firms—were not destroyed by the war or the military occupation, but survived fairly intact to provide institutional leadership and support for economic reconstruction.[14] But these institutions of capitalist economic development could perform only if political leadership, both German and Allied, decided to take the free market rather than the socialist path to economic reconstruction. The desire to rebuild as quickly as possible in the face of a perceived Soviet threat meant a decision in favor of the capitalist market economy.

The general success of this system during the past fifty years has been described. Its long-run consequences, particularly in producing and sustaining inequality and rigid social stratification, are now being grappled with in the political arena. The potential that the issue of inequality has in politics can be seen in many surveys in which solid majorities of Germans state that economic rewards have not been justly distributed in the Federal Republic.[15]

West Germany's Left, especially during the 1960s and 1970s, was sharply critical of the postwar decision to restore a capitalist system, which had proven so helpless in the face of the Nazi onslaught and, indeed, had in some cases collaborated with the Nazis. For the New Left, Germany had missed the opportunity between 1945 and 1949 to lay the foundations for a truly socialist society. After 1945 the Old Left advocated the expropriation and socialization of industry, banks, and other commercial institutions and the creation of a state-controlled planned economy. According to this view there is a close connection between capitalism and the Hitler dictatorship, and by restoring capitalism the Western Allies and postwar German leaders also restored the fascist potential.

It is difficult to evaluate this interpretation of postwar German development. There is little doubt that for the sake of rapid economic reconstruction a decision was made to use established economic resources rather than to build a new economic order from scratch. There is also little doubt that the free market or capitalist approach was, at least in the short run, extraordinarily successful. However, the German economy hardly qualifies as a "pure" capitalist system. As in other advanced Western countries, government plays a major economic role through subsidies, regulation, and in some cases capital investment.[16] In 1998, for example, the federal government paid out over $20 billion in subsidies to groups such as farmers, home builders and owners, the aerospace industry, shipbuilders, and coal and steel companies. The Land of Lower Saxony is a major stockholder in the Volkswagen automobile firm. National and state governments are also heavily involved in communications and the coal and steel industries, as well as in housing and transportation. In spite of the trend toward privatization of state-owned enterprises (discussed in Chapter 8), there is still a considerable mix of public and private components in the economy.

Germany's postwar economic elites have assumed a more active political role than at any other time in German history. But this role has been distinctly supportive of the liberal Republic. Business and industrial elites, once subordinate to traditional Prussian and then to radical Nazi political leadership, finally found political responsibility thrust upon them in the Bonn Republic. Like their counterparts in other advanced industrial societies, they have been concerned above all with stable political conditions and have supported the pragmatic, middle-of-the-road policies the Republic has thus far pursued. In this sense Germany's economic elites did after 1945 what they should have done in 1871—assumed their share of responsibility for the conduct of politics, instead of deferring to the traditional Prussian elites in political matters. Thus far in the Federal Republic, the economic elites have shown no inclination to support or be associated with any extremist political movement or philosophy.

RELIGIOUS COMPOSITION

At birth most West Germans become members of either the Roman Catholic or the Protestant Church. This division, an aftermath of the Reformation, follows regional lines: northern and eastern Germany are predominantly Protestant, whereas in the southern and western regions adherents of the Roman Catholic faith are in the majority. In the prewar Reich, Protestants outnumbered Catholics by a ratio of about 2 to 1. The loss of the heavily Protestant (80 percent) Eastern territories and the postwar division of the remaining (also Protestant) territory meant that both confessions had about equal strength in the former West Germany. This parity brought Roman Catholicism out of its minority status and ended Protestant preeminence among political elites. Nonetheless, Catholics still remain underrepresented among Western business, cultural, and educational elites.

In the former East Germany only about one-third of the population report any religious affiliation, with Protestants (27 percent) far outnumbering Catholics (6 percent). Thus in the unified country the ratio of Protestants to Catholics is about 43 to 35; the remainder of the population is not affiliated with either church. These changes have important implications for the relative strength of the political parties and the outcome of certain major issues such as abortion.

Since the influx of foreign workers and residents, which began in the 1960s, Germany has also become home to a growing Muslim population. By 1999 there were almost three million practicing Muslims in Germany, making Islam the third largest religion. Germany's Muslims are organized into over three hundred mosques, all but two of which are in West Germany. The two East German mosques are in Leipzig and Dresden. Unlike the Protestant, Catholic, and Jewish religions, these three million Muslims receive no financial support from the state.

The importance of religion in the lives of West Germans and their attachment to the respective churches, as measured by church attendance, is at best moderate. Only approximately 10 percent of Germans over age 16 attend church services "regularly" (at least twice a month). Only about 5 percent of Protestants are in this category, as compared to 20 percent of Catholics.[17] Church attendance also varies strongly by age and gender; women and older individuals are far more likely to attend regularly than are men and youth. The strength and character of religious beliefs also vary significantly by confession. For example, only 44 percent of Protestants believe in life after death, as compared to 63 percent of Catholics. Among East German Protestants, only 25 percent believe in life after death, as compared to 54 percent of East German Catholics.[18]

Interconfessional hostility appears minimal; solid majorities of both Catholics and Protestants support some sort of union between the two churches. The presence of subcultural "in-group" values within the two confessions has been declining. In 1901, 91 percent of all marriages were between couples of the same faith; in 1938, this had declined to 81 percent; and by 1987, only 53 percent of newly married couples belonged to the same faith.[19] Numerous surveys have found that the majority of the population does not perceive any significant conflict between Catholics and Protestants. The appearance of biconfessional political parties and labor unions in the postwar period has also reduced interconfessional conflict and hastened the social and political integration of German Catholics.

Although religion may not play a prominent role in the lives of most Germans, the two churches, as social institutions, are closely involved in politics. Unlike the United States, Germany has no strong tradition of church-state separation. Since the Reformation, the religious and regional division of the country has meant that the dominant church in any given area was dependent on existing state authority, that is, on the respective princes who acted as protectors of the faith in their territories. This dependence on state authority made both churches (but especially Protestantism, having no international ties) essentially conservative institutions oriented to the status quo. In exchange for their support, the princes also granted a variety of special privileges to the churches (tax-free land, bishops' residences, salaries), many of which are still in effect.

Certainly the most important privilege, and one that makes German churches among the most affluent in the world, is the church tax. This is computed as a percentage (about 9 percent) of an employee's income tax, automatically withheld from paychecks, and then transferred to their coffers.[20] The tax guarantees churches a steady, inflation-proof flow of funds because it is linked to the income tax, which rises with wage and salary increases. To avoid payment of this tax, a citizen must officially "contract out" of his or her church by filing the appropriate documents with state officials. By so doing, however, the citizen will probably have a difficult time securing the services of clergy for baptisms, weddings, and funerals, as well as gaining admission to church-run homes for the aged or securing help from the churches' charities.

Nonetheless, the number of members choosing to opt out of the church tax has increased sharply in recent years; between 1989 and 1995 the Catholic Church lost over 800,000 tax-paying members and the Protestants lost 1.5 million. In 1995, when a new unification solidarity surtax went into effect, as did a 1 percent increase in social security payments to finance a new long-term nursing care program, a record number of Germans dropped out of the church. The amount of church tax they saved was about equal to the new nonoptional taxes.

As one of the few social institutions to survive Nazism and the war with its reputation fairly intact, the church actually increased its political influence after the war in spite of the largely secular, materialist character of West German society. Because the churches were regarded by military occupiers as untainted by Nazism, the best way to get permission during the occupation period for opening or reopening a business or starting a newspaper or a political party was to have ample references from, or some affiliation with, one or both churches. According to one authority, "The immediate postwar years saw the German churches at their most influential since the Reformation."[21] As we will discuss in Chapter 5, both churches have since made extensive use of this influence.

Religion in Eastern Germany

East Germans are far less likely to belong to any church or to accept any basic beliefs of Christianity than are West Germans. Only 7 percent of West Germans have not been baptized or have left the church, as compared to 66 percent of East

Germans. Belief in God is held by 61 percent of West Germans, but by only 21 percent of East Germans. Approximately 50 percent of adults in the "old" Federal Republic believe in life after death, as compared to only 14 percent of the new residents of the enlarged Federal Republic.[22]

Thus unification has made Germany a more secular society. Whether East Germany will experience a religious "revival" in the coming years as its citizens are free to determine their religious preferences remains to be seen. It is remarkable that over one-third of the East German population has retained an affiliation to the church in spite of forty years of official opposition—if not hostility—to religion. The schools, youth organizations, media, and of course the Communist party pressured citizens of the former GDR to leave the churches or avoid any contact with them.

AGE AND FAMILY STRUCTURE

The frequent and sudden changes in modern German political history have affected the present age distribution of the population. As Figure 3.2 shows, low birth rates occurred during and at the end of the two world wars and during the economic depression of the 1930s. These low birth rates affected the distribution of both men and women; thus by the 1990s the 40–50, 55–65, and 70–75 age groups were all underrepresented in the population relative to other groups.

Casualties from the two world wars also produced a shortage of males, which was especially noticeable among those over age 55. In the immediate postwar period, the combined effect of war losses and low birth rates produced an underrepresentation and shortage of younger males in the work force, hence the need to import foreign workers to alleviate a severe labor shortage. In 1946–1947, for example, in the 20–25 year-old age bracket there were 171 women for every 100 men; in the 35–40 year-old group there were 153 women for every 100 men. Between 1939 and 1946 the proportion of males between the ages of 15 and 40 dropped from 59 percent to 49 percent.[23] A constant feature of German age structure throughout the postwar period, then, has been a shortage of males in the economically productive stages of the life cycle and a surplus in the "dependent" age groups. The low birth rates of the past ten years have further increased the dependent proportion of the population.

Overall modern Germany is thus an aging society. Low birth rates, longer life spans, and migration have produced an absolute and relative increase in the elderly population. Between 1950 and 1993 the number of residents over 60 years of age increased by 51 percent; the elderly proportion of the total population also jumped from less than 15 percent to over 20 percent.[24]

Major generational differences in political attitudes and behavior have become noticeable only since the late 1960s. The various generations, according to most analyses, exhibited a high degree of agreement on major political and social topics during at least the first two decades of the Republic's history.[25]

This was due in large part to the familial solidarity and almost exclusive concentration on material reconstruction that characterized the postwar period. As a re-

FIGURE 3.2   Age structure of the population

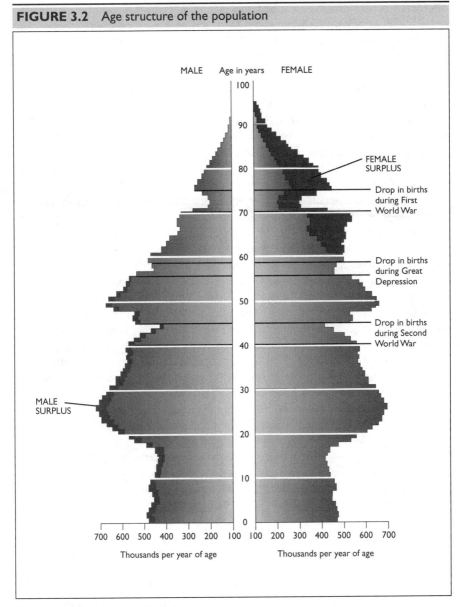

Source: German Information Center.

sult, little political communication and hence conflict took place between generations. For most Germans, the family "came to be regarded as the last stable focus in
a world of vast destruction, and vital interests returned to the sphere of the family."[26]
Given the overriding concern for maintenance of the nuclear family, politics as a

subject of possible disagreement between parents and children and hence a threat to familial solidarity was a taboo topic.[27] Also, the concern for economic betterment extended across all age groups and left little room for discussions about political issues, much less political participation.

The confrontation and "overcoming" of the National Socialist past, urged by Western occupiers and German intellectuals and an obvious topic for intergenerational discussion and debate, was postponed until the student and youth protest movement of the late 1960s. The New Left's critique of "monopoly capitalism" as practiced in the Federal Republic was linked to charges that German big business had supported and encouraged the Nazis. Many students, usually from middle-class backgrounds, defended their radical views in debates with their parents by reminding them of their support for the National Socialists.

Generational differences in other political areas also became apparent at this time. Younger age groups, generally those under age 30, were far more likely to support the Brandt government's innovative foreign policies, begun after 1969, than were older age groups. Attitudes toward major domestic reform issues such as codetermination in industry (see Chapter 5) and education were also divided significantly along age lines. Differences in more basic political dispositions such as liberalism and conservatism were also discovered by researchers. For example, a 1970 study found Germans under age 30 almost three times more likely to describe their basic political position as "left" than were their fellow citizens over age 60.[28] In a 1971 poll of parents and their children over age 16, 34 percent of the parent group ranked high on measures of authoritarianism as compared to only 8 percent of their children. And although 24 percent of the parent group were classified as politically "liberal," 41 percent of their children were in this group.[29]

This period also saw the reduction of the voting age to 18 and an increasing tendency on the part of younger voters to prefer the Social Democrat (SPD) and Liberal (FDP) parties over the Christian Democrats (CDU). In the 1983 and 1987 federal elections, young voters provided the new Green political party with the majority of its support. The Social Democrats in 1990 made a strong appeal for the support of young voters and were able to make inroads into the young Green vote. In 1998 both the Greens and the SPD did well among younger voters.

Family Structure

The postwar period witnessed an increase in the importance of the family as a social institution, as well as a change in authority relations within the family. As we have discussed, most Germans after 1945, in the face of the widespread collapse of traditional beliefs and values, withdrew to the family, "the last outpost of social security."[30] Yet this was a different, less authoritarian family structure than had existed earlier in German political history. Parental, especially paternal, authority had suffered a decline through National Socialism and the war. In some parts of postwar Germany, up to one-third of all children were being raised in fatherless homes. If the fathers did return from war and imprisonment, they were in many cases

largely dispirited and unable to orient themselves in the post-defeat conditions, thus further impairing their prestige. . . . Men having been indoctri-
nated to feel as "supermen" were, in varying degrees, unable to deal in a
dignified manner with the occupation forces in the role of subordinates,
often discrediting themselves in the eyes of their wives through awkward
obsequiousness.[31]

These postwar changes have had important consequences for German politics.
Wartime and postwar research on the family, especially that conducted by American social scientists, contended that the typical family was father-dominated and
had not changed significantly since the Industrial Revolution.[32] Father domination
and authoritarianism were then linked to the success of the Nazi movement and the
apparently strong emotional support that Hitler could count on until almost the last
months of the war.

Postwar research on the family has challenged this argument, as well as the assumption that there is a clear-cut relationship between the power structure within
the family and the support or nonsupport of particular political systems. In a 1959
comparative study of five nations, approximately 30 percent of the German respondents reported that their parents' home was "father-dominated" whereas only 17 percent judged their own families to be so governed. The percentage of "partnership
families" increased between generations from 39 percent to 63 percent.[33] The same
study found fewer father-dominated families in West Germany than in either Mexico or Italy. An analysis of these five-nation data showed that among respondents
growing up before 1917, only 29 percent recalled having had "some influence" in
family decisions, whereas 65 percent of those who grew up (i.e., who reached their
sixteenth birthday) between 1948 and 1953 reported that they had influence in family decisions.[34] Other postwar work on the family has also discovered a consensual
style of decision making to be the most frequent. The great majority of young people stated that they "got along well" with both parents and felt free to discuss any
problem with them.[35]

As Table 3.4 shows, public opinion on the topic of "who should run the marriage," also has changed significantly since the 1950s. In 1954 only 40 percent of
males and 54 percent of females felt that both husband and wife should have
"equal rights" in a marriage, and 42 percent of the men questioned and 28 percent of the women thought that the "man should have more say." By 1979, however, two-thirds of the males and almost three-fourths of the females took
the "equal rights" position. The "male chauvinist" proportion had dropped to 10
percent among men and only 6 percent for the women in the survey. Thus the
general climate of opinion on this topic has changed markedly over the quarter-
century period.

This steady increase in a decision-making style based on partnership, which has
apparently been taking place since the turn of the century in spite of rapid and sudden changes in political systems (empire, Weimar Republic, Nazi dictatorship, Bonn
Republic), suggests that there is no direct relationship between familial authority

TABLE 3.4   Equality in marriage, 1954–1979

Question: Do you feel that both husband and wife should have equal rights in a marriage, or do you feel the man should have more to say?

	1954		1979	
	Males	**Females**	**Males**	**Females**
Equal rights	40	54	67	74
Man should have more to say	42	28	10	6
Undecided, "it depends"	18	18	23	20

Source: Institute für Demoskipie, *Allensbach Report,* June 1979, p. 6.

relations and the specific structure of the political system. The "authoritarian-father thesis" cannot explain Nazism. Most students of family authority relations attribute the partnership style not to any political system or policy but to the effects of industrialization and modernization—specifically the entrance of the married woman into the labor force and the larger socioeconomic environment, which, it is argued, increases her power within the family. Thus the present style of decision making is a further indication of the modernization of postwar social structure.

THE EDUCATIONAL SYSTEM

The stratified character of German society is in part the result of an educational system that historically has given a basic education to all, but advanced academic training to only a few. Both the German academic high school (*Gymnasium*) and the universities were designed to educate a small elite for leadership positions, with the rest of the population being given only a general education sufficient to enable them to perform satisfactorily at lower levels of the society and economy. This traditional system and the manner in which children were selected for attendance at the higher schools reflected and perpetuated the existing class alignment.

Basic Structure

Most German education still operates on the traditional three-track pattern once common to many European societies. After four years (ages 6 to 10) of compulsory primary school, the 10-year-old child continues on one of three tracks:

1. Five to six more years in a general school (*Hauptschule*) followed by three to four years of both part-time classroom instruction and vocational training in a company. Between the ages of 18 and 19 this group then enters the work force on a full-time basis. They cease full-time education at the age of 16 or 17.[36]

2. Attendance for up to six years at a general high school (*Realschule*), which combines academic and technical training. Depending on the student's aptitude and course of study, Realschule graduates can transfer to the *Gymnasium* (academic high school) and the university.

3. Entrance into a Gymnasium for nine years of university preparatory education culminating in the *Abitur* (a degree roughly comparable to an American junior college diploma) and the right to attend a university.

The first two years in any track are considered an orientation period; transfers between various tracks are possible. Until the late 1960s, only about 40 percent of German children pursued tracks two or three, and less than 20 percent ever reached the university. Thus for most children full-time schooling ceased after only nine to ten years of school. The early school-leaving age meant that a career decision had to be made relatively early in life. Many working-class children, who had to make such a decision at age 15 or 16, had few options and probably had little input in the decision. By the 1980s, however, the proportion of the youngest age cohort in tracks two and three had risen to over 60 percent as the various reform policies of the state and national governments began to have an impact.[37]

There has been a strong class bias in the entire system. Both the Gymnasium and the university have been largely preserves of the middle class. According to one study conducted in the 1970s, working-class children had only an 8 percent chance of attending a Gymnasium, as compared to a 67 percent chance for the offspring of middle-class parents. Moreover, even the working-class child who did reach the Gymnasium had only about a 12 percent chance of reaching the university, as compared to a 50 percent chance for middle-class children.[38] Thus even in the Gymnasium the children of working-class parents were less likely to complete the course of study and gain entrance to the university. In the 1982–1983 school year only 20 percent of Gymnasium graduates were the children of working-class parents, one of the lowest levels among industrial societies.[39] It should thus not be surprising when surveys reveal that about three-fourths of manual workers are the sons of manual workers and that only about one out of every four holders of nonmanual occupations (white collar, civil servant, self-employed, free professional) comes from a working-class family.

In the immediate postwar years, the Allied occupiers, together with reform-minded Germans, planned extensive changes in this system through the introduction of comprehensive secondary schools, which were to provide greater educational opportunity. For a variety of reasons (not the least of were the Cold War and Allied reluctance to avoid radical social and economic changes that might hinder German economic reconstruction and rearmament), traditionalist, antireform forces prevailed, and the movement for change dissipated. Antireform elements also saw a relationship between the planned comprehensive school and the Unified School system introduced in the Soviet zone (East Germany).

By the mid-1960s public concern with the quality and performance of the educational system rose to unprecedented levels. International comparisons of student achievement and educational quality presented the German system in a poor light.

The federal government, which, according to the constitution, was clearly subordinate to the states in the field of education, began to seek a larger role in educational policy. The result was a 1969 constitutional amendment that assigns to the national government some responsibilities for overall educational planning and innovation—from kindergarten to the university. (Ironically, in the country that gave the institution of the *Kindergarten* to the world, there is sufficient space and personnel for only two out of every three *Kinder* [children].)

The key component of plans for restructuring and reforming the system has been the merger of the three-tracked secondary system into a single comprehensive school (*Gesamtschule*). All children, regardless of social background, would attend this school until at least the age of 16. At that point, children with a more vocational orientation would graduate with a first-level Abitur and would then proceed to vocational training and full-time occupations. The second level (upper secondary) of the Gesamtschule would consist of three more years of academic study and would culminate with a higher-level Abitur, followed by university attendance or full-time employment. Thus the tracking of students would be avoided until at least the age of 16 rather than the present age of 10 in some states. The purpose, of course, is more equality of educational opportunity and hence more social mobility. This relationship between education and equality of opportunity makes the comprehensive school issue more politically controversial than the reform of preschool education, vocational training, or university education. Fearing "unmitigated egalitarianism" and reduced standards, and valuing a more stratified, hierarchically ordered society, conservatives (including many Gymnasium teachers) have opposed most reform plans. The Christian Democrats have essentially taken the conservative position on this issue. The Social Democrats, on the other hand, are generally supportive of the comprehensive school and overall education reform.

Since 1969 the comprehensive school has been introduced in all states. By 1998 there were approximately 490 integrated comprehensive schools with about 550,000 students, of which roughly 80 percent were in states governed by the SPD. Comprehensive schools have also been introduced in the five new states of the former East Germany. However, this is a policy issue that still divides the political parties.

The general trend in all states is toward more flexibility between the tracks and greater opportunity. Since 1950 the proportion of all Germans with some educational experience beyond the basic level (track one) has increased from 18 percent to almost 45 percent. Indeed, by 1991 for the first time in German history there were more young people attending colleges and universities than there were in vocational (trainee) programs.[40] More students, regardless of their social background, are now offered a wider variety of programs and schools as Germany adapts its educational system to the needs of an advanced industrial society.[41]

Education in East Germany. The five new states in the former East Germany have had to restructure their educational systems to the West German pattern. This is a massive task involving the establishment of new schools and curriculum, and teacher retraining. In addition to the standard academic subjects, the communist system included programs designed to indoctrinate young people with Marxist-

Leninist ideology and thus produce the "new Socialist man and woman."[42] Indeed, the influence of the party was pervasive. Many teachers and almost all school administrators were party members. The great majority of children belonged to communist youth organizations, and most adolescents joined the Free German Youth, the East German version of the Soviet Young Communist League.

With the help of the West German states, many East German teachers have undergone retraining courses. New Western textbooks appeared in most schools by the 1992–1993 school year. Many East German teachers have been on probationary status, which gives them the opportunity to demonstrate that they can adapt to the demands of education in a free society. By the late 1990s most, but by no means all, were given permanent status in the new system. At the administrative level—principals and assistant principals—many were dismissed or demoted. In East Berlin, for example, at the beginning of the 1991–1992 school year only 46 of about 700 pre-1989 administrators were in their old positions. It is estimated that about 30,000 of the 185,000 East German teachers and administrators were replaced.[43] By 1995 at the college and university level about two-thirds of the 140,000 employees of the old system were dismissed because of their conduct during the communist regime, their inability to meet western standards, or for budgetary reasons.[44]

MASS MEDIA

As a highly developed industrial society, Germany has an extensive mass media structure that has made Germans among the most politically informed people in the world.[45] Approximately 70 percent of the population views the half-hour evening newscasts of the major networks. Political news comprises about one-third of these telecasts. Also, political reports in daily newspapers are read by roughly 60 percent of the adult population.[46] But an increasing concentration of newspaper and magazine ownership and a certain bureaucratic blandness (induced by the structure of public control) in radio and television's political reporting have become problems in the media's relationship to the political system.

The Press

Germany has approximately 350 daily newspapers with a combined daily circulation of about 32 million. However, only one-third of these have their own complete editorial staff. The remainder have local staff and advertising facilities and rely on wire-service reports or reports from other papers in their chains for state, national, and international news. Moreover, almost 60 percent of daily readers consume the journalistic products offered by the Springer publishing company. Until his death in 1985, Axel Springer used his press empire to oppose left-wing foreign and domestic politics, especially as they affected business interests and the possibility of German unification.

In terms of national newspapers, Germany is limited to one mass-oriented tabloid, the *Bild Zeitung* (literally, "Picture Newspaper"), and several quality, "elite" papers. *Bild,* the flagship of the Springer chain, with a daily circulation of

4.4 million and an estimated daily readership of over 12 million (about one-fifth of the adult population), is a skillfully edited blend of sensational sex, crime, and populist politics. Claiming to speak for the average citizen in advocating "common sense" politics, the paper treated the conciliatory approach to the Soviet Union and Eastern Europe of the Social-Liberal coalition during the 1970s as a sellout of German interests and at times imputed traitorous behavior to government policymakers in this area. But *Bild* can also take more conservative politicians to task, as it did Chancellor Kohl in 1991 when he reneged on his campaign pledge of "no new taxes" to finance unification.

Another favorite target of the Springer press has been "radicals" and "leftists" in the schools, universities, and political parties. The paper—indeed the entire firm—was the focus of student demonstrations during the late 1960s and early 1970s. The Springer press portrayed the students as the irresponsible, spoiled offspring of an overly tolerant middle class playing into the hands of the communists. The students and many intellectuals have in turn charged *Bild* and the Springer chain with deliberate distortion of the news in a way that contributes to the apolitical tendencies of some citizens.

The major national elite daily newspapers, all with circulations between 275,000 and 500,000, are the conservative to middle-of-the-road *Frankfurter Allgemeine Zeitung;* the more reformist *Süddeutsche Zeitung* (published in Munich); the avowedly left-liberal *Frankfurter Rundschau;* and the one quality paper in the Springer chain, *Die Welt,* which was once a highly respected publication before Springer undertook his active involvement in politics.

Although their editorial orientations differ, these papers present a high level of reporting with strong coverage given to politics as well as business and financial news. In recent years a new national daily, *Die Tageszeitung,* or simply *taz,* has become the major voice of the alternative media. Its editorial position is close to the Greens, the environmentalist, feminist, and peace movements.

Prior to unification, all of East Germany's major daily papers were under the control of the Communist party and its allied organizations: trade unions, women's and youth groups, and the bloc parties. With unification, most of the GDR's seventy dailies were bought out by or were merged with West German media organizations. By 1998 more than half of the 8 million daily newspaper circulation in the former GDR was accounted for by five West German publishing companies.

Periodicals.   The best-known political periodical is the weekly news magazine *Der Spiegel* ("The Mirror"), with a circulation of over 1 million. Similar to *Time* or *Newsweek* magazine in appearance, *Der Spiegel* prides itself on a crusading, critical, iconoclastic style. Its founder and publisher, Rudolf Augstein, the liberal counterpart to Axel Springer, has been active in politics as an adviser and parliamentary candidate. In recent years the magazine has become the leading practitioner of aggressive investigative reporting in the Federal Republic. The various scandals dealing with the financing of political parties,including the Flick affair (see Chapter 6), began with extensive exposes in *Der Spiegel.* To the dismay of the West German Left and some of his own editors, Augstein strongly supported Chancellor Kohl's "rush to unity" in 1989–1990.

Since 1993 *Der Spiegel* has had to contend with a powerful competitor, *Focus,* a product of the Burda publishing group. Within a year the new weekly, published in Munich, attained a circulation of 600,000 and made strong inroads into *Der Spiegel*'s circulation and, above all, advertising revenue. *Focus* aims at a younger audience, is less opinionated than *Der Spiegel,* and makes much greater use of color and graphics.

Television and Radio
Mindful of the Nazis' abuses of the airwaves, the Constitution assigns sole responsibility for radio and television to the constituent states. Both media are administered by state-based, nonprofit public corporations, which are to be free from direct political influence. These corporations, however, are supervised by boards of control representing the major "social, economic, cultural, and political forces," including political parties and interest groups.

There are currently ten such broadcasting corporations, acting for the sixteen Länder. They form the Association of Public Broadcasting Corporations in the Federal Republic (ARD), constitute the First Network of German television, and also produce cooperative radio programs. A second television network (ZDF) was established in 1962. Both public radio and television are financed largely through monthly fees charged for each household.

The political parties exert considerable influence on broadcasting corporations through the presence of their representatives on the stations' governing councils. Some of the regional corporations are identified as either "red" (SPD), such as Bremen or Hesse, or "black" (CDU/CSU), such as the Bavarian and Southwest (Baden-Württemberg, Rheinland-Palatinate) Broadcasting Corporations. Proportional CDU-SPD-FDP influence characterizes the North German Broadcasting Corporation (NDR). The Second National Television Network (ZDF) generally tends toward a pro-CDU position. Thus far only the West German Corporation (WDR), financed largely by the state of North Rhine–Westphalia, has remained relatively free of significant party influence.

All these corporations, with the exception of the Second Network, are responsible for producing a common national program. The contribution of each regional corporation is determined by its size and income. This sometimes causes conflict between the regional networks. Programs produced by "red" stations critical of Christian Democratic political leaders or policies have been rejected by stations in CDU-dominated states. The "black" stations, or commentators close to the Christian Democrats, have at times returned the favor with programs critical of the Social Democrats. Nor has the Second Network been free of political influence. In 1991 a leading commentator for ZDF was transferred, apparently owing to his excessive criticism of Chancellor Kohl.

Following unification, the five new East German states established their own public broadcasting corporations.[47] The states of Saxony, Thuringia, and Saxony-Anhalt formed the Middle German Network (MDR), which became part of the First Network (ARD). This new network is based in Leipzig. The small northern state of Mecklenburg–West Pomerania joined the North German Network (NDR). Significantly, the only eastern state that did not join with other new states, or with those in the "old"

Federal Republic, to form a network was Brandenburg, the sole eastern state in 1991 not governed by the Christian Democrats. It formed the East German Network (ORB). The Second Network has also established studios in the five new states.

In 1983 the government of Chancellor Kohl introduced a variety of proposals for private radio and television stations and began to install cable facilities throughout the country. In 1985 a private channel, SAT-1, which is partly owned by the Springer company, began cable and satellite telecasts. Its main output was light entertainment and feature films, with some news material. The new channel was jointly owned by the Springer company and the Leo Kirch organization. Kirch has become a major figure in the new private television market.[48] Shortly after the introduction of SAT-1, a second private station, RTL-plus, began its programs. The public networks have also added cable-satellite stations. By 1998 over 17 million households, or more than half the country's 80 million viewers, were able to receive the new stations.[49] In the past the Social Democrats have generally opposed private radio and television networks, fearing an excessive commercialization of the media. The notion that the mass media have a responsibility for educating citizens and elevating the cultural level of the nation, rather than merely providing entertainment, is still supported by many Social Democrats.[50]

Since their introduction, however, the private and cable networks have been very successful in drawing viewers away from the public stations. Many Germans seem to prefer American-style entertainment programs over traditional cultural and educational offerings ("MTV over Wagner"). The popularity of the commercial networks has forced the public stations to adapt their programming to the mass entertainment or American model, much to the disappointment of many intellectuals. Ratings and advertising revenue are now closely watched by the public networks even though the core of their revenues still come from user fees.

Like their public counterparts, the large private networks have been identified with specific parties and candidates. Most media observers consider SAT-1 to be pro-CDU and especially positive toward the Kohl government (1982–1998), whereas RTL was more critical of the chancellor. According to one study, SAT-1 during the 1994 election campaign gave almost four times more television coverage to Kohl than to Rudolf Scharping, his opponent.[51]

The success of the private media companies has put the public stations on the defensive. Why, critics ask, should Germans pay monthly fees, set by law, to finance stations they increasingly do not watch? The Christian Democratic party has been at the forefront of the current dissatisfaction with the public stations. Many Christian Democrats advocate privatizing the state-run stations or greatly reducing their budgets.[52]

SUMMARY AND CONCLUSION

The Federal Republic of Germany today is a more socioeconomically modern, integrated society than was the Germany of the empire, the Weimar Republic, or the Nazi dictatorship. The postwar loss of territory in the east to the Soviet Union and Poland and the 1949–1990 division of the nation also meant the loss of several major headaches that had plagued political systems in the past: the dominance of Prussia; regional conflicts; an inner-directed Catholic subculture; an antidemocratic, militaristic landed nobility; and Great Power pretensions in foreign policy. Wartime destruction and postwar refugee migration meant a new, modern postwar economic plant staffed by an abundant supply of proficient labor, in many cases composed of refugees from the "lost territories." Economic success and prosperity brought an easing of class tensions and the end of working-class social isolation. Ironically and albeit at a frightful cost, the Nazis left German society in a condition more favorable to liberal democracy than they had found it.

These changed socioeconomic conditions now constitute an environment that is more conducive to the growth of support for the Republic than was the case during Germany's first attempt at political democracy, the Weimar Republic. The dominance of achievement-oriented, materialistic, and individualistic values may cause intellectuals to dismiss the Federal Republic as provincial and philistine, but they have made Germany more governable as a political democracy.

As we will discuss in the next chapter, a consensus on the key values and norms of political democracy, not present in 1949, has developed in the Federal Republic during the past five decades. As a result of this consensus, the leaders and those who are led are better prepared to deal with the social, economic, and political challenges of unification and the other policy problems of the twenty-first century than were earlier generations.

Notes

1. German political leaders have generally avoided addressing this problem, fearful of reviving memories of the Third Reich when Hitler encouraged large families as part of his racist program. During the 1987 election campaign, Chancellor Helmut Kohl alluded to the birth rate problem by encouraging Germans to adopt a positive attitude toward children and large families.
2. Federal Statistical Office, Wiesbaden. Statistics on the number of East Germans who have moved to the West are no longer kept, but it is estimated that an additional 250,000 have moved to the West since unification.
3. See the comments by the historian Jürgen Kocka in *The Economist*, May 21, 1994, p. 10.
4. Federal Statistical Office, "Frankreich—Deutschlands wichtigster Handelspartner im Jahr 1998," March 11, 1999 (Internet edition). Among individual countries, France and the United States are Germany's most important trading partners.
5. Germany is self-sufficient in grain, sugar, beef, and milk. Fruits, vegetables, poultry, eggs, and pork are its major food imports. Friedrich Golter, "Aufgaben der Landwirtschaft in einer modernen Industriegesellschaft," *Aus Politik und Zeitgeschichte*, no. 42 (October 18, 1986): 30.
6. Organization for Economic Cooperation and Development, *Economic Surveys: Germany* (Paris, 1991), p. 48; *Agrarbericht 1995*, cited in *Frankfurter Allgemeine Zeitung*, February 8, 1995, p. 1, Federal Statistical Office.
7. Arnold J. Heidenheimer, *The Governments of Germany* (New York: Thomas Y. Crowell, 1971), pp. 197–198. See also Arthur Gunlicks, *Local Government in the German Federal System* (Durham and London: Duke University Press, 1986), Chapter 7.
8. Daniel Bell, *The Coming of Post-Industrial Society* (New York: Basic Books, 1973), p. 17.
9. Federal Statistical Office, Wiesbaden.

10. David P. Conradt, "The Electorate, 1980–1983," in *Germany at the Polls: The Bundestag Elections of the 1980s,* ed. Karl H. Cerny (Durham and London: Duke University Press, 1990), p. 48.

11. Carl Graf Hohenthal, "Die Billigkonkurrenz aus dem Ausland macht dem deutschen Bergbau zu schaffen," *Frankfurter Allgemeine Zeitung,* March 13, 1997, p. 3.

12. Norbert Sturm, "Die im Schatten zahlen nicht," *Süddeutsche Zeitung,* March 6, 1998 (Internet edition).

13. Until October 1991, when most subsidies were ended, East Germans paid on average substantially less for rental property than their counterparts in the West. This would reduce the differences reported in Table 3.3. In the next few years, however, rents in Eastern Germany will rise to approximate Western levels.

14. Karl W. Roskamp, *Capital Formation in West Germany* (Detroit: Wayne State University Press, 1965), pp. 53ff.

15. General Social Survey, Zentralarchiv für empirische Sozialforschung, *Codebook,* 1984, p. 51.

16. German governments have also played an active role in organizing rescue operations for industries and major corporations facing a severe economic crisis. Although such bail-outs are relatively rare in the United States (e.g., the Lockheed and Chrysler loan guarantees), German national and state governments since the early 1960s have come to the aid of the coal and steel industry, shipbuilding, automobile companies, and major electronics firms. Governments have used devices such as loan guarantees, tax write-offs, subsidies, and even direct grants to major industries in order to save the companies and the jobs they provide. In some cases political officials, together with business, labor, and banking leaders, have formed a "crisis cartel" to fashion comprehensive, long-term solutions to the problems of key industries such as shipbuilding and electronics. For an analysis of several corporate crises in West Germany, see Kenneth Dyson, "The Politics of Corporate Crises in West Germany," *West European Politics 7,* no. 1 (January 1984): 24–46.

17. *Der Spiegel,* no. 10 (March 6, 1995), p. 76.

18. EMNID 1990 surveys cited in *Das Profil der Deutschen* (Hamburg: Spiegel Verlag, 1991), p. 74.

19. M. Rainer Lepsius, "Sozialstruktur und soziale Schichtung in der Bundesrepublik Deutschland," in *Die Zweite Republik,* ed. Richard Löwenthal and Hans-Peter Schwarz (Stuttgart: Seewald Verlag, 1974), p. 264; and John Ardagh, *Germany and the Germans* (New York: Harper and Row, 1987), p. 231.

20. Receipts from the tax amount to about $11 billion annually. The government retains about 3 percent of these revenues to cover the administrative expenses related to the collection of the tax.

21. Frederic Spotts, *The Churches and Politics in Germany* (Middletown, CT: Wesleyan University Press, 1973), p. x.

22. EMNID surveys cited in *Das Profil der Deutschen.*

23. O. Jean Brandes, "The Effect of War on the German Family," *Social Forces* 29 (1950): 165.

24. Computed from figures cited in Juliane Roloff, "Alternde Gesellschaft in Deutschland," *Aus Politik und Zeitgeschichte,* no. 35 (August 23, 1996), p. 3.

25. Elisabeth Noelle-Neumann and Erich Peter Neumann, *The Germans: Public Opinion Polls, 1947–1966* (Allensbach: Verlag für Demoskopie, 1967), pp. 34ff.

26. Eugen Lupri, "The West German Family Today and Yesterday: A Study in Changing Family Authority Patterns" (Ph.D. dissertation, University of Wisconsin–Madison, 1967), p. 37.

27. Friedrich Tenbrück, "Alltagsnormen und Lebensgefühle in der Bundesrepublik," in Löwenthal and Schwarz: *Die Zweite Republik,* pp. 289–310.

28. Institut für Demoskopie, Study No. 2060.

29. Manfred Koch, *Die Deutschen und ihr Staat* (Hamburg: Hoffmann and Campe, 1972), p. 45.

30. Helmut Schelsky, "The Family in Germany," *Marriage and Family Living 16,* no. 4 (November 1954): 332.

31. Brandes, "The Effect of War on the German Family," p. 165.
32. See, for example, Bertram Schaffner, *Fatherland: A Study of Authoritarianism in the German Family* (New York: Columbia University Press, 1949), pp. 15ff; David Rodnick, *Postwar Germans: An Anthropologist's Account* (New Haven: Yale University Press, 1948), pp. 123 ff; David Abrahamsen, *Men, Mind, and Power* (New York: Harper, 1947), pp. 154ff.
33. Lupri, "The West German Family Today and Yesterday," pp. 41–46.
34. *Ibid.*
35. Koch, *Die Deutschen und ihr Staat*, pp. 102, 121.
36. Germany has a highly developed system of vocational education, which some observers consider a key to its postwar economic success and a major factor in the relatively low level of unemployment among young people. All students who have finished the general education track, or who have dropped out of Realschule or Gymnasium programs, must attend a vocational or trade school up to the age of 18. About 60 percent of the classroom instruction is focused on vocational subjects and the remainder on general academic subjects. This classroom work is confined, however, to one or two days a week. Thus most of the students' time is spent with hands-on training in the business enterprise. The trainees are paid a modest wage by the sponsoring company. Training is offered in about 400 occupations or trades ranging from baker to computer specialist. The vocational program is completed when the trainee passes a theoretical and practical examination conducted by an examining board of experts in the field. Susan Stern (ed.), *Meet United Germany* (Frankfurt: Frankfurter Allgemeine Zeitung Information Services, 1991), pp. 151–153. Some experts recommend this type of vocational education system for other countries including the United States. See William E. Nothdurft, *School Works* (Washington, D.C.: The Brookings Institution, 1989).
37. Statistisches Bundesamt, *Datenreport 1989* (Bonn: Bundeszentrale für politische Bildung, 1989), p. 56.
38. Hans W. Weiler, "The Politics of Education Innovation: Recent Developments in West German School Reform" (Report to the National Academy of Education, October 1973), pp. 43ff.
39. Der Bundesminister für Wissenschaft und Bildung, *Strukturdaten, 1986/1987,* Bad Godesberg, 1986, p. 62.
40. *Der Spiegel, no.* 50 (December 9, 1991), p. 36. University education in Germany, as in many other European countries, is free. Students pay only a nominal registration fee. Grants and loans are available to students from lower-income families to cover the costs of room and board.
41. By 1998 in the former West Germany, 37 percent of students were attending either the Gymnasium or the comprehensive school. Only 34 percent were in the Hauptschule, with the remainder attending Realschulen. Thus almost two of every three children were in academic tracks. Some experts now maintain that there are too many children at this level. See Reiner Scholz, "Das Gymnasium—Hauptschule der Nation, *Die Zeit,* no. 51 (December 20, 1991), p. 11.
42. The official term was "comprehensive, educated humanist socialist personality." See Bernd-Reiner Fischer and Norbert Schmidt, "Das zweifache Scheitern der DDR-Schule," *Aus Politik und Zeitgeschichte,* nos. 37–38 (September 6, 1991): pp. 27–36 for a discussion of GDR educational philosophy.
43. *Der Spiegel,* no. 37, (September 9, 1991), p. 119.
44. Nina Grunenberg, "The Roof Still Leaks in the Physics Department," *Education and Science*, no. 2 (1994), p. 119.
45. See 1991 World Values Study, Interuniversity Consortium for Political Research, Ann Arbor, MI, 1991.
46. Eurobarometer Survey, no. 35 (April 1991).
47. For an excellent account of the changes in the media of the former GDR from the collapse of the communist regime through the unification process see Joseph E. Naftzinger, "Transitioning from Communist to Free Media in Central Europe: The Example of East German Television and Radio," unpublished manuscript, Washington, D.C., December 1991.

48. Nathaniel Nash, "A Dominant Force in European TV," *New York Times,* August, 28, 1995, p. D1.

49. Federal Statistical Office, Wiesbaden, Press Release, Nov. 17, 1996. Thus far only about one-third of those households that can receive the cable program have actually chosen to be connected to the system.

50. Former Chancellor Helmut Schmidt (1974–1982) was especially critical of private, commercial television. In 1979 he attempted to halt the installation of an experimental cable television network and the broadcast of German-language television programs from Radio Luxembourg's satellite. Schmidt contended that a "flood" of commercial television programs would be damaging to German family life and "change the structure of our democratic society." His anti-television campaign included a proposal that Germans abstain one day each week from watching television. There was little interest in his plan.

51. Institut für Demoskopie, Survey No. 6033 cited in *Information zur politischen Bildung*, No. 260 (Fall 1998), p. 47.

52. Alan Cowell, "Germans, Too, May Trim Public TV," *New York Times,* February 9, 1995, p. A6.

CHAPTER

4

Political Culture, Participation, and Civil Liberties

According to many historians, Germany's first experiment with political democracy at a national level, the Weimar Republic, failed because it was a "republic without republicans." The formal structures of political democracy—representative institutions, free elections, constitutional guarantees of civil liberties—were present, but the political attitudes and values of many Germans were not supportive of these structures. According to this view, most Germans during Weimar longed for either a restoration of the monarchy or a similarly strong authoritarian system to return the country to economic prosperity and great power status. As discussed in Chapter 1, the founding of the Federal Republic likewise met with little popular enthusiasm. Hence some Germans and foreign political leaders, as well as scholars, were uncertain in 1949 about the prospects of the postwar system. Once again, as during Weimar, the constitutional structures of democracy were present, but what about the political attitudes that lay behind the constitution? Would Germans, through their attitudes and behavior, accept and support this new system, or would they remain indifferent or even embrace antisystem ideologies and movements?

This chapter explores the question by examining the development of German political culture—that is, German attitudes and values toward politics and German political behavior—since the founding of the postwar state. We will seek to determine how Germans think and feel about the republic and how they have acted or behaved toward the new system since 1949. Of particular importance since 1949 are the support and maintenance of civil liberties and human rights as well as the treatment of minority groups.

In this chapter we also will examine the political culture of the Federal Republic's newest citizens: the 16 million inhabitants of the former German Democratic Republic who lived for forty years under a one-party dictatorship, but who, through West German television and radio, were well informed about the development of democracy among their Western cousins. Are East Germans different in their political attitudes and values? Or did they experience vicariously the changes that took place in

West Germany and need only an opportunity to express freely their support for democratic values and institutions? Did they become "republicans without a republic"?

POLITICAL VALUES

National Identity

As a linguistic, ethnic, and cultural unit, the German nation is one of Europe's oldest. Britain, France, and other European states had resolved the questions of political and geographical boundaries as well as the criteria for membership in the national community by the late eighteenth century. Yet the questions of what Germany is and who the Germans are have never been resolved in a political sense. A single German state incorporating all peoples who identify with the German nation has never really existed, with one possible exception: Hitler's short-lived and ill-fated *Grossdeutsches Reich* (Great German Reich), established after Nazi annexations of Austria and the Sudetenland. Even the much-heralded unification and establishment of a Second Reich under Prussian leadership in 1871, which brought twenty-five German political entities into one federation, united most but by no means all German-speaking peoples in Europe. The successors to the Second Reich, the Weimar Republic and the Nazi Third Reich, maintained the territory of the unified nation-state and, in the Nazi case, briefly extended its borders. Yet by 1945, after only seventy-five years as a unified nation-state (albeit with three different types of political systems), the problem of national identity and the future of the German nation as a political unit had to be resolved once again.

National identity, the sense of belonging to a particular national community—usually sharing a common physical territory, language, history, and cultural values—has been present among Germans for at least as long as it has among many other European nations. This general national identification has not been linked, however, with a stable unified state and political system. Thus, to ensure its own stability, each succeeding political system has sought unsuccessfully to broaden the scope of national identification to include a commitment to the given state. An attachment to a particular state and political system has been the missing component in the German sense of national identity. As Donald Devine has pointed out, national identification in the United States includes identification with and support for certain political symbols (the Constitution, flag, national anthem) and ideals (individual liberty, property, equality). To be an American also has meant support for a particular state form and political system: a liberal, democratic republic. Socialism, communism, monarchy—all other possible political forms—are not a legitimate part of the American national identity.[1] Such a linkage between national identity and specific state form has never been present in Germany.

The Republic proclaimed in 1949 was, like its predecessors, faced with the problem of creating and fusing a commitment to a particular political form with an existing national identity. The presence of a competing German state (the GDR) within the same territory as that of the prewar Reich and its capital in the communist part of the historic center of the Reich complicated the task. West German leadership compounded the problem at first by officially encouraging support for the values of the liberal democratic constitution but not for the specific West German state. Thus, in effect, West German leadership until recently was urging citizens to become democrats but not to develop too strong an attachment to the Federal Republic, because it was only "provisional" until all Germans were reunited within a single democratic state with Berlin as its capital. Until that time, however, this provisional West German state also claimed to be the only legitimate representative of all members of the German nation within or outside its borders. This viewpoint was not shared by the leaders of communist East Germany, but apparently it had widespread support among East German citizens.[2]

In spite of these difficulties, to what extent has a national identity with a political component developed since 1945? In the immediate postwar period, for understandable reasons, many wanted to forget about being German. A few enthusiastically embraced the "European idea," a politically united Europe with no national borders, or gladly submitted to the Americanization that was so apparent in popular culture. Most simply reduced their scope of allegiance to the self, the family, and perhaps the local community. This mass withdrawal to the primary sphere (or *privatization,* as some social scientists have termed it) gave German leaders considerable freedom of action but also imposed limits on the intensity of commitment or identification they could require from their citizens.

This condition could not last indefinitely, and there are signs that Germans are rediscovering the larger national community and at the same time developing a specific identification with the Federal Republic.[3] As Table 4.1 shows, the proportion of Germans who are proud of the postwar political system has increased substantially over the past thirty years. In 1959 only 7 percent expressed pride in some aspect of the political system. Among Americans at that time (1959), the level of pride in political institutions was 85 percent; and among British respondents, 46 percent were proud of their country's political order. By 1978 the German level of pride in their political system had

TABLE 4.1   Sources of national pride, 1959–1988 (in percentages)

	1959	1978	1988
Political institutions, constitution	7	31	51
Economy	33	40	50
Social welfare programs	6	18	39
Characteristics of the people	36	35	na
Contributions to science	12	13	37
Contributions to the arts	11	10	22
Other, no answer	43	39	50

Source: For 1959 and 1978: David P. Conradt, "Changing German Political Culture," in *The Civic Culture Revisited,* ed. Gabriel Almond and Sidney Verba (Boston: Little Brown, 1980), p. 230; for 1988: German General Social Survey, cited in Peter Mohler "Der Deutschen Stolz: Das Grundgesetz," *Informationsdienst Soziale Indikatoren,* no. 2 (July 1989), pp. 1–4.

risen to 31 percent, and in 1988 fully 51 percent of respondents expressed pride in the postwar constitution and political order. Note that by 1988 the political system was the area in which Germans had the most pride; it had overtaken the economy, which in 1978 had been the greatest source of postwar German national pride. Support for specific national symbols has also grown since 1949. The proportion of Germans stating that they feel "joyful" or "happy" when they see their black-red-gold national flag has increased from 23 percent in 1951 to almost 60 percent in 1992.[4] Solid majorities of Germans now consider national feelings of patriotism and pride to be important.

Germans also have become increasingly critical of the United States, the once protective big brother who could do no wrong. This is also indicative of a growing sense of identity and independence. It began during the Vietnam War when criticisms of American foreign policy became, for Germans, quite vocal, even reaching the point where the then-finance minister and later chancellor, Helmut Schmidt, while in the United States in 1971, criticized American policy. Differences over policies in the Middle East also became apparent as Germany attempted to maintain a posture of neutrality throughout most of the 1970s.[5] A similar pattern can be seen in the German reaction to American policies following the Soviet invasion of Afghanistan in 1979. The Schmidt government did not unconditionally support Washington's request for sanctions against the Soviets, including a boycott of the 1980 Olympic games. Instead, it warned against "overreaction," "alarmism," and a "backslide" into a cold war. Germany clearly felt slighted and not properly consulted before many decisions on the part of the Carter administration. The widespread opposition in the early 1980s to the stationing of new NATO intermediate-range missiles in Germany was also an expression of this emerging national identity. According to one observer, "the rejection of 'American missiles'—even missiles originally urged by a West German government and ratified by NATO . . . is seen [by the missile protestors] as an assertion of national self-reliance against an unreliable American tutelage."[6]

The question of national identity and German-American relations was also involved in the 1985 controversy surrounding the visit of President Reagan to a German military cemetery in the small town of Bitburg. The presidential visit, taking place forty years after the end of World War II, had been proposed by Chancellor Kohl as a symbolic gesture of German-American reconciliation. After it was discovered that the cemetery also contained the remains of forty-nine SS troops, Reagan came under heavy pressure from American Jewish and veterans' groups to cancel the visit. However, Reagan refused, citing his commitment to Kohl and the strong support this "noble gesture" had in the Federal Republic. Kohl, who was pressed privately by the White House to propose an alternative to the cemetery visit, rejected any changes in the presidential itinerary.

In Germany almost three-fourths of the adult population supported the Bitburg visit. Significantly, only the Green political party called for its cancellation. Although the Social Democrats, the major opposition party, sharply criticized the manner in which the Reagan visit was organized, they did not advocate the abandonment of the presidential gesture to Germany's war dead. Generally, Germans were surprised at the intensity of the American reaction. For many Germans born since 1945, the Third Reich and World War II belong to a dark past that should no longer have any influence on the country's international stature and prestige. According to this view, Germany in the past fifty years has earned the right to be accepted as an equal within the Western community of nations.

In recent years several conservative intellectuals and political figures, some with ties to the Kohl government, have argued that the Federal Republic is hindered in its dealings with other nations by its lack of a national identity and pride comparable to those found in other European countries.[7] They contend that the major obstacle to the development of such an identity is an excessive focus on the Third Reich by historians, educators, and the media, which burden younger generations with an unjustified sense of guilt. The conservatives stress that German history is long and complex and that even during the period 1933–1945 there were phenomena other than National Socialism. A country that is obsessed with guilt, they argue, will be incapable of dealing with the challenges of the future. To counteract this, conservatives want to create and stress common positive historical memories and traditions.

Many liberal and social democratic intellectuals have been critical of what they believe is an attempt by conservatives to gloss over, or to relativize, the singularity of the Nazi experience and especially the Holocaust. The debate has been particularly intense among several leading historians and social scientists. This *Historikerstreit* (historians' dispute) attracted national attention in 1986 when a leading social philosopher, Jürgen Habermas, accused two historians of seeking to trivialize the Nazi period. He linked their efforts to a larger movement among conservative historians to create a new view of the past that would "limit the damage" done by the Third Reich and give Germans confidence and pride.

Although he did not deny the need for a sense of national identity, Habermas urged Germans to focus their patriotism and pride on the open, democratic society that has been created since 1945:

> The creation of such a society was the greatest achievement of the postwar generation, for it opened Germany unconditionally to the political culture of the West. . . . The only patriotism that will not alienate us from the West is constitutional patriotism. Unfortunately, a tie to universal constitutional principles that is based on conviction has only been possible in Germany since, and because of, Auschwitz. Anyone who wants to drive the blush of shame over that deed from our cheeks by using meaningless phrases like "obsession with guilt," anyone who wants to call Germans back to a conventional kind of identity, destroys the only reliable basis of our tie to the West.[8]

Habermas's charges were sharply denied by the historians, and the debate continued for several months in the pages of West Germany's leading newspapers and periodicals. This *Historikerstreit* and the Bitburg incident illustrate how difficult and sensitive the question of national identity had become in the Federal Republic.

Legitimacy

Like many new states, the Federal Republic was also confronted with the problem of acquiring legitimacy. Would the inhabitants of the Western occupation zones accept and obey the authority of the new state? Would the policies of the new state be consistent with what most citizens regard as right and wrong? In spite of national division from 1949 to 1990 and a constitution (Basic Law) never subjected to direct popular approval, there has been no serious challenge to the authority of the Federal

TABLE 4.2   Changes in attitudes toward previous regimes (monarchy and dictatorship) and key values of the Federal Republic (political competition and representation), 1950–1997 (in percentages)

Questions	1950	1951	1952	1953	1954	1955	1956	1957	1958	1959	1960
Restore monarchy?											
Yes	—	32	—	—	22	—	—	16	—	—	—
No	—	36	—	—	51	—	—	60	—	—	—
Don't know	—	32	—	—	27	—	—	24	—	—	—
Hitler, one of Germany's greatest statesmen?											
Yes	—	—	—	—	—	48	43	—	—	42	34
No	—	—	—	—	—	36	37	—	—	41	43
Don't know	—	—	—	—	—	16	20	—	—	17	23
A new Nazi party?											
Support	—	—	—	16	—	—	15	11	11	11	—
Oppose	—	—	—	62	—	—	61	66	64	62	—
Indifferent	—	—	—	22	—	—	24	23	25	27	—
Political competition. It is better for a country to have:											
One party	25	23	21	20	19	15	11	12	12	12	11
Several parties	53	60	68	66	69	74	76	77	77	76	79
Undecided, other,											
no answer	22	17	11	14	12	11	13	11	11	12	10
Do members of a parliament represent:											
Personal interests	—	32	26	—	17	—	—	—	17	—	—
Party interests	—	14	14	—	10	—	—	—	8	—	—
General interest	—	25	33	—	39	—	—	—	41	—	—
Other, no answer	—	29	27	—	34	—	—	—	34	—	—

Source: Institut für Demoskopie, Allensbach, West Germany. These and all other public opinion polls cited in this study were obtained from the Institut. Sole responsibility for the presentation, analysis, and interpretation of these data rests with the author.

Republic. Indeed, the overwhelming majority of West Germans consider the institutions and processes of the Federal Republic as legitimate. Support for this statement can be found in part in the high levels of voter turnout and the concentration of electoral support in the parties committed to the Republic. Extremist, antisystem sentiment is confined to small percentages of the electorate. Direct challenges to the Republic's authority have been limited to Communist and neo-Nazi parties in the 1950s and 1960s and to the small but very active urban terrorist groups that have plagued police and courts since the late 1960s (discussed in greater detail later in this chapter).

The legitimacy of the Federal Republic, especially in its early years, was based in part on the absence of any credible alternative. After experiences in this century with

1961	1962	1963	1964	1965	1966	1967	1968	1977	1978	1990	1994	1997
—	—	—	—	11	—	—	—	—	—	—	10	—
—	—	—	—	66	—	—	—	—	—	—	75	—
—	—	—	—	23	—	—	—	—	—	—	15	—
30	37	35	29	—	—	32	—	—	31	26	—	24
43	44	44	44	—	—	52	—	—	56	67	—	71
27	19	21	27	—	—	16	—	—	13	7	—	5
—	8	—	—	—	7	6	—	7	—	—	—	—
—	71	—	—	—	74	78	—	79	—	—	—	—
—	21	—	—	—	19	16	—	14	—	—	—	—
11	—	—	—	—	—	8	7	6	5	3	—	7
73	—	—	—	—	—	82	81	90	92	89	—	86
16	—	—	—	—	—	10	11	4	3	8	—	7
—	—	—	11	—	—	—	—	—	15	—	—	—
—	—	—	7	—	—	—	—	—	3	—	—	—
—	—	—	51	—	—	—	—	—	55	—	—	—
—	—	—	31	—	—	—	—	—	27	—	—	—

monarchy, the Weimar Republic, and Nazism, postwar Germans had no historically successful alternative to put forward. They were quite willing to take, in essence, what the Allies offered (a liberal, parliamentary system in only part of the former Reich). However, this decline in support for past political systems and the resultant increase in support for the current regime were part of a developmental process affected by both the passage of time and the performance of the new system.

Through opinion surveys in which West Germans were questioned periodically about their attitudes toward two of the past political systems, monarchy and the Hitler dictatorship, and their support for key principles of the current regime, we can examine the character and sources of this process. Table 4.2 presents the responses to questions about monarchy and the Hitler dictatorship from 1950 to 1997. In 1951, thirty-three years after the collapse of the Hohenzollern dynasty, almost one-third of the adult population favored its restoration. Nevertheless, fourteen years later the support for the monarchy had dropped to only 11 percent. Much of this decline, according to one analysis, was due to the simple passage of time; those with living memories of the Hohenzollerns constituted an ever smaller segment of the population.[9] Some of this decline, however, was related to the policy successes of the postwar system.

This is even more apparent in attitudes toward Hitler and the Nazi party. When asked whether Hitler would have been one of the greatest German statesmen had it not been for the war, almost one-half of the adult population in 1955 answered affirmatively; by 1967 this number had dropped to less than one-third, with a majority flatly rejecting the proposition. Age is an important factor in explaining this change. Each age group socialized since 1949 was progressively less likely to support the Hitler dictatorship than were older generations who grew up under earlier regimes.[10]

Also, when national samples on nine different occasions between 1953 and 1977 were asked how they would react if a new Nazi party attempted to come to power, a similar trend was apparent. Potential support for neo-Nazism dropped from 16 percent in 1953 to only 7 percent in 1977. The percentage of respondents who would actively or passively oppose such a party increased from 62 percent to 79 percent over the same period. Perhaps more important, by 1977 almost 60 percent of the adult population stated it would do "everything possible" to see that a new Nazi party would not come to power. In addition to age, the steady drop in support was a result of economic prosperity and other policy successes of the first chancellor, Konrad Adenauer—German acceptance into the European Community, NATO, and the integration of ten million postwar refugees. The effects of political education in the schools apparently also were a factor in producing this decline. In short, there was some support for past regimes in the early 1950s, but it diminished over time with the growing effectiveness of the Bonn system. By the 1960s the Republic, originally legitimated by Allied occupation, could stand on its own by virtue of its performance.

Thus far we have accounted for the legitimacy of the postwar system through the absence of a credible alternative to what the Western Allied occupiers established in 1949 and the performance of the postwar system—above all, economic prosperity, effective executive leadership, and policy successes. What, however, would happen if for some reason its performance faltered? Does the regime now have some reserve of citizen goodwill it could fall back on in crisis situations? Is there support for this regime that is not specific or policy oriented? Have Germans over the past fifty years developed a more affective, if not emotional, commitment to this regime, which could see it through hard times? These hypothetical questions are difficult to answer. Nevertheless, the available material suggests that this rain-or-shine support has developed and that the postwar Republic is more than a fair-weather democracy. Our evidence for this assertion comes from two general sources: the ever-present public opinion poll, and the actual behavior of Germans at both elite and mass levels during political crises of the recent past.

Democratic Values, Processes, and Institutions

The decline in popular support for past political regimes has indeed been paralleled by a steady increase in support for the values, processes, and institutions of the Federal Republic. The essentially passive acceptance of the postwar system for a basically negative reason—because everything else had failed—was displaced by a more active, positive orientation to the new Republic. Moreover, by the late 1960s the levels of popular support had become sufficiently high and diffuse that some observers were describing the Federal Republic as "institutionalized" and "established."[11] The process can also be illustrated through public opinion data covering key values of liberal democracy (freedom of political conflict and competition) and its central institution and process (representation of the popular will via a legislative assembly).

Conflict and Competition.   The inability of liberal democracy to take root in Germany in the first half of the twentieth century has been explained by numerous scholars as the result of an absence of popular understanding of the role of conflict and competition in democratic politics. Germans, it has been said, long for no-conflict solutions to social and political problems. Unlike citizens in the classical democracies of the United States and Britain, Germans do not, according to the German sociologist Ralf Dahrendorf, recognize that differences of opinion and interest in politics are inevitable. Thus they have not concentrated on (1) managing conflict through the creation of institutions that guarantee its expression, or (2) the development of rules acceptable to conflicting parties; they have sought instead to eliminate the causes of conflict by searching for "absolute solutions" to social and political problems without ever considering whether such solutions actually exist.[12] This aversion to conflict has made Germans at both elite and mass levels unable to accept the need for opposition parties or extensive bargaining within and between parties in parliament. It has instead made them "expert-oriented" and "legalistic," with an administrative conception of politics.[13]

Available evidence suggests, however, that if aversion to political conflict was characteristic of attitudes in the past, this aversion has diminished greatly over the past fifty years. Between 1964 and 1990 the proportion of West Germans who considered "the conflicts between different interest groups and their demands on government" as "damaging to the general welfare" dropped from 74 percent to 53 percent.[14] National samples of adult citizens were asked on eighteen separate occasions between 1950 and 1997 whether "it is better for a country to have several parties, so that a variety of different opinions can be represented, or only one party, so that as much unity as possible exists." The proportion of the adult population supporting political competition was only 53 percent in 1950; attitudes toward this key value of liberal democracy were still mixed and ambivalent. By the late 1970s, however, 92 percent of the public supported the principle of party competition. Moreover, explicit support for a one-party system dropped from about one-fourth of the population in the early 1950s to less than one-tenth by the early 1970s.[15] These trends suggest that the value of political competition is now firmly established in the political culture.

Representation and Parliament.   According to most theories of democracy, the central institution for political democracy in large societies is the legislative assembly in which the various interests and opinions are represented. Do Germans feel they are represented in parliament? Do they support, in theory at least, this important institution? Once again, available data show steady gains in popular support for this key process and institution. In 1951 about half of the adult population stated frankly that if they sent their representative a letter, it would not be read or perhaps might not even reach him or her. Twenty-one years later, only about one-fifth of the population held this view. By the mid- to late 1960s, most citizens felt that their communications with representatives would be read and acted on.[16] When asked in surveys conducted between 1951 and 1965: "What do you think of the Bundestag in Bonn as our representative assembly?" the proportion evaluating it as "excellent," "basically good," or "fair" increased from 66 percent in 1951 to 86 percent by 1965.[17]

As Table 4.2 indicates, the belief that parliamentary deputies are primarily concerned with the "general interest," rather than their personal interests or those of their party, has steadily increased. In 1951 only one-fourth of the adult population felt that the parliamentary deputies were concerned above all with the interests of the population as a whole. By 1978 this had more than doubled, increasing to 55 percent. The proportion of the electorate that attributed a primary concern with either personal or party interests to the parliamentary deputies dropped during this period from 46 to 18 percent.

Thus support for key political values, a central political process (representation), and the major republican institution (parliament) had by the late 1960s reached levels at which it was possible to speak of a consensus on liberal democracy in modern Germany. And although the increase in support for the system and the decline in positive feelings for past regimes have been the result of both generational changes and the performance of the postwar system, the important point for our purposes is that by the end of the period covered in these surveys, all major social, economic, and political groups ranked high in their support of political competition, their sense of representation, and their support of the parliament. Support—at least for the liberal Republic established in 1949—has become diffuse, not significantly related to any particular group or policy of the government. These principles and processes have become accepted norms for the conduct of politics in the Federal Republic.

While support for democratic principles and values remains high, Germans have become increasingly critical of the performance of their political institutions and representatives and more distant from political parties. From 1972 to 1996 the proportion of West Germans with a favorable attitude toward parliamentary deputies dropped from 63 percent to 25 percent.[18] "Disappointment" with the political parties rose from 34 percent in 1991 to 51 percent by 1997.[19] Ironically, much of this increased criticism is an expression of the maturity and sophistication of German citizens. They expect more from their political institutions and leaders than they did a generation ago and in recent years the performance of the political system has been below expectations. Nonetheless the major unknowns about German politics no longer revolve around the possibility of reverting to an authoritarian or even a fascist past but, rather, to the future scope of democracy.

DEMOCRATIC SUPPORT IN EAST GERMANY

With the collapse of the communist regime in East Germany in 1989 and the subsequent unification of the two German states, the Federal Republic was once again, as in 1949, faced with the task of integrating millions of citizens whose only concrete political experience had been with authoritarian and totalitarian regimes. Since 1933 citizens in the former East Germany had been governed by either the Nazis or the Communists.

Did a distinct East German political culture emerge during the forty-year division of the nation? Do East German attitudes and values show the impact of decades of indoctrination in Marxist-Leninist ideology? Or did East Germans vicariously experience the democratic development of their cousins in the West? Did East Germans not demonstrate their own commitment to democracy in their revolution of 1989–1990?

Since unification this question has been the subject of extensive scholarly research. The growing body of evidence presents a mixed picture. East Germans since 1989 have voted in large numbers for democratic parties. The relative success of the former Communist party, the Party of Democratic Socialism, since 1994 has been restricted largely to Easterners who had benefitted from the old system or who felt they had been unjustly treated in the economic and social dislocations of the unification process. Surveys conducted in 1990 before unification found few differences between the two populations in their general support for democratic values. Approximately 90 percent of East and West Germans agreed that democracy required a political opposition, civil liberties, the rule of law, freedom of speech and expression, and free elections.[20]

Since the 1990 unification, however, as East Germans have confronted the harsh realities of unemployment, increased crime rates, and the indifference, if not hostility, of some of their Western cousins, their support—both specific and abstract—for political democracy has declined, whereas West Germans remain very supportive of liberal democracy as practiced in the Federal Republic. In May 1990 almost 80 percent of East Germans agreed with the statement that "democracy is the best form of government," and over 40 percent considered the democracy "that we have in the Federal Republic" the best form of government or state. By July 1991 abstract support had dropped to 70 percent, and only 31 percent of East Germans considered the Federal Republic the best form of government. Among West Germans, both abstract support (86 percent) and specific support (80 percent) were about equal. Among younger Germans, these differences were even greater: Only 25 percent of East Germans under age 30, as compared to 72 percent of young West Germans, considered the Federal Republic's democracy to be the best form of government.[21]

The effects of a forty-year division are also noticeable in the differing conceptions of German history held by citizens of the two regions. In several surveys since 1988, West Germans were asked whether there was anything in their history that distinguished them from other countries, "something that can really be termed German history." As Table 4.3 shows, among those West Germans who believed there was something that distinguished German history, about half mentioned National Socialism, Hitler, and the Third Reich. The many wars in German history and the country's postwar division were the second and third most frequently mentioned distinguishing characteristics. When East Germans were asked the same question in 1990, 1992, and 1996, however, a much smaller percentage mentioned the Third Reich or National Socialism as a distinguishing feature of German history.[22] Note also from Table 4.3 that there appears to be some indication of a convergence between East and West on this question as the Eastern reference to the Third Reich has increased while the Western level at least between 1992 and 1996 declined. For East Germans, the country's frequent wars and postwar divisions were the most important factors setting Germany apart from other nations. These differences reflect, in part, the divergent approach the two regimes took to the past. East Germans were told by their leaders that they bore

TABLE 4.3   Historical identity: West-East Germany

Question: Is there anything in our history that distinguishes us from other countries, I mean something that can really be termed *German* history?

	West			East		
	1989	1992	1996	1990	1992	1996
Yes (percentage)	59	59	69	67	60	68

Question: And what do you think is special about our history, what distinguishes our history from the history of other countries?

	West (percentage)			East (percentage)		
	1989	1992	1996	1990	1992	1996
The Third Reich, National Socialism, Hitler.	52	52	44	5	11	13
Germany was a divided country, the Berlin Wall.	11	11	15	36	30	37
Many wars in the history of Germany; Germans have started wars, German military leaders.	23	22	29	36	36	33
Reconstruction after the war.	6	8	5	2	3	1
Character traits (love of order, hard-working, etc.)	5	4	4	13	5	3
Other, don't know	22	18	9	16	24	9
Total*	119	115	106	108	109	96

*Multiple responses were possible.

Source: Institut für Demoskopie, Survey Nos. 5014, 9010, *Jahrbuch,* IX, p. 385.

no responsibility for the Third Reich. Hitler and the Nazi regime were portrayed as the inevitable result of German and international capitalism. The German Democratic Republic, as the first socialist state in German history, represented a clean break from this militaristic and fascist past. In the West, attempts were made in the postwar period to confront the legacy of Hitler and National Socialism and to accept responsibility for the Holocaust. West German media and schools, especially in the past twenty years, have given extensive coverage to the Third Reich. At least publicly, West Germans appear more sensitive about this period in German history than do East Germans.

East Germans still retain more positive attitudes toward "socialism" and a more class-oriented conception of society than do West Germans. Table 4.4 presents the

TABLE 4.4   Attitudes toward socialism and inequality, West-East Germany, 1994 (percentage agreement)

Question:	West	East
Socialism is basically a good idea that was only badly carried out.	44	81
Class differences still determine whether one will be on the top or the bottom of society.	63	91
Germany is an open society. Ability and education now count more than social background.	75	54

Source: Allegemeine Bevölkerungsumfrage der Sozialwissenschaften (Cologne: Zentralarchiv für empirische Sozialforschung, 1994, Study No. 2400).

1994 responses from West and East Germans to selected questions. Over 80 percent of East Germans as compared to 44 percent of West Germans agreed with the statement that "socialism is basically a good idea that was only badly carried out." The economic dislocations of the unification process, especially the sharp jump in unemployment and the many plant closings, have taken their toll of East German views of the market economy. Between 1990 and 1996 the proportion of Easterners with a positive opinion of the Federal Republic's economy dropped from 77 percent to only 24 percent.[23] These negative experiences with the market system also extend into other attitudes toward Western society. Over 90 percent of East Germans, for example, consider one's social background (i.e., the social class of one's parents) to be the most important factor in determining where one will end up on the social ladder. They are less likely than West Germans to consider the Federal Republic an open society in which ability and education count more than the social class of a person's parents. The pattern of responses presented in Table 4.4 has not changed significantly since these questions were first asked in 1990.[24]

East Germans also seem to have a more simplistic, "either/or" conception of democracy than do West Germans. According to one study, they see democracy either as a very elitist system (i.e., one in which the chancellor or state must take care of them) or as a very participatory system in which they must demonstrate to secure their demands. Democracy as a system in which intermediate organizations such as parties, interest groups, and parliament play key roles of channeling citizens' demands into policies is still less understood in the East than in the West.[25]

However, there are also signs of convergence in the political culture of the once-divided nation. Although East Germans are generally less trusting of the basic institutions of liberal democracy such as parliament, the courts, and local government than are their Western cousins, the gap is narrowing, as Table 4.5 indicates. Between 1990 and 1992 the proportion of East Germans expressing trust in the justice system increased from 30 percent to 54 percent. Other increases were found in attitudes toward the Constitutional Court, local government, and the police. The convergence in levels of trust in parliament and the federal government, however, was due more

TABLE 4.5   The narrowing trust in institutions gap: West-East Germany, 1990–1992 (percentage trust in institutions)

	1990			1992		
Institution	West	East	Difference	West	East	Difference
Police	91	52	−39	84	53	−31
Constitutional Court	87	49	−38	80	63	−17
Justice	81	30	−51	67	54	−13
Parliament	83	49	−34	60	46	−14
Local administration	83	36	−47	56	51	−5
Federal government	75	55	−20	52	55	+3
Television	64	76	+22	43	52	+9

Source: For 1990, Institut für angewandte Sozialforschung (INFAS) surveys cited in Ursula Feist and Klaus Liepelt, "Auseinander oder Miteinander? Zum unterschiedlichen Politikverständnis der Deutschen in Ost und West," in Hans-Dieter Klingemann and Max Kaase (eds.), *Wahlen und Wähler. Analysen aus Anlaß der Bundestagswahl 1990,* Opladen: Westdeutscher Verlag, 1994, p. 601.

to a decline in trust among West Germans than to any substantial increase on the part of East Germans. But a 1999 survey, which once again asked about the respondents' trust in the government and parliament, found that East-West differences were narrowing, especially among younger Germans. Among those under 25 there was, for example, only a 3-point difference in the level of their trust in parliament, but in the 55 and older age group the East-West difference grew to 15 points. Thus, ten years after unification we see some signs of convergence.[26]

Even though they were able to watch democracy in the West on television, East Germans are still new at participation in democratic politics. Their memories of the political, social, and economic system under which they lived from 1949 to 1989 will probably distinguish them from citizens of the former Federal Republic for some years to come. But as the social and economic integration of unified Germany—including, of course, new generations of East Germans who have only experienced a unified country—continues, these differences should diminish. This assumes, of course, that the unification process, especially its economic dimension, moves the East toward the Western level. As in West Germany during the 1950s and 1960s, the performance of the new democratic order will be a key factor in the political integration of the former East Germany.

POLITICAL INTEREST AND INVOLVEMENT

The General Pattern

The formal, legal rules of the Federal Republic have thus far placed few participatory requirements on citizens beyond periodic voting. This leaves major responsibility for system maintenance, policy innovation, and development to political elites. Most Germans in 1949 probably did not want it any other way. The immediate post-war period witnessed a widespread withdrawal from public and political matters and an almost exclusive concern with private and familial affairs—and above all with material acquisition. Many Germans had their first political experiences during the Weimar and Nazi periods; these experiences were for the most part not positive. The ordinary German who joined the party after 1933, caught up in the initial enthusi-asm for National Socialism and Hitler, may well have found himself or herself after 1945 unemployed and their bank accounts and other assets frozen during denazifi-cation, in addition to the myriad other calamities suffered by all Germans in the im-mediate postwar years. In short, many "little people," political innocents, got burned by politics and were reluctant to try again. Hence, beyond the limited and hardly taxing act of voting, there have been relatively low rates of participation in activities such as party organizations, election campaigns, and public causes.

Formal participation in elections, however, is high by both European and Ameri-can standards. Turnout in national elections has ranged from 91 percent in 1976 to 78 percent in 1990, averaging about 86 percent over fourteen elections. Turnout in state and local elections has averaged 60 to 70 percent, also much higher than for corre-sponding subnational elections in other advanced industrial societies. Yet participation in elections, although high in frequency, has been low in intensity. Survey research con-ducted in the 1950s and 1960s found that most German citizens traditionally go to the polls more from a sense of duty or because "it is the usual thing to do" than from a be-lief that they are in fact helping to decide the personnel and policies of government.[27] Moreover, most studies of German political behavior have found that those citizens who are interested in politics and discuss political issues with any frequency restrict such activity to their families and very close friends.[28] The overall pattern throughout the 1950s and 1960s was one of privatization, with little involvement beyond voting.

There is growing evidence, however, that the traditional pattern has changed. Economic prosperity and rising educational levels have given more people the re-sources of knowledge, conceptual ability, and time necessary to participate in poli-tics. Trend data on a variety of items—interest in politics and "talking politics," and an inclination to join a political organization—show a steady increase in the politi-cization of German citizens.[29]

New Forms of Political Participation: Citizen Groups and Movements

The emergence of widespread citizen initiative and action groups outside the party sys-tem is another phenomenon indicative of growing mass confidence in the role of the citizen. Some of these groups were in evidence as early as the mid-1960s, but they were voter initiative groups in support of particular parties and candidates, and in some cases their spontaneity and freedom from the existing parties were in question. In 1972 there were more than 300 voter initiative groups supporting the SPD. The movement was led by nationally prominent writers and artists, not by average concerned citizens. Of greater interest for our purposes are the local initiative groups organized by citizens to protest and remedy a particular local problem: arbitrary increases in mass transit fares;

inadequate children's playgrounds, kindergartens and schools; and air and water pollution. These groups are indicative of new patterns of political participation that contradict the traditional characterization of Germans as politically passive, relying only on intermittent, indirect participation through voting or formal contact with the state bureaucracy. Most of the groups concentrate on one issue and tend to be free from any encompassing ideology. Nevertheless, they reflect the inability of the established party system and the institutions of local government to meet key needs of the citizenry. Petitions, demonstrations, and protest marches are all part of their tactical arsenal.

These groups had their precedent in the widespread demonstrations during the late 1960s over the Emergency Laws,[30] the Vietnam War, and university reform; they are to some extent the adult version of the student protest movement.[31] The focus then shifted to the local level, the one least penetrated by the national political parties, where the problems of outmoded school systems, environmental decay, inadequate zoning, and land use regulations exceeded the capacities of most local governments and officials.

In 1977, however, a large-scale citizen initiative protest over the construction of nuclear power plants was organized at the national level. A few years later a nationwide peace movement emerged, initially directed against the proposed deployment of middle-range nuclear missiles in Germany. The peace movement, allied with some elements of the Social Democratic party, played a major role in the eventual collapse of the Social-Liberal government in 1982. These new social movements were soon joined by increasingly assertive women's rights organizations. In recent years segments of Germany's elderly population have organized into a Gray Panther movement. All these movements have had close ties to the Green political party, but they have also been careful to guard their independence. Also common to all groups is a dissatisfaction with the established institutions and processes of the postwar system.

The success of citizen initiative groups and the new social movements, together with the increases in political participation already described, seem to indicate that Germans are ready for a more direct democracy than that envisioned in the Basic Law. Proposals have indeed been made for more citizen involvement and influence, especially at the local level through referenda, petitions, the right to recall public officials, and even state financial support for citizen groups. Surveys indicate that the public supports a less elitist constitutional structure. In a 1990 study, for example, over 80 percent of the adult population in both the former East and West Germany endorsed referenda for important policy issues. Over half felt that "democracy works best when people have the opportunity to directly represent their interests and concerns."[32] Thus most Germans now want more opportunities for political participation than are permitted under the current constitution.

CIVIL LIBERTIES AND HUMAN RIGHTS

Unlike the United States, Britain, or France, Germany does not have a strong civil libertarian tradition. German political and legal theory has for the most part emphasized the duties of the individual vis-à-vis the state rather than the state's responsibilities to protect individual liberties. Indeed, as Leonard Krieger has pointed out, German political thinkers have defined liberty largely in collectivist terms.[33] That is, the individual was considered "free" only within the confines of the collective or state, and obedience to its rules and regulations ensured his or her freedom and personal development. To be sure, this state, according to German political tradition, was to be a *Rechtsstaat,* a state based on the rule of law, and great attention was given to the detailed legal codes that defined individual rights and duties and delimited state authority. The interpretation of these laws and their social and political effect traditionally restricted, rather than enlarged, individual freedom. The Rechtsstaat tradition also produced an excessive legalism, which resulted in many unjust statutes that were steadfastly adhered to in the name of the rule of law. The Nazi seizure of power, the persecution of Jews, and many other acts of the Nazi dictatorship were thus all considered "legal."

During the extensive student demonstrations of the late 1960s, courts used the old provisions of the penal code against disturbance of the public order to punish protesters who were exercising rights of free expression guaranteed in the Basic Law. Furthermore, the postwar prosecution of war criminals was consistently delayed and complicated by the retention of laws and regulations, passed before and during the Nazi era, that protected judicial and bureaucratic wrongdoers. There is no culturally ingrained sympathy for the underdog. The German humanistic tradition is, above all, abstract and philosophical, not pragmatic.

Evidence also suggests that the rule of law is less likely to apply to lower-status, disadvantaged groups than to the more established, prosperous segments of the community. Foreign workers, the very young, the elderly—in short, the weak in this society—have been subjected to various, albeit subtle, forms of discrimination and neglect in spite of the welfare state. The upper-middle-class character of the judiciary creates a situation, especially in criminal cases, in which one class in effect sits in judgment of another class about whose lifestyle it knows or understands relatively little.[34] The procedures, rules, jargon, and bureaucratic red tape of the criminal justice system are beyond the comprehension of many citizens. Nevertheless, public awareness and sensitivity to the importance of civil liberties has become substantial in the Federal Republic. In surveys conducted between 1964 and 1991, more than 90 percent of the adult population consistently agreed that "every person should have the right to express his opinion regardless of what the majority thinks."[35]

In its first twenty articles, the constitution or Basic Law lists an impressive array of fundamental and inalienable rights and liberties (see Appendix, pp. 238–287). Equality before the law—the prohibition of any discrimination based on gender, race, language, national origin, religion, or political persuasion—is guaranteed in Article 3. Freedom of religion (broadly defined to include any belief system) and the right to refuse armed military service for reasons of conscience are granted in Article 4. Civil rights relating to freedom of expression and information via speech, writing, pictures, broadcasts, and films are enumerated in Article 5. Censorship is rejected, although "general laws" dealing with the protection of youth (obscenity) and "personal honor" (slander and libel) limit this freedom. Explicit academic freedom (teaching and research), conditional on loyalty to the constitution, is granted in Article 5 (paragraph 3). Article 5 also clearly guarantees freedom of assembly, association, and movement; the privacy of mail and telephone messages; and the right to petition.

Finally, in an extraordinary departure from German constitutional tradition, Article 20, as amended in 1968, declares that "all Germans shall have the right to resist any person or persons seeking to abolish the constitutional order, should no other remedy be possible." In a 1974 speech commemorating the July 20, 1944, plot to assassinate Hitler, Chancellor Helmut Schmidt specifically referred to this article as one that would legalize armed resistance against any authority that violated the individual liberties enumerated in the basic rights of the constitution.

Civil Liberties Controversies

In its first fifty years the Federal Republic has had several major controversies involving alleged government violations of these basic constitutional freedoms.

The Spiegel Affair.   The most publicized and dramatic civil rights case during the past fifty years involved a government raid in 1962 on the offices of the newsmagazine *Der Spiegel* and the arrest of its two major editors. The government charged that the magazine had illegally procured and published secret defense documents and planned to publish more—hence the police raid and arrests. The minister of defense responsible for the police action had been a frequent target of the magazine. Perhaps not coincidentally, the magazine had also begun an exposé of alleged corruption involving the minister in connection with aircraft purchases and government-sponsored military housing projects.

The government argued that a strong suspicion of treason justified extreme measures. The German press, the opposition party in parliament, and sizable segments of the governing coalition felt otherwise. The minister of justice, who had not been informed of the action, resigned; his party, the Free Democrats (FDP), threatened to leave the government if the defense minister did not resign. His subsequent resignation and the quashing of the government indictment by the Federal Appeals Court closed the case for all practical purposes. The nearly unanimous opposition of the press and the response of some, but not all, elements of public opinion were indicative of considerable support for freedom of the press, or at least opposition to overt, heavy-handed attempts at censorship reminiscent of an earlier era. Clearly, after this incident any government would be more reluctant to use such tactics against a critical press; and indeed there has not been a recurrence of this type of government behavior.

The "Radicals" in Public Service Issue.   A civil liberties controversy in the 1970s involved the employment of "political radicals" (e.g., communists, neo-Nazis) by the state. The issue became political when New Left groups within the Social Democratic party supported the radicals' right to public employment and successfully opposed the party establishment's hard line in this area. This enabled the conservative Christian Democrats to charge that the Social Democrats were allowing left-wing teachers and bureaucrats to flood the civil service and ultimately undermine the constitutional order. Most cases in the 1970s involved allegedly radical teachers in elementary and secondary schools. In one Hessian community, for example, four schoolteachers taught communist "popular front" slogans to their pupils. When more than five hundred parents refused to send their children to school, two teachers were immediately dismissed and the other two suspended.[36] In a high school geography class in Bremen, the teacher sent his pupils into various neighborhoods to photograph homes and apartments and interview their occupants about their lifestyles, finances, and sociopolitical attitudes in order to illustrate the class structure of the community. Irate homeowners in the city's more affluent sections protested the "Nazi-like tactics," and the instructor was suspended. Many of these young teachers had attended universities during the "salad days" of student protest and New Left influence. Now active as teachers and administrators, they embarked, in their own way, on the "long march through the institutions."

In 1972 the federal government and the *Ministerpräsidenten* (chief executives) of the states issued an executive decree that was supposed to establish unified national policy in this area until formal legislation could be passed by the parliament. Although each case was to be examined and resolved separately, some general guidelines were given. An applicant for public employment who was engaged in "anticonstitutional" activity was not to be hired. If an applicant was a member of any organization that was unconstitutional, that alone was to be grounds for doubting whether he or she would support the "free democratic order." Thus any member of such a group, usually the Communist party or the radical-right National Democratic party (NPD), would normally have his or her employment application rejected. For those already in the public service, membership in such organizations could be grounds for dismissal. For manual workers and white-collar employees in public service without civil service status, the relevant sections of trade union contracts would apply.

This decision represented a hard-line approach to the question of political extremists in the civil service. It also reflected the fears of the Social Democrats of being portrayed by the opposition as "soft on radicalism." Critics charged that the decree could be interpreted to mean that even ordinary or nominal membership in groups such as the Communist party or NPD would mean a denial of or dismissal from employment. Furthermore, "anticonstitutional" activity could be construed to mean everything from participating in street demonstrations to blowing up the Capitol. The entire decree, it was argued, would encourage denunciations and petty spying of civil servants on one another, reminiscent of the Nazi era. Opponents of the decree also charged that it violated Article 3 of the Basic Law, which prohibits discrimination on the basis of political views and grants equal access to public jobs. In spite of these objections, a 1975 decision of the Federal Constitutional Court (see Chapter 8 for a description of this court) essentially upheld this policy, although the court emphasized that membership in radical groups would have to be substantiated by other "anticonstitutional" activity to justify dismissal from public service.[37]

In practice, the "unified" statement was differentially applied in the various states. In those governed by the Social Democrats, no civil servants were dismissed for mere membership in radical organizations, although a leadership or office-holding function was grounds for removal. In states governed by the Christian Democrats (CDU), on the other hand, membership alone was sufficient for dismissal. One CDU-governed state, the Rhineland-Palatinate, advocated a nationwide system of security checks. Another, Bavaria, maintained dossiers on teachers and college professors. A teaching intern in the Bavarian city of Augsburg was dismissed because (1) he took part in a demonstration during which "communist slogans" were shouted, and (2) as a student he had been a member of the Socialist German Student League (SDS). Between 1972 and 1975, only approximately 300 citizens were denied public employment, and only approximately 50 out of almost 3.7 million public employees were removed from public service because of "radical" political activities.

By the late 1970s, an increasing number of party and government officials at all levels had become convinced that the 1972 decree was a mistake and that the existing security clearance practices were unfair and in need of major revision. The SPD mayor of Hamburg in late 1978 announced that Hamburg, like its sister city-state of Bremen, would no longer routinely request that the Office for the Protection of the Constitution provide information on all candidates. Several months earlier the SPD minister of education in Berlin had declared that the 1972 decision of his party to support the decree was wrong and that Berlin would change its procedures. In January 1979, the SPD-FDP coalition in Bonn also abolished the practice of automatically checking each application with security agencies. A month later a CDU-governed state (the Saarland) also abandoned the routine check. Clearly, a combination of experience with the policy, the reaction of public opinion (especially among the younger, educated segment of the population), and foreign criticism of the Federal Republic had produced a trend away from the policy. On balance, however, the entire controversy inhibited the expression of unpopular ideas and the support of minority political movements. It illustrates the capacity of even democratic regimes to produce authoritarian policies. However, the eventual abandonment of the policy also shows that the postwar democracy can learn from its mistakes.[38]

Civil Liberties and the Census.   In the early 1980s a planned national census became another major civil liberties issue. The last complete census had been taken in 1970. For budgetary reasons a new census, planned for 1980, was postponed until 1983. The law authorizing the census was unanimously passed by the parliament with little debate or controversy. But citizen initiative groups and the new Green political party (see Chapter 5) initiated a campaign against the census, which they regarded as an unnecessary intrusion by the state into the private lives of citizens. Specifically, the anticensus groups were critical of provisions in the law that would allow officials, including police and security agencies, to compare the new data with domicile registration information already collected by local and regional authorities. In short, information given by individuals to the census takers could be shared with the police and other public bodies.

The anticensus movement was denounced by the interior minister as a "minority of extremists seeking to undermine the system."[39] But in 1983 the Federal Constitutional Court, responding to a petition by census opponents, issued an injunction halting the census, which had been scheduled to begin that same month. Finally, in December 1983, the court in a major decision unanimously struck down many of the provisions of the 1982 law. The court objected to the open-ended character of the law's language, which it ruled did not set sufficient limits on the state's authority to question its citizens. The court also ruled unconstitutional the statute's provision for the sharing of data among government agencies. In addition, the introduction of a single identification number for each citizen, which could be used to retrieve personal data from a variety of files, was rejected by the court. The government and parliament had to draft a new law that satisfied the constitutional standards set by the court. Most civil libertarians and constitutional lawyers praised the decision as an important advance for civil liberties in the Federal Republic.[40]

In 1985 a revised law, which met the objections of the court, was passed by the parliament, and the census finally took place in 1987. Some Green leaders continued to oppose the new law and called for citizens to boycott the census. The Greens contended that the law still did not offer protection against the misuse of the data. The other parliamentary parties, including the Social Democrats, strongly criticized the Green boycott as a clear violation of the law.

"The Great Bugging Attack."   The major civil liberties case of the 1990s has been the issue of electronic surveillance by police and security forces. Since the end of the Cold War, Germany, as well as other Western European countries, has experienced sharp increases in organized crime activity including drug traffic, automobile theft, and extortion. Existing laws, which reflect the postwar German effort to avoid the abuse of police power that took place during the Nazi era, greatly restricted the ability of security forces to undertake the types of investigations common in other European democracies. Wire-taps, search warrants, and other surveillance techniques could be conducted only after extensive judicial examination. German police forces felt handicapped by these procedures and requested help from the Kohl government.

The result was a 1998 constitutional amendment (Article 13) and subsequent law, which were also supported by the Social Democrats (then the opposition), that grants police greater powers to plant bugging devices in private homes. Such eavesdropping practices had been constitutionally prohibited. In the view of the police, however, such bans on telephone taps and mail intercepts had hindered efforts to combat terrorism and organized international criminal bands. Following protests from the media and civil liberties groups, the legislation was amended to exclude journalists, lawyers, members of parliament, clergy, and medical doctors from any electronic snooping. This was still not enough to satisfy some critics, including the minister of justice, who resigned in protest over the legislation. The new law will certainly be challenged in the courts and its future is still in doubt.

THE STATUS AND ROLE
OF KEY SOCIAL GROUPS

Foreign Workers

The most significant and conspicuous minority group in the Federal Republic comprises foreign workers and their families. Germany's fabled postwar economic boom was due in part to a large labor supply created by the forced migration of almost 10 million refugees from territories annexed by the Soviet Union and Poland, together with the influx of 3 million additional refugees from East Germany that continued until the Berlin Wall was put up in August 1961. These additions to the labor supply initially compensated for the loss of labor from the war. Yet by the early 1960s the economy's need for labor could no longer be met internally, and workers from Europe's poorer regions were recruited extensively by business with government assistance.

The number of foreign workers, or "guest workers" (*Gastarbeiter*), as they were euphemistically termed at the time, increased from about 110,000 in 1957 to more than 2.5 million by 1973. Although the recessions of 1974–1976 and 1981–1983 reduced their number to about 1.7 million, foreign workers still account for approximately 8 percent of the total work force and roughly 15 percent of the total manual work force.[41] In 1999 the three largest "exporting" countries were Turkey (30 percent), the former Yugoslavia (18 percent), and Italy (12 percent). Spain, Greece, and Poland also sent sizable contingents. In many large German cities, such as Frankfurt, Munich, Stuttgart, and Hamburg, foreign workers constitute from 15 to over 20 percent of the total work force and probably 30 to 40 percent of the manual work force. Foreign workers have usually been assigned tasks that Germans are no longer willing to perform: street cleaning, common labor, grave digging. About 50 percent of Frankfurt's and 80 percent of Munich's sanitation workers are foreign laborers. Although those in major industries receive the same pay as German workers, wage discrimination in smaller firms is not uncommon.

Even in large firms, foreign workers are usually found in the lowest-paid manual occupations. This is due partly to their poor vocational training (by German standards) and language difficulties, and also to discrimination on the part of German employers. Nonetheless, most foreign workers are covered by government health, security, and pension programs and, where applicable, are unionized. Thus, although holding low-paying jobs, they do not constitute a subculture of poverty in the Federal Republic. German churches, labor unions (by requiring equal pay for equal work), and charitable organizations have also alleviated some of the more pressing problems of foreign residents.

When foreign workers, after a year or so of employment, bring their families into Germany, their problems are compounded. The education of their children has been particularly difficult. Should the children be educated and socialized completely as Germans, or should special school classes with native teachers be established—at least in language and social studies? In many cases the parents themselves are not able to indicate their preferences or future plans, much less those of their children. Many of the children have spent most or all of their lives in Germany. Yet their parents cling to the goal of someday returning to their home country and thus want their children to retain its language and values. As a result the children grow up in a sort of twilight zone—they master neither their parents' culture and language, nor the German. Many drop out of school and, urged on by their parents, attempt to secure some kind of employment to augment the family's finances. While about 90 percent of German young people between the ages of 15 and 19 are enrolled in school, only 61 percent of foreign children in that age group attend school.[42] But in recent years the tightened job market has made it difficult for untrained foreign youth with poor German language skills to find employment. The result is a growing body of unemployed adolescents, especially in the large cities. The potential for social unrest in this situation should be obvious, especially to British and American readers.[43]

In spite of the declining influx of foreign workers in recent years, their higher birth rate and the arrival of family members have actually increased the total number of foreign residents. By 1999 there were over 8 million foreign residents, with only about 2 million in the work force. The number of foreign dependents has grown from 1.4 million in 1973 to over 6 million by 1999. In some large cities such as Frankfurt, up to half of all newborn children are from families of foreign workers.

Thus there are now two and even three generations of foreign residents in Germany. After the United States, Germany is the world's most popular haven for immigrants.

Several proposals have been made to improve the status of the foreign workers and their families. One involves giving the franchise to foreign workers for local elections. This would, it is argued, make local officials more responsive to their needs. In 1989 the states of Schleswig-Holstein and Hamburg passed legislation that allowed foreign residents to vote in local elections. The Christian Democrats in these states challenged the constitutionality of the law before the Federal Constitutional Court. (See Chapter 8 for a discussion of this court.) In October 1990 the Court declared the law unconstitutional, arguing that "the people" referred to in the constitution are German citizens. If foreign residents are to vote in German elections, it would require a constitutional amendment. In 1992 the constitution was indeed amended to give some foreign residents (those who are citizens of European Union countries) the right to vote in local elections. This amendment (Article 28) was passed to comply with the new agreements on European unity passed at the European Union summit conference in the Dutch city of Maastricht in 1991. But foreign residents who are not citizens of European Union countries still cannot vote regardless of how long they have lived in Germany.

The current Schröder government, which came to power in 1998, passed legislation in 1999 that makes it much easier for foreign residents to acquire German citizenship. But the government also seeks to restrict future waves of immigrants. The new citizenship legislation replaced the 1913 law, as amended in 1990, which based citizenship on lineage or blood. German-born children of foreigners now have an automatic right to citizenship if at least one of their parents has been living in Germany since age 14.[44] The waiting period for naturalization of foreign residents will be reduced from fifteen to eight years and dual citizenship will be allowed until the child reaches adulthood (age 23) at which time one citizenship must be chosen. It is estimated that this 1999 law will result in up to 4 million new naturalized citizens and will enfranchise over one million new voters.

Foreign Residents and Political Asylum.   Since the late 1980s Germany has become the target country for hundreds of thousands of foreigners fleeing economic and political oppression. In 1991 alone almost a quarter of a million foreigners sought political asylum in the Federal Republic, three times the level of any other European country. Article 16 of the Basic Law contains one of the most liberal asylum laws in the world. The framers of the constitution in 1949, many of whom became political refugees themselves during the Third Reich, wanted the country's borders to remain open to any refugee from political persecution. Most of the current asylum seekers, however, are fleeing for economic and not political reasons. All applicants are entitled to due process under German law; and even though most applications are rejected, the legal process can last for months and even years. In the interim, the foreigners are the beneficiaries of Germany's generous welfare state.

The growing number of asylum seekers, the poor economic situation in the former GDR (especially for young people), and a general shortage of affordable housing throughout the country were important factors in outbreaks of violence against asylum seekers that erupted in 1991. Beginning in the former East Germany, gangs of skinheads and young neo-Nazis attacked the hostels and apartment buildings that house the foreigners. The gangs, who threw rocks and bottles at the residents, were supported in some cases by local residents who cheered them on. The decision by local officials in one East German town to evacuate the foreigners spurred similar attacks in other areas, including many in West Germany. In October 1991 alone, authorities registered over nine hundred attacks on foreign residents, the most extensive violence against foreigners seen in Germany since the Third Reich.

The incidents sparked demonstrations by many Germans against the violence and in support of the foreigners. All major political leaders condemned the attacks, but the then-Chancellor Helmut Kohl was criticized by many for not participating in the pro-foreigner demonstrations and for not speaking out more forcefully in support of the asylum seekers. Responding to growing public pressure, the government, with the support of the opposition Social Democrats, passed a constitutional amendment (Article 16) in 1993 that restricts the asylum right. The new legislation retains the constitutional guarantee of protection against political persecution, but it seeks to exclude persons who attempt to enter the country for largely economic reasons. It also speeds up the administrative procedures at the borders. Persons from countries where there is no internationally recognized political persecution can be turned away at the borders. Also, asylum seekers who enter the Federal Republic from any European Union country can be denied asylum. Thus a legitimate political refugee living in France cannot apply for asylum in Germany; he or she must remain in France. Numerous human rights groups in Germany opposed the amendment, but it brought Germany's policy into line with that of most of its European neighbors and the United States. Passage of the amendment took the wind out of the sails of the xenophobic Republicans and other far-right groups. By 1994 the number of asylum applications had dropped by 60 percent.

The new Schröder government wants to further reduce the number of immigrants. After the break-up of the former Yugoslavia in 1991–1995, Germany took in over 300,000 refugees, more than all other European countries combined. This additional burden cost the government about $11 billion at a time of rising deficits and high unemployment. By 1999 all but 80,000 of these refugees, mainly from Bosnia, had been sent home. There is now a growing consensus across all major parties and interest groups that the "boat is full" and Germany can no longer be the target country for refugees from throughout Europe. Thus in 1999, after 250,000 Albanians were expelled from Kosovo, Germany quickly announced that the refugees should stay in Albania, Montenegro, or Macedonia and not be transferred to Western Europe. It is revealing of this new attitude that the most vocal proponent of the "boat is full" argument is Schröder's Interior Minister, Otto Schily, a former Green who once advocated an open-door immigration policy.

Women

Politics in Germany, as elsewhere, has traditionally been a man's business. German women have been less likely to participate in all political activities—voting, "talking politics," party membership, campaigning, candidacy—than men. The classic functions assigned to women in German society, neatly summarized by the three K's—*Kinder* (children), *Kirche* (church), and *Küche* (kitchen)—have left little room for explicit political roles and have been slow to change. The traditionally subordinate status of women in politics was also evident in surveys that found most women expressing more confidence in a man as the representative of their political interests than in a woman. Only approximately 30 percent of a national sample in 1975 felt that women could represent women's political interests better than men; among university-trained women, however, this proportion was higher. A 1983 study among the nations of the European Community found German respondents more likely to take a male chauvinist position on the question of women in politics than were citizens in other major West European countries.[45]

Yet since the late 1960s a greater awareness and visibility of women in politics has become apparent. The elections of 1972 and 1976 showed that the Christian Democrats could no longer count on receiving lopsided majorities from female voters. It was especially among Catholic women that the Social Democrats were able to make exceptional gains. Public attitudes toward women in politics also showed significant change; between 1965 and 1987, the proportion of men who "liked the idea" of a woman becoming politically involved rose from 27 to 68 percent. As Table 4.6 shows, between 1966 and 1988 the proportion of men who agreed that "politics is a man's business" dropped from 44 percent to 23 percent; among women during the same period, agreement declined from 32 percent to 15 percent. Solid majorities of both men and women now reject the notion that "politics is a man's business."

Although women continue to be underrepresented among the membership of the political parties, there is a trend toward increased female involvement. From 1971 to 1985 the number of active women members in the political parties increased from about 200,000 to 440,000. By 1985 about one-fourth of all SPD members were female and more than one-fifth of CDU/CSU members were women. In the smaller parties women made up over 40 percent of the Green membership and about one-fourth of the FDP membership.[46] In the 1998 election, 207 women (31 percent of the total) were elected to the parliament, the highest number in the history of the Federal Republic. In Britain and the United States, by contrast, women make up only about 10 percent of the national legislature.

In recent years women have been elected to top posts, including the presidency of the national parliament and Germany's version of the American Supreme Court, the Federal Constitutional Court; five of the sixteen judges on this court are also women; and a record five women joined the Kohl government as cabinet ministers following

TABLE 4.6   "Politics is a man's business": West Germany, 1966–1988 (in percentages)

	1966		1974		1988	
	Men	*Women*	*Men*	*Women*	*Men*	*Women*
Agree	44	32	31	28	23	15
Disagree	42	51	62	65	62	73
Undecided	14	17	7	7	15	12

Source: Elisabeth Noelle-Neumann and Renate Köcher (eds.), *Jahrbuch der Öffentlichen Meinung*, Vol. IX (New York and Frankfurt: K.G. Saur Verlag, 1993), p. 620.

the 1994 election. Since 1983 the proportion of women in the national parliament, the *Bundestag,* has more than tripled. Women now make up a majority of the deputies from the Green and PDS parties. In 1988 the Social Democrats adopted a rule that at least 40 percent of party officials be female; since 1998 the party rules call for a 40 percent female quota for all legislative seats. This quota system now applies at all levels—local, state, and national—of the party organization.[47] The Christian Democrats in 1994 also proposed a quota plan to increase female representation throughout the party's organization and parliamentary delegations. The federal government and many states now have cabinet ministries to address specifically the discrimination against women and the more general problem of equal opportunity for both men and women.

Income differences, however, between men and women remain substantial. White-collar males in industry earned in 1998 about 40 percent more than females. Differences among male and female manual workers were also considerable; male manual workers earned about 30 percent more than their female counterparts. The income differences are largely the result of the high proportion of women in lower-paying jobs. For example, only 10 percent of women in manual occupations were skilled workers in 1993, as compared to 55 percent of male blue-collar workers. Among white-collar employees, 9 percent of females were in supervisory positions, as compared to 36 percent of men.[48]

The German executive suite is still largely a male preserve. A 1993 study found that the country's 626 largest companies had approximately 2,300 men, but only 7 women, on their managing boards.[49] In 1993 a law was passed that will increase female representation at the top levels of government agencies. The legislation requires government agencies to create and carry out plans to promote women in each department with the goal of "eliminating the underrepresentation of women in hiring and promotion."

Legal discrimination against women has also hindered the progress of the women's movement, German-style. The nineteenth-century civil code put married women especially in a subordinate position. According to the "marriage and family law," a husband could divorce his wife if she took employment without his permission, and a woman could not legally retain her maiden name after marriage. Not until 1974 were these provisions repealed. Moreover, a liberalized abortion law passed by the parliament in 1974 with strong support from women's rights groups was, in a 6 to 2 decision, declared unconstitutional by the Federal Constitutional Court in 1975. The court's decision touched off protest demonstrations, especially in large cities, and a bomb exploded in the court's building in Karlsruhe. Nonetheless, the attempted reforms in the legal status of women, noticeable since 1969, are indicative of a greater sense of political awareness among women and a capacity of the system to respond, although with mixed success, to their needs.

Women in a United Germany.   The condition of women in the former GDR differed from that of West German women in two important respects. First, almost all women (about 90 percent) in the East, as compared to about half in West Germany, were in the paid work force. Second, state support for child care was more comprehensive and more generous in the East than were corresponding programs in West Germany. East German women could leave their jobs after the sixth month of pregnancy and remain at home for up to one year after the birth of a child with full pay. Free or low-cost child care was usually available at the women's work places, because many firms operated child-care facilities for their employees. In addition, East Germany had a liberal abortion law that allowed abortion on demand through the first trimester of pregnancy. Of course, pay levels in the East were about two-thirds less than those in the West. Women in the East also had to contend with long lines at stores and chronic shortages of many consumer goods.

The declining economic situation in the East has been especially troublesome for women. In many cases they have been the first to be laid off or put on part-time status. By early 1992 almost 60 percent of female workers in some industrial cities were out of work. Yet as the economy begins to improve in the East, women are still among the last to be rehired. Moreover, most formerly state-owned firms have closed their child-care facilities in an attempt to cut costs and make their enterprises more competitive. Thus their women employees must find adequate and affordable child care. The pro-choice East German abortion law expired in December 1992, and a generally pro-choice all-German abortion law was declared unconstitutional in 1993. This decision was considered particularly unjust to East German women. It is little wonder that East German women are more likely to consider themselves "worse off" since unification than are East German males.

Youth

The postwar baby boom, which did not begin until after 1948, and a relatively high birth rate during the 1960s, have resulted in 35 percent of the population being under 30 years of age. To these young Germans, the traumatic experiences of depression, war, defeat, and foreign military occupations are events to be studied in history classes, not living memories. After all, the postwar generation has grown up in a politically stable and economically prosperous society. However, that society has never been youth-oriented and for the most part has been ill-prepared for the youth culture that has emerged.

But, like their counterparts in other Western societies and older German citizens, young Germans in general are not a hyperpoliticized, ideologically radical element in a staid, middle-class society. Their rate of participation in elections is below that of older age groups. In 1990, for example, only 63 percent of voters under 25 years of age went to the polls, as compared to 84 percent of voters over age 45. In the former East Germany, only 55 percent of voters under age 25 cast their ballots. Further, the youth organizations of the major parties in the West count less than 5 percent of the 18- to 29-year-old group among their ranks.[50] Surveys of young people show that they are concerned above all with employment prospects, the quality of their education, vocational training, individual happiness, and a sense of fulfillment—goals with which their elders could hardly disagree.[51]

Although they are not particularly involved in political matters—much less radical causes—young Germans are more likely to have opinions supportive of liberal democratic values and innovative reform policies than are older age groups. In recent years, young people have also been more likely to vote for the Social Democrats and, above all, Green political parties rather than for the more conservative Christian Democrats. Not surprisingly, these parties have campaigned strongly for the youth vote. In one state, Lower-Saxony, the Social Democratic–Green government lowered the minimum voting age for local elections from 18 to only 16.

Official concern about youth questions and the organization of young people has been evident in all German governments since 1949. This is expressed by the presence of a Family Ministry with a separate Youth Department, several major white papers on youth, and a variety of legislative programs relating to the activities and problems of young people (vocational education, mental health, scholarship programs, child labor laws). For the state, "youth" is a bureaucratic category, a group like the elderly, refugees, farmers, or labor. Most traditional solutions to problems of drug abuse, juvenile delinquency, school truancy, and unemployment among young people that are proposed by various governments tend to revolve around the organization of youth in a variety of cultural, religious, recreational, labor, and educational associations, all subsidized by the state. Approximately 40 percent of young Germans age 15 to 24 belong to at least one of these types of organizations.

Attempts at political education designed to create a "critical, active citizen" are characteristic of most of the groups; indeed, some political educational programs are required to receive state subsidies for their other activities. Whether this extensive state concern with young people is effective has yet to be determined. Given the reported increases in drug abuse, alcoholism, and crime, the traditional official youth programs appear to be insufficient.

Since the 1980s the weak economy has produced record high unemployment among young people. The government and the private sector have attempted to increase the number of apprenticeship positions, and Chancellor Kohl even made a personal commitment to secure a training position for every applicant. The very high level of support given by young people to the Greens in 1987 (67 percent of Green support came from voters under age 35) was in part a reaction to the economic situation. In addition to the missile and peace issues, there was an economic component in youth support for the Greens.[52]

Young Germans, both Eastern and Western, have been less concerned about unification than their elders. Indeed, in East Germany the students, who were a privileged group in the former GDR, were not as involved as other young people in the events that eventually toppled the communist system. Only politically reliable young people were allowed entrance into East German universities. Many younger East Germans were also more likely to have developed an identification with the communist state than were older age groups.[53] Young people in West Germany benefitted from the post-unification economic upturn in the "old" Federal Republic, whereas their counterparts in the East experienced sharply increased unemployment and rapidly changing educational conditions. By the end of 1994, unemployment in the East among young people reached almost 35 percent. High unemployment among Eastern young people is frequently cited as a major factor in their proclivity to support right-wing radical groups and engage in violence against foreigners. In the early 1990s about 14 percent of East Germans under age 30 reported that they would "probably" or "definitely" move to the West in the near future.[54] Indeed, the integration of East German youth into the democratic political and social order has been an important task confronting the political system.

Refugees and Resettlers

Over 20 percent of West Germans came to the Federal Republic as refugees or expellees from the Eastern territories lost to the Soviet Union and Poland after World

War II, other parts of Eastern Europe, or—between 1949 and 1989—the former East Germany. The absorption of this mass of almost 14 million homeless (and in many cases impoverished) people was a major problem for the young German state, which was already overcrowded and unable to adequately feed and house its pre-1945 population. But within two decades this group had become integrated into German society—a major accomplishment of the postwar system. Today they represent neither a social nor an economic problem; hence, as refugees, they have little political relevance.

Since 1988 almost 3 million ethnic German resettlers from Eastern Europe and the former Soviet Union have emigrated to the Federal Republic. For decades the Federal Republic had urged Poland, the Soviet Union, and other Eastern European countries to allow their nationals who by virtue of their language, ancestry, or education profess to be German to resettle in the Federal Republic.

Article 116 of the Basic Law makes these settlers, many of whom do not speak German, eligible for immediate and full citizenship. Thus the descendants of eighteenth- and nineteenth-century German settlers can appear in Germany and become citizens. Many of them, however, have suffered persecution and discrimination as the price for maintaining their German heritage. Considering the problems of unemployment and housing shortages, the arrival of these distant cousins has evoked some resentment among native Germans. Others, pointing to Germany's low birth rate and aging population, welcome them as a positive demographic development.

Political Radicals and Extremists

The legitimacy criteria for extremist movements have been higher in the Federal Republic than in other Western European societies. Citing the Weimar, Nazi, and East German experiences for support, both West Germany's postwar occupiers and the political elites of the Federal Republic have had a relatively low tolerance for any individual, group, or movement that advocated radical changes in the basic structure of the political, social, or economic order. In short, it has been difficult to be an extremist in West Germany and—in comparison to France, Italy, and Britain—relatively easy to be labeled as such by the established parties, courts, and other institutions.

The framers of the Basic Law in 1948–1949 gave the Federal Constitutional Court the power to ban any political party whose program or policies in the judgment of the court threatened the basic structure of the Republic. Under this provision, the court in the 1950s did outlaw one right-wing party and the German Communist party. Thus the Basic Law did not leave the fate of allegedly extremist parties to the electorate but, rather, to the courts.

In addition to constitutional prohibitions against extremism (defined as opposition to the "basic free democratic order"), Germany and its constituent states have established offices for the Protection of the Constitution (*Verfassungsschutz*); these are charged with investigating individuals and groups suspected of undermining the system. The national office is under the Interior Ministry. It publishes an annual report to the parliament that catalogues extremist activity (political parties, acts of political violence) and assesses any trends. At times, critics have charged that the government has misused the office for political purposes.

The Radical Right.   Between 1949 and 1969 a variety of right-wing parties and organizations, many of which were led by former Nazis or people with close ties to former Nazis, came to and departed from the political scene. Most of the groups were small, but they could be very noisy and, given Germany's past, drew considerable attention, especially from foreign observers.

At the 1969 election one of these organizations, the National Democratic party (NPD), made a strong effort to gain representation in the national parliament. Securing only 4.3 percent of the vote, it failed to clear the 5 percent hurdle necessary for entrance into the legislature. After 1969 the party quickly faded; at the 1976 election it received less than 1 percent of the vote, and between 1970 and 1974 it lost all its seats in several state parliaments. During the 1970s various other nationalist and right-wing organizations mounted protests against the government's policy of detente with the Soviet Union, East Germany, and Eastern Europe, but little was heard from them following ratification of the treaties.

In 1989 a new radical right party, the Republicans, burst on the political scene at state elections in Berlin, a local election in Frankfurt, and the election of deputies to the European parliament. Led by a former member of the Waffen-SS (the military wing of the elite guard), the party attracted enormous media attention. Its success was due largely to its strong anti-foreigner theme, that is, the party's hostility to foreign workers, residents, and even ethnic Germans who since 1988 have been allowed to emigrate in increasing numbers from the Soviet Union and other Eastern European countries. Voter interest in the Republicans, however, dropped quickly in the wake of the unification movement during 1989–1990. Following losses in several state elections the party's support fell to less than 2 percent, well under the 5 percent needed to enter parliament. At the December 1990 all-German election, the Republicans received only 2.2 percent of the vote.

The issue of foreign residents and, especially, the flood of asylum seekers discussed earlier in this chapter remained an important item on the political agenda after the 1990 election. In 1992 at a state election in Baden-Württemberg the Republicans received 11 percent of the vote and once again returned to the headlines. The party's long-run future, however, remains largely dependent on how the major parties deal with the foreign resident issue. Since passage of the 1993 constitutional amendment restricting the asylum right, the party's support has once again dropped sharply.

Since unification, groups of young skinheads and neo-Nazis have formed in the new Eastern states. Although constituting only a small proportion of East German youth, they have attracted widespread media coverage for their attacks on foreigners and noisy, sometimes violent rallies at which racist and extremist nationalist themes are presented. By 1997 German authorities estimated that about 3,900 of the 7,600 "violence-prone right-wing extremists" (including skinheads) in the entire country came from the five new Eastern states and Berlin.[55]

These groups are less a political problem than they are an expression of the frustration felt by some young people who are uncertain of their future. They also represent a reaction against the ritualized anti-fascism enforced under the communist regime. The appearance of these groups, however, underscores the importance of economic and social reconstruction as a requisite to democratic stability in the new states.

The problem of unification has also given new life to radical right parties. Capitalizing on high unemployment and anti-foreigner sentiment in the East, several extreme right-wing parties scored successes at state elections. Although there are few foreign residents in the new Eastern states, these parties have been able to convince especially younger East Germans that their economic problems are the result of the country's generosity toward foreign immigrants. The most successful extreme right-wing party in the East has been the German Peoples Union (DVU). Based in the West German city of Munich, the DVU is the personal creation of a longtime and prominent member of West Germany's nationalist fringe, Gerhard Frey. Two other right-wing parties that have attracted some support in the Eastern states are the *Republikaner* or Reps and the somewhat revived National Democratic Party (NPD). Both of these parties have their origins in West Germany and indeed scored some minor successes at the state level over the past thirty years. None of these three radical-right parties, however, came close to entering the national parliament in the 1998 election; the combined percentage for all three parties was only 3.3 percent. In spite of its ability to grab some headlines at state elections, the far right has held little interest for Germany's voters in national elections. Indeed, Germany, unlike France, Italy, Austria, and some other members of the European Union, is not represented in the European Parliament by any delegates from far-right parties.

Although the prospects of a resurgent Nazi movement still stimulate the imaginations of some novelists and screenwriters, no right-wing, much less neo-Nazi, organization has ever emerged since 1949 in sufficient strength to seriously challenge the legitimacy of the Republic. Although Germany's record in the early postwar years of removing former Nazis from key public positions or preventing their reemployment was checkered, the simple fact is that by the 1990s such individuals were either dead or very elderly and retired, or had by their subsequent behavior repudiated their past affiliations.

The Radical Left.   The focus of media and public attention shifted in the late 1960s from right-wing, neo-Nazi movements to the various revolutionary Marxist groups and radical terrorist organizations that emerged mainly in large cities and on university campuses.

In the immediate postwar period, the remnants of what had been Germany's ideological left wing during the Weimar Republic—old-guard socialists, radical intellectuals, pacifists, and socially committed church members (especially on the Protestant side) were frustrated as the anticipated moral regeneration and drastic change in the structure of society, economy, and polity did not take place. Original hopes for a "humanistic socialism" were thwarted as a middle-class, materialist, and elitist ethos came to dominate the politics of the new Republic. The radical dissenter became isolated, an oddball in the affluent society.

This postwar rejection of the ideological left and its identification in the minds of many West Germans with Stalinism and the East German dictatorship contributed to the rigid, uncompromising opposition of the New Left to the parliamentary system of the Federal Republic.[56]

Isolated, its ideology spurned by all major parties and leaders, the New Left in the 1960s developed a socialist theory that rejected and denied legitimacy to the liberalism embodied in the postwar system. The Cold War, West German rearmament, Vietnam, the Social Democrats' (SPD) acceptance of the market economy, and Adenauer's foreign policy all intensified the Left's opposition to the parliamentary system. The SPD's entrance into a grand coalition in 1966 with its longtime adversary, the Christian Democrats, was the last straw and marked the beginning of significant radical left activity.

By 1969 the internal divisions over ideology and tactics, the massive indifference if not opposition of the West German "proletariat," and the increasing tendency to violence among factions of the movement greatly weakened the New Left. The Socialist-Liberal election victory of 1969 and the end of the Grand Coalition also took the wind out of the radical argument that the Republic was on the verge of a fascist takeover. Nonetheless, the New Left in its own way contributed to the increased politicization of West German citizens evident since the late 1960s. The new emphasis on "discussions" rather than speeches by political leaders, as well as the increased readiness of a traditionally passive citizenry to use the rights of free expression to protest unpopular governmental action and seek redress and reform (so evident in the citizen initiative movement already discussed), were to some extent influenced by the innovative and often audacious tactics of the "extraparliamentary opposition."

Where have all the radicals gone? Like their American and British counterparts, many took teaching and research positions at colleges and universities; and some became active in the Social Democratic party, the Greens, the trade unions, churches, journalism, and other middle-class occupations. Several splinter groups from the movement, however, resorted to guerrilla-type violence in an apparent attempt to bring down the state. Terrorist activities began in the 1970s with bank robberies, kidnappings, and murders. By June 1972, with the capture of the so-called hard-core Baader-Meinhof band (named after two leading figures in the movement), terrorist activity subsided. In 1974 the death in prison of one of the terrorists, through the consequences of a hunger strike, touched off the murder of a West Berlin judge. In 1975 another splinter group kidnapped the leader of the Christian Democrats in West Berlin shortly before the city elections and as ransom demanded the release of several terrorists from West German jails.

In 1977 terrorist activities assumed new dimensions when, over a five-month period, a series of well-planned attacks on major government and business leaders took place. The chief federal prosecutor (equivalent to the American attorney general or the British director of public prosecution) and the head of a major bank were assassinated, and in September the director of the Federation of German Industry was kidnapped and later murdered. The terrorists had the support of numerous sympathizers who provided them with falsified identification papers, escape automobiles, conspiratorial hideouts, and other logistical support. Money was secured largely through periodic bank robberies.

Following the collapse of the East German communist regime in 1989–1990, another aspect of the West German terrorist scene became known. For almost fifteen years the East German Secret Police (*Stasi,* see Chapter 2) sheltered, trained, and gave extensive material support to terrorists in the Red Army Faction (RAF). At least two RAF attacks in 1981—one at the U.S. airbase in Ramstein that injured seventeen people, and an attempted assassination of a U.S. Army general—were led by terrorists who had been trained for the operations in East Germany. Terrorists involved in the 1977 murders of a leading banker and industrialist were provided with new identities and lived for twelve years in the former GDR.

In 1989 the RAF claimed responsibility for the car-bombing murder of Germany's leading banker, Alfred Herrhausen of the Deutsche Bank. A close advisor to Chancellor Kohl, Herrhausen was an early and enthusiastic supporter of German unity. In 1991 the RAF struck again when Detlev-Karsten Rohwedder, the director of the Trusteeship Authority (Treuhand), the huge agency charged with privatizing the former GDR's economy (see Chapter 8), was murdered at his home in West Germany. But by the early 1990s the Red Army Faction had only about twenty hardcore or commando-level members living underground. Officials estimated that they were supported by roughly two hundred militants and four hundred sympathizers who distributed propaganda and provided logistical support.

In 1998 the Red Army Faction (RAF) suddenly announced that it had disbanded. Authorities considered the statement authentic. In its history the RAF was responsible for the deaths of at least thirty people, including prominent political and business figures. Five fatal attacks dating from 1985 remain unsolved. In its statement the RAF expressed no regret toward its victims.

SUMMARY AND CONCLUSION

The much-discussed postwar political stability of the Federal Republic is now rooted in a solid attitudinal consensus on the values, processes, and institutions of liberal democracy. Bonn, in contrast to Weimar, is not a republic without republicans. Moreover, since the mid-1960s there has been an ever closer fit between citizen attitudes and values and actual behavior. Germans at elite and general public levels have become more interested in politics and more inclined to use politics as a means of social change and personal development. Consider the following: Since 1966, three alternations of government and opposition have taken place without straining the system; widespread citizen initiative groups have emerged to campaign for social and political issues, especially at the local level (housing, education, the environment); election campaigns have seen extensive citizen participation and involvement; the party system has become more polarized and conflictual within the rules of the game; the intensity of political debate, both inside and outside of parliament, has increased as major innovations in foreign and domestic policies were attempted. Finally, none of the economic recessions of the past thirty-five years produced any noticeable increases in antisystem sentiment or movements. In short, the institutions and processes of liberal democracy are being used extensively without any perceptible stress on the basic structure of the political order. The stability of the German political system has been supplemented by a vitality in political life not apparent during the Republic's early years.

Can this democracy now integrate 16 million new citizens who have lived under authoritarian regimes for almost sixty years? This is the challenge facing the Federal Republic as it enters the twenty-first century. Thus far, East Germans have shown substantial support for the institutions and processes of liberal democracy. But like West

Germans in the 1950s, they must also experience the successful performance of this democratic order. In the next few years the economic dimension will be especially important for the integration of the East into the democratic political culture of the West. Another key factor in the democratic development of the former German Democratic Republic will be the capacity of the party system and interest groups to channel the demands of these citizens and produce meaningful policy outcomes. We now turn to an examination of the Federal Republic's party system and its interest groups.

Notes

1. Donald J. Devine, *The Political Culture of the United States* (Boston: Little, Brown, 1972), pp. 347ff.
2. Walter Friedrich, "Mentalitätsswandlungen der Jugend in der DDR," *Aus Politik und Zeitgeschichte,* nos. 16–17 (April 13, 1990): 25–37.
3. This takes several forms. There has been, for example, a renewed interest among historians and the media in Prussia and its influence on German history. The immediate post-World War II period, during which the "switches were set" (*Weichenstellung*) for the formation and evolution of the Federal Republic, also has attracted the serious attention of historians.
4. Elisabeth Noelle-Neumann and Renate Köcher, eds., *Jahrbuch der Öffentlichen Meinung,* Vol. IX (Munich and New York: Saur Verlag, 1993), p. 397.
5. From 1976 to 1988 the proportion of foreign oil that the Federal Republic imported from the Middle East declined from 90 percent to 49 percent.
6. James M. Markham, "German Missile Protests: Mixed Signals for Kohl," *New York Times,* October 24, 1983, p. A3.
7. Elisabeth Noelle-Neumann and Renate Köcher, *Die verletzte Nation* (Stuttgart: Deutsche Verlagsanstalt, 1987).
8. Jürgen Habermas, "Eine Art Schadensabwicklung," *Die Zeit,* July 11, 1986, reprinted in *Historikerstreit* (Munich: Piper Verlag, 1987), pp. 75–76.
9. G. Robert Boynton and Gerhard Loewenberg, "The Decay of Support for Monarchy and the Hitler Regime in the Federal Republic of Germany," *British Journal of Political Science* 4 (October 1974): 488.
10. *Ibid.,* p. 485.
11. Lewis J. Edinger, "Political Change in Germany," *Comparative Politics* 2, no. 4 (July 1970): 549–578.
12. Ralf Dahrendorf, *Society and Democracy in Germany* (New York: Doubleday, Anchor Books, 1969), pp. 137–138.
13. *Ibid.,* p. 146.
14. Unpublished survey data collected by Professor Rudolf Wildenmann, Mannheim University.
15. David P. Conradt, "West Germany: A Remade Political Culture?" *Comparative Political Studies 7* (July 1974): 222–238.
16. *Jahrbuch der Öffentlichen Meinung, 1965–1967,* Vol. IV (Allensbach: Verlag für Demoskopie, 1968), p. 182.
17. Cited in Gerhard Loewenberg, *Parliament in the German Political System* (Ithaca: Cornell University Press, 1967), p. 429.
18. Elisabeth Noelle-Neumann and Renate Köcher, *Jahrbuch der Demoskopie. Band X (1993–1997),* Munich: K.G. Saur Verlag and Verlag für Demoskopie, 1997, p. 822.
19. *Jahrbuch der Demoskopie. Band X,* p. 889.
20. Petra Bauer, "Freiheit und Demokratie in der Wahrnehmung der Bürger in der Bundesrepublik und der ehemaligen DDR," in *Nation und Demokratie,* ed. Rudolf Wildenmann, (Baden-Baden: Nomos Verlagsanstalt, 1991), pp. 99–124; Institut für Demoskopie, "Die Unterstützung der Demokratie in den neuen Bundesländern," unpublished manuscript, Allensbach, 1991, pp. 26–29.

21. Institut für Demoskopie, Survey no. 5050.
22. When this question was asked again in April 1995, the proportion of East Germans mentioning the Third Reich increased to 19 percent. There appears to be a slow trend toward convergence. In some areas, however, the East-West conceptions of history remain quite different. In the same April 1995 study, about 70 percent of West Germans stated that the United States had played the decisive role in the defeat of the Nazis in World War II; 24 percent credited the Soviet Union with the victory. Among East Germans, however, 87 percent considered the Soviet Union's role decisive and only 23 percent viewed the United States as the decisive factor in the defeat of the Nazis. See Elisabeth Noelle-Neumann, "Der geteilte Himmel," *Frankfurter Allgemeine Zeitung,* May 3, 1995, p. 5, for additional survey data on differing East-West conceptions of history.
23. Elisabeth Noelle-Neumann, Renate Köcher, *Jahrbuch der Demoskopie. Band X (1993–1997).* Munich: K.G. Saur and Verlag für Demoskopie, p. 670.
24. A 1995 survey also found substantial differences between East and West Germans in this area. When asked whether the "social system in the Federal Republic is just," only 19 percent of Easterners replied positively as compared to 48 percent of Western respondents. Over half (53 percent) of East Germans in 1995 considered the Federal Republic to be an "unjust" society, as compared to 28 percent of West Germans. Institut für Demoskopie surveys cited in Elisabeth Noelle-Neumann, "Kein Schutz, keine Gleichheit, keine Gerechtigkeit," *Frankfurter Allgemeine Zeitung,* March 8, 1995, p. 5.
25. Ursula Feist, "Zur politischen Akkulturation der vereinten Deutschen. Eine Analyse aus Anlaß der ersten gesamtdeutschen Bundestagswahl," *Aus Politik und Zeitgeschichte,* nos. 11–12 (March, 1991): 21–32.
26. *Eurobarometer,* No. 51 (March–April, 1999).
27. Sidney Verba, "Germany: The Remaking of Political Culture," in *Political Culture and Political Development,* ed. L.W. Pye and S. Verba (Princeton: Princeton University Press, 1965), pp. 130–170.
28. Erwin K. Scheuch, "Die Sichtbarkeit politischer Einstellungen im alltäglichen Verhalten," *Kölner Zeitschrift für Soziologie und Sozialpsychologie,* Sonderheft no. 9 (1965): 169–214.
29. David P. Conradt, "Changing German Political Culture," in *The Civic Culture Revisited,* ed. Gabriel Almond and Sidney Verba (Boston: Little, Brown, 1980), pp. 231–240.
30. In 1968, after years of discussion and debate, the parliament passed a series of laws and constitutional amendments prescribing the conduct of government in emergency situations. Mindful of how the conservative nationalists and later the Nazis had abused the emergency provisions of the Weimar Constitution after 1930, various groups such as trade unions, student organizations, and some intellectuals mounted a vigorous opposition to the proposed legislation. Strong criticism was also leveled against the Social Democrats, who while in the parliamentary opposition had vetoed previous attempts at emergency provisions, but who in 1968, as a governing party, supported the laws.
31. Horst Zillessen, "Bürgerinitiativen im repräsentativen Regierungssystem," *Aus Politik und Zeitgeschichte,* no. 12 (March 23, 1974): 6.
32. Institut für angewandte Sozialforschung, *Politogramm,* October 1990.
33. Leonard Krieger, *The German Idea of Freedom* (Chicago and London: University of Chicago Press, 1957).
34. Theo Rasehorn, *Recht und Klassen—Zur Klassenjustiz in der Bundesrepublik* (Darmstadt: Luchterhand Verlag, 1973).
35. This question is a standard item in the "Democracy Scale" originally developed by Professor Max Kaase. For comparisons between East and West Germans, see Petra Bauer, "Freiheit und Demokratie in der Wahrnehmung der Bürger in der Bundesrepublik und der ehemaligen DDR." (See note 20.)
36. *Der Spiegel,* no. 15 (April 9, 1973); *Die Zeit,* no. 43 (September 27, 1974).
37. *Der Spiegel,* no. 30 (July 28, 1975), pp. 28–29.
38. For a thorough analysis of this issue, see Gerard Braunthal, *Political Loyalty and Public Service in West Germany* (Amherst, MA: University of Massachusetts Press, 1990). The

relevant decisions of the Federal Constitutional Court are discussed in Donald Kommers, *The Constitutional Jurisprudence of the Federal Republic of Germany* (Durham, NC, and London: Duke University Press, 1989).

39. Interior Minister Zimmermann, quoted in *Die Zeit,* no. 52 (December 30, 1983), p. 5.

40. Hans Schuler, "Der Staat darf nicht alles wissen," *Die Zeit,* no. 52 (December 30, 1983), p. 5. The court's decision and strong opposition from civil libertarians also caused the government to reconsider the proposed introduction of a computerized identification system for all citizens. Under the plan each adult would receive a coded plastic card containing a variety of personal data that could be read out by any authority with the appropriate computer terminal. Opponents argued that the identification system, like the census data, could be easily abused by police and security forces.

41. In 1973 the Federal Republic, in cooperation with other European Community states, stopped recruiting foreign workers. Since then only family members of foreign workers already in Germany or foreigners with special qualifications have been allowed to enter legally.

42. Wolfgang Jeschek, "Integration junger Ausländer in das Bildungssystem kommt kaum voran," Deutsche Institut für Wirtschaft, *Report No. 24* (1998).

43. For evidence on the growing influence of Islamic fundamentalism on the 450,000 Turkish young people (15–21 years of age) in the Federal Republic see Wilhelm Heitmeyer, Helmut Schröder, Joachim Müller, "Desintegration und islamischer Fundamentalismus," *Aus Politik und Zeitgeschichte,* nos. 7–8 (February 7, 1997), pp. 17–31.

44. The old law allowed the children (under age 23) of foreign residents to become naturalized citizens provided that they have lived in the Federal Republic for at least eight years and have attended German schools for at least six years.

45. Eurobarometer Survey, no. 23, April 1983.

46. Beate Hoecker, "Politik: Noch immer kein Beruf für Frauen," *Aus Politik und Zeitgeschichte,* nos. 9–10 (February 28, 1987): 5; and *Das Parlament,* no. 32 (August 10, 1985), p. 11.

47. Since the 1980s many local, regional, and state governments have appointed *Frauenbeauftragte* (ombudswomen) to oversee antidiscrimination and equal opportunity programs. In Berlin, for example, an affirmative action program was established for the civil service in 1991. Its goal is a 50 percent representation for females in public employment.

48. Federal Statistical Office (ed.), *Datenreport* (Bonn: Bundeszentrale für politische Bildung, 1994), p. 339ff.

49. *Manager* magazine cited in Ferdinand Protzmann, "In Germany, the Ceiling's Not Glass, It's Concrete," *New York Times,* October 17, 1993, p. 16. A similar study eleven years earlier found only two women at the top level of German companies.

50. Walter Jaide and Hans-Joachim Veen, *Bilanz der Jugendforschung* (Paderborn: Ferdinand Schoningh Verlag, 1989), p. 202.

51. Jaide and Veen, *Bilanz der Jugendforschung,* pp. 214–232; for data from a 1997 study of young people see Arthur Fischer, Richard Münchmeier, *1997 Shell Jugend Studie,* Hamburg: Shell Jugend Stiftung, 1997. This study finds some decline in support for the Greens among young voters. Increasingly the Greens are also seen as an "establishment" party.

52. David P. Conradt and Russell J. Dalton, "The West German Electorate and the Party System: Continuity and Change in the 1980s," *Review of Politics* 50, no. 1 (January 1988): 3–29.

53. Bettina Westle, "Strukturen Nationaler Identität in der DDR und der BRD," unpublished manuscript, Mannheim University, July 1991, p. 14.

54. EMNID survey cited in *Der Spiegel,* no. 31 (July 29, 1991), p. 46.

55. Federal Office for the Protection of the Constitution figures cited in *Frankfurter Allgemeine Zeitung,* September 19, 1998, p. 3.

56. Kurt Shell, "Extraparliamentary Opposition in Postwar Germany," *Comparative Politics* 2, no. 4 (July 1970): 659.

5 The Party System and the Representation of Interests

The postwar party system differs in structure and function from that of the empire and the Weimar Republic. Structurally, the number of political parties seriously contending for parliamentary representation has dropped to only four or five, in contrast to the twelve to twenty-five parties represented at various times in the Reichstag between 1871 and 1933. The extremist, regional, and small special-interest parties that made stable coalition government so difficult during the Weimar Republic either did not reappear in 1949 or were absorbed by the major parties by the elections of 1953 and 1957. Functionally, postwar German parties have become key carriers of the democratic state and have assumed an importance and status unprecedented in German political history. Before the creation of the Federal Republic, democratic political parties, fragmented and narrowly based, were not, for the most part, major forces in political life. Many of the important decisions were made by the executive, the bureaucracy, the military, and the economic elites—not by democratic political parties. Frustrated and thwarted in their quest for governmental and specifically executive power, the parties concentrated more on ideological differentiation and the construction of their extraparliamentary organizations than on the more practical matter of organizing government. The presentation of meaningful alternatives to the electorate, the ability to translate party policy into governmental programs, and the control of governmental leaders were functions rarely performed by German parties.

THE PARTY STATE

The Federal Republic, on the other hand, has been termed a *party state*. German political scientist Kurt Sontheimer provides a clear definition of this term:

> . . . all political decisions in the Federal Republic are made by the parties and their representatives. There are no political decisions of importance in the

German democracy which have not been brought to the parties, prepared by them and finally taken by them.[1]

Political parties in the Federal Republic became agencies that made nominations and fought elections with the goal of controlling the personnel and policies of government. They no longer stood on the sidelines.

The postwar parties antedated the Republic. Indeed, they created it and have penetrated key institutions as never before in German history. Relatively untainted by Nazism (they were all outlawed in 1933), the parties began work early. Between 1945 and 1950, with considerable amounts of patronage at their disposal, they ensured that not only parliament but the bureaucracy, the judiciary, the educational system, the media, and later even the military were led directly or indirectly by their supporters. Even today, few German generals or civil servants would dare attempt to "go public" with criticism in any controversial area without the protection of a party/political figure. Moreover, these democratic parties were distrustful of what an American would term "independents." In Germany, to be independent has historically meant to be "above the parties," and those "above the parties" have usually sided with the authoritarian-statist tradition. Hence the parties opposed the efforts of American occupiers to establish a Federal Personnel Office along the lines of the nonpartisan American Civil Service Commission to staff, especially the upper levels of the bureaucracy, with "independents." To postwar German party leaders, a nonpartisan civil service meant at best a bureaucracy indifferent to the democratic system, and at worst one opposed to it. Today, after fifty years of democratic politics, the highest positions in the state bureaucracy, the educational system, and even the radio and television networks are mainly given to people who are active party members.[2]

The strength of this party system was also shown during the unification process. When it became apparent that the indigenous East German democratic forces could not compete with the well-organized Communist party apparatus during preparations for the country's first free election in 1990, the West German parties quickly moved across the recently opened border and organized the campaign. In the March 1990 election, East Germans could chose from the full range of parties available to West Germans. The losers in this process, however, in addition to the Communists, were the native East German democratic revolutionaries, who had risked their lives to bring down the Communist regime. Only about 5 percent of East Germans supported these groups in the election.

The constitutional source of this strong position held by the parties is found in Article 21 of the Basic Law, which states that "the political parties shall take part in forming the political will of the people. They may be freely established. Their internal organization must conform to democratic principles. They must publicly account for the sources of their funds." It is rare for any democratic constitution to mention political parties in such detail, much less assign them a function. Article 21 goes on in paragraph 2, however, to grant the Federal Constitutional Court the right to prohibit any party that does not accept the constitution:

Parties which by reason of their aims or the behavior of their adherents seek to impair or abolish the free democratic basic order or to endanger the existence of the Federal Republic of Germany, shall be unconstitutional. The Federal Constitutional Court shall decide on the question of unconstitutionality.

In other words, a political organization, exercising the rights of free speech and freedom of assembly, that opposes the constitutional order may be outlawed. Indeed, in the 1950s two political parties—the Communists and a neo-Nazi party—were banned by the court under this provision. Many constitutional scholars and political scientists questioned the wisdom of this action, arguing that the ballot box is the best place to defeat extremist groups in a democracy. But its inclusion in the constitution indicates the determination of the leaders of Germany's democratic parties to avoid a recurrence of Weimar conditions and to close the system to all extremist movements. The reluctance of any government since the mid-1950s to use the constitution to outlaw later radical movements, such as the right-wing National Democrats in the 1960s or the Republicans in the late 1980s, indicates the greater confidence of German political elites in not only the viability of the Republic's institutions but also the judgment of its electorate.

The constitutional recognition given to the parties is the major rationale for the extensive state support they receive, especially for election campaigns (see Chapter 6). Each of the major parties also has a quasi-official foundation that sponsors extensive domestic political education projects and engages in "political developmental" work in several less-developed countries. The overall thrust of the foundations' overseas work tends to be directed toward establishing goodwill for the Federal Republic, especially in the Third World, by supporting the training and development of native democratic parties and interest groups. Political education in the sense of training party and interest group officials and functionaries is also included in this overseas work. The SPD's Friedrich Ebert Foundation has supported the Social Democratic parties of Spain and Portugal while those countries were still under dictatorial control. The training and support of trade unionists in developing countries is another area of activity for the foundation. Similar projects, in some cases oriented to more center or conservative political movements, are sponsored by the CDU's Konrad Adenauer Foundation, the CSU's Hans Seidel Foundation, and the FDP's Friedrich Naumann Foundation. Since 1989 the Green party has established its own foundation, the Heinrich Böll Foundation, which support projects identified with the Green program (i.e., environmental problems, women's issues, and human rights organizations). In 1999, the Party of Democratic Socialism (PDS), the successor to the former ruling Communist party of East Germany, also received funds to establish a foundation, the Rosa Luxemburg Foundation, named after one of the founders of the German Communist party. Opposition to granting the PDS a foundation weakened after the party received 5 percent of the vote at the 1998 election. Almost all of the funds for these party foundations come from the state. In 1996 they received almost $450 million for their activities.[3]

The achievement of the "established" parties (SPD, CDU/CSU, FDP[4]), the only three who have been in the parliament continuously since 1949, is all the more remarkable when one considers the general indifference of the vast majority of West Germans during the postwar period to politics and parties, as well as the antiparty attitudes of traditional statists. What postwar party elites have succeeded in doing is to all but erase the image many citizens had of parties as ineffective, unreliable, and incapable of meeting key citizen demands.

This system of strong parties, or the "party state," is not without its shortcomings or critics. It is, for example, difficult for new interests, parties, and movements to gain a political foothold. The influence of the grass roots is also limited by the parties' hierarchical structure. The emergence in the 1970s of a significant citizen initiative movement and later a new political party, the Greens, outside the boundaries of this party system illustrates the extent to which some important issues, such as nuclear power, housing, and urban planning, have not been dealt with by the parties to the satisfaction of large groups of involved citizens.[5]

There is also increasing evidence that the established parties have abused and manipulated the laws governing their financing. In the 1980s several leading officials from the Free Democrats were indicted for illegally receiving campaign funds. In 1981 all major parties prepared a law that would have legalized many of their past excesses in the financial area. Only the ensuing public uproar caused the proposed law to be withdrawn. A new law passed in 1988 was declared unconstitutional by the Federal Constitutional Court (see Chapter 8) in 1992. The Court ruled that the parties were far too liberal in their allocation of public funds for their activities. It also ruled that state subsidies cannot exceed the amounts the parties raise themselves.

By 1999, public subsidies to the political parties accounted for over half of their total income. No other democracy is so generous in its support of parties through public funds as the Federal Republic. Because the parties control both the state and national parliaments, which allocate these funds, there are few means to control independently their ever-increasing demand for taxpayer support. In 1993 Federal President von Weizsäcker (see Chapter 7) publicly criticized the parties for their misuse of public funds and blamed them for the growing distrust of political leaders and institutions and the decline in voter turnout. The parties, he charged, consider the state to be their private treasury; he called for stricter campaign finance laws and a reduction in state subsidies for the parties.

In late 1999 a major scandal involving the finances of the Christian Democratic Union during the Kohl era (1982–1998) provoked renewed public and media criticism of the parties. Allegations of kickbacks from defense contractors, secret foreign bank accounts, money laundering schemes, and falsified financial records severely damaged the CDU and the reputation of former Chancellor Helmut Kohl.

The Party System

THE CHRISTIAN DEMOCRATS

For most of its history, the Federal Republic has been governed by a political party that, like the Republic itself, was a distinctly postwar creation. The Christian Democratic Union (CDU) and its Bavarian affiliate, the Christian Social Union (CSU), represented the efforts of widely divergent groups and interests to seek a new beginning following the Nazi catastrophe and postwar occupation.

Between 1945 and 1948, small groups of political activists made up of former Weimar Center, Liberal, and Socialist party members, together with Catholic and Protestant laity, organized throughout Germany. The dominant theme in the motivations of these disparate interests was the need for a new party based in part on the application of general Christian principles to politics. It was felt that the traditional differences between Protestants and Catholics had to be bridged, at least at the political level, to create a new movement that could be a powerful integrating force in the new political system. Also, by stressing its ties to the churches, this new party linked itself to the one pre-Nazi social institution that survived the war with some authority, legitimacy, and organizational strength.

In its early years, the CDU was programmatically committed to wide-ranging socioeconomic reform, particularly in the British zone. The major statement of the party, the Ahlen Program of 1947, indeed called for the nationalization of large industries and rejected the restoration of many prewar capitalistic structures in the Federal Republic. In addition, Article 15 of the Basic Law—which permits, with proper compensation, the socialization of land, natural resources, and the means of production—was supported by the chairman in the British zone and future chancellor, Konrad Adenauer.

What happened between 1947 and 1949? Essentially the success of Erhard's 1948 currency reform, which ended postwar inflation and the black market; the end of Allied dismantling of German industry; American opposition to "socialist policies"; and the realization that the Christian Democrats, given the strength of the Socialists, had little freedom to maneuver on the left of the political spectrum all together made the CDU shift toward a more center-right than center-left position. In short, there was by 1949 room for a middle-of-the-road, center party with a conservative economic policy and a major party to the right of the SPD, but not for another center-left party. The Union's performance at the first federal election in September 1949, the economic boom that began with the Korean War in 1950, and the foreign policy successes of Chancellor Adenauer solidified the more conservative course.

Nonetheless, the party remained remarkably open to a wide variety of political viewpoints. Apart from a general commitment to the "social free market economy" (a sort of capitalism with a heart) and a pro-Western, anticommunist foreign policy, the Christian Democrats avoided any specific policy orientation, much less ideology. To its critics, this was opportunism; to supporters, however, the party's pragmatic, bargaining approach to politics represented a welcome relief from the ideological rigidity that had characterized many Weimar parties. It thus provided a home for liberals, socialists, conservatives, Catholics and Protestants, north and south Germans, rural, urban, industrial, and labor interests, all held together by, above all, the electoral successes of Chancellor Adenauer. The CDU became a prototype for what Otto Kirchheimer termed a "catchall party," a broadly based, programmatically vague movement that capitalized on the mass economic prosperity of postwar Europe.[6]

The stunning victories of the party in the 1953 and 1957 elections were essentially personal triumphs for Adenauer. The CDU's dependence on the popularity of the chancellor was to prove a short-run advantage but a long-run liability. In riding the crest of his personal popularity, the Union did not take the necessary steps to strengthen its organization and depersonalize its appeals to retain its position after Adenauer's inevitable departure. At the 1961 election, Adenauer's age (85), thirteen years of governmental responsibility, and a "new look" SPD began to erode the party's electoral base. The Christian Democrats lost their absolute majority, and as a condition for a coalition with the Free Democrats, Adenauer had to agree to step down by 1963. His successor, Ludwig Erhard, had never been a party leader and had little real political power within the Union. Indeed, after the war he had toyed with the idea of joining the FDP. But as the architect of postwar economic prosperity, he did possess an electoral appeal that the Union gratefully employed at the 1965 election. With the 1966 recession, however, Erhard's status as an "electoral locomotive" declined and, with that, his position in the party and his chancellorship.

With no strong, electorally successful chancellor to hold it together, the party's numerous factions and wings began to struggle among themselves for control of the organization. Taking the SPD into the government in 1966 (the Grand Coalition) kept the party in power until 1969 but failed to halt the steady decline in its image among many voters as the only party capable of governing Germany at the national level. For the first time in its history, the CDU/CSU in 1969 found itself without a leader, without a program, and, above all, without power.

The Union in Opposition, 1969–1982

Yet the closeness of the CDU/CSU defeat in 1969 (the party fell only 13 seats short of an absolute majority) provided the Union with sufficient reasons *not* to prepare for its new role as the parliamentary opposition. Although its percentage of the vote declined, the CDU in 1969 remained the largest single party. The Union's leadership insisted that, as the largest party, it was entitled to form the government, a privilege denied them by the "manipulations" of a "desperate" FDP and SPD. Thus the party concentrated much of its effort between 1969 and 1972 on short-range tactical maneuvers designed to split the coalition parties or at least gain enough support from discontented government deputies to erase the coalition's small majority and return the Union to power without new elections. To this end, the party attempted unsuccessfully to unseat the Brandt government in May 1972 by means of a "constructive vote of no-confidence" (see Chapter 7). Instead of concentrating on the development of its organization, program, and leadership, the party sought to topple the government and take a shortcut back to political power.

After the decisive SPD-FDP victory in the 1972 election, however, the CDU/CSU could no longer deny the necessity of accepting its role as the opposition party. Yet the Union in opposition still lacked leadership, policy, and organizational consensus. After three years of intraparty maneuvering, Helmut Kohl, the young *Ministerpräsident* of the state of Rhineland-Palatinate emerged in 1975 as the party's new leader and 1976 chancellor candidate. In the 1976 election the CDU/CSU made impressive gains but nonetheless narrowly missed returning to power. This 1976 electoral performance was interpreted as a defeat by Kohl's foremost challenger in the party, the leader of the Bavarian CSU, Franz-Josef Strauss. Barely six weeks after the election, Strauss attempted to separate the CSU from the Union and make it a new national party. Pressure from party members in Bavaria and Kohl's threat to campaign against the CSU in Bavaria finally forced Strauss to abandon his plans before the start of the new legislative term. The Kohl-Strauss conflict overshadowed the important improvements the CDU had made in its organization and its sophisticated and effective 1976 election campaign.

With his Bavarian CSU solidly behind him, Strauss was able to convince the more conservative elements within the CDU, especially in states like Baden-Württemberg and Hesse, that he deserved a chance as chancellor candidate and could indeed win. Many CDU activists, ideologically opposed to the Bavarian, nonetheless also began to accept the idea of a Strauss candidacy. They reasoned that given the high popularity of Chancellor Schmidt and the solid record of his government, the CDU/CSU, regardless of its candidate, was bound to lose in 1980. Why not let Strauss have his chance and thus, after his inevitable defeat, be rid of this source of so much tension and division within the Union? This argument was quite persuasive for a sufficient number of moderate and liberal party leaders and Strauss was elected as the Union's 1980 chancellor candidate.

The Union's decisive defeat in 1980 was absorbed at the leadership level with relatively little intraparty rancor. Strauss returned to Bavaria, and Kohl retained his position as national chairman of the CDU and parliamentary floor leader. His loyal support of Strauss in the campaign increased his stature within the CSU and among CDU conservatives. Kohl's performance as opposition leader in the *Bundestag* also improved.

The Return to Power

By early 1982 it was apparent that the Social-Liberal coalition would not last until the next scheduled election in 1984. Now the unchallenged leader of the party in Bonn, Helmut Kohl carefully maintained his good relations with the Free Democrats and especially their leader, Hans-Dietrich Genscher. In September 1982 the Free Democrats left the Schmidt cabinet. Shortly thereafter they joined with the CDU and removed Schmidt, replacing him with Kohl. After thirteen years in opposition, the Christian Democrats had returned to power.

Six months later at the March 1983 election, the CDU/CSU had all the advantages of incumbency without any of its disadvantages. From the chancellor's office, Kohl could campaign against the thirteen years of Social Democratic rule and optimistically point to the new beginnings that his government now wanted to make if the electorate would give it the opportunity. Although the economy continued to decline after October 1982, the Union disclaimed any responsibility, dismissing even the record high unemployment levels of early 1983 as its *Erblast,* the burden inherited from the Socialists. The Greens, a political party formed in the late 1970s, were portrayed as Luddites who would destroy rather than create jobs. An "ungovernable" SPD-Green coalition would thus mean economic disaster. The CDU/CSU promised a better future through its policies of reduced spending, increased consumer taxes, and tax incentives for business.

In the 1987 election the Christian Democrats campaigned on the record of the Kohl government. The party emphasized that it had brought Germany back to economic prosperity, reduced the federal deficit, cut taxes, and restored the Federal Republic's status both as a dependable ally of the United States and as a major force in the European Community. Nonetheless, attaining 44 percent of the vote, the

CDU/CSU dropped to its lowest level since 1949. Intracamp switching to the FDP, low turnout among farmers protesting the government's agricultural policies, and overconfidence among its activists were the major factors cited by the party leadership in explaining the outcome. The Union also lost votes to the SPD because of the persistently high unemployment level among manual workers.

The Christian Democrats and Unification

As West German political parties began to participate in the East German political process in early 1990, the outlook for the Christian Democrats was bleak. The East German CDU, which for a brief period after 1945 was an independent party with some association to Christian Democrats in other parts of the country, became a puppet or "bloc" party, one of four that the Communists allowed to operate as a democratic facade for the regime. It did count among its members some East Germans who tried to improve the existing system from within, or who saw the party as a refuge from the one-party system, that is, a means of expressing a small degree of independence, without being pressured to join the Communist party. There were also some devoutly religious East Germans among the party's members. The leadership, however, was totally corrupted by the Communists. In exchange for obediently following the communist line, they were given luxurious (by East German standards) homes, automobiles, generous salaries, and some patronage.

The West German CDU at first avoided any formal contact with this "bloc CDU" in the East. But after the East CDU changed its leadership in the wake of the GDR's collapse and as the date for East Germany's first free parliamentary election approached, Chancellor Kohl and the West CDU began to reassess their relationship to their errant East German cousin. Kohl and his advisors contended that while the old leadership was hopelessly compromised, the rank and file membership was basically sound. Once opinion polls in the East showed that the Social Democrats, a new but "clean" party, held a commanding lead, Kohl put together an "Alliance for Germany" composed of two new opposition groups, the German Social Union, the Democratic Breakthrough, and the "reformed" East German CDU. With Kohl as the de facto leader, the Alliance won a solid victory at the March 1990 East German parliamentary election. The East CDU's large membership and organizational infrastructure served the Alliance well at the subsequent state elections in October 1990 and the all-German poll in December. The CDU became the dominant party in four of the five East German states and with 44 percent of the vote, it remained the largest party in unified Germany.

Soon after the 1990 victory, however, the Union's electoral fortunes, as measured in polls and state elections, declined sharply. The announcement in February 1991 that the costs of unification would indeed require tax increases prompted a "tax lie" campaign by the opposition, which bore fruit at state elections throughout 1992 and 1993.

It was not until the June 1994 European parliamentary election that the CDU could reverse two years of electoral decline. That victory was presaged by steady improvements in the party's standing in public opinion polls since early 1994 and by public perceptions of an improving economy. The economic upturn thus came just in time and was just enough to give Kohl and the CDU a narrow victory in the October 1994 national election.

The 1998 Election: The End of the Kohl Era

In spite of their 1994 victory, the Christian Democrats showed the effects of their long tenure in office. Chancellor Kohl's dominance of the national organization left little room for new leaders to emerge. At the state level the party continued to decline. By 1997 they were the major governing party in only four of the sixteen states. Younger party leaders wanted Kohl to step down before the 1998 election in favor of Wolfgang Schäuble, the leader of the CDU's parliamentary group, but Kohl, Western Europe's senior statesman, insisted on running again. It was a huge mistake. The party ran a lackluster campaign and could not overcome the "Kohl must go" theme of the opposition. After sixteen years in power, many Germans were simply tired of the "old man." Also, unlike 1994, the economy did not improve in 1998 and the unemployment issue badly hurt the CDU. In the eastern states voters turned on Kohl and the CDU with a vengeance. After giving the Christian Democrats lopsided support in the elections of 1990 and 1994, which were still dominated by the unification theme, Eastern voters deserted the Union in droves; CDU support in the East in 1998 dropped by more than 30 percent. Kohl accepted defeat gracefully and stepped down as leader of the party shortly after the election. He was replaced by Wolfgang Schäuble, the longtime crown prince of the party.

THE SOCIAL DEMOCRATS

The only major Weimar political party to reemerge in the Federal Republic was the Social Democratic Party of Germany (SPD). The SPD maintained an executive committee in exile throughout the Nazi period. Together with members who had survived within Germany, it was able to reestablish its national organization in relatively short order after 1945.

In view of the party's unequivocal opposition to National Socialism (the SPD was the only party to vote against Hitler's Enabling Act in March 1933) and its strong organization, it appeared that the SPD would soon become Germany's natural governing party with the resumption of democratic politics at the national level. These expectations were not fulfilled, because the party at the first parliamentary election in 1949 fell far short of an absolute majority and by 1953 was clearly subordinate to the enormously successful CDU under Adenauer.

Why did the SPD fail during the immediate postwar period to become Germany's major governing party? Most analysts attribute this to (1) the party's leadership and, specifically, its national chairman after 1945, Kurt Schumacher, (2) its incorrect reading of German public opinion on key foreign and domestic policy issues, and (3) the unexpected appeal of Adenauer and the free-market economic policies of Economics Minister Ludwig Erhard.[7]

Following the disastrous 1953 and 1957 federal elections, in which the party received less than one-third of the vote, major changes in policy, leadership, and strategy were advocated by an increasing number of SPD state leaders, particularly in Hamburg, Frankfurt, and Berlin. The major leaders of this reform movement were Herbert Wehner, Willy Brandt, Karl Schiller, and Helmut Schmidt. These reformers flatly argued that the party would be permanently consigned to the "30 percent ghetto" unless it made major changes. Their analysis of the election defeats and public opinion polls showed that the SPD had several substantial electoral barriers to surmount.

First, large segments of the electorate had doubts about the SPD's foreign policy, specifically, its commitment to NATO and the pro-Western, anticommunist policy initiated by Adenauer, which was so strongly supported by the electorate during the 1950s. By 1960 the great majority of West Germans accepted the Western orientation of the Bonn Republic, and the reformers were convinced that the SPD must also commit itself to NATO and the Western alliance. Second, there were doubts about the patriotism of the Socialists. Were they really "German" enough or still "wanderers without a country," as Kaiser Wilhelm had once termed them? Third, the party's working-class image, its formal commitment to Marxism, and its generally proletarian style made it difficult for middle-class electors to identify with it. Fourth, the SPD's commitment to the "social free-market economy" was still questioned by large segments of the electorate who feared that the party would experiment with the highly successful economic system and thus endanger prosperity. Finally, the party's anticlerical past remained a significant obstacle among many Catholic voters. The SPD's attempt to integrate its members via numerous suborganizations—youth, women, adult education, mutual assistance, sports, newspapers, magazines—made it appear to many as an ersatz religion, a whole way of life competing with the churches for the hearts and minds of the working class. The reformers clearly wanted to de-emphasize this dimension of the SPD's public image.

At its 1959 convention in Bad Godesberg, the SPD formally abandoned many of the policies and procedures that hindered its support among Catholic and middle-class electors. Its commitment to the Western alliance and anticommunist policies, seen in the administration of Berlin Lord Mayor Willy Brandt, who was elected national chairman a year later, were underscored at this convention. Moreover, the party at Bad Godesberg dropped those sections of its program calling for the nationalization of the means of production and compulsory national economic planning. Finally, at Bad Godesberg, the party repeated its 1954 statement on Christianity and socialism, in which it maintained that Christianity together with classical and humanistic philosophy were the intellectual and moral roots of socialist thought. In short, the SPD now saw no contradiction between socialism and Christianity; the party was firmly committed to the constitutional guarantees respecting the freedom of religion as well as state support for religious institutions.

The SPD's new look was rewarded by the electorate with increased support in 1961 and 1965. But, while gaining on the Christian Democrats, the Socialists remained well behind the CDU and had no national political power or responsibility. The SPD during the 1960s was concerned above all with "embracing the middle," that is, appealing for middle-class support by stressing its allegiance to the free-market economy and the Western alliance. Major policy differences with the Christian Democrats were avoided. Instead of policy, the SPD focused on its leader, Willy Brandt. Much younger than Konrad Adenauer, Brandt was projected as a dynamic, reform-oriented, yet reliable personality who would build on the accomplishments of the (aging) postwar leadership. While this strategy brought electoral gains, national political responsibility came only after the collapse of the Erhard government in 1966 and the subsequent Grand Coalition with the Christian Democrats.

The Return to Power

By entering into a coalition with its long-time opponent, the Social Democrats propped up a severely divided and leaderless Christian Democratic Union. The pact with the CDU, in which the Union still retained the chancellorship, was opposed by a sizable proportion (about 40 percent) of the SPD's membership and some top leaders, among them Willy Brandt. The main strategist of the party during these years and the key architect of the Grand Coalition, Herbert Wehner, successfully argued that such a coalition would finally give the party the opportunity to show its critics that it could govern Germany efficiently and responsibly, indeed better than the Christian Democrats. Moreover, successful performance in the coalition could set the stage for becoming the largest party after the elections of 1969 or 1973.

These arguments prevailed, and the Social Democrats in 1966 entered a national government for the first time since 1930. The party used its opportunity well. Almost all of the SPD ministers in the coalition performed successfully; one of them, Economics Minister Karl Schiller, had spectacular policy successes that even surpassed those of Brandt, who had become foreign minister.

It was Schiller who received major credit in the minds of the electorate for leading the economy out of the 1966–1967 recession.[8] Applying essentially Keynesian policies of increased government spending, tax reductions, and lower interest rates, Schiller by 1969 had restored the economy to full health. Mainly through these efforts, for the first time in German history, economic prosperity and the Social Democrats were closely associated by large segments of the electorate.

Complementing Schiller's successes in economic policy, Foreign Minister Brandt began what was to become known after 1969 as *Ostpolitik,* the normalization of relations by West Germany with Eastern Europe and the Soviet Union. Social Democratic ministers in justice and social welfare also got high marks for their work.

The party was rewarded in 1969 with a further 3.5 percent increase in its share of the popular vote. Much of this increase came from middle-class electors supporting the Social Democrats for the first time in their lives. The 1969 gains enabled the party to become the dominant partner in a "small coalition" with the Free Democrats under the chancellorship of Willy Brandt.

With their foreign policy successes after 1969, the strong personal appeal of Brandt, and continued economic growth and prosperity, the Social Democrats in 1972 became the strongest party and, together with the Free Democrats, increased their parliamentary majority from 12 to almost 50 seats. The long march out of the "30 percent ghetto" of the 1950s was over. Political power and responsibility, however, brought new tensions.

Electoral success and governmental power had come largely through the party's conscious move into the center of the political spectrum, where, as we shall discover in Chapter 6, "the votes are." But success also brought increased criticism from both young and old socialists that the SPD had sold its ideological or Marxist soul for political power. Dormant since the Bad Godesberg reforms, the SPD's left, composed of Young Socialists (about 180,000 members), "old" Marxists largely from the trade union movement, and some intellectuals, had sprung to life in 1966 over the coalition with the bourgeois CDU. The left argued that the party, instead of trying to persuade the electorate of the need for an extensive restructuring of the economy and society along Marxist lines, had taken the easy route to political power by being content simply to represent diverse social groupings and classes without changing the power relationships between them. In short, the party had been opportunistic and not much better than the Christian Democrats. This division deepened still further after Helmut Schmidt became chancellor in 1974. It played a major role in the party's fall from power in 1982.

Electoral Decline and Opposition, 1976–1998

In 1976 the SPD suffered its first decline in support at a national election since 1957. The 1974–1976 recession and the disillusionment with the slow pace of detente with Eastern Europe and the Soviet Union, together with the party's internal organizational and programmatic disputes, had a negative impact on its electoral fortunes. With the prospects of a return to the opposition looming larger, the party's leadership attempted to unite behind the Schmidt government, whose parliamentary majority was reduced to only ten seats. The key integrating figure in the party became its national chairman, Willy Brandt, who had retained this post after his resignation in 1974.

The party was also disappointed with the results of the 1980 election. In spite of the high personal popularity of Chancellor Schmidt, the SPD gained less than 1 percent over its 1976 total. It was the Free Democrats, the junior partner in the governing coalition, who profited the most from Schmidt's popularity. The SPD left sharply criticized the Schmidt government for cutting social programs but raising defense expenditures in the new budget. At one point in 1981 Schmidt threatened to resign unless the left factions within his own party ceased to undermine his government's policies.

In September 1982 the Schmidt government collapsed, and the Social Democrats, after almost sixteen years as a governing party, went into opposition. This was followed five months later, in the 1983 election, by the party's worst electoral performance (38.2 percent) in almost twenty years. In 1983 the SPD campaigned for the first time since 1965 as an opposition party and was led by a new chancellor candidate, Hans-Jochen Vogel, who had less than six months to prepare for the role. The party's leadership responsible for the campaign held to the belief that there was a majority "to the left of the CDU." By emphasizing the "new politics" issues of the environment, nuclear power, and opposition to the NATO decision to station new intermediate-range nuclear missiles on German soil, they believed that sufficient support could be attracted from Green voters and new voters, which would make an SPD-Green alignment numerically if not politically possible. But by moving to the left to attract Green support, the SPD lost important segments of its traditional core electorate: skilled workers and lower- and middle-level white-collar and technical employees.

In 1987 the SPD selected the Minister-President of North Rhine–Westphalia, Johannes Rau, as its chancellor candidate. Rau had won a decisive victory two years earlier in his state, Germany's largest, and had defeated not only the CDU, but had also prevented the Greens from entering the state parliament. His winning state campaign became the model for the party's 1987 effort. Rau's personal qualities were emphasized while issues and conflicts with the opposing parties were downplayed.

The Rau candidacy meant that the SPD would seek an absolute majority of the national vote, thereby avoiding the question of a coalition with the Greens. Rau also pledged that he would not allow himself "to be elected Chancellor with the votes of the Greens" in the event that the party fell short of the absolute majority. Both of these decisions lacked credibility for most voters. Surveys found that less than a third of the electorate believed that the SPD could win an absolute majority and that only about 40 percent agreed that Rau would indeed reject Greens' support if needed after the election.

The strategy also failed because the party's left wing undercut Rau's centrist approach. At the pre-election party congress, the left passed resolutions repudiating the party's earlier support for nuclear energy and pledged to shut down the Federal Republic's nuclear plants within ten years. Shortly after this conference, the SPD suffered major defeats at state elections in Bavaria and Hamburg. Rau's candidacy collapsed. The party's vote at the 1987 election dropped to 37 percent, its lowest level since 1961. For the second time in the 1980s the party returned to opposition as internally divided as it was at the beginning of the decade.

The SPD and the Unification Process

The 1989–1990 unification both surprised and divided the SPD. For years the party had sought to improve the concrete living conditions of East Germans by negotiating with the Communist regime. The contact with the GDR leadership, however, also gave the Communists a certain legitimacy and status in the view of many Germans. When the revolution began, the SPD was ill-prepared. While the party had good contacts with the now-beleaguered GDR "elite," it had few if any with the "street" (i.e., the fledgling democratic opposition, including the churches). The "rush to unity" that followed the opening of the Wall also divided the party. Many members under the age of 45, like most younger Germans, had no living memories of a united Germany. They had accepted, at least tacitly, the permanence of the division, or believed that it could be overcome within a united Eastern and Western Europe.

In the 1990 election, these SPD activists, including the party's chancellor candidate, Oskar Lafontaine, were unable to recognize the appeal German unity had in the West and its fundamental importance for the new voters in the East. Older Social Democrats, such as the former chancellors Willy Brandt and Helmut Schmidt, enthusiastically supported unification and had few problems with the euphoria this issue generated. Lafontaine's lukewarm approach to this issue hurt the SPD at the 1990 election, especially in the East, where the SPD received only 24.5 percent of the vote. Overall, its total of 33.5 percent represented the party's worst performance since 1957.

But while the SPD was hurt in 1989–1990 by the "upside" of the unification issue, by mid-1991 it was benefiting from its "downside," namely voter discontent in the West over the tax increases needed to finance unification and voter unhappiness in the East with the slow pace of economic reconstruction. From January to June 1991 the SPD won three straight state elections, allowing it to control nine of the sixteen state governments and hold the majority in the Bundesrat (see Chapter 7).

In 1994 the SPD attempted, with Rudolf Scharping, the chief executive of the state of the Rhineland-Palatinate and the party's fifth candidate since 1983, to avoid its fourth straight loss. In the early going Scharping did well on the campaign trail. His campaign focused on the economy and record-high unemployment. But an upturn in the economy in early 1994 took the wind out of the party's sails. The SPD did increase its vote over 1994, but still fell short.

The New Center and the 1998 Victory

In 1995 Scharping was removed from his position as party leader at the SPD's party convention. Although he had been elected by a vote of the party's members in 1993, several other SPD leaders, led by Oskar Lafontaine, pushed through a change in the party's rules at the convention and dumped Scharping. The SPD, the rebels argued, was badly in need of new leadership and direction. Internal polls found that only about 30 percent of the electorate still supported the party. The SPD was unable to take advantage of a weak and aging Kohl government. Something had to be done. Scharping was replaced by Lafontaine, but the question of who would lead the party in 1998 was left open.

Following the 1995 "Putsch" convention, the party's fortunes at state elections and in public opinion polls improved. Support for the Kohl government continued to decline as unemployment increased and the economic growth remained sluggish. Lafontaine had unified the party, but the SPD still needed a candidate to challenge Kohl in 1998. The prime contenders were Lafontaine and the popular chief executive of Lower Saxony, Gerhard Schröder. Both men wanted the job. Lafontaine yearned for another chance at Kohl and Schröder was convinced that he was the only Social Democrat who could defeat Kohl. Lafontaine also enjoyed the support of the party's rank-and-file activists, but Schröder's poll numbers were much better. The candidate question was not resolved until March 1998, six months before the national election, when Schröder was reelected decisively at the state election in Lower Saxony.

In 1998 the SPD tried for the fifth time to defeat Kohl. How did they finally get it right?

1. The party decided that job one was to win the election. Internal ideological and policy squabbles were put aside as the SPD concentrated on winning. A professional campaign organization was set up modeled on the efforts of Bill Clinton in the United States and Tony Blair in Britain. A new advertising agency was employed to give the party a new look.

2. The party was determined to present a united front. German voters do not like their party to be divided internally; they want it to be united. Personal and policy differences were put aside at least for the campaign.

3. In Schröder, the party had a strong candidate. Young, but not too young, media savvy, compatible with the party's new pragmatic style, Schröder fit nicely.

4. In its program the party moved into the middle, where the votes are. Schröder left much of his program purposefully vague. He promised to build a "new center" that would get the economy moving without causing too much pain for voters used to the generous welfare state.

5. Relying heavily on polls, the Schröder campaign was focused above all on Kohl: "Kohl must go!" was the chant that drew the loudest response at his rallies.

This approach was successful. With 41 percent of the party vote and 298 seats, the SPD achieved its best result since 1980. And for only the second time in the history of the Federal Republic, the party received more votes than the Christian

Democrats. Now, after sixteen years in opposition, Schröder and the Social Democrats must show that they can govern and can above all reduce Germany's double-digit unemployment rate.

Old Left Meets New Center: The Lafontaine-Schröder Conflict

The 1998 victory, however, did not end the conflict between Schröder and Lafontaine. Their differences were put aside for the sake of the election campaign, but soon after the victory they resumed their struggle, this time within the new government. Lafontaine was appointed finance minister, and as chairman of the party, he was the strongest single member of the Schröder cabinet; many within the party actually considered Lafontaine more powerful than Schröder.

The differences between the two leaders were most apparent in economic and tax policy. Lafontaine, with the support of the party's old left and the trade unions, advocated an unabashed demand-side approach to economic growth: higher wages, increases in social-welfare payments, lower interest rates. While advocating tax cuts for lower- and middle-income groups, he did little to relieve high labor costs for business and actually planned to increase taxes on large business firms. Schröder's policies were aimed at making German business more competitive in the global economy: lower taxes, more investment incentives, and fewer government regulations. At times Lafontaine appeared to be leading his own separate government as he criticized the slow pace of decision making under Schröder.

The conflict finally came to a head in March 1999 when, at a cabinet meeting, Schröder, in a statement apparently directed at Lafontaine, announced that he would not support any new legislation that was directed against business. He was referring to Lafontaine's proposal to tax the cash reserves of energy and insurance companies. The next day Lafontaine abruptly announced his resignation from the government and the leadership of the party. An emergency meeting of the SPD Presidium then nominated Schröder as the new party chairman. In April 1999 a special party congress elected him to the post, albeit with the lowest majority (about 75 percent) in the postwar history of the party.

Lafontaine's departure gave the Schröder government a second chance after its fitful and ineffective start. Its much-heralded tax reform package was strongly opposed by business interests and had to be changed. The proposed citizenship law, which allowed children born in Germany of foreign parents to hold dual citizenship, also had to be changed. The planned dismantling of Germany's remaining nuclear power plants, a key issue for the Greens, has been put on hold. Lafontaine's departure now gives Schröder a freer hand in governing. It also puts the responsibility for success or failure squarely on his shoulders.

THE FREE DEMOCRATS

Located ideologically somewhere between the two major parties is the only small party to survive the steady reduction in the number of serious contenders for parliamentary representation since 1949: the Free Democratic Party (FDP). The Free

Democrats have never received more than 13 percent of the party vote in any national election. Between 1957 and 1987 they did not win a single winner-take-all district contest with the CDU and SPD.

Yet the FDP has played a role in the German political system far out of proportion to the size of its electorate. It has participated in fifteen of the nineteen cabinets formed at the national level since 1949. From 1949 to 1956 and from 1961 to 1966, it was the junior coalition partner of the CDU/CSU; between 1969 and 1982 the Free Democrats were in a coalition with the SPD, and from 1982 to 1998 the party was again aligned with the Christian Democrats. Thus the FDP has been in power for thirty-eight of the Republic's first fifty years. In government it usually receives about twice as many seats in the cabinet as it would be entitled to based on its vote. According to one analysis, the FDP has also had a disproportionate influence on government spending policies. The authors conclude that "the most useful document a German voter should consult at election time in order to anticipate the shape of public spending under the next government is the program of the FDP."[9] Finally, two of the seven presidents of the Republic, Theodor Heuss and Walter Scheel, have been Free Democrats.

The party owes its *survival* to an electoral system that ensures parliamentary representation on a proportional basis to any party that secures at least 5 percent of the popular vote. But its extraordinary *success* is a result of its position as the needed "pivot" party in the parliament. Simply put, the FDP has held the balance of power in the Bundestag following most federal elections. Because both major parties have, with one exception (the CDU in 1957), failed to win an absolute majority of seats, they are faced with three alternatives in the postelection coalition negotiations: (1) a coalition with the FDP, (2) a "Grand Coalition" with the other major party, or (3) opposition. Obviously, the first of these has been far more attractive to the major parties than the latter two. This gives the FDP an enviable bargaining position, assuming that the party is willing to consider a coalition with either major party and that the major parties have roughly the same number of parliamentary seats.

The party regards itself as the legitimate heir to the tragic German liberal tradition. Historically, German liberals have been divided between (1) a conservative, nationalist wing, one with strong ties to large industrial interests and an ambivalent commitment to parliamentary democracy, and (2) a progressive, or left, wing centered in the southwest and the Hanseatic cities (Hamburg, Bremen), whose support for parliamentary government took precedence over nationalism and the authoritarian imperial system. Thus, unlike liberals in Britain or France, German liberals as a whole were not staunch supporters of parliamentary government and the liberal state. During the turbulent last years of the Weimar Republic, the vast majority of the liberal parties' supporters defected to the right-wing parties, including, above all, the Nazis. The small band of liberal deputies remaining in the Reichstag after the last free election of March 1933 voted for Hitler's Enabling Act.

It was not until the formation of the FDP in 1948 that the two tendencies in German liberalism were united within one organization, and unity in terms of policy has remained a rare commodity in the party's postwar history. The nationalist, or right wing, held the upper hand during the 1950s when, in coalition with the CDU/CSU, the party was to the right of the Union, especially in economic policies. Even at this time, however, its opposition to Catholic Church influence within the CDU/CSU and to Adenauer's pro-Western orientation, which the Free Democrats claimed neglected if not abandoned reunification, differentiated the party from its much larger partner.

The FDP's drift to the center-left and hence toward the SPD in the mid-1960s took place as much for tactical as for policy reasons. As a junior coalition partner, it always ran the risk of suffering a fate similar to that of the other small parties: absorption by the CDU/CSU. Thus, it had to seek to retain its identity vis-à-vis the CDU/CSU by either pulling out of the coalition, as it did in 1956 and 1966, or stressing its differences with its major partner, especially prior to elections.

Following the Grand Coalition between the SPD and CDU/CSU in December 1966, the FDP became the sole opposition party for the first time in its history. Key party leaders at this time, such as Walter Scheel, federal president from 1974 to 1979, and Hans-Dietrich Genscher, foreign minister since 1974, sought to demonstrate through a series of policy and leadership changes that the party was not a mere satellite of the CDU/CSU. Their purpose was not only to gain votes from SPD and CDU/CSU supporters discontented with the Grand Coalition, but also to demonstrate to the Social Democrats that it could at some future time be an acceptable and reliable coalition partner. The party's positions on foreign-policy issues, such as its support for the normalization of relations with Eastern Europe, for educational and legal reform became increasingly consistent with those of the Social Democrats. In moving toward the SPD the Free Democrats lost much of their "old" middle-class clientele, but gained the support of younger, "new" middle-class voters living in large metropolitan areas who wanted an end to two decades of CDU/CSU rule.

After the 1980 election, the Free Democrats agreed to a renewal of their coalition with the SPD. Soon thereafter, however, it became apparent that the FDP was attempting to loosen its ties with the Social Democrats in preparation for another switch in coalition partners—this time back to its old ally from the 1950s and 1960s, the Christian Democrats. The FDP and the SPD were unable to agree on the type of economic policies needed to deal with the recession that began in the Federal Republic after 1980. The SPD supported a variety of pump-priming measures—tax cuts, public works projects—while the Free Democrats pushed to reduce state spending, especially on welfare programs, and stimulate private sector investment through tax concessions to business.

The formal break took place in September 1982, but the party was by no means united in dropping the SPD and joining the Christian Democrats. About a third of the party's parliamentary delegation and a corresponding proportion of party members and voters opposed the switch. They charged the FDP with "betraying" Helmut Schmidt, and in state elections held in late 1982 the party dropped to only about 3 percent of the vote. By 1983, however, support from CDU/CSU voters via ticket-splitting and the return of some of its old clientele from the 1950s and 1960s enabled the party to secure 7 percent of the vote and thus remain in parliament and the government.

With 11 percent of the vote at the 1990 all-German election the FDP achieved the third best result in its history. This success was largely a tribute to the role the party's de facto leader, Hans-Dietrich Genscher, the longtime foreign minister and vice-chancellor, played in the unification process.[10] As FDP campaign speakers never tired of reminding voters: "Bismarck unified Germany with blood and iron. Helmut Kohl did it with Hans-Dietrich Genscher!" The Free Democrats moreover benefited from their "no new taxes" theme and did especially well in East Germany, from which Genscher fled in the 1950s.[11]

The FDP's fortunes steadily declined after the 1990 election. Between 1992 and 1994 it lost a record ten straight state elections as well as a critical local election in the country's largest state, North Rhine–Westphalia. This string of losses began with the departure in May 1992 of Genscher. Genscher was the most popular political leader in the Federal Republic and critical for the party's electoral future. While the unpopular decisions of the Kohl government and the poor economy also played a role in the party's decline, the Genscher factor stands out.

The FDP in the 1994 election was able to return to the Bundestag only with massive ticket-splitting by Christian Democratic voters (see Chapter 6 for a discussion of ticket-splitting). Over 60 percent of the party's voters actually preferred the Christian Democrats, but split their ballot to ensure that the coalition would survive.

The Free Democrats and the 1998 Election

In 1998 the Free Democrats, after twenty-nine years in power, went into opposition. While the party was able to surmount the 5 percent barrier, it ran a lackluster campaign devoid of popular leaders or an attractive program. Many in the FDP saw the defeat as an opportunity to rejuvenate the party. Freed from its ties to Kohl and the Christian Democrats, the FDP can now strike out on its own.

In its new role as the junior opposition party, the FDP faces three major challenges. First, it must rebuild its organization at the state and local level. The party is now represented in only five of sixteen state legislatures. At the local level the situation is equally bleak. In many cities the party is now longer represented in city councils. Second, it must develop policy alternatives that will distinguish it from the other parties. The party's leadership believes that there is an electoral market for a program that emphasizes lower taxes, less bureaucracy, less governmental regulation, and more freedom for business. The party, in short, wants to return to its free-market roots. Finally, the FDP must learn to compete with the Greens, who in many non-environmental areas advocate policies similar to the FDP. Increasingly the Greens are seen as a younger, more dynamic alternative to the Free Democrats.

THE GREENS

In 1983 for the first time since the 1950s a new political party—the Greens—secured representation in the parliament. The party began as the political arm of the citizen initiative group movement discussed in Chapter 4. In the late 1970s those groups concerned with the environment and especially with the danger of nuclear power plants established a national political party. In 1979 and 1980 the Greens entered two state parliaments but fared poorly in the national elections, receiving less than 2 percent of the vote. After 1980, however, the Greens' cause was greatly aided by the emergence of the NATO missile question, the planned deployment of new middle-range ballistic missiles in the Federal Republic. The nationwide peace movement that arose in response to the missile deployment plan was a major source of new support for the party. The peace movement also brought the Greens additional activists, many of whom had acquired extensive political experience in the Social Democratic party, the student protest movement of the 1960s, and various left-wing splinter groups. These new supporters, who came to the Greens less out of a concern with the environment and more because of the arms race and various socioeconomic problems such as inner-city housing and education, gave the movement its badly needed organizational and tactical expertise. The Greens entered state parliaments in Berlin (1981), Lower Saxony (1982), Hamburg (1982), and Hesse (1982). With the addition of these new supporters, generally termed the "alternative" movement, the Greens were in a position to challenge the established parties at the national level. Although the SPD made a major effort to capture the Green vote after its fall from power in 1982, the new party managed to enter the parliament with 5.6 percent of the vote.

With the twin issues of the environment and the NATO missile or "peace" question, the party made significant inroads in 1983 into traditionally SPD voter groups. Among young voters with some college or university educational background, the Greens received almost 25 percent in 1983. Throughout 1984 the party continued to gain voters at local and state elections as the Greens' emphasis on environmental protection and disarmament struck a responsive chord among voters dissatisfied with the established parties.

In the mid-1980s the Greens' electoral advance stalled. Divisions within the movement had become an issue. The critical problem was the party's relationship to the Social Democrats. Should the Greens seek power through a coalition with the SPD, or should they remain a protest movement uncontaminated by any association with the old, established parties? Most Green voters supported an alignment with the SPD. The party's activists and leaders, however, were divided. One group, the Fundamentalists (*Fundis*), has rejected any cooperation with the established parties, whereas a second wing, the Realists (*Realos*), have been willing to form coalitions with the SPD at state and national levels in order to achieve Green goals, if only in piecemeal fashion. In late 1985 the Realists appeared to have the upper hand as the Greens in the state of Hesse formed a coalition with the SPD and took over the Environmental Affairs Ministry.

The 1986 nuclear accident at Chernobyl in Ukraine brought the Fundamentalists back in control of the party. At their convention that year, the Greens passed resolutions calling for West Germany's immediate withdrawal from NATO, unilateral disarmament, and the dismantling of all nuclear power stations in the country. The Greens also refused to distance themselves from the violent demonstrations that had taken place at nuclear power plants and reprocessing facilities subsequent to the accident.

In the wake of the Chernobyl disaster, support for the Greens in public opinion polls doubled to over 12 percent. For a time it appeared that had the Greens decided to coalesce with the SPD, the two parties would have an absolute majority after the 1987 election. By mid-1986, however, the effects of Chernobyl began to wane, and the potential Green-SPD vote dropped from 53 percent to 43 percent. Although the Greens clearly gained support because of the accident in Ukraine, they also lost voters due to their radical positions on foreign policy, defense, and domestic issues. In spite of these problems, the Greens were able to increase their share of the vote at the 1987 election from 5.6 percent to 8.3 percent, the size of their parliamentary delegation growing from twenty-seven to forty-two deputies.

The Greens and Unification

Of all the parties, the Greens proved to be the least interested in and the least prepared for the political impact of unification. The great majority of their young electorate and more importantly their leadership had no memories of a Germany that was not divided. They were the least likely to have a sense of German national identity, thinking of themselves more as Europeans or even "citizens of the world." On November 9, 1989, when the Berlin Wall was breached, most members of the parliament in Bonn rose spontaneously and sang the national anthem. Most Greens did not, and those who did were criticized by their colleagues for this emotional display of "outmoded" national feelings. The Greens opposed the Kohl government's "rush to unity," which they argued disregarded the interests and needs of East Germany's indigenous democracy movement. They advocated a more evolutionary approach to unification within the context of the movement toward European unification. Some Greens even termed the government's unification policy an *Anschluss* or annexation of East Germany, a word which postwar Germans use almost exclusively to describe Hitler's 1938 takeover of Austria.

The Greens' leadership failed to understand the political impact of the widespread support that unification had in the electorate, even among its own voters. In 1990 two-thirds of Green voters supported unification. This stood in sharp contrast to the opposition of the party's parliamentary leadership, which voted against both unity treaties in the Bundestag. The 1990 campaign was dominated by this issue and the Green message was lost. With only 4.8 percent of the vote in West Germany, down from 8.3 percent in 1987, the party failed to gain representation in the all-German parliament. The Greens in the former GDR, running in coalition with East German citizen reform groups, did surmount the 5 percent barrier. Generally, the Greens in the East were more attuned to the importance of the unification issue than their counterparts in the West. Had the two parties run a combined list in 1990, the West German Greens, under the special provisions of the electoral law in effect for the 1990 election, would also have been represented.[12]

The End of the Long March:
National Political Power, 1994–1998

By 1994, with the euphoria of unification long gone, and now formally united with their East German equivalent—the Bündnis90/Green party—the Greens were well positioned to reverse the 1990 defeat. The Realist wing of the party, led by Joschka Fischer, was firmly in control, and the Greens since 1990 had been able to demonstrate in several state level coalitions that they could govern. Also, environmental issues continued to trouble more than enough voters to put the party over the 5 percent mark.

With 7.3 percent of the vote in 1994, the Greens became the first party ever to return to the parliament following a failure to surmount the 5 percent mark. As expected, the party did very well among younger, middle-class voters and students. Their East German wing, however, declined to less than 5 percent. After 1994 the Realist-Fundamentalist cleavage in the Greens was replaced with an even deeper division between the Western and Eastern wings of the party: the post-materialist, middle-class affluent West German Greens have little understanding for their Eastern counterparts. The core of the Eastern group is the Bündnis90, the former dissidents who played such a critical role during 1989–1990 in the collapse of communism.

The East Germans are still deeply concerned about coming to terms with the communist past, including a vigorous investigation and if possible prosecution of Communist officials. The Western Greens, with no personal experience of living under communist rule, would like the party to reach out to former Communists, especially the rank and file, who were relatively innocent of any association with the abuses of the Communist regime.

In 1998 the Greens, after twenty years, finally achieved what many of the early Greens never wanted: national political power. The original Greens of the 1980s were a protest party, an anti-party, whose origins can be traced to the extra-parliamentary opposition and counterculture of the 1960s, and the citizen-initiative groups and new social movements of the 1970s. Their "long march" to national political responsibility began in earnest in the mid-1980s when the more radical "eco-socialists" and peace movement supporters began to leave the party. By the early 1990s the Realists were in control and the party began to govern with the Social Democrats at the state level. This experience further strengthened the Realists in their intraparty struggles with the Fundamentalists, who were less interested in governing than they were in preserving the principles on which the party was founded: an end to atomic energy, disarmament, and a new anti-elitist political style.

The party's 1998 campaign, after a rocky start, aimed at a coalition with the Social Democrats. At its March 1998 convention the "Leftists," a new version of the old Fundamentalists, staged somewhat of a comeback by passing resolutions calling for increasing gasoline taxes to about $12 a gallon to finance a reduction in labor costs. Some members of the party also suggested that Germans restrict their overseas vacation trips by air to once every five years to reduce pollution.

The Realists, however, regained control of the campaign and attempted to limit the damage caused by the unpopular convention resolutions. The party's major campaign slogan—"The Change Must Be Green"—was designed to remind voters that only in coalition with the Greens could change, i.e., the removal of the Kohl government, take place, because the Social Democrats alone could not do it. Clearly, the party in tandem with the SPD wanted to ride the anti-Kohl wave into power.

With 6.7 percent of the vote and 47 seats the party achieved its goal. Following surprisingly brief and consensual coalition negotiations with the Social Democrats, the Greens received three ministries—Foreign Affairs, Energy, and Health—and several key policy commitments from their larger partner, above all, a promise that Germany would phase out its nineteen nuclear plants as soon as possible. The party must now show its supporters that it can govern at the national level while remaining faithful to its core ideals.

THE PARTY OF DEMOCRATIC SOCIALISM/LEFT LIST (PDS/LL)

The former ruling East German Socialist Unity (Communist) party changed its name during the revolution of 1989–1990 as well as its leadership and program. At the elections of 1990 and 1994 the party was able to secure parliamentary representation either through special one-time-only provisions of the electoral law (1990), or rarely invoked sections of the law (1994). But in 1998 the PDS did secure more than 5 percent of the vote and is now represented in the Bundestag with its own *Fraktion.* The key to the party's staying power has been the continued frustrations of many Easterners over the slow pace of economic reconstruction. The PDS is also the preferred party for those East Germans who benefited from the Communist regime, former party and state functionaries, military and secret police personnel, and managers and officials of now-defunct state-owned enterprises. The PDS at local and state elections between 1990 and 1998 was able to average about 20 percent of the vote in many Eastern regions. The party still has over 130,000 members (three-fourths of whom are retired), who have proven to be very effective grass-roots campaigners. The core of its membership and electorate is composed of former state and party functionaries, army officers, secret police employees, teachers, college and university instructors, and writers and intellectuals now displaced through unification. It has become the party of protest for those Easterners who are unhappy with the unification process. Its long-term future, however, depends on its ability to broaden its appeal.

The party's attempts to secure a foothold in the West have been hampered by numerous scandals involving its finances and leadership. Its most prominent leader, Gregor Gysi, has been accused of being an informer for the Stasi while ostensibly serving as a defense attorney for East German dissidents. The PDS also has one faction, the "Communist Platform" group, that openly advocates a Leninist strategy to radically change the political system.

In 1998 the PDS entered into its first governing coalition at the state level joining the SPD in Mecklenburg–West Pomerania. Since 1994 it has also "tolerated," i.e. not opposed, the minority SPD government in the Eastern state of Saxony-Anhalt. The decision to form a government with the former Communists was sharply criticized by many SPD members and leaders in other Eastern states, who question the party's commitment to democracy and the rule of law. Soon after taking office, the PDS contingent in the government demanded an amnesty for all former Communist officials indicted or convicted after 1990 for crimes committed during the forty-year Communist dictatorship.

The Representation of Interests

EXTENT OF INTEREST GROUPS

Germany is a densely organized society. Germans are used to organizations and accustomed to working with them for the satisfaction of individual and group needs. Numerous international surveys have found Germans to be more likely to use interest groups as a means of influencing government than citizens in other Western democracies such as the United States or Great Britain.[13] Currently, there are about 4 voluntary associations for every 1,000 inhabitants of the Federal Republic, or almost 240,000 in all.[14] This includes, however, thousands of local sport clubs and singing societies, whose explicit political activity is very limited and restricted to the local level. There are also various politically latent interests, such as those of consumers and foreign workers, that remain poorly organized and represented.

Importance and Style of Interest Representation

German political tradition and values, the consensual style of the new political parties, and the structure of the Federal Republic have all combined to make interest groups a vital factor in the policymaking process. Germany had interest groups long before the formation of the Reich, indeed before the formation of any sovereign political entity on German soil. A variety of associational groups representing occupations and economic interests can trace their origins to the corporate guilds of the Middle Ages. Composed of practitioners of a particular trade or craft (carpenters, bakers, cabinetmakers, butchers), these groups still perform regulatory functions for the state such as licensing and the supervision of training, and membership is compulsory for those desiring to practice the occupation legally. Almost all skilled artisans, in addition to those in the "free" professions (law and medicine), belong to these chambers, which also determine and enforce standards for the craft and control the recruitment of new members. Their legal responsibility for membership recruitment and conduct gives the chambers important political as well as economic power. They are all organized hierarchically from the local to national level. Thus their national leaders have considerable authority in dealing with the ministerial bureaucracy. The hierarchical, quasi-governmental character of these associations makes individual members dependent on the group's leadership for the furtherance of their interests. The national-level interest-group leadership thus becomes part of a larger elite structure within which informal bargaining plays a key role.

Most of the major occupational chambers also have members in the parliament, mainly in the delegations of the CDU/CSU and FDP. The Christian Democrats, for example, have a parliamentary group composed of about 45 deputies with direct affiliations with one or several of the chambers. It is estimated that about a third of the parliament's members represent their occupations.[15] Either they are professional interest-group employees assigned to represent their groups, or they are associated with certain trade, occupational, or professional interests on a part-time basis. The influence of interest groups in the recruitment of parliamentary candidates is to a great extent the result of the parties' dependence on groups for financial and electoral support. The electoral system, as we discuss in Chapter 6, also facilitates the nomination and election of these interested parliamentary deputies. Their efforts are particularly noticeable in committee work.

Perhaps more important than their role in the recruitment of parliamentary deputies is the access of interest groups to the ministerial bureaucracy. Such access allows them to influence the design of legislation. Major interest organizations are consulted in the drafting of laws affecting them as a matter of administrative procedure. The practice dates back to the early nineteenth century and reflects the strain of corporate or group, instead of individual, representation in the German political tradition, as well as the government's interest in the expertise of these groups and their cooperation in the implementation of policy.[16] During the Weimar Republic, access to the ministries was limited to nationally organized interest groups. This practice was also adopted in the administrative rules of the national ministries. It tends to accentuate the hierarchical character of German interest groups and the formal, quasi-legal character of interest-group activity.

This pattern of strong government/interest group/political party integration became more institutionalized during the late 1960s when the top representatives of government, business, and labor met in a "Concerted Action," a regular conference at which general economic conditions were discussed and guidelines for wages, prices, and economic growth were set. At these meetings business, labor, and the national government sought to reach a consensus on (1) what a reasonable wage increase would be for various workers, (2) the acceptable level of price increases, and (3) the amount of government spending and taxation necessary to ensure stable economic conditions and moderate—that is, noninflationary—economic growth. Although the Concerted Action disbanded in the late 1970s, as labor interests became dissatisfied with what they felt were the unreasonable sacrifices they were called on to make, informal labor/business/government contacts continued. The record levels of unemployment in the 1990s prompted Chancellor Kohl and later his successor, Gerhard Schröder, to call for an "Alliance for Jobs"—a cooperative program involving business, labor, and government that resembled the Concerted Action of the 1960s.

In 1998 Chancellor Schröder made the Alliance for Jobs the cornerstone of his efforts to find jobs for the more than four million unemployed. The Alliance consisted of the top leaders of the major business interest groups and trade unions together with the chancellor and the relevant members of the cabinet (Economics, Finance).

The Concerted Action, Alliance for Jobs, and the other formal interest-group and government contacts have prompted some observers to term Germany a "neo-corporatist" state.[17] *Corporatism* is an old term in social and political thought, referring to the organization of interests into a limited number of compulsory, hierarchically structured associations recognized by the state and given a monopoly of representation within their respective areas.[18] These associations become in effect quasi-governmental groups, training, licensing, and even exercising discipline over their members with state approval. The power of these associations is not determined by a groups's numerical size alone but also by the importance of its function for the state and community.

In addition to parliamentary recruitment and extensive consultations between government and interest groups, the practice of appointing group representatives to the many permanent ministerial advisory commissions and councils affords the interest groups still more input into the policymaking process. Finally, the highly developed system of semipublic institutions and administrative courts, discussed in Chapter 8, offers interest associations an additional opportunity to influence the policy process.

MAJOR INTEREST ALIGNMENTS

Business and Industrial Interests

In a society in which the stability and legitimation of new political institutions have been closely connected with economic prosperity, business and industrial interest groups enjoy considerable cultural support when they enter the political arena and make policy demands on the system. Regardless of which party or parties form the government, the interests and claims of German business will receive a thorough hearing. Indeed, a frequent charge of the left is that even the Social Democrats, when in office, are too receptive and accommodating to the interests of business.

In addition to their own national offices, the numerous local and state employer organizations are represented by three umbrella organizations with extensive facilities and staffs in the capital: the Federation of German Industry (*Bundesverband der Deutschen Industrie* [BDI]), the Federation of German Employer Associations (*Bundesvereinigung Deutscher Arbeitgeberverbände* [BDA]), and the German Industrial and Trade Conference (*Deutscher Industrie und Handelstag* [DIHT]).

The BDA tends to specialize in wage policies, whereas the Industrial and Trade Conference concentrates most of its efforts on maintaining the economic viability of small independent business owners and artisans. Thus neither organization is as politically active or visible on as broad a front as the Federation of German Industry, which focuses its activities on the government's national and international economic policies and is clearly the most influential and effective voice of business in national politics.

The BDI is a federation made up of thirty-nine individual industrial associations, which together have a membership of more than 90,000 firms. During the two decades of Christian Democratic rule, it enjoyed very close ties to the government and tended to get the edge in competition with trade unions for political advantage. Yet, given the commitment of all major parties to the social free market economy, the BDI has had little difficulty putting its proposals to the government when the Social Democrats have been in power.

Apart from its general support of German industry, the BDI evaluates all proposed legislation in any way related to business during all stages of policymaking, from ministerial drafting through parliamentary debate and even administrative implementation. In addition to sympathetic parliamentary deputies and general cultural support by virtue of its accomplishments, business interests command considerable financial resources, and their support or nonsupport—especially of the middle-class parties, the CDU and FDP—gives them added weight in electoral politics.

From 1969 to 1982, when the Social Democrats were in power, the BDI and other business groups concentrated most of their efforts on opposing government plans for parity representation or codetermination in industry (equal worker representation on a firm's board of control), *Vermögensbildung* (the building of capital resources among the general public involving some redistribution through compulsory profit-sharing), and tax reform. It also consistently resists extensions of the social welfare system that would increase employer contributions, and like its counterparts in the United States and Britain (the National Association of Manufacturers and the Federation of British Industry), it constantly implores the government to "hold the line" on spending. The BDI, as expected, has been very critical of labor unions, Young Socialists, intellectuals, and any other "radical" group that would weaken industry's position in West German society or undermine the market economy.

The collapse of the SPD-FDP government in 1982 and the return to power of the Christian Democrats were welcomed by the BDI. The plans of the Kohl government to encourage private sector investment and cut social programs were very consistent with BDI policy. The BDI's major problem in recent years, however, has been the unions' demands for a thirty-five-hour week as a means of reducing unemployment.

With the strong backing of the Kohl government, the BDI took a hard line on this question, which has increased the level of labor-management conflict.

Most BDI activity takes place in direct, small-group consultations with ministerial officials, parliamentary deputies, and governmental leaders. It has an extensive research department that supplies information to its member associations, the media, schools, and universities. Only rarely has it engaged in advertising campaigns to influence large groups of voters.

Since unification the BDI and other interest groups have attempted to assist the government in the conversion of East Germany's planned economy to a market economy. It also supports a variety of tax breaks and investment incentives to stimulate economic growth in the region. Its critics have charged that it is more interested in securing lucrative opportunities for large West German firms than in helping create an indigenous entrepreneurial class in East Germany.

Labor

The major German labor organization, the German Federation of Labor (*Deutscher Gewerkschaftsbund* [DGB]) is also a postwar creation. Previously, the German labor movement had been closely tied to political parties and their respective ideologies. In the Weimar Republic, socialist, communist, liberal, and Catholic unions all vied for the support of workers, thus politicizing and fragmenting the labor movement. Western Allied occupiers, particularly in the American zone, strongly urged the separation of the unions from the political parties and the establishment of a single, unified trade union federation that would emphasize the basic economic objectives of wages and working conditions rather than radical social and economic change. Many German labor leaders also wanted an organization less attached to parties, and in 1949 the DGB was founded. The DGB is composed of seventeen separate unions with a combined membership of almost nine million; the largest unit of the federation is the metalworkers' union (steel, automobiles, machinery), with about a third of the total membership.

Although the DGB's initial programmatic statements in 1949 had a decidedly Marxist tone (socialization of key industries, central economic planning), which reflected the majority position held in the new organization by former leaders of the Weimar socialist unions, the major emphasis in the union movement's work soon shifted to more pragmatic goals of a shorter work week and higher wages. In its new basic program of 1963, Marxist elements were abandoned for all practical purposes. Like its American counterpart, the AFL-CIO, the DGB now emphasizes collective bargaining to improve the economic status of the worker gradually within the existing social, economic, and political framework. Unlike American business unionism, the DGB has given strong backing to workers' representation and input into the decision making of the industrial firm through codetermination; according to this system workers would be represented on a company's board of control in equal proportion to the representatives of management and capital (stockholders).

This change in DGB policy, from a general support for Marxist-oriented policies to collective bargaining and workers' participation within the context of the market economy, is consistent with the general decline in socialist programs that followed the success of the liberal economic policies of the first Adenauer governments during the early 1950s. A similar transformation, as we have seen, also took place in the CDU/CSU after 1948 and in the SPD as of 1959.

Labor is represented in the parliamentary delegations of both major parties but its influence and sympathies lie far more with the Social Democrats than the CDU. Most SPD members (about 70 percent) eligible to join labor unions are members of the DGB-affiliated groups, and the unions indirectly account for a large portion of SPD revenue. About 35 to 40 percent of the SPD's parliamentary party have strong ties to the labor movement.[19]

Generally the labor unions have supported Social Democratic policies, although at times they have been impatient with the slow pace of the party's domestic reform programs. Nonetheless, union criticism of the SPD has generally been moderate. On balance, the DGB's relationship to the SPD is not as close as that of the British unions to the Labour party, yet closer than the AFL-CIO's ties to the Democratic party.

In 1998 the DGB made a major effort on behalf of the Social Democrats. After sixteen years of conservative rule, the unions felt that labor had not received its fair share of the economic pie. While income from investments had increased sharply during the Kohl years, labor's share had actually declined. It is estimated that the unions spent about $6 million in special funds to help finance the Schröder campaign.

Although there is a labor wing in the Christian Democratic Union led by deputies from the Rhine-Ruhr region, there is little or no labor influence in the Bavarian affiliate of the Union, the CSU, and over the past two decades the power of the labor wing has declined in the Union's internal councils. The DGB also goes to considerable lengths to maintain its independent, nonpartisan posture and points to its representation in the CDU as evidence of its willingness to support any party that will work to implement its programs.

The labor movement has come under increasing criticism in recent years from left-wing intellectuals for its alleged conservatism and allegiance to the status quo. Certainly it has been a disappointment to orthodox Marxists, who envisioned it as a key force for revolutionary change. The movement has also disappointed liberal and socialist reformers by its relative indifference to changes in areas such as education and civil rights (reform of the criminal code and liberalized abortion statutes, for example).

Unions in the Federal Republic are now faced with the necessity of branching out into new areas of activity if they are to continue as a major force in German social, economic, and political life. The proportion of unionized workers in the total work force, about 35 percent, has remained unchanged since the early 1960s. Because the constitution (Article 9, Section 3) prohibits the closed shop, new members must be recruited through the unions' ability to offer concrete benefits that come only through union membership. Many of these benefits, such as unemployment compensation, health, disability, accident, and pension programs, once private goods that could be obtained only through union membership, are now the province of the state, and as public goods, are available to all without affiliation with the union. Support during strikes is still provided by the unions, but given the low strike rate in Germany, this is a marginal benefit. Unions must seek ways to provide their members with programs that are not public goods. This is one factor behind their strong drive for a thirty-five-hour work week and for codetermination, under which *union* members would sit on a board of directors as the major representatives of workers. The unions also want to assume more responsibility for vocational education and for the administration of labor and social welfare programs.

Since the late 1970s the relations between labor and management have become more conflictual. Higher unemployment levels, reduced rates of economic growth, the weaker competitive position of German goods in some export markets, and automation have all contributed to this development. Unions in recent years have given greater priority to job security than to direct wage increases. As unemployment reached record levels in the early 1980s, the unions began their major campaign for a thirty-five-hour work week as one means to provide more jobs. The conflict level has also been heightened by the German employers' extensive use of the lockout in strike situations. This practice, legal in the Federal Republic, means that many workers not directly affected by the strike are barred from working.

Labor and Unification.   The collapse of the GDR also meant the end of the East German trade organization, the Free German Trade Union (FDGB), which had been under the complete control of the Communist party. Membership was compulsory, but the unions had no significant power. Strikes were forbidden and collective bargaining was unknown. The Eastern trade unions did administer a vast network of vacation homes and organized holidays for most of their nine million members. After the 1989–1990 revolution the leader of the FDGB was arrested and later tried and convicted on charges of corruption and misuse of union funds.

The West German unions moved quickly to organize Eastern workers. All major Western unions now have affiliate organizations in the former GDR. But in a newly freed society only about half of all East German workers have decided to join a union; this is still a higher figure than in the West (35 percent). West German trade union leadership finds itself in a difficult position in the East. Given the lower productivity prevailing in the East, wage parity with West German workers would mean that many former GDR firms would price themselves out of the market. Thus the unions have negotiated contracts, which on average, pay East Germans about 60–70 percent of what their Western colleagues earn. This has angered many East German workers, especially those in the service industries. Hospital workers, for example, have staged wildcat strikes and some have left for higher-paying jobs in the West. Until the Eastern economy improves, the unions will have great difficulty in delivering the benefits their new members expect.

Since 1991 the trade unions have experienced a steady membership decline. By 1996 total membership had dropped from 11.8 million in 1991 to 9.4 million. Most of the withdrawals have come from the East, where trade union membership was artificially high in the first years of unification. The original rush to membership in the East was in part based on the mistaken notion that trade union membership could somehow ensure job security. But in the West, membership has also declined due mainly to the loss of blue-collar jobs.[20]

Leadership problems have also plagued the union movement in recent years. Franz Steinkühler, head of the Metalworkers Union (the largest and most powerful member of the federation) and the most well-known labor leader in the country, had to resign following disclosures of insider trading while he was a member of the Supervisory Board of Daimler-Benz. The incident sparked the passage in 1994 of Germany's first-ever insider trading law.

Agriculture

As analysts of interest groups have long known, the effectiveness of a group's efforts is closely related to its internal cohesiveness and unity of purpose. The experiences of West German agrarian interests, the so-called Green Front (not to be confused with the Green political party discussed earlier in this chapter), substantiates this thesis. The vast majority of the Republic's 2.2 million farmers are organized into three organizations that constitute the Front: the German Farmer's League (*Deutscher Bauernverband*), the Association of Agricultural Chambers (*Verband der Landwirtschaftskammer*), and the *Raiffeisenverband,* a cooperative association involved in banking, mortgage loans, and retailing. In part because of their steadily dwindling number and increasing social isolation, agrarian interests are closely integrated and, unlike American rural interests, do not for the most part pursue conflicting aims. This united Green Front is probably the country's best organized lobby. In addition there are about fifty parliamentary deputies (most of whom are in the CDU/CSU) who form a relatively cohesive farm group within the legislature and dominate the parliament's agriculture committee.[21]

Mindful of past agrarian support for right-wing radical groups, including the Nazis, all parties have made major efforts to placate agriculture and meet its demands. Indeed, the influence of farm organizations probably increased under social-liberal governments (1969–1982). In an effort to secure the support of the FDP's right wing, the post of agricultural minister was assigned to a Bavarian conservative in 1969. Fearful of a break in the coalition, the Social Democrats, with little rural support themselves, were very generous and conciliatory to their strange bedfellow.

After more than forty years of large subsidies and structural change, German agriculture remains a major problem child of the economy. In comparison to France, Italy, and the Netherlands, it remains in a poor competitive position. The focus of farm interests has thus been on the protection and maintenance of the farm market through price supports and direct subsidies. Currently, almost half of the income of German farmers comes from national and European subsidies and price supports.[22] Germany's farmers want above all the continuation of the European Community's Common Agricultural Policy(CAP).[23]

The CAP program, introduced in 1967, ensures farmers high prices in a protected market. This is good news for the farmers but bad news for consumers. Germans and other West Europeans spend about 10 percent more of their income for food and tobacco than do North Americans. Most of this difference is due to the price support program.[24] In countries with larger sectors of the work force in agriculture, such as France and Italy, support for CAP is strong. But why in the Federal

Republic, which must import much of its food, does this policy encounter no significant opposition? Indeed, the high food prices caused by this policy have never been a major item on the German political agenda.[25] There are two major reasons for this paradox: (1) the highly organized agricultural interests in the Federal Republic, whose members constitute a critical voting bloc in many districts, and (2) the overall net gains to the Federal Republic from membership in the European Community. The Green Front has been a significant force in the parliamentary delegations of both the Christian Democrats and the Free Democrats. There has never been a time in the history of the Federal Republic when at least one of these parties did not hold national political power. Generally, German policymakers, regardless of party, accept the CAP because the losses to agriculture have been more than compensated for by profits from industrial exports to other European Union countries.

East German Agriculture.   Agriculture in the former East Germany is in a state of transition. Under the communists, almost all farmers were forced to join collective farms. Since unification, about 20 percent have reclaimed their land and are now attempting to become independent while about 60 percent are now reorganized into cooperatives. The remainder have left agriculture. Some farmland has also been leased or purchased by West German interests or is under the control of the successors to the Trusteeship Authority (see Chapter 8). In some cases the former members of the collective farms sold their shares to the new cooperatives at prices far below the actual market value of the land and equipment. Many former directors of the collective farms emerged after unification as the new and very prosperous leaders of these cooperatives. Currently, there are a variety of lawsuits and investigations into these sales. Many sellers claim they were cheated by the former communist collective farm directors.[26]

East Germany contains some of the country's richest soil and has become a productive and profitable agricultural region. But like other sectors of the economy, the collective farms were overstaffed. Before unification over 850,000 East Germans were employed in agriculture; by 1992 this had dropped to only 300,000. Over 150,000 former collective farm workers are unemployed and the remaining 400,000 have moved to other occupations.[27] Those remaining on East German farms, however, saw their income increase rapidly in the years following unification. By 1994 the average income of farmers in the East was actually higher than their colleagues in the West. This was due to the larger size of Eastern farms, special unification subsidies, and a reduced reliance on unprofitable livestock breeding in the former East Germany.[28]

THE CHURCHES

By law and custom the Catholic and Protestant churches occupy a privileged position in German society, which affords them extensive opportunities to exert influence in a wide range of public policy areas. In addition to the church tax, discussed in Chapter 3, both churches still receive an annual state subsidy, dating from the

Napoleonic wars, which now amounts to over $300 million. Church officials appointed by the state, such as military and hospital chaplains, are considered civil servants and are paid by the state. By 1999 there were also about 55,000 Jews out of a total Jewish population of almost 100,000 who were members of 65 Jewish congregations. Germany now has the fastest growing Jewish population in the world due mainly to emigrants from the former Soviet Union. The Jewish congregations also receive state support.

Germany's nearly three million Muslims and their more than three hundred mosques, however, receive no state financial support. With the new 1999 citizenship law (see Chapter 4), which will greatly ease the restrictions for foreign residents to become naturalized German citizens, the proportion of Muslims who can vote should also increase sharply. With the franchise, it is expected that these new voters will then press for state support of their religion.

Income from the church tax and additional state subsidies finance a wide variety of charitable activities. The two major churches through their social welfare organizations—the Catholic *Caritas* and the Protestant *Diakonie*—operate over 50,000 hospitals, nursing homes, nursery schools, and other welfare facilities for children, women, the elderly, and the unemployed throughout the country. These institutions employ over 700,000 people and make the churches Germany's largest private employer and provider of health and welfare services. The churches operate about 75 percent of all child care and elderly support agencies and one of every three hospitals. Charitable work among foreign workers and foreign missionary activity also benefit from public support.

All church-owned properties are tax-free. Both churches are by law represented on the boards of control of radio and television networks. Representatives of the churches are also found on numerous advisory commissions at both federal and state levels. Finally, both church bodies maintain offices in Bonn and Berlin that are responsible for ensuring that the churches' position is well represented in the government and parliament.

Although they share this common legal and political status, the two churches have differed in their approach to public policy. The German Catholic Church has traditionally been more active in pursuing specific policy aims than its Protestant counterpart. Well organized, with extensive lay organizations of more than 3 million members and a press with 25 million readers, German Catholicism has sought output from the political system consistent with its goal or claim that the Church has a right to intervene in certain political, social, and spiritual matters.

From 1949 to the mid-1970s the Catholic Church made a major effort to secure state financial support for separate Catholic and Protestant school systems. The Church insisted that parents had the right to send their children to a state-funded Catholic school. Unable to get a clear statement supporting separate schools for Catholics and Protestants in the Basic Law, the Catholic hierarchy relied on the 1933 *Reichskonkordat* (treaty) between the Vatican and the Nazi government, which guaranteed a state-supported religious school system. Most Protestant states, however, exercising their newly restored rights in the education field, established biconfessional public schools after the war, in some cases abolishing previously separate

Catholic systems.[29] By the 1970s these confessional schools had largely been phased out due to lack of support by parents and evidence that this "separate but equal" approach was inefficient and detrimental to educational quality. The Catholic Church lost the battle not because of the strength of the opposition but through massive desertions by its own troops, Catholic parents.

In addition to confessional schools, the church has actively sought extensive state support and recognition of the family, stiffer divorce laws, strict control over "obscenity" in films and magazines, and the continued prohibition of abortion for all but the most pressing medical reasons. As in the case of the church school issue, it has been losing the battle in all these areas. The Ministry of Family Affairs (a pet project of the church since 1949) was abolished in 1969 and became part of the Health and Youth Affairs Ministry. During the Grand Coalition (1966–1969), criminal penalties for homosexual relations between consenting adults, blasphemy, and adultery were removed. From 1969 to 1982 the Social-Liberal government, over strong and vocal Catholic opposition, has liberalized divorce, abortion, and pornography laws. A growing gap between the attitudes of the Catholic laity and the hierarchy, seen in increased Catholic support for the SPD during the 1970s, meant that the church leadership was unable to mobilize its membership in these policy areas. Moreover, the strong commitment and association the church has had with the Christian Democrats left it in the Social-Liberal years without any major direct influence on policy to the extent it enjoyed during two decades of CDU rule. In every election, with the exception of 1969, the Catholic hierarchy made clear its preference for the CDU and in varying degrees has regarded being a good Catholic and a good Social Democrat or Liberal as a contradiction, a position obviously not shared by a growing number of its members.

In contrast to Roman Catholicism, West German Protestantism—or more specifically its political arm, the Evangelical Church in Germany (EKD)—has placed greater emphasis on the support of the basic political values of the Federal Republic than on matters directly affecting the immediate interests of the church. Its major policy concerns, which it pursues less intensely than does the Catholic Church, have been with reunification, a nonconfessional labor movement, codetermination in industry, East-West detente, civil liberties, and education reform. Traditionally conservative on social-economic policies, the postwar leadership of German Protestantism, if not its members, has turned almost 180 degrees and now has the reputation of being a center-left progressive movement in domestic policies. Unlike the Catholic leadership, however, the Protestant hierarchy has been unwilling to make any of its policy pronouncements binding on its members and has kept lines of communication open to all parties.

In the former GDR, however, the Protestant Church pursued a more active political role. In the early postwar years it strongly opposed the communist attempts to eliminate religion as a force in East German society. Throughout the 1970s and 1980s it provided a base and a refuge for the country's small dissident movements. When mass opposition to the regime finally emerged in 1989, the church again provided the initial base of support. The famous Monday demonstrations in Leipzig began after a prayer service in the Nicholas Church. Many of the early democratic East

German leaders were Protestant ministers. During the GDR's first and last freely elected government, the foreign minister, defense minister, and development minister were members of the Protestant clergy.

Some members of the East German clergy, however, apparently collaborated in some way with the communist regime. One recent study of the East German Church contended that about 3,000 clergy cooperated with the *Stasi* (secret police) and allowed some church organizations to be infiltrated with secret police informers. Several bishops and the administrative chief of the Protestant Church, Manfred Stolpe, Minister-Präsident of Brandenburg since 1990, are alleged to have had ties to the Stasi. Since unification some churches have begun to investigate the clergy and church administrators. The full extent of church involvement in the regime's security apparatus must await the opening of the Church's archives.[30]

Both churches today find their traditional relationship to state and society in flux. The historically close relationship between the churches and state bodies, which has its roots in the aftermath of the Reformation, has brought most Germans to accept the traditional character of church-state relationships as legitimate. Criticism of state financial support and the advocacy of a clear separation of church and state have been restricted to small groups of liberal intellectuals centered in the larger metropolitan areas such as Hamburg and Berlin. Nonetheless, the sentiment that at least the church tax must be reduced or eliminated is growing. In recent years high unemployment coupled with an increase in the number of Germans leaving both churches have cut sharply into church revenues. In some regions church budgets for charitable work and day-care centers have been cut by over 20 percent and fewer seminary graduates are finding jobs.[31] Given the growing secularization of German society, which has been accelerated by unification, the restructuring of church-state relations will clearly be a subject of continued and increased debate in German politics.

SUMMARY AND CONCLUSION

The traditional, established interest groups in German society have, for the most part, adapted well to the postwar Republic and "party state." They have all become less attached to and less dependent on specific parties and now tend to concentrate on policy goals directly related to their major area of concern. As we have seen, business interests have discovered that they could flourish under Social Democratic governments just as they did under Christian Democratic governments. Agricultural interests, more pragmatic than during the Weimar Republic, saw the subsidies and protectionist policies so vital to their survival continued under Social Democratic and Christian Democratic governments. In short, there has been a high degree of consensus and cooperation between major interest alignments and the established parties.

But what of those interests not accommodated by the existing structures? To what extent is the institutionalized, hierarchical character of German interest groups, parties, and—as we discuss in Chapter 8—the bureaucracy, a help or hindrance to the development of popular attitudes favorable to participation and involvement in the political process? The emergence and success of citizen initiative groups and new social movements, discussed in Chapter 4, testifies to the presence of demands that neither established parties nor interest groups have met. The interests of foreign workers and residents, consumers, and working women have also been inadequately represented by existing institutions. Because membership in many occupational and professional groups is compulsory, or automatic, the constitutional provisions for intragroup democracy should be, but have not been, enforced. The same absence of democratic procedures also applies to decision making within the political parties.

These are by no means uniquely German problems. To some extent they are the result of a constitutional order that puts little confidence in the ability of the common man to meet the participatory requirements of political democracy. If established parties and interests have adapted well to this constitutional system, so cautious and conservative in its approach to popular participation, their next task may well be to respond and adapt to new demands from a citizenry no longer in its democratic political infancy.[32]

Notes

1. Kurt Sontheimer, *The Government and Politics of West Germany* (New York: Praeger, 1973), p. 95.
2. In a 1981 survey of elites, 68 percent of high-level civil servants were party members; the corresponding figure for the general population was about 4 percent. Data cited in Ursula Hoffmann-Lange, "Eliten zwischen Alter und Neuer Politik," in *Wahlen und politischer Prozess*, ed. H.D. Klingemann and Max Kaase (Opladen: Westdeutscher Verlag, 1986), p. 113.
3. *Das Parlament,* No. 10 (March 5, 1993: 9; *Der Spiegel,* No. 24 (June 9, 1997), p. 27.
4. SPD = Social Democratic party; CDU = Christian Democratic Union (in Bavaria, CSU = Christian Social Union); FDP = Free Democratic party.
5. Kenneth H.F. Dyson, *Party, State and Bureaucracy in Western Germany* (Beverly Hills and London: Sage Publications, 1977), p. 56. There are signs that the parties are attempting to make their organization more democratic. In June 1993, for the first time in its history the Social Democrats selected their new leader by a vote of the party membership. Two years later, however, they reverted to the traditional method and elected a new leader by a vote of the delegates at the party's convention. In May 1994 the Christian Democrats in the state of North Rhine–Westphalia, the largest in the Federal Republic, selected their new chairman by a vote of the membership.
6. Otto Kirchheimer, "Germany: The Vanishing Opposition," in *Political Opposition in Western Democracies,* ed. Robert A. Dahl (New Haven: Yale University Press, 1966), pp. 237–259.
7. Adenauer also received the unqualified endorsement of the United States throughout the 1950s. See Gordon Craig, "Die Bundesrepublik Deutschland aus der Sicht der USA," in *Deutschland Handbuch,* ed. Werner Weidenfeld and Hartmut Zimmermann (Munich and Vienna: Hanser Verlag, 1989), pp. 672 ff. During the 1953 German election campaign the then–American secretary of state, John Foster Dulles, declared that Adenauer's defeat would be a "catastrophe" for Germany.
8. David P. Conradt, *The West German Party System* (Beverly Hills and London: Sage Publications, 1972), pp. 18–21.
9. Richard I. Hofferbert and Hans-Dieter Klingemann, "The Policy Impact of Party Programs and Government Declarations in the Federal Republic of Germany." *European Journal of Political Research,* Vol. 18, No. 3 (May 1990), p. 300.

10. Genscher, who has been in the government since 1969, was the principal architect of the 1982 collapse of the Schmidt government. He was also involved in the 1984 plan to grant amnesty to those individuals and business firms under investigation for violating the party finance laws. Because of their smaller membership base, the Free Democrats are more dependent on larger contributions (and contributors) than the large parties. Only about 30 percent of the party's income comes from membership dues, as compared to about 40 percent for the major parties.

11. Like the Christian Democrats, the FDP also has a "bloc problem" in the former GDR. The Liberal Democratic Party (LDPD) was one of the four satellite parties in the GDR's National Front. When it merged with its West German counterpart in 1990, the unified FDP's membership and finances improved dramatically; the East FDP had in fact more members than the West German party. Moreover, the Liberals in the East also owned large amounts of valuable real estate, which was acquired under questionable circumstances, that is, expropriation. The national FDP has been reluctant to turn these properties over to the Trusteeship Authority. Numerous Eastern FDP officials have also had to resign because of their contacts with the secret police.

12. The two Green parties failed to form an alliance at the 1990 election primarily because Western Greens did not want to dominate their Eastern counterparts as the Christian Democrats and the Free Democrats did. There were also policy disagreements. The Eastern Greens, who were allied with the former GDR's democracy movement, were more concerned about unification than were the Western Greens. See E. Gene Frankland and Donald Schoonmaker, "Disunited Greens in a United Germany: The All-German Election of December 1990 and Its Implications," unpublished paper presented at the American Political Science Association, Washington, D.C., 1991.

13. Samuel Barnes, Max Kaase, et al., *Political Action: Mass Participation in Five Western Democracies.* Beverly Hills and London: Sage Publications, 1979.

14. Thomas Ellwein, *Das Regierungssystem der Bundesrepublik Deutschland* (Opladen: Westdeutscher Verlag), 1991, p. 438.

15. Ferdinand Müller-Rommel, "Interessengruppenvertretung im Deutschen Bundestag," in *US Kongress und Deutscher Bundestag,* ed. Uwe Thaysen, Roger H. Davidson, Robert G. Livingston (Opladen: Westdeutscher Verlag, 1989), p. 305.

16. Loewenberg, *Parliament in the German Political System,* pp. 285–286.

17. Gerhard Lehmbruch, "Liberal Corporatism and Party Government," in *Trends toward Corporatist Intermediation,* ed. Phillipe C. Schmitter and Gerhard Lehmbruch (Beverly Hills and London: Sage Publications, 1979), pp. 147–188; and Helmut Willke, "Zur Integrationsfunktion des Staates. Die Konzertierte Aktion als Paradigma in der neuen Staatstheoretischen Diskussion," *Politische Vierteljahresschrift 20* (September 1979): 221.

18. Phillipe Schmitter, "Interest Intermediation and Regime Governability," in *Organizing Interests in Western Europe,* ed. Suzanne Berger (Cambridge: Cambridge University Press, 1981), pp. 300ff.

19. One survey of West German elites found that 81 percent of all leading labor officials supported the Social Democrats while only 13 percent preferred the CDU/CSU. Ursula Hoffmann-Lange, "Eliteforschung in der Bundesrepublik Deutschland," *Aus Politik und Zeitgeschichte,* no. 47 (26 November 1983), p. 18.

20. *Das Parlament,* nos. 7–8 (February 10–17, 1995), p. 7; Statistisches Bundesamt (ed.), *Datenreport 1997,* Bonn: Bundeszentrale für politische Bildung, 1997, p. 171.

21. Two-thirds of the agriculture committee is composed of agricultural interest group officials. See Ferdinand Müller-Rommell, "Interessengruppenvertretung im Deutschen Bundestag," in *US-Kongress und Deutscher Bundestag,* Uwe Thaysen, et al. (Opladen: Westdeutscher Verlag, 1990), p. 312.

22. Federal Statistical Office. In the United States subsidies account for 30 percent of farm income.

23. The CAP was originally conceived at a time when Western Europe still had to import food. European farmers were encouraged to produce by fixed prices and guarantees from the European Community to purchase whatever the free market could not absorb. Once

Europe became self-sufficient in food production, however, the program was not modified but continued under the original assumption of a dependency on imported food. By early 1991 the European Community's stockpiles of surplus food included 17.2 million tons of grain, 560,000 tons of beef and 317,000 tons of butter.

24. Erich Andrlik, "The Farmers and the State: Agricultural Interests in West German Politics," *West European Politics 4,* no. 1 (January 1983): 104.
25. Andrlik, p. 108.
26. *Der Spiegel,* no. 24 (June 12, 1995), p. 133.
27. Federal Ministry of Agriculture, *Agrarbericht 1991,* Bonn, 1992, p. 14.
28. *Frankfurter Allgemeine Zeitung,* February 8, 1995, p. 1
29. In biconfessional or community schools, children of both confessions attend the same school but are given separate religious instruction (usually two to three hours per week) by representatives of the two faiths.
30. Gerhard Besier and Stephan Wolf, eds., *Pfarrer, Christen und Katholiken* (Berlin: Neukirchener Verlag, 1992) cited in *Der Spiegel,* No. 6 (February 3, 1992), pp. 40–41, 44–45; see also Ralf-Georg Reuth, *IM Sekretär. Die Gauck-Recherche und Dokumente zum "Fall Stolpe."* Frankfurt-Berlin: Ullstein Verlag, 1992
31. Edmund L. Andrews, "German Churches Hard Hit by Decline in Tax Revenues," *New York Times,* January 6, 1998.
32. The new Red-Green government elected in 1998 has promised to amend the constitution to allow for referenda at the national level. Referenda are seen as a means of increasing citizen interest and reducing their sense of powerlessness. The Greens have been especially supportive of more direct democracy at the national level. *Frankfurter Rundschau,* October 16, 1998.

6 Elections and Voting Behavior

The most common and extensive form of political participation in Germany, as in other industrialized societies, is voting. Indeed, in the absence of any significant plebiscitary components in the constitution, voting affords the German citizen the major formal means of influence in the policymaking process. Elections were held at the local and state levels as early as 1946 in the British and American zones, and the first national election in 1949 was regarded as a quasi-referendum on the constitution. Subsequent West German claims to be the sole legitimate representative of the German nation (East and West Germany) were based on the freely elected character of these governments. Thus the results of early local, state, and national elections were viewed primarily as indicators of system support and legitimacy. How many citizens would actually vote? And how many would support the democratic parties? The high turnout and the general rejection of neo-Nazi, Communist, and other extremist parties evidenced in these early elections were seen as securing the legitimation of the postwar system. The first free election in East Germany in March 1990 also legitimated the interim government and the subsequent unification process.

The other major functions that elections have for a political system—providing succession in leadership, influencing and controlling the policy decisions of government—were of lesser importance in the early years of the Republic. The elections of the 1950s and even the 1961 vote were largely referenda on Adenauer's leadership; the policy and personnel alternatives of the opposition parties played a subordinate role in these campaigns.

Since the mid-1960s, however, the policy, leadership succession, and control functions of elections have become more prominent at both the national and the state levels. In 1969, for example, the electorate effected the first alternation of government and opposition in the history of the Republic, ending twenty years of Christian Democratic rule. The near-miss of the Christian Democrats in 1976 and the Schmidt-Strauss "duel" in 1980 continued this pattern of hard-fought election campaigns, the outcome of which can directly influence the policies and personnel of government. In 1983 the electorate strongly endorsed the Christian Democratic–Free Democratic coalition that had taken office six months earlier when the government of Chancellor Schmidt collapsed. German voters in 1983 also brought the first new party since 1957 into the parliament, the Greens. In 1987, for the first time in the history of the Republic, both major parties lost support at the same election. Voters returned the coalition government of Helmut Kohl, but with a reduced majority.

In December 1990 at the first free all-German election since 1932, German voters strongly endorsed the unification policies of Chancellor Kohl and Foreign Minister Genscher. The government was returned with a record majority of 134 seats in the parliament. In 1994 Chancellor Kohl and his governing coalition were reelected for a fourth term, but with a greatly reduced majority of only 10 seats. In 1998 German voters for the first time in the fifty-year history of the Republic replaced an incumbent chancellor and his entire government. The Social Democrats returned to national power after sixteen years in the opposition and ended the Kohl era in German politics.

ELECTORAL MECHANICS

Elections to the national legislature must be held at least every four years but can be held sooner if the government loses its majority and requests the federal president to dissolve parliament and call new elections. This has occurred twice: in 1972, when the Brandt government, through the defection of several FDP and SPD deputies, lost its majority and the opposition was unable to secure a majority for a new government; and in 1982, when the Kohl government called for elections to legitimize the parliamentary developments that ended thirteen years of Social Democratic–Liberal rule. Elections to the various Länder parliaments are held every four or five years, but special elections can be called earlier. Usually state elections are held in off years, a procedure especially favored by the opposition party at the national level to mitigate "coattail" effects.

For elections to the national parliament, the Republic is divided into 328 constituencies with an average size of about 240,000 residents and 165,000 registered voters. Each district must be a contiguous whole, while respecting state and, if possible, county (*Kreis*) boundaries. The size of each district must not deviate by more than one-fourth from the national average. Thus there is considerable variation in district size. For the election scheduled in 2002 the number of districts will be reduced to 278 and all of the current district boundaries will be changed.

The Basic Law, as amended in 1970, grants universal suffrage and the right to hold public office to Germans 18 years of age or older. Germany has automatic registration based on residence records maintained by local authorities. If a citizen has officially reported his or her residence in the constituency (it is required by law to do so), he or she will automatically be placed on the electoral register, provided that the age requirement is met. Before election day, the voter will be notified of registration and polling place.

THE ELECTORAL SYSTEM

The procedures by which popular votes are converted into parliamentary seats, a country's electoral system, are more than just a technical problem best left to constitutional lawyers. Most political scientists and political leaders assume that the electoral law will affect the character and structure of its party system and hence its politics. Generally, there are two basic types of electoral systems: (1) a plurality system, usually with single-member districts as in Britain and the United States, according to which the party or candidate securing the most votes takes all; and (2) a proportional electoral system, by which a party's share of parliamentary mandates is proportional to its percentage of the popular vote. Most political scientists have argued that a plurality system encourages a concentration of popular support among a small number of parties and enables clear decisions to emerge from an election, making postelection coalition negotiations unnecessary. The proportional system, on the other hand, although more equitable in providing representation to small segments of opinion and group interests, is said to produce a fractionalization of the party vote and hence a multiparty system in which no single party secures a majority of the parliamentary seats and government by coalition must result.

The assumption that a certain type of electoral law is related to a particular type of party system and hence favors some parties more than others makes the electoral law question a partisan political issue. Small parties generally favor a proportional system because it would guarantee them some parliamentary representation even if their percentage of the popular vote was far less than a plurality. Large parties tend to support a winner-take-all system, confident of their ability to mobilize the marginal voter.

The German system has been termed a "personalized proportional law" with half of the 656 parliamentary deputies elected by plurality vote in single-member districts and the other half by proportional representation from Land (state) party lists. Each voter casts two ballots—one for a district candidate and the other for a party. The party vote is more important because it is used to determine the final percentage of parliamentary mandates a party will receive.[1] The seats won in the district contests are then deducted from this total. Thus the more district mandates a party wins, the fewer list seats it will receive.

An example from the 1998 election clarifies this procedure.[2] As Table 6.1 shows, the SPD in 1998 with 40.9 percent of the second ballot vote was entitled to 268 seats under pure proportionality. It had won 212 district contests and was thus due 56 mandates from its state lists. However, its final total of 86 list seats included 13 "excess" mandates because in some states, mainly in the East, it won 13 more district seats than it would be entitled to under proportional representation, and 17 additional seats from those of the small parties that did not surmount the 5 percent clause. The CDU/CSU, on the basis of its second ballot percentage,was entitled to 230 seats, but because it won 112 district contests, it received 133 mandates from the state lists, which included 15 additional seats from the small parties. The Greens secured 6.7 percent of the second ballot vote and received 47 seats, which included 3 from the smaller parties. The Free Democrats with 6.2 percent of the second ballot vote were entitled to 41 seats, all of which came from its state lists, and received 2 additional seats from the minor parties. The PDS in 1998 cleared the 5 percent mark for the first time and received 36 seats, including 2 from the minor parties.

TABLE 6.1   Distribution of seats in the 1998 election

Party	% 1st Ballot	% 2nd Ballot	No. of Seats Entitled under Proportional Representation	No. of District Contests Won (1st ballot)	No. of List Candidates Elected
SPD	43.8	40.9	268	212	86*
CDU/CSU	39.5	35.1	230	112	133
Greens	5.0	6.7	44	0	47
FDP	3.0	6.2	41	0	43
PDS	4.9	5.1	34	4	32
Minor parties	3.8	6.0	39	0	0
Total	100.0	100.0	656	328	341

*The SPD received 13 extra deputies because of its "excess" victories, mainly in the East German states.

In practice, then, this is a proportional representation system with three important exceptions to "pure" proportionality, all of which have played an important role in recent elections:

1. *The 5 Percent Clause.* A party must receive at least 5 percent of the vote in order to be proportionally represented in the parliament; hence the minor parties in our example, with about 6 percent of the vote, received no seats, and the 39 mandates they would have been allotted in a pure proportional system were given to the parties that secured parliamentary representation.

2. *The Three Mandate Waiver.* However, if a party wins at least 3 district (first ballot) seats, the 5 percent clause is waived and the party does participate in the proportional distribution.[3] The former East German Communist party, the Party of Democratic Socialism (PDS), owed its return to the parliament in 1994 to this little-known and seldom-used provision of the law.[4] By concentrating its resources in districts in the former East Berlin, the PDS did indeed win 4 seats and received an additional 26 mandates (or 6.5 for each district victory) from the second ballot distribution. Thus a vote for the PDS candidate in one of these four East Berlin districts was worth 6.5 times more than a first ballot vote for the parties that did surmount the 5 percent hurdle.

3. *The Excess Mandate* (Überhangmandate) *Provision.* If a party wins more direct mandates than it would be entitled to under proportional representation, it would retain these "excess" seats and the size of the parliament would be increased accordingly. Let us assume, for example, that the SPD in 1998 had won all 328 district contests but had received

only 40 percent of the second ballot vote. In a pure proportional system it would be entitled to only 40 percent, or 262 seats. According to the German system, however, it would retain all 328 district seats but receive no mandates from the proportional lists, and the total size of the parliament would be increased from 656 to 722. An enlargement of the parliament to this extent has never occurred.

Until 1990 this excess mandate provision was a little-known and relatively inconsequential component of the electoral system. Before unification the largest number of excess mandates was 5 in 1961, and in several elections there were none at all. But in 1990 the CDU won 6 such seats, and in 1994 the number increased to a record 16: the Christian Democrats received 12 and the Social Democrats, 4. Because of this provision, the government's "true majority" of only 2 seats grew to 10 when all the first district ballots were counted, and the Bundestag was "enlarged" from 656 to 672 members. In 1998 the number of excess mandates dropped to 13, all of which went to the Social Democrats. With a complete redistricting scheduled for 2002, the number of these excess mandates should decline.

This electoral system—through its provisions for two ballots and the extra seats in the event a party wins more direct district contests than it would be entitled to under proportional representation—could also facilitate a great deal of ticket-splitting, or "lending" of votes by supporters of two coalition or prospective coalition partners. Supporters of one party could cast their first ballot vote for its coalition partner, thereby ensuring it a high number of district victories; voters of the second party could return the favor by casting their second ballot for the coalition partner, thereby increasing its share of mandates from the state lists. Ticket-splitting of this type has become fairly widespread. During the Social Democratic–Liberal era (1969–1982) at national and state elections, many SPD voters, fearing that their junior coalition partner, the Free Democrats, would not surmount the 5 percent hurdle, "lent" their second ballot votes to the FDP. Because the FDP's district candidate had little chance for direct election, the Free Democratic voters in turn lent their first ballot votes to the SPD.

In 1994 and 1998, approximately 16 percent of German voters did indeed split their ballots. Ballot-splitting has become a key factor for the survival of the Free Democrats and, to an increasing extent, the Greens. In 1998 the Free Democrats were able to secure 6.2 percent of the second ballot vote only through massive assistance from Christian Democratic splitters; postelection surveys found that almost two-thirds of the FDP total came from voters who considered themselves Christian Democrats. These voters were attempting to ensure that the Free Democrats, and thus the Kohl coalition, would survive. For the Greens in 1998, support from first ballot Social Democratic voters made up about 54 percent of their second ballot vote.[5] The proportion of Green voters remaining loyal to their party with both sections of the ballot dropped from 56 percent in 1994 to 37 percent in 1998. Thus the Greens appear to be becoming as dependent on SPD ballot splitters as the FDP has been on CDU first ballot voters.

Proposals for the change of this electoral system have usually been toward a plurality system of the Anglo-American type, that is, plurality elections in single-member districts. Such a system, it is argued, would eliminate the need for coalition governments by creating clear winners (and losers) and thereby increase the electorate's role in the selection of a governing party; it would also eliminate the possibility of extremist parties, even those securing above 5 percent, gaining parliamentary representation with only a small percentage of the vote.

These proposals have been opposed most intensely by the Free Democrats, whose survival as a serious political force is dependent on the retention of the proportional system. Thus, before the party enters into any coalition with one of the major parties, it secures a pledge from its potential partner that the electoral law will not be tampered with. The Greens and the other small parties have also opposed any major change in this system.

NOMINATION AND CANDIDATE SELECTION

The electoral system is also an important structural factor influencing the recruitment and nomination of candidates to the parliament. The party list section of the ballot allows parties to bring into parliament, through a high position on the list, representatives of interest groups and experts with specialized knowledge who would for various reasons (personality, background) have a difficult time winning a grassroots campaign. A district campaign, on the other hand, affords candidates an opportunity to establish their personal vote-getting appeal and can provide a second chance for personalities left off the state list or given a hopelessly low position. Moreover, a strong district following gives an incumbent a measure of independence from the state or national party organization.

Yet in spite of one-on-one district contests (the personalized part of the electoral system), most Germans vote for a party label rather than a personality. In 1987, for example, about 60 percent of a representative sample of the electorate stated that the most important factor in their vote was their attachment to a party "with whose basic policies I agree." An additional 20 percent based their vote on particular issues rather than on any general attachment to a party. Only 13 percent mentioned the candidates of the parties as the determining factor in their vote.[6]

Constituency candidates, by law, must be nominated after a secret ballot election, either by all party members in the district or by a district selection committee that has itself been elected by the vote of the entire membership. This nomination must be made not more than one year before the election. The official nomination papers must also contain minutes of the selection meeting, together with attendance records and voting results. The enforcement of these legal provisions, however, has thus far been left to the parties.

The selection of candidates for state lists takes place at party conventions held six to eight weeks before election day. The construction of these lists is usually a controversial matter in which the various factions struggle and bargain to receive positions high enough to ensure election or, in most cases, reelection. There is a tendency for even those candidates running in supposedly safe districts to seek the safety net provided by a high list position.

At the district level, the entire process of candidate selection is, according to most observers, a relatively decentralized procedure in which local party oligarchies and issues play a more important role than the construction of state lists. The grass-roots organizations are very sensitive to pressure from above and jealously seek to maintain their power. Indeed, there are reports that especially at recent elections, national "prominents" seeking a district nomination feel handicapped by the so-called local matadors and under pressure to prove themselves sufficiently in touch with the base. Moreover, the district selection process is becoming more conflict-laden. This development reflects the influence of new members in the local party organizations and the emergence of contending ideological factions at the grass-roots level.

Criteria for Selection

How does an aspiring German politico become a candidate for parliament? Because most nominees are incumbents, the most obvious qualifications are previous experience and performance. In the absence of national experience, however, a good record in some local or Land office is an important qualification. About half of all district candidates have held local office, and about one-fourth have had some experience at the state level. The reputation as a good party man or woman (i.e., being a loyal, hard-working partisan, especially in local party work) will further enhance the aspirant's prospects. The political culture values expertise, so occupational and educational experience is a further qualification. Finally, the degree of interest-group support for a particular candidate and the character of the expected opposition are also at work in the local nomination process.

A good position on the state list (second part of the ballot) usually requires one or more of the following: state or national prominence, the support of top leaders of interest groups vital to the party (especially important in the CDU/CSU), leadership positions at the state or national level in auxiliary organizations of the party (youth, women, farmers), and the support of important ideological groupings within the organization. Because the top three names on each party's state list will be printed on the ballot, most state party organizations try to have the most prominent national or state leaders in these slots to aid in voter recognition. The use by some district candidates of the list as a safety net, and the ability to do so, usually also requires senior leadership status in the party. In some cases a candidate in a hopeless district, who has nonetheless done a good job of campaigning in the area over several elections, will be rewarded eventually with a good list position.

Proposals for reform of the nomination system have focused on the introduction of American-type primary elections, the stricter enforcement of the provisions of the party law governing the selection process at both district and state levels (secret ballots, public announcements of meetings), and the establishment of nationwide candidate lists at the parties' national conventions. Given the growth in grass-roots participation in party affairs, reform proposals are likely to gain increasing support.

ELECTORAL POLITICS AND CAMPAIGN STYLES

As in other advanced Western societies, the style of election campaigns in Germany has become strongly influenced by professional advertising and public relations techniques. All major parties contract with ad agencies for the design of the campaign appeals: Slogans, posters, television spots, and newspaper and magazine advertisements are pretested to achieve, if possible, the desired effect on the target group of voters.[7] Nonetheless, it would be erroneous to assume that the German version of Madison Avenue is a behind-the-scenes power. The message, or main themes, of a campaign are for the most part the decision of the parties, with the public relations and advertising experts largely determining the manner in which these themes are presented.

The extensive, well-developed media structure and the close, well-financed relationship between major interest groups and the parties ensure that the voters will be subjected to a massive barrage of electoral propaganda. In addition to daily press, radio, and television news coverage, parties are given free time for political spots on radio and television. Special election previews, with commentary and analysis, are standard fare during the final four to six weeks before the election. From 1972 to 1987 televised debates between the leaders of the parties represented in the parliament highlighted the final stage of the campaign. (At the 1990 election, however, Chancellor Kohl and the Christian Democrats declined to take part in the "elephant round," as the Germans term the debate between the top leaders, fearing that the media exposure would enhance the standing of the former East German Communist party, which would have been entitled to participate.) Mass mailings, posters, and advertisements are also employed extensively. As in other political areas, the German voter has been well informed about the candidates, parties, and issues.

In the last three decades electoral politics have also been characterized by a steady increase in public involvement during the campaign. Traditionally, German voters have been rather passive and reticent during campaigns, dutifully absorbing information channeled to them by the media and party organizations. Discussions among family and friends, attendance at election meetings, and the public display of partisan preferences were restricted to only a part of the electorate. Since the late 1960s, however, public interest and involvement in elections have taken on new forms and reached higher levels than during previous campaigns. The proportion of voters reporting that they discussed the elections with family or friends almost tripled between 1969 and 1976. New forms of public involvement included widespread voter initiative groups and the public display of partisan preferences through bumper stickers.[8] Voter initiative groups were first organized by the novelist Günter Grass on behalf of the SPD on a small scale in the elections of 1965 and 1969, and they were in evidence in some local and state elections between 1969 and 1972. In the federal election in 1972, citizen groups were working for all parties, although most of them tended to favor the Social Democratic–Liberal government.[9] These groups organized rallies, staffed information booths in downtown shopping areas, sponsored advertisements, distributed literature and campaign buttons, and generally attempted to stimulate voter interest and activity in the campaign. They have since become commonplace during campaigns. These various signs of interest, popular concern, and involvement indicate that Germans have acquired a fuller understanding of the citizen role and of the potential for political change available through political participation.

CAMPAIGN AND PARTY FINANCE

As in the United States, election campaigns in Germany have become very expensive. Unlike those in most other modern democracies, however, German political parties are the recipients of extensive governmental subsidies with which they finance a large part of their organizational and campaign work. In 1998, for example, public subsidies constituted over one-third of the total income reported by the parties represented in parliament and over 50 percent of that received by the smaller parties.

State subsidies began in 1959 with a modest annual allotment of about $2 million to the three parties. By 1965 this had increased to $20 million, including the addition of subsidies from some states. In 1967 a new law provided a public subsidy of about a dollar for each vote received by any party gaining at least 2.5 percent of the popular vote at the preceding election. Thus by 1976 the federal government alone paid out over $60 million to the parties contesting federal elections. The 1967 law also required the parties to file annual statements of their finances and to disclose the names of all individuals contributing more than $10,000 in any one year, as well as all corporations contributing more than $100,000. The Federal Constitutional Court (see Chapter 8) later ruled that the law was unconstitutional in a number of ways. It ordered the minimum percentage needed for a party to receive subsidies to be dropped to 0.5 percent (about 250,000 votes) and also required that the disclosure ceilings be lowered. The reduction of the minimum percentage means that public subsidies are a major source of funds for smaller parties such as the Greens and the Free Democrats. In 1992 the Court ruled that public funding for the parties cannot exceed the amount they raise themselves through contributions and membership dues.

However, the costs of the expensive election campaigns and party bureaucracies are far from covered by state funds and membership dues. The parties seek to meet these expenses through large, tax-deductible contributions from business and other interest groups. As in other developed democracies, there is a real danger that political favors will be anticipated or actually promised by the parties in exchange for financial support. In 1982 and 1983 a series of reports in *Der Spiegel* revealed that the giant Flick business group had contributed large sums to the three major parties with the expectation that the company would receive a favorable ruling from the economics ministry in a tax case.[10] At stake were about $175 million in taxes that the Flick company sought to avoid paying. The economics minister had indeed interpreted the tax laws to Flick's advantage. In 1983 both the minister and his predecessor were indicted on charges of misusing their office by accepting financial contributions for their party (the FDP) from Flick.[11] In late 1999 a major scandal involving the Christian Democrats and former Chancellor Kohl again focused public attention on the role of money in election campaigns. Kohl admitted that he kept special secret bank accounts to finance campaigns and strengthen his hold on the party. It is alleged that these funds came largely from arms dealers and other firms that profited from government contracts.

THE PATTERN OF FEDERAL ELECTIONS, 1949–1998

The results of the fourteen national elections held since 1949, including the three (1990–1998) all-German elections, are presented in Figure 6.1. These data reveal five major characteristics of German voting behavior over the past fifty years:

1. The hegemonic position of the CDU/CSU in the party system from 1953 to 1965, due above all to the party's spectacular electoral victories in 1953 and 1957.

2. The steady increase in support for the SPD between 1953 and 1972, averaging about 3 percent in each election, which brought the party up to parity with the Christian Democrats.

3. The gradual decline of smaller parties ("Other") between 1949 and 1980, whose percentage of the poll dropped from 28 percent in 1949 to about 2 percent in 1980.

4. The competitive and less predictable character of elections since 1983. Long-term trends have been replaced by short-term fluctuations from election to election.

5. The decline of the two largest parties since the late 1980s and the slow but steady increase in smaller parties.

In the first federal election in 1949, twelve parties secured parliamentary representation, but only two—the CDU/CSU and the SPD—received more than 25 percent of the popular vote. The CDU/CSU campaigned on the twin issues of the Republic's

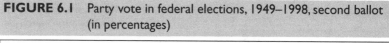

FIGURE 6.1   Party vote in federal elections, 1949–1998, second ballot (in percentages)

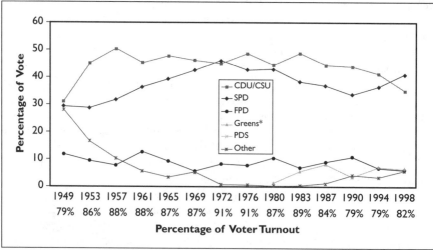

*1990 combined East-West vote.

integration into the Western alliance abroad and the market economy at home. "We don't want any socialism in Germany" was its major slogan. With the exception of the Communist party, which secured 5.7 percent of the vote and 15 parliamentary seats, all other smaller parties generally agreed with these two Christian Democratic positions. The differences between them and the Union were far less than between them and the Social Democrats. If one combines the CDU/CSU's 1949 vote and that of the smaller, nonleftist parties in that first election, the total—44.3 percent—is similar to the total achieved by the Union alone in the elections of 1953 and 1957.

The elections of 1953 and 1957, which brought the Christian Democrats to the pinnacle of their electoral success, represented the continuation of the 1949 pattern. By this time, however, the policy successes of the Adenauer-led government began to take their toll on the small, regional, special-interest parties, whose support steadily dwindled. The CDU gains resulted above all from its absorption of these smaller parties rather than from gains from the SPD. The Social Democrats' policy alternatives—neutralism in foreign policy and a socialist planned economy at home—were rejected decisively by the majority of the electorate. By absorbing the smaller parties, the CDU/CSU greatly simplified the party system and reduced the possibility of a reversion to the unstable multiparty system of the Weimar Republic.

The early successes of the Christian Democrats provided the impetus for the SPD's transformation from a narrowly based, ideologically committed socialist movement to a heterogeneous, pragmatic, center-left party of reform. This process, described in Chapter 5, produced steady electoral gains after 1953, and by 1972 gave the SPD a larger share of the popular vote than the CDU received. Most of the SPD gains over these years, however, came from Christian Democratic voters and new voters, not from the ranks of the minor parties. The SPD, unlike the CDU, had no small parties on the left of the spectrum to absorb. Until 1972 the CDU was able to compensate for losses to the SPD by gains from minor parties. Had it not been for this reservoir, the Union's decline between 1965 and 1972 would have been even more apparent.

The tenacity of the FDP and its ability to avoid the fate of other third parties is, in addition to the electoral system, largely the result of its function as an alternative for CDU/CSU and SPD voters who are temporarily dissatisfied with their party. During the FDP's coalitions with the Union from 1949 to 1956, and again from 1961 to 1966, there was considerable movement between the electorates of these two parties. Essentially, those CDU/CSU voters who were somewhat dissatisfied with their party would vote for the FDP as a means of sending the big party a message without leaving the middle-class camp and going all the way over to the opposition, the SPD. During its coalition with the Social Democrats (1969–1982), the FDP sought the support of SPD voters who were unhappy with their party but did not want to remove it from power. The FDP has thus acted as a type of opposition within the coalition, a "corrective" to the major partner.

The 1976 federal election saw the return of the Social Democratic–Liberal coalition that had governed Germany since 1969, but with a majority of only 10 seats, down sharply from the advantage of 46 seats held after the November 1972 poll. The opposition Christian Democrats, led for the first time by their new chairman, Helmut Kohl, not only regained their status as Germany's largest single party but also achieved their highest proportion of the party vote since 1957 and reversed the steady gains the Social Democrats had achieved at every election since 1957.

In the 1980 federal election the SPD-FDP coalition, due largely to a strong performance by the Free Democrats, won a decisive victory over the Christian Democrats led by the controversial Franz-Josef Strauss. The Free Democrats increased their share of the vote from 7.9 to 10.6 percent. The electorate decisively rejected the Strauss candidacy but did not endorse the Social Democrats, preferring instead to return a stronger "liberal corrective" to the SPD. The CDU/CSU, in spite of a 4.1 percent drop in its vote, remained the strongest party.

In 1980 the three established parties also had to contend with a nationwide environmentalist political party. In the late 1970s a variety of environmentalist groups, with a common opposition to the government's plan for expansion of nuclear energy plants, banded together to form the Green political party. In October 1979 the Green party gained entrance into the parliament of the city-state of Bremen, and in March 1980 it surmounted the 5 percent hurdle in the relatively large state of Baden-Württemberg. The Greens had a strong protest component to their image, and this helped them skim votes from all the established parties—but especially the SPD and FDP—in state and local elections. In 1980 they were unable, however, to overcome the charge of being simply a single-issue protest movement with no capability to assume or share responsibility for the myriad tasks and problems of government. The established parties also stole some of the Greens' thunder by adding stronger environmental protection sections to their election programs.

After the 1980 election, the NATO missile question and the resultant nationwide peace movement gave the Green party new momentum and put the Greens into three more state parliaments by 1982. In the March 1983 elections the Greens, with 5.6 percent of the vote, became the first new political party to enter the parliament since the 1950s. Their electoral success in 1983 was due above all to the strong support they received from younger voters, especially those with college or university backgrounds. The Greens' success in 1983 and those of the PDS in 1994 and 1998 also indicate that the electoral system does not place insurmountable barriers to new political parties.

In the 1987 election voters returned the ruling Christian Democratic–Free Democratic coalition, but with a reduced majority. For the first time in postwar German electoral history, both major parties lost support in the same election. The combined CDU (44 percent) and SPD (37 percent) share of the vote dropped to 81 percent, the lowest since 1953. The Free Democrats increased their vote to 9 percent, and the Greens' proportion of the vote rose to over 8 percent. Voting turnout, generally among the highest in Western Europe, dropped to 84 percent, the lowest level since the first federal election in 1949.

Unified Germany Votes: The 1990–1998 Federal Elections

1990 Federal Election. On December 2, 1990, German voters elected 662 deputies to the twelfth national parliament (*Bundestag*) since the founding of the Federal Republic. Approximately 140 of these deputies represented the 16 million inhabitants of what had been, until October 3, 1990, the German Democratic Republic. Although this election was the twelfth for the Federal Republic, it was the first time that the Eastern citizens participated in a federal election and the first free, "all-German" poll since 1932. The election was also the culmination of a unification process that had begun in November 1989 with the opening of the Berlin Wall and the subsequent collapse of the East German regime.

Two quite different electorates went to the polls on December 2, 1990. West Germans had been participating in democratic elections at the local, state, and national levels for over forty years. East Germans, following the collapse of the Communist regime, had participated in only three free elections: the parliamentary (*Volkskammer*) elections in March 1990, the local elections in May, and the state assembly elections in October.

Unification was the central theme of the election campaign. The ruling coalition of Christian Democrats and Free Democrats led by Chancellor Kohl emphasized that it had fulfilled the charge of West Germany's 1949 Basic Law (constitution): the unity of the nation in peace and freedom, which had eluded fifteen previous governments during the past forty years. The CDU stressed that it was Kohl's leadership that had secured widespread international support for unity and accelerated the pace with which the entire process was completed. The Free Democrats claimed that the lion's share of the credit belonged to their leader, Foreign Minister Hans-Dietrich Genscher. The Social Democrats countered by charging that the government had rushed into unification without considering its economic and social costs and by largely ignoring the legitimate right of East Germans to be more involved in the process. The SPD chancellor candidate, Oskar Lafontaine, the young minister-president (chief executive) of the Saarland, was slow to grasp the significance of unification for the campaign. He belongs to a generation that had known only a divided Germany, and he assumed that unification was not an issue with broad electoral appeal. Lafontaine focused on younger voters who were less emotionally involved with unification than were their elders.

The Greens were even more skeptical about unification than were the Social Democrats. The party's relatively young electorate was less concerned about "Germany" than were voters of the other parties. The Greens wanted the indigenous East German opposition groups to have more time to find a third way between the Stalinist communism of the old East Germany and what they considered the anti-environmentalist capitalism of the West.

After a year of unprecedented political developments, many voters were tired of politics and the campaign was generally routine, if not dull. As expected, the Kohl government was returned, with an increased majority of 134 seats in the new 662-seat parliament. Within the governing coalition the big winners were the Free Democrats, who achieved the third best result in their history.

The opposition parties were the big losers in 1990. The Social Democrats, securing only 33.5 percent of the vote, dropped to their lowest level since 1957. SPD losses were heavy among middle-class voters—including skilled manual workers, the traditional core of the party's electorate. In the new Eastern states the party received less than one-fourth of the vote. This poor performance of the SPD in the East was in part a reaction to Lafontaine's lukewarm attitude toward unification. But it also reflected the party's organizational weakness in the new states. In 1946, when the SPD was forced to merge with the Communists into the Socialist Unity Party, it lost its property and membership. In 1989 the party had to start from scratch. Although the Christian Democrats and the Liberals (FDP) functioned as puppet parties under the communist system, they did have, by Western standards, large memberships and substantial real estate holdings. After the collapse of the Honecker regime, the leadership of these parties resigned and their holdings passed into the hands of their West German counterparts.

The big surprise of the 1990 election was the failure of the West German Greens to return to parliament. With 4.8 percent in West Germany, down from 8.3 percent in 1987, the party failed to clear the 5 percent hurdle needed for representation in parliament. The party was hurt by its opposition to the unification policies of the Kohl government. It also suffered from low turnout among its supporters and defections to the SPD.

In the East, the former Communist party, now renamed the Party of Democratic Socialism/Left List (PDS/LL), did secure enough votes under special provisions of the electoral law to enter the new parliament. East German parties needed to receive only 5 percent of the vote in the former territory of the GDR to enter parliament. With about 11 percent in the East, but only 2.4 percent nationwide, the PDS cleared this barrier, as did a coalition of East German Greens and former GDR dissidents (Alliance 90).

1994 Federal Election.   In 1994 German voters selected the membership of the Bundestag for the thirteenth time since the founding of the Federal Republic in 1949. For the electorate in the five new states of the former German Democratic Republic (GDR), it was only the second national election and the first since the social and economic upheavals of unification began in early 1991.

The 1994 election produced mixed results for all parties, large and small. There was neither a clear winner nor a clear loser. The ruling coalition returned to power, but with a greatly reduced majority of only 10 seats, down from 134 in 1990. To carry their small and weakened partner, the Free Democrats, over the 5 percent line, the Christian Democrats had to give up about 4 percent of their vote to the Liberals. The Social Democrats, with 36 percent of the vote, finally ended their string of three straight declines in national elections. But they nonetheless lost their fourth straight national election. The SPD offered the electorate only a weakly defined programmatic alternative to the government, and its leader, Rudolf Scharping, was unable to compete on even terms with the chancellor once the campaign heated up.

Among the small parties the Free Democrats, with only 6.9 percent of the vote (due mainly to splitting by CDU voters), did return to the Bundestag, but on the same election day they lost another three state elections. The Greens became the first party ever to return to the Bundestag following a failure to clear the 5 percent hurdle. The PDS achieved its goal of returning to the parliament, but the party remained insignificant in the West.[12]

The 1998 Election: The End of the Kohl Era.   In September 1998 the Social Democrats and Greens finally succeeded in toppling the Kohl-led CDU-FDP coalition that had governed for sixteen years. For the first time in the history of the Federal Republic an entire sitting government was replaced. Previous power shifts, i.e., those of 1969 and 1982, had involved only one of the coalition parties leaving after an election. The 1998 election was also the first time that German voters replaced an incumbent chancellor.

Unemployment was by far the major campaign issue and the area in which the Kohl government was most vulnerable to opposition criticism. By early 1998 over 4.8 million Germans, or about 11.5 percent of the work force, were officially unemployed. This represented an increase of almost 100 percent over the 1990 level. Since the 1990 unification over 3 million jobs have been lost; 2.5 million of those were in the East. High unemployment has also meant increases in poverty and welfare (*Sozialhilfe*) recipients. Since 1994 the number of people below the poverty level set by the European Union has jumped from 6 to 7 million. The number of Germans on welfare has increased from 1 million in 1983, the first year of the Kohl government, to 3 million in 1998.

But the poor economy was not the only reason for Kohl's defeat. After sixteen years German voters had grown tired of Chancellor Kohl and wanted at least a new face, if not new policies. The "Kohl must go" theme, the portrayal of an aging leader increasingly out of touch with younger voters, was very effective. Kohl's younger and more telegenic rival, Gerhard Schröder, was consistently ranked ahead of the chancellor in polls throughout the campaign. Indeed, Schröder's appeal cut across party lines, with about 10 percent of Christian Democrats preferring Schröder over their own candidate.[13]

Kohl and the Christian Democrats suffered massive losses in the East. With an unemployment level approaching 20 percent, almost double the national average, Eastern voters who had supported Kohl and the Union in 1990 and 1994 were now looking for alternatives. Many felt betrayed by Kohl's vision of flowering landscapes, full employment, prosperity and high-tech powered growth. Manual workers, those hit hardest by unemployment, left Kohl and the CDU in droves; between 1994 and 1998 the proportion of East German workers voting for the Christian Democrats dropped from 52 percent to only 32 percent, about the same level of support that West German voters gave the CDU.[14] Generally, there were signs of a convergence in the two electorates in 1998 not noticeable in 1990 and 1994. Several important differences remain, above all the continued high level of support in the East for the former Communist party.

BASIC ORIENTATIONS OF THE ELECTORATE

Ideology
The absence of major electoral support for parties proposing drastic changes in the political and economic order of the Federal Republic, and also the success enjoyed by the Social Democrats since they moved more to the center of the political spectrum, indicate that the electorate has thus far had little interest in extremist or ideological parties and politics. The Christian Democrats during the 1950s and 1960s were a middle-of-the-road party par excellence, and they were essentially joined by the Social Democrats in the early 1960s. Survey data on the ideological orientations of the electorate tend to substantiate this interpretation. Figure 6.2 presents the

1416182022242526272829303132333435363738394041424344454647484950515253545556575859606162636465666768697071727374757677787980

FIGURE 6.2   Ideological self-estimate of the electorate, 1996

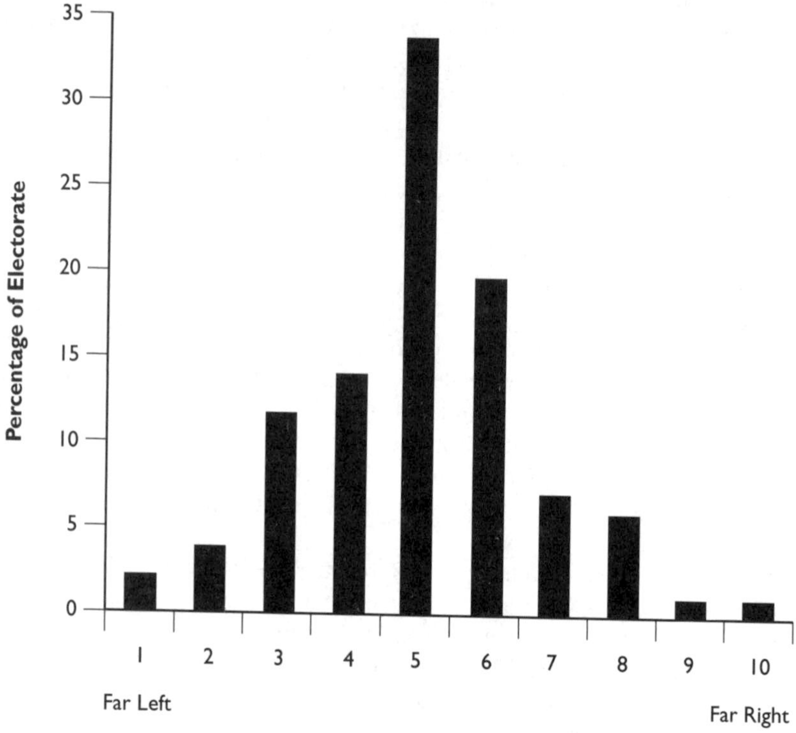

Source: ALLBUS, 1996.

TABLE 6.2   Continuity and change in voting behavior, 1980–1998 (in percentages)

	1980/1983	1983/1987	1987/1990*	1990/1994	1994/1998
Supported the same party at both elections	66	64	56	54	55
Changed party choice between elections	24	24	23	24	23
New voters/ nonvoters	10	12	21	22	22

*1987–1990 figures are for West Germany only.
Source: Forschungsgruppe Wahlen survey nos. 472, 551, 720, 864, Forschungsgruppe Wahlen, *Bundestagswahl 1998.* I am indebted to Dr. Dieter Roth for these data.

ideological self-image of the electorate in 1996. Respondents were asked to rank themselves along a 10-point scale ranging from "1" (far left) to "10" (far right). As Figure 6.2 shows, the majority of the electorate positions itself in the middle of the left-right continuum. Given these orientations, electoral success in the Federal Republic clearly resides in the vital center of the political spectrum.

Party Preference

As Table 6.2 indicates, most Germans still tend to vote for the same party from election to election, although the percentage remaining faithful to their parties has declined steadily from 66 percent in 1983 to 55 percent at the 1998 election. Thus, the dynamic segment of the electorate, or swing vote, has expanded from 34 percent to 45 percent over this period.

The consistency of support is roughly similar for the major parties, with both managing to retain approximately 75 percent of their supporters between elections. The Free Democrats, however, have had the most unstable electorate by far; the party has generally been able to hold only about 40 percent of its voters from the previous election.

DETERMINANTS OF VOTING BEHAVIOR

Sociodemographic Factors

Social class, usually measured through occupation, and religion are the two most important demographic factors structuring the party vote in West Germany. The hard core of the Social Democratic electorate is composed of manual workers. In 1998 they preferred the SPD to the middle-class parties in West Germany by about a 60 to 40 ratio. The Christian Democratic Union, on the other hand, enjoys a high level of support (60 percent) among independent nonmanuals (professionals, the self-employed), including farmers. The Free Democrats have received their strongest support from white-collar workers or salaried nonmanuals, sometimes referred to as the "new middle class," in contrast to the CDU's "old middle class."

In terms of the religious factor, the overall relationship in the West has also been quite clear: Christian Democratic support is greatest among Catholics, especially those with a strong attachment to the church, which is usually measured by church attendance. On the other hand, the Social Democrats and Liberals receive disproportionate support from Protestants with moderate or weak attachment to their religion. Because Protestants, as compared to Catholics, are less likely to attend church regularly and apparently are less attached to their church, it may well be more accurate to term SPD and FDP supporters more *secular* than CDU/CSU voters.

Thus far in East Germany's short electoral history, the relationships of social class, religion, and voting found in the West have yet to develop. In the East most working-class voters in various elections from March to December 1990 supported the Christian Democrats. In the March 1990 parliamentary elections, for example, approximately 55 percent of manual workers in the East supported the

CDU or its conservative allies. At the December 1990 federal election, approximately 60 percent of manual voters voted for the CDU or the FDP.[15] In the industrialized southern regions of Saxony and Thuringia, worker support for the West German middle-class parties was higher still. In 1998, however, these differences diminished. Eastern voters are beginning to converge with their Western cousins. The Social Democrats, for example, made substantial gains among Eastern blue-collar voters.

Religion in the East has also thus far played a different role in structuring the party vote than it does in the West. The religious cleavage in the East falls between Protestants and Catholics on the one hand, and those with no religious affiliation on the other. Both East German Catholics and Protestants have given strong support (60–70 percent) to the Christian Democrats. But over half of the East German population, as compared to 15 percent in the West, has no religious affiliation. This group is far more likely to vote for the Social Democrats or the old Communist party (PDS). These differences may well change as the East German electorate matures and the Social Democrats, together with the trade unions, organize and mobilize East German workers. As the churches reorganize in the East there may well be an increase in religious affiliation, or at least a return to pre-communist levels. In these early elections East Germans appear to be motivated more by factors other than social class and religion.

Some analysts have also argued that the 1998 election was the first "normal" vote for Eastern Germans. The elections of 1990 and 1994 were influenced by the exceptional atmosphere created by unification. East Germans temporarily forgot their forty years of socialization under a system that emphasized a strong state and social and economic equality. In 1998 Easterners returned home to the "left" parties, Social Democrats and PDS. One election, of course, hardly constitutes a trend, and only time will tell whether the Social Democrats have replaced the Christian Democrats as the dominant party in the Eastern states.

Three other demographic factors of some importance are age, gender, and the voters' place of residence (rural community, urban-metropolitan area). Generally, younger voters entering the electorate for the first time (especially since 1980) have been more likely to support the SPD or the Greens than the CDU/CSU. Since 1983 the overall importance of the age factor increased sharply as the Greens made a successful appeal to new and young voters. Approximately one of every five new voters in 1983 supported the Greens; among the rest of the electorate the party received the vote of only about one of every twenty voters. Age, rather than class or religion, was the most important determinant of support for the Greens. At the 1998 election, however, support for the Greens among young voters declined. As the Greens become an established party with an aging leadership and membership, they become less appealing to new voters.

There have been sizable differences in the party vote of men and women, at least until 1972. In four elections held between 1957 and 1969, the percentage of women supporting the CDU/CSU exceeded that of males by about 10 percentage points. Female support for the SPD, however, was on the average about 6 percent below that of males. It is ironic indeed that Germany's "left" party, which consistently fought for women's suffrage, was not rewarded at the polls. If the electorate had been composed only of males, the SPD would have become the strongest party by 1965 instead of 1972.

This tendency toward disproportionate support for the CDU among females was halted in the 1972 election, as the difference in male-female support for the CDU/CSU dropped to only 3 percent. In the case of the SPD, the male-female difference declined to only 1 percent in 1972 and 1976. In 1980 the Social Democrats for the first time actually received more support from females than from males. In the 1990 and 1994 elections there was no significant gender gap in the unified German electorate.

These demographic variables, then, form the major structural determinants of voting behavior. Yet by themselves they do little to explain the dynamics of this behavior and, specifically, the factors that produce social changes in party support between elections and over the course of several decades. To explain these aspects of voting behavior, most analysts explore the dynamic interrelationships of *social change* and *electoral choice,* together with opinions of candidates, party policies, and issues. A fuller understanding of voting and its function in the political system must also take these factors into account.

VOTER DYNAMICS

Social Change
As we have seen, most manual workers (about 60 percent) support the Social Democrats, and most Catholics support the Christian Democrats. What, then, of Catholic workers? Or unionized, low-paid, white-collar workers? SPD support is strongest among younger voters, manual workers, Protestants with marginal attachments to their church, and residents of large metropolitan areas; CDU/CSU support is centered in older age groups, women, middle-class workers, Catholics with strong attachments to the church, farmers, and voters in small towns. What about young Catholic women living in metropolitan areas? These groups of voters are referred to by social scientists as *cross-pressured—* their socioeconomic positions expose them to conflicting political communications. Their support for any one party tends to be less constant than that of voters with consistent attributes, for example, older Catholic women living in villages or young manual workers with little interest in religion living in metropolitan areas. The size of the cross-pressured segment of the electorate has been estimated at approximately 30 percent. Moreover, it is growing as German social structure becomes more complex.

Another important source of change can be found in the class and religious composition of the electorate. As discussed in Chapter 3, the size of both manual worker segments of the work force has declined in the postwar period, whereas the number of Germans in new middle-class occupations has increased greatly. New middle-class voters are generally more likely to change their vote from election to election than are voters in manual or old middle-class occupations. This

TABLE 6.3   Party vote by class, 1987–1998 (in percentages)

Party	Old Middle Class				New Middle Class				Working Class			
	1987	1990	1994	1998	1987	1990	1994	1998	1987	1990	1994	1998
CDU/ CSU	70	57	56	56	47	44	38	31	33	44	37	30
SPD	16	18	17	18	37	33	36	42	59	47	45	48
FPD	8	18	14	12	6	17	8	7	2	6	4	3
Greens, others	6	7	13	14	10	6	18	20	6	3	14	19

Source: INFAS (Institut für angewandte Sozialforschung) Surveys, 1983–1987. Each survey contains 5,000 to 6,000 cases, random samples. Cited in Ursula Feist and Hubert Krieger, "Alte und neue Scheidelinien des politischen Verhaltens," *Aus Politik und Zeitgeschichte*, no. 12 (March 21, 1987): 38; for 1990, Forschungsgruppe Wahlen Survey No. 715; for 1994, Forschungsgruppe Wahlen, *Bundestagswahl 1994* (Mannheim, 1995), p. 21; for 1998, Forschungsgruppe Wahlen, *Bundestagswahl 1998*, (Mannheim, 1998), p. 22.

development is shown in Table 6.3, which presents the party preferences of the three class groups since 1987. The old middle class remains largely the preserve of the CDU and the FDP, with these two parties combined receiving about 70 percent of the vote. In 1994 the smaller parties, especially the Greens and in the East the PDS, took some votes away from the established parties among this group. The long-term decline in the size of the old middle class, however, reduces its importance in explaining aggregate change.

The expanding new middle-class part of the electorate has been more volatile since 1987 than has the old middle class or the working class. In 1998 this group turned from the CDU to the Social Democrats. Until 1994 the Union, although declining overall, was generally able to hold its share of this voting group. The FDP, after leaving its coalition with the SPD in the early 1980s, lost support among this group. In 1990 its vote rose to record levels in part because of strong support from the former East Germany's fledgling middle class. The Social Democrats, after several years of decline, saw their share of the new middle-class vote increase from 36 percent in 1994 to 42 percent in 1998. The Christian Democrats, however, dropped from 38 percent to 31 percent. The Green proportion of the new middle-class vote in 1998 rose to a record high of 20 percent. In 1983, when they first cleared the 5 percent mark and entered the parliament, they received only 6 percent from this group.[16]

Among working-class voters there are also signs of growing volatility. At the 1994 election both the Christian Democrats and the Social Democrats lost support among this group. Even though the Social Democrats remain the strongest party, they have now seen their support among manual workers decline from 55 percent

TABLE 6.4 Support for the CDU/CSU by religion, 1980–1998 (in percentages)

	1980	1983	1987	1990	1994	1998
Catholics	56	65	51	56	55	47
Non-Catholics	32	40	33	39	40	32
Difference	24	25	18	17	15	15

Source: Forschungsgruppe Wahlen, election surveys. The 1990, 1994, and 1998 figures do not include the former East Germany.

in 1987 to 45 percent in 1994. The smaller parties have been the major beneficiaries of the declining working-class support for the large parties. In 1998, however, the Social Democrats made strong gains among manual workers in the East who now support the party at about the same level as their West German counterparts. But the former communists in the East are still strong competitors for the manual worker vote.

The growing secularization of the Federal Republic has also changed the significance of the religious factor in voting behavior. In the 1950s more than 40 percent of the electorate attended church on a weekly basis; by the time of the 1994 election less than 20 percent attended church as regularly.[17] Among German Catholics, regular church attendance declined from 54 percent in 1953 to 28 percent in 1994.[18] Although churchgoing Catholics were about as likely to vote for the Christian Democrats in 1994 as they were in the 1950s, their numbers, and therefore the aggregate impact of religion on the vote, have declined.

This trend can be seen in Table 6.4, which presents the support level for Christian Democrats since 1980 among Catholics and non-Catholics. The majority of German Catholics continue to vote for the CDU/CSU, but the overall importance of religion for the party has dropped. In 1980 the CDU/CSU received almost 25 percent more support among Catholics than among non-Catholics; by 1998 this gap had narrowed to only 15 percent. Fewer and fewer voters are exposed to the social and political cues of a religious milieu, and therefore they turn to some other source in making their voting decisions.

Candidates: The Chancellor Bonus.   As in other Western societies, the incumbent government has a distinct advantage over the opposition. Its ability to dominate the news, announce new programs such as tax reductions and pension increases, and proclaim foreign policy successes, all timed to the campaign and election, are well-known tactics in British and American politics that are also practiced in Germany. The announcement of new policies, subsidies to various interest groups, and trips to the United States for special conferences (and lots of photographs) with the U.S. president are standard pre-election procedures for any chancellor.

The government also benefits from certain features of the political culture. Germans like to perceive their government as strong and decisive, as something certain in a world of uncertainty, something they can count on to protect and maintain the social order. These orientations provide an advantage for any incumbent government, and any chancellor quickly learns to tap these cultural supports of governmental authority.

When Willy Brandt challenged Adenauer for the chancellorship in 1961, the electorate (according to public opinion polls) preferred the incumbent by a 3 to 2 margin. When Brandt ran against the then-popular Chancellor Ludwig Erhard in 1965, Brandt fell further behind; Erhard was preferred by a 5 to 2 margin. Even in 1969, when Brandt as foreign minister campaigned against Chancellor Kiesinger, Brandt could not overcome the handicap of opposition; Kiesinger was the electorate's favorite as chancellor by an almost 2 to 1 margin. In 1972, however, Brandt, as the incumbent, enjoyed a similar advantage over his Christian Democratic rival, Rainer Barzel. From 1949 to 1969 it was the CDU/CSU that benefited from this bonus, whereas from 1972 to 1980 the SPD and its chancellor candidates, Brandt and Helmut Schmidt, were the beneficiaries. In 1994 the incumbent Helmut Kohl was preferred over his challenger, Rudolf Scharping, by about a 55 to 45 margin.

In 1998, however, the chancellor bonus disappeared as Kohl's challenger, Gerhard Schröder, maintained a strong lead over Kohl throughout the campaign. It appears that there are limits to the "bonus." After sixteen years in office, Kohl in 1998 was hardly helped by his incumbency. It is also very unlikely that any future chancellor will exceed Kohl's tenure.

Party Policies.   The policies and programs of a party are another dynamic factor affecting voting behavior. The SPD between 1957 and 1972 made steady gains of about 3 percent in each federal election. Most of this increase came from new voters and from middle-class voters who had previously supported the bourgeois parties. This growth in support was related to changes in SPD policies since the late 1950s. The party made a major effort to attract middle-class support by abandoning the more radical or Marxist components of its programs (nationalization of industry and banks, and national economic planning) and attempted to project itself as a modern, innovative party that nevertheless accepted the basic characteristics of the postwar social and economic order. Moreover, when the Social Democrats did come to power at the national level through the 1966 Grand Coalition (discussed in Chapter 5), they assumed the Ministry of Economics and thus were afforded the opportunity to demonstrate to the electorate that the party could outperform the CDU/CSU and was not a group of irresponsible radicals who could not handle money and finances. Thus the policies and behavior of the party, as surveys have shown, reduced the impact of social class and effected changes in voting behavior to the net benefit of the SPD.

The personnel and strategy decisions of the parties can also influence electoral outcomes. For example, the selection of Franz-Josef Strauss by the CDU/CSU as its chancellor candidate in 1980 was a major factor in the party's subsequent electoral defeat.[19] The SPD's decision in 1983 to all but ignore the unemployment issue and emphasize noneconomic issues such as the NATO missile decision was another strategic error that cost the party sizable blue-collar support.[20] During the 1987 campaign, both parties made questionable strategy choices. The Christian Democrats underestimated the extent of discontent among farmers, many of whom stayed home.[21] The SPD's decision to seek an absolute majority, with Johannes Rau conducting an American-style campaign, lacked credibility in the view of most voters.[22] To compound the problem, the party essentially abandoned this approach about two months before the January 1987 vote. In 1990 the SPD badly misread public opinion on unification. Its ambivalent approach was out of step with the generally positive attitude most voters had about the unification process. In 1998 the CDU/CSU should have replaced Helmut Kohl as its chancellor candidate. Kohl's decision to run one more time was a critical factor in their defeat. The union in 1998 also was unable to convince voters that it had a solution for the problem of mass unemployment.

Issues.   In preelection surveys in 1994 and 1998, national samples of voters were given a list of policy issues or problems. Each voter was asked to name the issues that were personally "very important" to him or her. Table 6.5 ranks the issues according to the percentage of respondents stating that the particular issue area was personally "very important." If 60 percent or more of the sample regarded the issue as very important, its salience was coded as high; if 40–59 percent, as medium, and if 0–39 percent, as low.

In 1994 and 1998 economic issues, above all unemployment, topped the list of voter concerns. Environmental protection, a major concern in 1990 and 1994, was nowhere to be found in 1998. The post-1990 revelations of widespread environmental

TABLE 6.5   Rank order of major campaign issues by salience to the electorate, 1994 and 1998

	Issue	
Salience	1994	1998
High (above 60%)	Unemployment Environmental protection Housing Crime	Unemployment
Medium (40–59%)	Asylum seekers Taxes	Asylum seekers Law and order
Low (0–39%)	Unification Security of pensions Peace	Security of pensions Environmental protection Taxes

Source: For 1994: Forschungsgruppe Wahlen Survey No. 848; for 1998, Politbarometer data, Forschungsgruppe Wahlen, *Daten zur Bundestagswahl am 27. 09. 1998*, Federal Press Office, Bonn.

damage in the East had made this question "very important" to almost three-fourths of the voters in 1994. Two other materialist issues, the security of the pension system and economic growth, were important in the minds of most voters, especially those in the former GDR, where unemployment soared following the July 1990 currency union.

As in the United States in 1996, the 1998 German election was focused on domestic issues, particularly the economy. In survey after survey preceding the election, voters in the West overwhelmingly considered unemployment the most important problem. Of course in the East it has been the top problem almost since unification in 1990, as the number of employed East Germans dropped from 9.2 million to 6.2 million. Whereas in past elections—especially those of 1990 and 1994—noneconomic issues such as the environment, "law and order," or "peace" (missiles, disarmament) have equaled or surpassed economic issues in importance, this was not the case in 1998.

Until early 1994 the public's view of the economy was generally very negative. But beginning in April and May 1994, public perceptions of economic improvement jumped dramatically; one polling group, for example, found that from February to May the proportion of the electorate that believed the economy was improving doubled from 26 percent to 52 percent.[23] In 1998 there was a slight upturn in the economy during the final weeks of the campaign, but this time it was too little too late for Helmut Kohl's Christian Democrats. In 1994 on the eve of the election almost 40 percent of voters believed that the Kohl government could deal effectively with unemployment; four years later as voters went to the polls only about 20 percent still had such confidence in the government.[24]

SUMMARY AND CONCLUSION

In spite of an electoral law that supposedly encourages a multiparty system, German voters over the past fifty years have concentrated their support in two major parties and two small but important "third" parties. After two decades of governments dominated by the Christian Democrats, the electorate in 1969 used the ballot to give the longtime opposition party, the Social Democrats, the major share of political responsibility for the first time. Throughout the 1950s the center-right parties (the CDU plus small middle-class parties) secured about 70 percent of the popular vote and the center-left SPD secured only 30 percent, but by 1980 the distribution of preferences had changed to about 55 percent for the center-left and 45 percent for the center-right. Yet in 1983 the electorate gave the Christian Democrats their highest vote total in twenty-six years. The Social Democrats, after sixteen years in power, were dropped back to their vote level of 1965. Moreover, the SPD monopoly over the center-left of the electorate was broken as the first new party in thirty years, the Greens, gained entrance to the parliament. Voters have also increasingly turned away from both major parties—the Christian Democrats and the Social Democrats now command the allegiance of only about three-fourths of the electorate. Finally, since 1990 Germany's new voters in the East have further complicated the electoral landscape. About one Eastern voter in five has supported the former Communists and Eastern voters, especially at the elections of 1994 and 1998, have shown a declining interest in such "Western" parties as the Free Democrats and the Greens.

These changes in voter behavior have been accompanied by a growing politicization and mobility of the electorate. Interest in elections, knowledge and concern about issues, and readiness to switch party allegiance have increased. Voters are drifting from their once-firm demographic moorings as the concrete performance of parties, their leadership, and their treatment of policy issues become relatively more important in determining voting behavior than is social class or religion. This is, then, an electorate that is both (1) stable in the sense of supporting prosystem parties over time, and (2) in transition in the sense of becoming more sophisticated about issues and policies and more willing to use the ballot to effect political change and secure the desired policy outputs.

Notes

1. This was not true, of course, for the voters in the few districts the PDS was trying to win in 1994 and 1998. In those seats, the first ballot was more important.
2. Most voters do not understand this system. In one survey, only 30 percent correctly identified the second ballot as more important than the first; 14 percent believed the first was more important than the second (a not entirely incorrect answer for PDS voters in some East Berlin districts in 1994); 48 percent stated that the two ballots were equally important; and the remaining 8 percent of the sample knew nothing about the system. Institut für Demoskopie survey, cited in *Frankfurter Allgemeine Zeitung,* October 5, 1994, p. 5.
3. This is, strictly speaking, not an exception to proportionality, but the application of proportionality if the three-district victory requirement is met.
4. For the 1990 election a one-time only modification of the electoral law was in effect. In order for the smaller parties in the former East Germany to have a better chance to enter the national parliament, they were required to secure a minimum of 5 percent in either the new East German states, the "old" West Germany, or the country as a whole. East German parties were also allowed to submit joint or combined lists in order to increase their chances of meeting the 5 percent minimum. Had the West German Greens cooperated with their East German counterparts, they would have been in the parliament with about 33 seats. These special provisions were added to the electoral law at the insistence of the Federal Constitutional Court, which threw out a law favored by the large West German parties that the Court ruled was unfair to the East Germans.
5. Forschungsgruppe Wahlen post-election surveys cited in *Bundestagswahl 1994,* Report No. 76, October 21, 1994, p. 16 and *Bundestagswahl 1998,* Report No. 91, September 30, 1998, p. 16.
6. Institut für angewandte Sozialforschung, *Politogramm. Bundestagswahl 1987* (Bonn–Bad Godesberg: INFAS 1987), p. 75.
7. See D. M. Farrell and M. Wortmann, "Party Strategies in the Electoral Market: Political Marketing in West Germany, Britain and Ireland," *European Journal of Political Research 15* (1987): 297–318, for an account of the role of marketing specialists in German campaigns.
8. Max Kaase, "Die Bundestagswahl 1972: Probleme und Analysen," *Politische Vierteljahresschrift* 14, no. 2 (May 1973): 158. For more recent campaigns see David P. Conradt, "The 1994 Campaign and Election: An Overview," in *Germany's New Politics,* ed. D. Conradt, et al. (Providence and London: Berghahn Books, 1995), pp. 1–18.
9. Institut für Demoskopie, *Jahrbuch der öffentlichen Meinung, 1968–1973* (Allensbach: Verlag für Demoskopie, 1975), vol. V, p. 337. For corresponding 1976 data, which show

that CDU groups were about as frequent as those campaigning for the Social Democrats, see Elisabeth Noelle-Neumann, "Kampf um die öffentliche Meinung" (manuscript, Institut für Demoskopie, Allensbach, Germany, 1977), p. 25.

10. Between 1977 and 1980 the then–opposition leader and later chancellor, Helmut Kohl, received about $65,000 from the Flick company for his party, the Christian Democrats. The Social Democrats received several large contributions during the same period, largely through their Friedrich Ebert Foundation.

11. The Flick company had sold its share of Daimler-Benz stock at a large profit by reinvesting the money consistent with the provisions in the tax laws that exempt profits from taxation if they are invested in a way that benefits the German economy. The German Foreign Investment Law also allowed a tax exemption for funds invested in non-German projects, provided that such investments through technology transfers or the international division of labor helped the German economy. Flick invested most of the Daimler-Benz profits in the American firm W.R. Grace and Company. In its petition for tax exemption, the Flick firm in 1978 stressed the technical know-how Germany would acquire from the American firm. Flick also emphasized that it would eventually acquire a "dominant" position in the Grace firm. Two years later, however, only three of the thirty-three Grace board members were German.

12. Most analysts found that the party's vote was related to the following demographic and attitudinal characteristics: above-average education, a nostalgia for the old GDR, a feeling of being discriminated against by the West, and strong support for the ideological principles of socialism. For an excellent analysis of the PDS vote, see Jürgen W. Falter and Markus Klein, "Die Wähler der PDS bei der Bundestagswahl 1994," *Aus Politik und Zeitgeschichte,* nos. 51–52 (December 23, 1994): 22–34.

13. Forschungsgruppe Wahlen, *Bundestagswahl 1998,* Mannheim, 1998, pp. 55–63.

14. Kai Arzheimer, Jürgen W. Falter, "Annäherung durch Wandel? Das Wahlverhalten bei der Bundestagswahl 1998 in Ost-West Perspective." *Aus Politik und Zeitgeschichte,* no. 52 (December 18, 1998), p. 39.

15. Forschungsgruppe Wahlen, *Bundestagswahl 1998,* Mannheim, 1998, p. 22 ff.

16. Although the Greens have an anti-technology image, which is partially deserved, the party in 1998 did better among white-collar employees in high-tech occupations than it did among those working in low-tech or traditional technology occupations.

17. Institut für Demoskopie, Survey No. 061; Renate Köcher, "Nachhut oder Vorhut?" *Frankfurter Allgemeine Zeitung,* April 5, 1995, p. 5.

18. Forschungsgruppe Wahlen, *Politbarometer,* October 1994, p. 2.

19. Jürgen W. Falter and Hans Rattinger, "Parteien, Kandidaten und politische Streitfragen bei der Bundestagswahl 1980" (unpublished manuscript, Bundeswehr Hochschule, Munich, June 1981), p. 85.

20. David P. Conradt and Russell J. Dalton, "The West German Electorate and the Party System: Continuity and Change in the 1980s," *Review of Politics* 50, no. 1, p. 6.

21. Institut für angewandte Sozialforschung, *Politogramm: Bundestagswahl 1987* (Bonn–Bad Godesberg: INFAS, 1987), p. 114.

22. Surveys cited in *Der Spiegel* 40, no. 22 (1986): 42, 43.

23. Conradt, "The 1994 Campaign and Election," p. 15.

24. Politbarometer data, Forschungsgruppe Wahlen, cited in *Daten zur Bundestagswahl am 27. 09. 1998,* Federal Press Office, Bonn.

7 Policymaking Institutions 1: Parliament and Executive

In the preceding chapters we have surveyed the historical, socioeconomic, cultural, organizational, and behavioral contexts in which the German political process takes place. We now turn to an examination of the process itself and to its outcomes: governmental policies. The provisional character of the new state created in 1949, the traditional weakness of representative institutions in Germany, the particular circumstances of Allied occupation, and the authoritarian character of the first chancellor, Konrad Adenauer, led to a decision-making process in the early years of the Republic that was clearly dominated by the executive. Since the early 1970s the parliament and the judiciary have become more assertive. Unification, the move of the government and parliament to Berlin, and the growing importance of the European Union also could produce new patterns of policymaking.

At the outset it must also be kept in mind that Germany is a less centralized state than either Britain or France and that the sixteen states that constitute the Federal Republic play important roles, which are more fully discussed in Chapters 8 and 9. In addition, at the national level, which concerns us in this chapter, the states have direct influence on policymaking through the *Bundesrat,* or federal council, an institution whose role has undergone considerable change in recent years. Finally, like other members of the European Union, the Federal Republic has transferred policymaking authority in some areas such as agriculture and (since 1999) the money supply to European institutions.

There are three major national decision-making structures: (1) the parliament, or *Bundestag;* (2) the federal council, or Bundesrat; and (3) the federal government, or executive (the chancellor and the cabinet). In addition, a federal president, indirectly elected and having little independent responsibility for policy, serves as the ceremonial head of state. Each of these institutions has some precedent in the German political tradition, and their contemporary roles reflect in part the influence of this tradition.

Legislative Institutions

THE BUNDESTAG:
THE MAIN POLITICAL BATTLEGROUND

In theory, the center of the policymaking process in the German political system is the Bundestag, or parliament. The Basic Law assigns to it the primary functions of legislation, the election and control of the federal government (chancellor and cabinet), the election of half of the membership of the Federal Constitutional Court, and special responsibilities for supervision of the bureaucracy and military. Its 669 members are elected at least every four years and are the only directly elected political officials in the constitutional structure. In practice, however, this parliament, like its predecessors—the *Reichstag* of the empire (1871–1918) and the Weimar Republic (1919–1933)—has had a long uphill struggle to realize the lofty authority assigned to it in the constitutional documents. Prior to 1949, parliamentary government had both a weak tradition and a poor record of performance in the German political experience.

During the empire, the Reichstag was hindered in the performance of its control and legislative functions by a Prussian-dominated upper house and a government whose chancellor was appointed by the monarch. This, together with executive control of the military and bureaucracy, left the parliament with the power of the purse as its main source of influence, but with little direct initiative in the policymaking process. The chamber's posture toward the government was defensive and reactive, and although the government had to seek some accommodation with Reichstag opinion, there was little parliamentary control over the government. The policy successes of the legendary Bismarck, particularly in foreign policy, awed even the most antimonarchical deputy and intensified the reputation of the executive as a branch that *acted,* whereas the parliament only *talked.*

The Weimar Constitution of 1919 greatly enhanced the power and function of the parliament. The executive (chancellor and cabinet) was now directly responsible to the lower house and could be removed by a vote of no confidence. In what most analysts regard as a major error, however, the framers of the Weimar system also created a strong, directly elected president independent of parliamentary control. This dual executive of president and chancellor, only one of which could be directly controlled by parliament, created the conditions for conflict and competition between the chancellor and parliament on the one hand, and the president and state bureaucracy on the other. The former became identified as Republican institutions; the latter, especially after the 1925 election of the promonarchical, authoritarian Paul von Hindenburg as president, as anti-Republican. This arrangement also put the cabinet somewhere between the chancellor and the president, which encouraged both executives to vie for its support. Thus executive responsibility was not clearly fixed.

In addition, the growing polarization of politics during the Weimar period steadily reduced the strength of pro-Republican parties in parliament. After the first parliamentary election in 1919 about three-fourths of the deputies belonged to parties more or less committed to the Republic, but in the last elections of 1932 most deputies belonged to parties (Nazi, Nationalist, and Communist) committed to the destruction in one way or another of the very institution and constitution they were supposed to support. Parliament became increasingly immobile; successive governments in the early 1930s had no parliamentary majority supporting them, yet neither could the parliamentary opposition secure a majority for a new government. The strong president, however, at the request of the chancellor, could and did rule by decree, hardly an ideal situation for a fledgling democracy. Through the incessant attacks of the anti-Republican parties, especially the Nazis and Communists, but also through their own inexperience and ineptness in the ways of democratic politics, the pro-Republican parties and the parliament itself became identified in the public mind as weak, ineffective, indecisive—a *Quasselbude* (gossip chamber), as the Nazis' propaganda chief, Josef Goebbels, termed it.

The world economic collapse between 1929 and 1930, combined with the government's feeble response, all but ended the parliamentary system. Lacking a majority, the government was unable to act without the crutch of presidential decrees. Government by executive fiat made the legislature superfluous. Finally, by approving Hitler's Enabling Act in March 1933, it ceased to function as a lawmaking body and became merely an occasional forum for the dictator's public pronouncements.

The Bundestag, established in 1949, inherited this tragic parliamentary tradition. Unlike earlier parliaments, however, in theory at least it no longer had to compete with an executive over which it had no direct control. For the first time in German constitutional history, the Basic Law assigned sole control over government and bureaucracy to the parliament. Although this control function of the parliament was undercut by the strong leadership of Chancellor Adenauer during the early years of the Republic, the Bundestag since the mid-1960s has begun to assume a role in the policymaking process more congruent with its formal and legal position.

The Parliament's Two Homes: Bonn (1949–1999) and Berlin

German legislators in Bonn met in the most unpretentious surroundings of any modern parliament. The chamber itself was first built in 1949 as an addition to a former teachers' college. Until 1970 most deputies had to share offices, which were once classrooms, with one or two of their colleagues. From 1988 to 1992 the parliament convened in a restored waterworks building while the old chamber was being completely rebuilt. The city of Bonn, with 300,000 inhabitants crowded into an area suitable for 150,000, was by no means a capital city in the classic European sense. Most deputies did not maintain homes in Bonn but lived in rented rooms or apartments and returned to their homes and families on weekends. For some members, life in Bonn was somewhat similar to their student days, with rented rooms and landladies. Some parliamentarians even slept in their offices to save costs.

The Bonn-Berlin Debate.   After unification in 1990 a lively debate began over whether the Bundestag should move to Berlin, the official capital, or remain in Bonn. A growing number of political leaders from other states and cities contended that the postwar federal system would be weakened by moving all government offices from Bonn to Berlin. The cost, estimated at over $70 billion, was also frequently cited as a factor against a move to Berlin. In spite of its disadvantages, Bonn is associated with West Germany's postwar transformation into a stable democracy and a model member of the Western community of nations. For some, Berlin is a symbol of Germany's militaristic, authoritarian, and totalitarian past—the Prussian Kaisers and Hitler all waged war from Berlin. Berlin's supporters countered that it was unfair to blame an entire city for the acts of a few individuals many years ago. They pointed to Berlin's steadfast commitment to Western values during the darkest days of the Cold War. The city, located in the former GDR, also needed the economic boost that the parliament and government would bring.

On June 20, 1991, following an emotional eleven-hour debate, the Bundestag voted by a narrow margin to return the seat of government and the parliament to Berlin. In the vote the deputies were not bound by party discipline, but only by their individual consciences. Support for both cities cut across party lines. Chancellor Kohl supported Berlin, but his finance minister wanted the government to remain in Bonn. The decision for Berlin was one of the most important in the chamber's history. It affirmed the parliament's commitment to integrate the Eastern states into the larger Federal Republic as soon as possible. It was not until 1996, however, that concrete plans for the actual move to Berlin were finalized. The parliament, chancellor, and ten of the government's fifteen ministries finally moved to Berlin in 1999. Ministries for education, foreign assistance, environmental affairs, science and technology, and agriculture will at least for the time being remain in Bonn.

Mindful of Berlin's past image as the city where the emperor and Hitler attempted to dominate Europe by military force, the city's planners, together with Germany's political leadership, have attempted to design the old/new capital in an open, international, and avant garde style. The design of many buildings has been entrusted to renowned international architects such as Sir Norman Foster. He was in charge of renovating the old Reichstag, the home of the "new" Bundestag. The Chancellery, President's Office, and other governmental structures will be adorned with numerous works of art, commissioned after international competitions. This "public-art spending spree," according to one authority, is "unrivaled in modern times." The total budget for Berlin artwork exceeds the amount that the United States government has spent during the past thirty-five years. Over 140 artists from around the world are involved in creating new pieces for the public buildings. The main facade of the parliament, for example, will be adorned with a $1-million mural by the renowned American artist Ellsworth Kelly. Many of the new works will not shirk from attempting to deal with Germany's totalitarian past. Most significant in this area is the planned national memorial to Jewish Holocaust victims, which will be built south of the Brandenburg Gate.[1]

Structure and Organization

The key organizing agents of the Bundestag are the parliamentary groups of the political parties, or *Fraktionen* (caucuses). A Fraktion is a group of parliamentary members all belonging to the same party. From an organizational and operational standpoint, the parliament is composed of these Fraktionen and not individual deputies. The size of a party's Fraktion determines the size of its representation on committees, the number of committee chairpersons it can name, and the amount of office space and clerical staff it receives, as well as its representation on the important executive bodies of the chamber, the Council of Elders and the Presidium.[2] Although there have been independent deputies not formally affiliated with any party, they have invariably had "visiting rights" with a Fraktion.

The importance of the political parties in organizing the work of the chamber also extends to the relationship between the leadership of the parties and the individual deputy. As in Britain, party discipline, and hence party voting, are high in the parliament: Approximately 85 to 90 percent of all votes are straight party votes, with all deputies following the instructions of the Fraktion leadership or the results of a caucus vote on an upcoming bill. Free votes, when the party gives no binding instructions to its deputies, are rare. Nonetheless, the constitution guarantees that a deputy who cannot support his or her party can leave its Fraktion and join another without having to resign, at least for the duration of the legislative period.

The daily agenda of the chamber is determined by the Council of Elders—in essence a steering committee—composed of the Bundestag's president (always a member of the largest Fraktion), the four vice presidents, and twelve to fifteen representatives of all Fraktionen. The council schedules debates, allots time to each party, and assigns committee chairmanships to each in proportion to its parliamentary strength. A second executive body in the Bundestag is its Presidium, consisting of the president and vice presidents of the chamber. The Presidium is responsible for the overall administration of the chamber, from its furnishings to the recruitment of clerical and research personnel. In theory, partisan factors play a lesser role in the conduct of its business than they do in the Council of Elders.

Committees.   Parliamentary committees are more important in Germany than in Britain or France, yet less important than in the U.S. Congress. The Bundestag has twenty-two standing committees. Both the partisan composition and leadership of these bodies are proportional to party strength in the chamber. Thus, unlike in the American system, the opposition party or parties have a share of committee chairmanships. In addition, German committees cannot pigeonhole or reject bills, but must examine them, take testimony, and, if necessary, propose amendments to the entire house. The activities of committees generally reflect the parliament's self-image as a responsible critic of the government but not a rival force. Committees do not have the large independent staffs of their American counterparts. In meetings, most of which are closed to the public, the drafts of legislation are frequently explained to the lawmakers by the ministerial officials who wrote the bill. Until recently, parliamentary committees were not aggressive in the use of their investigatory and information-gathering powers. This resulted in part from the chamber's traditional deference to the government and state bureaucracy and in part from the party loyalty of the committee majority to the government. This latter phenomenon is common to parliamentary committees in unitary systems, where support for the government inhibits the independence of the committee and parliamentary majority, especially in the exercise of their control function.

The Members

The members of the Bundestag constitute part of Germany's political elite. The chancellor, almost all cabinet ministers, and all parliamentary state secretaries (the minister's political assistants) are drawn from its ranks. Thus the social background of these 669 people reveals something about the quality and characteristics valued by the prevailing elite culture and by that relatively small group of party leaders at national, state, and district levels who, through their control of the nomination process, play a key role in Bundestag recruitment.

The social background of Bundestag deputies has changed dramatically between the first Bundestag in 1949 and the fourteenth Bundestag, elected in 1998. Almost half of the first parliament (1949–1953) was composed of employees (manual and lower-level white-collar workers) dependent on wages for a livelihood.[3] The value placed on this type of individual declined rapidly after 1949, and by 1961 less than 15 percent of parliamentary deputies came from this relatively modest occupational background. Since 1961 and even after the Social Democratic victories of 1969 and 1972, this proportion has not increased.

Two specific occupational groups that by the 1980s were especially prominent in the chamber were civil servants and interest group leaders. Together these two occupations accounted for over 60 percent of the membership.[4] And civil servants are represented at a rate about ten times greater than their proportion in the population at large. Unlike in Britain or the United States, a German civil servant can be elected to legislative office (local, state, or national) without resigning from the service. Indeed, the existing civil service regulations encourage standing for public office. A government employee desiring to run receives a six-week leave of absence with full pay during the election campaign. If elected, he or she takes additional leave for the duration of the legislative term. Moreover, while on parliamentary leave, the civil servant receives pension credit and normal promotions. The potential conflict of interest between civil servants serving as parliamentary deputies with, among other duties, the responsibility for setting civil service salary scales has as yet not prompted any change in the laws.[5]

Apart from these incentives, the strong representation of state officials in parliament is also consistent with the expert, administrative orientation to politics that characterizes German political culture. As Gerhard Loewenberg has pointed out:

> In a society noted for the early development of a modern bureaucracy, government is still widely regarded as a purely administrative matter. From this, it is an easy step to the conclusion that administrators are the best qualified occupants of any governmental position, and that the parliamentary mandate is a type of administrative office.[6]

Interest group leaders and functionaries from business, industry, agriculture, and labor constitute another major part of the chamber's membership. Like civil servants, they have had extensive experience with bureaucratic structures and procedures. One study found that over half of all members of parliament from 1972 to

1987 had some paid or unpaid (voluntary) function in an interest group.[7] Among the middle-class parties, the CDU and FDP, almost 70 percent of their deputies held some office in an interest group.[8] Interest group representatives were also very prominent in the Labor, Transportation, and Family and Health committees.[9] Thus almost 70 percent of the deputies can be said to have essentially bureaucratic backgrounds as civil servants or interest-group representatives. This leaves workers, housewives, farmers, and even those in business and professional occupations heavily underrepresented in the chamber. Unable to take temporary leave from a job or career, they are at a comparative disadvantage to those in occupations strongly related to the activities of parliament.

The new deputies from the former GDR who entered the parliament following unification in 1990 have occupational backgrounds quite distinct from their West German colleagues. Almost one-third of this group are either natural scientists, engineers, physicists, or chemists, as compared to only about 5 percent of the members from West Germany. East Germans in these positions were less likely to be tainted or discredited by associations with the Communist party and above all the secret police (*Stasi*).[10] Many lawyers and civil servants in the former East Germany, as well as intellectuals and university professors and teachers in the social sciences and humanities, were in some way compromised by the Stasi regime.

In addition to changes in occupational backgrounds, the educational level of the deputies has steadily increased. Between 1949 and 1983, the proportion of Bundestag members with some education beyond the basic eight-year *Volksschule* increased from 70 percent to 95 percent; by 1998, about 30 percent of the members held doctoral degrees. Younger deputies are most likely to enter the chamber with this higher educational background. Finally, the proportion of women in the parliament has increased steadily from less than 10 percent in 1949 to over 30 percent in 1998. This is one of the highest proportions of female members in any European parliament. In Britain, by contrast, only 18 percent of MP's (members of parliament) are female; in the United States less than 15 percent of Congress members and senators are women.

These trends apply to all parties in the chamber from 1949 to 1998. Indeed, in terms of social background, the first Bundestag in 1949 was actually more representative of the total population than were succeeding parliaments. German parliamentarians have become more an internally unified professional elite, distinct from the general population by social background and training. These developments certainly facilitate a consensual policymaking style at the elite level and are indicative of a certain political maturity. They also relate to the increased assertiveness of the chamber vis-à-vis the executive in recent years. Yet the increasingly closed character of the membership also raises serious questions about democratic representation and the access of especially disadvantaged social groups to the decision-making centers of the system. Whether the addition of members from the former East Germany will change this pattern remains to be seen. Thus far, Easterners have been content to follow the lead of their more experienced West German colleagues. But regardless of party, they have tended to emphasize the unique and critical problems faced by their constituents in the new East German states.

Electing and Controlling the Government

The Bundestag elects the federal chancellor. Unlike the procedures under the Weimar Constitution, the chamber does not elect specific ministers but only the chancellor, who then appoints the cabinet ministers. Although this election is by secret ballot, it follows strict party lines and has, with the exception of the CDU/CSU's unsuccessful attempt to bring down the Brandt government in 1972, provided few surprises.

The parliament's efforts to control the government and state bureaucracy are, of course, far more complex than the election of the chancellor. One important control procedure is the question hour, a practice adopted from English parliamentary practice, in which a deputy orally questions the relevant minister or the minister's representative about a particular problem. These questions vary considerably in tone and content. Many deal with citizen complaints, which a deputy can take for mutually beneficial publicity to the "highest level." Others deal with more fundamental questions about the direction of governmental policy. Since 1949, use of the question hour has increased dramatically. During the first Bundestag—in retrospect, the pinnacle of executive domination—members asked the government only about 400 questions over four years. By the fifth Bundestag (1965–1969), this had increased to about 10,500; and during the seventh Bundestag (1972–1976), almost 19,000 questions were put to the government by the deputies.

To supplement the question hour, an *Aktuelle Stunde* (an hour devoted to current developments) procedure was added in 1965. According to this procedure a group of deputies (usually from the opposition) can petition the Bundestag leadership and the government for a question period about a particularly pressing problem. Deputies may also submit to the government written questions to be answered in writing and inserted in the record. If at least twenty-five deputies submit such a petition, it is regarded as a minor inquiry needing no parliamentary debate; if at least thirty deputies submit a written question, it becomes a major inquiry, and a plenary debate must be held on the question and the government's reply. Almost 40 percent of all major inquiries were made during the first Bundestag (1949–1953). This was a time of great debates about the fundamental principles and policies of the Republic: the Western Alliance, European integration, federalism, rearmament, and the market versus the planned economy.

A further control procedure is the chamber's right to investigate governmental activities and its power to demand the appearance of any government or state official. Upon the request of at least one-fourth of the deputies, an investigating committee must be formed, with partisan composition proportional to party strength in the entire house. Therein lies one of the major problems of parliamentary investigating committees in a unitary system with disciplined parties. The possibility that its findings may embarrass the government and hinder the committee members' own political careers is an impediment to the more freewheeling investigatory practices found under separation-of-power systems with loose party discipline, as in the United States.

Furthermore, there is at best a weak tradition for parliamentary investigations in Germany. The historical relationship of subordination to the executive, the cultural bias in favor of the state bureaucracy, and the relatively inadequate staffing of parliamentary committees have worked against the effective use of the investigatory function as a means of control.

Finally, the most drastic form of parliamentary control is a formal vote of no confidence in the chancellor and his cabinet. Because of the stable, disciplined parties and the Basic Law's positive or constructive vote of no confidence (discussed later in this chapter), this procedure has been used only twice in the chamber's history.

The Parliament in the Post-Adenauer Era

Since the 1960s the parliament's use of its investigative powers and its efforts to increase public knowledge and involvement in its work have become more extensive. Although public committee hearings (the English word has been adopted) on proposed legislation, for example, have been possible since 1952, little or no use was made of this provision until the mid-1960s. In the fourth Bundestag (1961–1965) only four bills were given public committee hearings, but in the fifth parliament (1965–1969) about sixty public hearings on proposed legislation were held. Public debates have become more lively and focused, partly because of increased issue conflict between the parties and the reduction of time limits for speakers. Television coverage of important debates also has enhanced the image of the chamber. Debates can now be scheduled according to policy areas—for example, one week on foreign policy, the next on education. Thus the government can be questioned about a specific set of problems over an extended period.

The overall effect of these changes has been to make the parliament a more independent if not sovereign institution, but it should not be exaggerated. The initiation of legislation is still for the most part the responsibility of the chancellor and the cabinet. Party discipline and the hierarchy within the Fraktionen still limit the impact of the lone deputy. Only about 40 percent of bills introduced by individual deputies, most of a private and marginal character, are passed, in comparison to 85 percent of those introduced by the government.[11] In addition, the conditions associated with the often-discussed decline of parliament in other countries—the increasingly technical character of government that requires expertise available only in the executive, the alleged necessity for speedy decisions, and the strict discipline imposed by modern mass parties—are also prevalent in Germany.

In terms of its influence vis-à-vis the executive, the Bundestag now occupies a middle position when compared to the U.S. Congress and the British Parliament. It is not as independent of the executive as is the U.S. Congress, but neither is it as controlled by the government as the British House of Commons. The Bundestag supplies the government with a working majority, but through a strong committee system and the prevalence of coalition governments it has been able also to maintain some independence from the executive. In the preparation of bills, even government bills, the Bundestag has more influence than the House of Commons. The German chancellor, in contrast to the British prime minister, also has less influence on the day-to-day schedule and agenda of the parliament. The German executive must engage in more informal negotiations with the leadership of the parliamentary parties than in Great Britain. The Bundestag in committee can make major changes in a government bill without forcing the government to

TABLE 7.1   Trust in parliament: major European countries, 1999

	Germany	Britain	France	Italy	EU*
Tend to trust	45	36	37	30	41
Tend not to trust	42	48	48	55	49
Don't know	13	16	15	15	11
Total	100	100	100	100	100

*Fifteen-nation European Union average.
Source: *Eurobarometer*, no. 51 (Spring 1999), p. B3.

resign; numerous bills submitted by the government have in fact been extensively rewritten by the parliament with both government and opposition parties influencing the bills' final form.[12]

The Bundestag has secured a firm position in the Republic's political life. The great majority of Germans regard it as a necessary and important political institution.[13] Citizen belief in the responsiveness of the institution also has grown over the past decades. When asked in 1951 whether a parliamentary deputy would respond to their letter, almost half of a national sample thought they would receive no answer; by 1983 the proportion of the electorate with such a pessimistic assessment of parliamentary responsiveness had dropped to only 19 percent.[14] As the data in Table 7.1 show, the German parliament has also fared well in comparison to the legislative assemblies of other major European countries, most of which have stronger democratic and parliamentary traditions than Germany. The proportion of Germans who believe they can trust the Bundestag is actually higher than in Britain or France. The German proportion is also comparable to the average found in the fifteen-member European Union. Given the history and pre-1949 record of German parliaments, this is a substantial achievement.

THE BUNDESRAT: THE "QUIET" SECOND CHAMBER

Located close to the Bundestag is Germany's second legislative body, the Bundesrat, or federal council. Few non-Germans are aware of its existence, much less importance. Even many Germans do not know how powerful this institution can be in the legislative process. The purpose of the Bundesrat is to represent the interests of the states (*Länder*) of the federation in the national legislative process. It is the continuation of a tradition that extends back to the Bundesrat of the empire. The unified Reich established in 1871 was possible only after Bismarck and the Prussians had made certain concessions to the states—specifically, a strong representation in Berlin and the right of states to implement state-related national policy. In effect, this bargain of 1871 meant that Berlin would rule but that the states would administer the rules. The framers of the Basic Law, many state officials themselves with strong Allied and especially American encouragement, returned to the federal structure of the empire and Weimar Republic and in some ways gave the Länder, now without Prussia, more influence than they had in either of the two earlier regimes.

Each state has 3 to 6 votes in the Bundesrat, depending on size, for a total of 68. The delegate from each state must cast the state's votes as a unit, on instructions from the state government. Thus the state's delegate is not free to vote as he or she sees fit, nor is the parliamentary opposition in these states represented in the Bundesrat. The 68 votes of the Bundesrat are apportioned as follows: the four most populous states (North Rhine–Westphalia, Bavaria, Baden-Württemberg, and Lower Saxony) each receive 6 votes; the middle-sized states (Hesse, the Rhineland-Palatinate, Schleswig-Holstein, Berlin, and four of the new Eastern states, Saxony, Thuringia, Saxony-Anhalt, and Brandenburg) have 4 votes each; the four smallest states (the Saarland, Hamburg, Bremen, and the Eastern Land of Mecklenburg–West Pomerania) receive 3 votes each. The degree of malapportionment in the Bundesrat ranges from 1 vote for every 233,000 inhabitants of Bremen to 1 vote for every 2.8 million citizens of North Rhine–Westphalia. Thus although the Bundesrat does not represent the states as equal units (as the U.S. Senate does), the smaller states are still clearly favored in the distribution of votes.

Prior to unification in 1990 the number of votes allotted to each state ranged from 5 votes for the large states to 3 for the smallest states.[15] Under this arrangement the four large states had 20 of the chamber's 41 votes, more than enough to veto any measure requiring a two-thirds majority. Thus the small states could not gang up on the large states and force them to pay for programs they opposed.

With unification, however, this existing formula would have left the big four with only 20 seats in a chamber of over 60 and hence unable to block legislation. In negotiations with East Germany that preceded the October 1990 unification, the four largest West German states insisted on a new formula that would preserve their veto power. After extensive bargaining, with Bavaria taking the lead for the other large states, the current formula was incorporated into the August 1990 Unity Treaty as an amendment to Article 51 of the Basic Law. The large states now have 6 instead of 5 votes and, with a total of 24 seats, can still block legislation requiring a two-thirds majority. Party politics had little to do with this compromise. It was largely a question of the large and richer states acting to preserve their positions within the enlarged federation.[16]

Functions

According to the Basic Law, the Bundesrat can initiate legislation, and it must approve all laws directly related to the states' responsibilities, such as education, police matters, state and local finance questions, land use, and most transportation issues. In addition, any legislation affecting state boundaries, national emergencies, and proposed constitutional amendments requires Bundesrat approval.

In practice, however, the Bundesrat, at least until 1969, has rarely initiated legislation or exercised its veto powers.[17] Its influence in the policymaking process has nevertheless increased since 1949, and especially since 1972 it has become a more politicized institution. This somewhat paradoxical development is due largely to changes in (1) the actual composition of the chamber's membership, (2) the determination of those areas in which the Bundesrat has an absolute veto, and (3) the party control of the two chambers of parliament, the divided government of Germany between 1972 and 1982 and from 1991 to 1998.

Formal vs. Actual Composition of Membership. In its early years, the Bundesrat was more an administrative than a policymaking institution—or, as one authority has said, it was "between" politics and administration.[18] Because the states have to administer much of federal law, the Bundesrat has been mainly concerned with examining governmental legislation from the standpoint of how the states would implement it. This function of the institution was related to the types of people who actually did the work of the chamber: state-level civil servants who had been deputized by the formal members, state political officials. Thus, with the exception of the monthly plenary sessions, state-level civil servants have far outnumbered politicians in the chamber.

Most civil servants come from the ministries of the formal Bundesrat members. Originally the framers of the Basic Law included this deputation provision (contained in Article 51) with the expectation that it would be used only rarely, when regular members could not attend committee and plenary sessions because of state commitments. In practice, however, in the Bundesrat's committees, where most of the work takes place, bureaucrats outnumber politicians (the ministers sent by the states) by about a 15 to 1 ratio.[19] Thus at a typical Bundesrat session there are few, if any, political heavyweights. This makes the chamber quite different from the much larger and very politicized Bundestag. According to one authority, "The Bundesrat's meetings are always quiet, never interrupted by applause, seldom in the spotlight of public attention."[20]

When ready for a formal vote, the draft legislation is presented to the plenary session, which usually approves pro forma the result of the committee's work. Thus, in practice, the Bundesrat does not reject bills outright; but early in the policymaking process, after committee study, it would recommend changes in legislation designed to facilitate its implementation at the state level. In most cases, the expert advice of the Bundesrat does produce revisions or withdrawal by the government of the proposed legislation, thus making an outright veto unnecessary but also testifying to the influence of the states, through their governmental administrations, on the national policymaking institutions.

Expansion of Veto Power. The framers of the Basic Law anticipated that only about 10 percent of all federal legislation would require Bundesrat approval and hence be subject to the chamber's veto. In practice, however, through bargaining in the legal committees of each house and judicial interpretation, the scope of the Bundesrat's absolute veto power has been enlarged to the point at which it can now veto

roughly 60 percent of all federal legislation.[21] This unforeseen development occurred largely because many federal laws that refer to matters not subject to Bundesrat veto nonetheless contain provisions that set forth how the states are to
administer and implement the legislation. Citing Article 84 of the Basic Law, the
states have argued that because they are instructed as to how the federal legislation is to be administered, the legislation requires Bundesrat approval in both its substantive and procedural aspects. This coresponsibility theory has generally been
supported by the courts. Thus if the law affects the states, even if only in its
administrative aspects, the entire law falls under the Bundesrat's veto power. This
has also, in most cases, applied to any subsequent extension of or amendments to
the legislation that the Bundesrat may propose. Administrative decrees and regulations issued by the government require Bundesrat approval under this interpretation.

The enlargement of Bundesrat power, however, has prompted some students of
constitutional politics to propose that the powers of the Länder and federal government be more explicitly stated in the constitution. And in an important decision in
September 1974, the Federal Constitutional Court ruled that legislation that amends
existing statutes does not need Bundesrat approval if the original legislation has
passed the chamber previously.

Divided Parliamentary Control.   From 1972 to 1982 and again from 1991 to 1998
the Bundestag and the Bundesrat were controlled by different parties. Although in
opposition in the Bundestag, the Christian Democrats from 1972 to 1982 held a majority in the Bundesrat. During this period some Christian Democratic leaders argued that the Bundesrat would be an ideal instrument with which the party could
block, or at least force revisions on, government programs.[22] In spite of its slim advantage in the chamber, the CDU/CSU delegates voted *en bloc* against the Brandt
government's treaties with the Soviet Union and Poland and its transportation program, as well as its urban finance and tax reform, land use, and liberalized divorce
and abortion bills. In areas where the Bundesrat had an absolute veto, the CDU/CSU
delegations forced major compromises on the government and in some cases—such
as the higher education planning law (1974)—completely blocked the proposed
government bill.[23] The Bundesrat also vetoed several key policies of the Schmidt
cabinet, including a proposed tax increase and the government's bill on radicals in
public employment. Although in the majority, however, the CDU/CSU did not attempt to draft and introduce alternative programs to those offered by the government
in the Bundestag. Its efforts were concentrated largely on delaying legislation and
forcing changes on the government.[24]

Between 1991 and 1998 the Social Democrats were the majority party in the
Bundesrat, although the Christian Democratic government held a slim majority in
the Bundestag. The Social Democrats used their majority to block or force changes
in a variety of government initiatives. The 1993 Solidarity Pact, which refinanced
the costs of unification and increased taxes, was passed only after concessions were
made to the Social Democrats. In 1994 the chamber rejected the abortion law passed
by the Bundestag because it required women seeking an abortion in the first
trimester of pregnancy to be counseled. The constitutional amendments proposed by

the Constitutional Commission in 1994 (see Chapter 10 for a description of these amendments) were also blocked by the Bundesrat even though they passed the Bundestag. The Kohl government's plans for the deregulation of many economic activities and the loosening of restrictions on part-time employment also had little chance in the SPD-controlled Bundesrat.

The most controversial Bundesrat vote in recent years was the 1997 veto of the Kohl government's tax reform legislation. The government had proposed a very comprehensive tax reform package designed to make German business more competitive in the global economy. It was the cornerstone for Kohl's response to record high unemployment and stagnant economic growth. The Kohl government charged the SPD with pursuing a "blockade policy" with its Bundesrat majority and with acting against the interests of the states, including those that it governed, in order to pursue a national strategy designed to defeat Kohl at the 1998 election.

It would be difficult, however, to develop the Bundesrat into a coequal second chamber. Neither the constitution nor the structure and tradition of the house favors such a development. The constitution does not provide any legal mechanism for the Bundesrat to bring down the government elected by the Bundestag. In addition, the strength of each party group always depends on state-level political conditions, which can change rapidly. Because there are now sixteen different state elections every four years, most majorities in the Bundesrat would be very unstable. For the Bundesrat to become a consistently effective opposition to the government in the Bundestag, the state leaders who control the delegations must also be willing to accept directives from the national leadership.[25] Generally, where there has been considerable interparty unity at both the state and national levels and a clear partisan division—such as in education (comprehensive school, university reform) or land policy—Bundesrat opposition has been strong and successful. But many issues still do not fall into these categories. The CDU-controlled Bundesrat has rejected bills that the CDU in the Bundestag has approved; similarly, the Bundesrat has unanimously passed some legislation opposed by the CDU in the Bundestag. The Social Democrats have had similar experiences. In 1992 the new Eastern Land of Brandenburg, governed by an SPD-led coalition, supported an increase in the value-added tax (a form of sales tax levied on products or services as value is added to them in the production and distribution process) in spite of the strong opposition on the part of the national SPD leadership. The prospect of more revenue for the economic reconstruction of their state was more appealing to the Brandenburg Social Democrats than was the unity of the national party. Shortly after taking office in 1998, Chancellor Schröder's proposed tax legislation was strongly opposed above all by the larger states, including those governed by his own party. Thus the party itself must be in agreement if the Bundesrat is to become an effective instrument of opposition.

If, however, the parliamentary (Bundestag) opposition ever achieved a two-thirds majority (46 delegates) in the Bundesrat, it could at least temporarily wreak havoc with the government's program. In that case any Bundesrat veto, regardless of whether the proposed legislation is in the states' area of competence, could be overridden by the government only if it could muster a two-thirds majority in the

Bundestag. All these developments and potential future changes make the current Bundesrat a much more political institution and thus a greater object of controversy than it was in the early years of the Republic.

Executive Institutions: Chancellor and Cabinet

CHANCELLOR DEMOCRACY

In framing the Basic Law of the Federal Republic, the delegates to the parliamentary council centered executive authority in the chancellor. Unlike under the Weimar Constitution, the chancellor does not share executive power with a strong president, nor do the provisions of the Basic Law make the chancellor as vulnerable to shifting parliamentary alignments as were the Weimar executives. In some respects the German chancellor's constitutional position is similar to that of the chancellor under the Imperial Constitution, although his powers over cabinet ministers and the Länder are not as extensive.

The position of the chancellor as the chief executive of state is defined in Article 65 of the Basic Law:

> The Federal Chancellor shall determine, and be responsible for, the general policy guidelines. Within the limits set by these guidelines, each Federal Minister shall conduct the affairs of his department autonomously and on his own responsibility. The Federal Government shall decide on differences of opinion between Federal Ministers. The Federal Chancellor shall conduct the affairs of the Federal Government in accordance with rules of procedure adopted by it and approved by the Federal President.

It is the chancellor who also appoints and dismisses cabinet ministers, whose primary political responsibility is to the chancellor's policies and not to the parliament. The power of the chancellor to set guidelines and his sole responsibility for the appointment and removal of ministers place him in a stronger position than his Weimar counterparts. Although ministers are not subordinate to the chancellor, as under the Imperial Constitution, the Bonn chancellor supervises their work and has veto power over their decisions if they contradict his general guidelines. Moreover, unlike the case in the Weimar system, the parliament cannot remove individual ministers, but must vote no confidence in the chancellor before the cabinet is also dismissed.[26]

The framers of the Basic Law also made it more difficult for the parliamentary opposition to bring down a chancellor than was the case during the Weimar Republic. A parliamentary majority against him does not suffice; the opposition must also have a majority in favor of a new chancellor before the incumbent chancellor is dismissed. This positive vote of no confidence was added to protect the chancellor from the shifting and unstable parliamentary alignments that brought down many Weimar chancellors.

In practice, as discussed in Chapter 5, the unstable multiparty system of Weimar, which the framers of the Basic Law had in mind when drafting the constructive vote of no confidence, has not reemerged. The concentration of electoral support in two large, well-disciplined parties and two or three smaller parties has ensured most chancellors firm parliamentary majorities. The positive vote of no confidence has been attempted only twice. In April 1972 the Christian Democrats filed a no confidence motion against Chancellor Brandt and nominated their parliamentary leader, Rainer Barzel, as the new chancellor. The CDU's leadership was convinced that it had enough support from its own ranks and from dissatisfied members of the Free Democrats to remove Chancellor Brandt. The motion failed, however, as the parliament in a dramatic secret ballot split 247 to 247, with 2 abstentions. Apparently one or two of the CDU members either abstained or voted for Brandt. In October 1982, however, the Christian Democrats, with the help of the Free Democrats, did successfully employ the constructive no-confidence vote when an absolute majority of the parliament voted to remove Helmut Schmidt and replace him with Helmut Kohl. About five months later, the electorate gave its stamp of approval to this change as the Kohl government (CDU/CSU–FDP) was returned with a large majority.

The chancellor is constitutionally superior to the cabinet, whose members serve at his pleasure and not that of the parliament. Yet the exact division of responsibility between chancellor and minister is, in theory, difficult to determine. After giving the chancellor responsibility for the overall direction of government policy, Article 65 goes on to state that "within this policy, each minister conducts the affairs of his department independently and under his own responsibility." This has been interpreted to mean that the chancellor cannot interfere in the day-to-day affairs of a department, deal directly with a civil servant within a department, or bypass a minister and issue direct instructions to a department.[27] But the chancellor can dismiss a minister or order him or her directly to rescind or abandon a particular policy or planned policy on the basis of this guideline authority. In addition, in times of war the chancellor assumes supreme command of the armed forces from the defense minister.

The chancellor, however, will rarely give formal instructions to a minister. The communication of chancellor guidelines usually takes place through cabinet discussions, informal face-to-face contacts, and advisory memoranda from the chancellor's office to the ministries. The ministries, in turn, are required to keep the chancellor's office informed of developments in their areas, and the chancellor must clear all ministerial statements.

Thus the ministers are constitutionally more than civil servants, but less than British cabinet ministers. They do, however, have legal and administrative responsibility, and in practice, through their positions in the party and coalition and through procedures such as the question hour in parliament, they have also acquired political responsibility.

The Chancellor's Office

Consistent with his constitutional position, the chancellor has facilities and staff that exceed those of the British and French prime ministers but are less than those of the American or French presidents. The chancellor's office has a staff of about 500, headed by either a cabinet minister without portfolio or a high-ranking civil servant. The office is organized into departments, usually directed by senior civil servants, that correspond to the cabinet ministries and act as a liaison between the chancellor and the respective ministry. The chancellor's office has above all a right to information, and its key officials, with daily access to the chancellor, are among the most influential members of the government. The office is also a type of institutional watchdog over the various ministries to ensure that the chancellor's guidelines and cabinet decisions are indeed being carried out.[28]

When one considers the constitutional position of the chancellor and adds to it the strong personality, popular appeal, and authoritarian style of its first incumbent, Konrad Adenauer, the origins of the term *chancellor democracy* become evident. With presidential-like control over the cabinet, the bureaucracy, and his political party, Adenauer was able in fact to bypass parliament in many policymaking cases. Adenauer, supported by Article 65 (which he interpreted liberally to his benefit), dominated his cabinet and led the government unlike any chancellor during the Weimar Republic. His relationship to his ministers was not unlike that of an American president to his cabinet members or that of the Imperial chancellor to his state secretaries.

The Cabinet

In forming a cabinet, the chancellor has to consider (1) the commitments made to his coalition partner, (2) the demands of the various factions within his own party, and (3) the objective needs of each position in relation to the qualifications of the various candidates. Most students of German leadership would agree that the first two criteria have outweighed the third criterion in the cabinet selection process. Cabinet size has ranged from sixteen during the first Adenauer government (1949–1953) and the current Schröder cabinet to twenty-two in the Erhard governments (1963–1966). Expansion of cabinet size beyond eighteen seems invariably connected to coalition and internal party considerations—that is, some important faction or personality demands to be accommodated. For example, in 1990 the Free Democrats, after increasing their vote from 9 to 11 percent, requested an additional minister. Chancellor Kohl also had to find room in his new cabinet for several representatives from the former East Germany. To create more cabinet posts, an existing ministry may also be divided.

The major ministries, however, have remained relatively intact or have expanded through consolidation. They are: foreign affairs, defense, finance, interior (internal security, police), justice, labor, economics, agriculture, and transportation. Others were created over the past three decades and have grown in importance: foreign assistance, education, science, health, the environment, women's issues, and urban affairs.

Generally, the classic ministries—foreign affairs, defense, finance, interior, and justice—are the most important cabinet posts. Their incumbents are correspondingly viewed as the strongest cabinet members and the heirs apparent to the chancellor.

Cabinet Ministers.   German cabinet ministers, like their counterparts in Britain and France, have usually achieved their rank after an extensive and successful apprenticeship in parliament, a party, or a professional career. Analyses of the social and political backgrounds of cabinet members have found four major pathways to ministerial office:

1. through a successful rise up the *party* hierarchy and into the circle of ministerial candidates;
2. through successful *occupational* experience, especially in business, the free professions, or interest group administration;
3. through *local and state officeholding* or *civil service* experience, especially in areas such as justice, finance, and economics; and
4. through *expert status* in an important field such as science or education.[29]

Given the number of qualified applicants, achieving ministerial office is in itself a considerable accomplishment and brings a variety of additional political and administrative responsibilities as well as substantial personal power and prestige. A minister inherits the traditionally strong German respect for state authority. Responsible for the "house," as a ministry is commonly termed, he or she receives a substantial salary (about $200,000 annually plus a generous expense allowance) and pension, not to mention a chauffeur-driven Mercedes limousine. Moreover, the minister's power and influence within the party usually are also enhanced by ministerial office. A minister's power within the cabinet depends on his or her political support within the party, his or her relationship to the chancellor, and the nature of the specific issue. Formally, the finance minister is the only member with special power. He or she can veto, with the support of the chancellor, any proposal that deals with public spending. This is a major reason why the finance ministry is consulted early in the drafting of spending bills.

As a cabinet member, the minister belongs to the top governmental elite and is, together with the chancellor and ministerial colleagues, collectively responsible for all acts and policies of the government. Yet in practice the necessity of coalition governments and the heterogeneity of German parties have greatly reduced cabinet solidarity. On numerous occasions, cabinet ministers have disagreed publicly with their colleagues. It is not unusual for a chancellor, through top aides, to leak criticisms of the ministers to the news media.

The German cabinet, unlike the British, is not a "working cabinet" in which government policy is openly discussed, debated, and finally determined. As one authority has observed, "its role is limited to a final political check on the general lines of governmental policy. Decisions are approved, rather than made by, the cabinet."[30]

The strong constitutional position of the chancellor and the ambition of most cabinet ministers to achieve still higher status in the government combine to give the institution a relatively low profile. Thus the cabinet is more a loose board of managers than a policymaking body.[31] The cabinet minister is aided by at least two state secretaries: (1) a career civil servant responsible for the administration of the ministry, and (2) another—a parliamentary state secretary (similar to a junior minister in the British system)—who assists in the political and representational tasks of the minister. Yet German ministers, unlike their British counterparts, must be both policy specialists and politicians. The Germans do not have the neat British division between the politically responsible cabinet minister and the administratively responsible permanent secretary.

Chancellor, Parliament, and the Military

Throughout most of German history the military has played a major role in state and society. From the rise of Prussia in the eighteenth century to final military defeat in 1945, "the army, rather than the political forces of the society, traditionally provided the impetus toward national independence and greatness, and thus the army has always been the dominant partner in its relations with civilian authorities."[32] Military values of order, obedience, dedication to duty, and hierarchy were also diffused throughout the rest of society. The army (at least its leadership) thought of itself as "the school of the nation," an institution uniquely qualified to inculcate the proper values of citizenship and patriotism in succeeding generations of German youth.

Germany's conquerors in 1945 were determined to eliminate the political and social influence of the military and to prevent the reemergence of Germany as a significant military power. By the early 1950s these same wartime Allies, now split into opposing camps, were in the process of rearming their former enemy. The Cold War had made Germany too important a territory to remain unarmed or neutral.

In the immediate postwar years, however, there was little public support for an independent army or even one integrated into a supranational European defense force. Rearmament, which began in the mid-1950s, was strongly rejected by opposition parties in the parliament but also by significant elements in the ruling Christian Democratic Union, the churches, labor unions, and many intellectuals. The army, in view of its collaboration with the Nazis, was a discredited institution. Fears of a reemergence of militarism and a new military elite, which would attempt to play an independent political role, were also widespread.

Civilian control of the military was thus of prime importance when the parliament, after long and sometimes bitter debate, finally approved the establishment of a West German army in 1956. During peacetime, supreme command of the armed forces is vested in the defense minister, who is expected to work closely with the defense council, a subcommittee of the cabinet. In wartime, the chancellor becomes commander-in-chief. Parliamentary control operates largely through its supervision of the military budget and the Bundestag's commissioner for military affairs, a type of ombudsman who is empowered to hear the complaints and grievances of soldiers and to protect their constitutional rights. The officer corps has not become a politically powerful elite, and its influence in policy matters has been subordinate to elected political leadership. By the 1970s most Germans perceived the military as another public service institution with specific functional tasks, somewhat like the railways, police, or post office.[33]

In the 1980s, however, the emergence of a nationwide peace movement and the widespread protests over the deployment of new missiles in the Federal Republic had an impact on the status of the military in society. Public induction ceremonies for new recruits were the scene of sometimes violent demonstrations by peace movement activists. The number of petitions for exemption from military service also increased. In some areas, teachers and school authorities have denied recruiting officers access to school classes unless peace groups receive equal time. In a 1982 survey, only 35 percent of the adult population stated that they would be willing to fight for their country in the event of a war. In contrast, almost 70 percent of American and over 60 percent of British respondents were willing to fight.[34]

The Military After Unification.   Unification and the related end of the Cold War have dramatically changed the military. The former East Germany's National Peoples Army (NVA) became part of the *Bundeswehr* in October 1990. The NVA was once considered one of the strongest and most effective armies in the Warsaw Pact. But following the collapse of the communist regime, the East German army also began to disintegrate. Between the fall of the Berlin Wall and unification, the army's size dropped from 170,000 to about 100,000. Many high-ranking officers resigned, took early retirement, or were dismissed because of their association with the communist system. The remainder were put on probationary status pending a review of their backgrounds and qualifications for service in the Bundeswehr.

As a condition of unification, the Federal Republic, in treaties with the Soviet Union and the Western occupying powers, agreed to reduce the combined size of unified Germany's armed forces from 600,000 to 370,000 by 1994. This was accomplished largely at the expense of the former East German army. By 1995 only about 12,000 officers and troops of the old NVA had survived the review process and had been assigned a place in the downsized, unified army. The Federal Republic also took over huge stockpiles of military equipment, supplies, and ammunition, including some of the most advanced armaments in the military arsenal of the former Soviet Union. By 1995 most of these supplies and equipment had been destroyed, sold, or given to allies.[35]

Unification, the end of the Cold War, and budgetary constraints have also prompted proposals for rethinking the role of the military. Some defense specialists have advocated the abolition of the draft and the creation of a smaller volunteer army of about 200,000 troops. They point out that Germany is now surrounded by friendly countries and fellow NATO members or future NATO members such as Poland, Hungary, and the Czech Republic and need not focus on defending its eastern borders against a massive ground attack. Many of Germany's allies, such as Britain, France, the Netherlands, and Spain, have abolished the draft, and like the United States, are relying on smaller, mobile, high-tech military forces to meet their defense needs and international obligations. A smaller army would also save money—an important consideration for the new Schröder government. Budget problems and the increased popularity of alternative national service for draft-age Germans has reduced the current size of the Bundeswehr to about 325,000, well under the 370,000 limit established in the unification treaties.[36]

Chancellor Democracy under Adenauer

During his fourteen-year tenure, Konrad Adenauer established the procedures and style of chancellor government, with which all subsequent incumbents of the office have had in some way to contend. His early successes in dealing with the Western occupation powers; the integration of West Germany into Europe; the reconciliation with France; and the rapid economic recovery that began shortly before his first term and became an economic boom by the mid-1950s gave him a record of accomplishment that enabled him to dominate parliament on many important matters, especially foreign policy. Impatient with the delays and indecisiveness of government by committee, he frequently made commitments (e.g., to the Allied occupiers on German rearmament) without any prior consultations with his cabinet, much less the parliament. He was also very adept at keeping the various wings and factions of the Christian Democrats in balance and under control, while at the same time discouraging their organizational and programmatic development. For all practical purposes, the party was run from the chancellor's office.

Adenauer was also able to bring his new state bureaucracy under control and make it responsive to his demands. His chief aide in this area was Hans Globke, a former high-ranking official in the Prussian bureaucracy, who played a major role in rebuilding the postwar civil service along traditional lines.[37] Indeed, some observers have argued that Adenauer placed far more confidence in his government's top civil servants than he did in his cabinet ministers, whom he tended to regard as a necessary evil of party politics.[38]

In Adenauer's chancellor democracy, the general public played a minor role. Deeply pessimistic about the capacities of the German people to measure up to the demands of democratic citizenship, he wanted their support but not their involvement. In short, Adenauer wanted to govern, and he did not want the parliament, his party, his cabinet ministers, or the public to bother him while he went about his business. His message to the electorate was, in essence: "Go about your private affairs, rebuild your lives, concentrate on regaining and improving your economic position, and leave the politics to me." Many citizens accepted and indeed welcomed this approach, even though it meant that much of the state building and the resolution of major problems, such as reunification and social reforms, would have to be postponed until after the Adenauer era.[39] However, Adenauer did make a major contribution toward the institutionalization of the Federal Republic in that he convinced most citizens that a republic could be strong and effective, and that strong state authority and firm leadership could operate within a democratic framework and give West Germans what they desperately wanted in the postwar period: security and economic prosperity. Through his authoritarian, paternalistic style, he sold West Germans on the Second Republic.[40]

The Heirs of Chancellor Democracy

None of the first three chancellors after Adenauer—Ludwig Erhard, Kurt-Georg Kiesinger, and Willy Brandt—lasted more than five years. As Table 7.2 shows, there also has been a trend toward younger political leaders. Helmut Kohl became chancellor at the age of 52 and exceeded Adenauer's tenure, governing for a record sixteen years.

Adenauer's immediate successor was Ludwig Erhard, the father of the economic miracle, who had been a self-designated heir ever since the late 1950s and whom Adenauer ceaselessly criticized publicly and privately as ill suited for the top job. In retrospect, Adenauer was probably correct.

Erhard never had any close contact with his party organization and did not consolidate his position within the CDU/CSU. He was, as one observer put it, more of a guest in the CDU.[41] Proud of his accomplishments as economics minister and aware of his great electoral appeal, he considered the party secondary to his government and never attempted to gain the support of its key factions. He attempted to project himself as a *Volkskanzler,* a people's chancellor, above the parties. This posture left

---

TABLE 7.2   German chancellors: 1949–2000

Name	Party	Term of office	Age at assumption of office	Age at Nazi seizure of power (1933)	Percentage of adult life (after 18) under democratic regime before becoming chancellor*
Konrad Adenauer	Christian Democrat	1949–1963	73	57	24
Ludwig Erhard	Christian Democrat	1963–1966	66	36	56
Kurt-Georg Kiesinger	Christian Democrat	1966–1969	62	29	65
Willy Brandt	Social Democrat	1969–1974	56	20	60
Helmut Schmidt	Social Democrat	1974–1982	56	15	63
Helmut Kohl	Christian Democrat	1982–1998	52	3	100
Gerhard Schröder	Social Democrat	1998–present	54	0	100

*Including the Weimar Republic

him in a very vulnerable position when Germany's first serious postwar recession in 1966 took the luster off his reputation as the guarantor of economic prosperity. After Christian Democratic defeats in key state elections in 1966, the Erhard government fell—ostensibly because of the departure of the junior coalition partner, the Free Democrats, but more through the internal maneuvering for power within the various factions of the Union. A stunned, disbelieving Erhard, still somewhat of a political innocent, retired to elder statesman status.

The chancellorship of Erhard's successor, Kurt-Georg Kiesinger, was inextricably connected with the rise and fall of the Grand Coalition between the SPD and the CDU/CSU. Kiesinger had been a Bundestag deputy from 1949 to 1958, specializing mainly in foreign policy. Finding the road to national prominence in Bonn too crowded, he returned to his native state of Baden-Württemberg and became its chief executive. When the Erhard government collapsed eight years later and the CDU/CSU desperately needed a new chancellor candidate who would also be acceptable to the Social Democrats in the likely event of a Grand Coalition, Kiesinger became the ideal person simply because he had the fewest outright opponents in either party. It was a case of absence making the heart grow fonder, or at least of not making it more antagonistic.

As chancellor, Kiesinger had the very difficult task of leading a government in such a way that none of the three main players—he, his party, and its partner, the Social Democrats—would be too successful. Partisanship might have caused the strange alignment to break up before 1969, something both parties feared. He became, in the words of the government's press secretary, "a walking mediation committee." This structurally induced, honest-broker style of leadership gave some of his ministers considerable freedom of action; and as discussed in Chapter 5, the Social Democrats in the government took full advantage of the opportunity. After the 1969 election and the SPD-FDP government, Kiesinger became a liability to the Christian Democrats. After a decent interval he stepped down from the titular leadership of the party. Whether he could have been an effective national leader was never determined because, given the character of the Grand Coalition, he never had a chance.

The First SPD Chancellors: Willy Brandt and Helmut Schmidt

Willy Brandt.   In 1969, Willy Brandt became the fourth chancellor of the Federal Republic. In terms of policy innovation, controversy, foreign stature, and significance for the political system, Brandt ranks as one of Germany's most important postwar leaders. Born in the north German city of Lübeck, he became active in social democratic politics as a teenager and was forced to flee Germany for Norway and later Sweden shortly after the Nazi seizure of power. He thus is the only chancellor born before or during World War II not to have lived in Germany during the Third Reich. Returning to Germany in 1945 as a Norwegian press attaché in a Norwegian military uniform, he resumed German citizenship and became active in Social Democratic politics in Berlin. Identified with the reformist, pragmatic wing of the party, Brandt rose rapidly in the organization and became lord mayor in 1957. Soviet pressure against the isolated city of Berlin intensified in the late 1950s and made it a major source of East-West tension. As its mayor, Brandt acquired a national and international reputation as a young, dynamic, progressive, yet non-Marxist and anticommunist leader. This image coincided with the SPD's new look after 1959. Brandt was elected national chairman in 1964 and became the party's chancellor candidate in 1961 and again in 1965. His defeats in these two elections, during which he was subjected to numerous personal attacks regarding his illegitimate birth and his wartime activity—which to some Germans made him a traitor—almost caused his retirement from national politics. The collapse of the Erhard government and the Grand Coalition, however, compelled his return to the national scene as foreign minister in the Kiesinger government.

As foreign minister, he laid the foundations for the new relationship that the Federal Republic would develop with the Soviet Union, Poland, East Germany, and other East European states. Although limited somewhat by the demands of coalition politics, Brandt was able to establish himself as a competent, innovative foreign minister and in so doing erased much of the "loser" image he had acquired in his unsuccessful bids for the chancellorship.

Immediately after the 1969 election, Brandt seized the initiative and formed a coalition government with the Free Democrats in spite of an SPD-FDP majority of only 12 seats. He thus became the first SPD chancellor since 1930. Between 1969 and 1972, Brandt and Foreign Minister Walter Scheel effected a major transformation of West German foreign policy through treaties with the Soviet Union, Poland, and East Germany. During this period, some domestic reforms were also made in social welfare programs, the pension system, and the criminal legal code. But although promising a government of internal reform, most of the government's domestic program was postponed because of its weak and dwindling parliamentary majority. Following the 1972 election, which gave the government a solid working majority of almost 50 seats, the unfinished domestic projects (e.g., codetermination, capital resources reform, urban renewal, education, and tax reform) were placed high on the political agenda.

Yet to the considerable disappointment of SPD supporters, the government in the first year and a half following the 1972 victory did not use its parliamentary majority to move forward in the domestic field with the same decisiveness it had demonstrated three years earlier in foreign policy. This relative inactivity was explained in part by the government's attempt to curb inflation through ceilings on government expenditures and the postponement of new programs. Personality and party political factors were also involved. After 1972, it became apparent that neither Brandt nor Scheel had expertise or interest in domestic affairs. Brandt had little knowledge of economics or finance and disliked much of the detail work and bargaining associated with domestic politics. In addition, unlike in foreign policy, there were serious differences between the coalition partners over major domestic issues such as codetermination, tax, and education reform.

The arrest of an East German spy on Brandt's personal staff in April 1974 was the final blow in a series of setbacks since his triumph in November 1972. The East

German agent, a resident of the Federal Republic since 1957, had been under suspicion by security agencies for almost a year before the actual arrest. Brandt had been privately informed of this but apparently acceded to the requests of security officials to keep the agent on his staff. Following consultations with the SPD leadership and the Free Democrats, Brandt assumed full responsibility for all errors connected with the affair and resigned as chancellor in May 1974.

Brandt's five-year tenure was distinguished above all by his foreign policy of reconciliation with Eastern Europe and the Soviet Union, for which he was awarded the Nobel Peace Prize in 1971, only the fourth German so honored. As the first chancellor with an impeccable record of uncompromising opposition to Nazism, he contributed greatly to the Republic's image abroad as a society that had finally overcome its totalitarian past. In spite of shortcomings in domestic policies, the Brandt chancellorship at least was one in which many innovations and long-overdue reforms began to be discussed and programs formulated.

Helmut Schmidt.   Less than two weeks after Brandt's resignation, Helmut Schmidt became the fifth chancellor of the Republic. Schmidt had been the strongest figure in Brandt's cabinet and was his designated successor. He had been finance minister (1972–1974), defense minister (1969–1972), chairman of the SPD's Fraktion (1966–1969), and interior minister in his native Hamburg (1961–1965). In these posts Schmidt acquired the reputation of a very capable—some would say brilliant—political decision maker. He was also criticized for having what some regarded as an overbearing, arrogant, cold personal style. Schmidt clearly lacked the emotionally warm image of Brandt, yet he is given higher marks for his concrete performance.

Schmidt was identified with the Federal Republic's mainstream. A pragmatic, problem-solving approach to politics, with a basic acceptance of the main features of the economic and political system, characterized his political philosophy. Schmidt assumed the chancellorship in the midst of the worldwide economic recession that followed the 1973 Arab oil embargo and subsequent astronomical rise in oil prices. His expertise and experience in national and international economic affairs and his ability to take charge in crisis situations, such as the 1977 terrorist hijacking and commando raid (see Chapter 4), soon became apparent. Within two years, inflation was brought under control and unemployment was reduced from more than 1 million to less than 700,000 (still well above pre-1973 figures). Moreover, the country's international balance of payments remained in the black. By 1979, before the second oil price shock, Germany was in fact experiencing a modest economic boom while neighbors continued to suffer from the impact of high energy prices and inflation.

Unlike Brandt, Schmidt had little patience with the SPD's left. A strong supporter of the market economy, he maintained a close relationship with the Federal Republic's economic and industrial elite. Indeed, in 1980 he was even seen by many CDU voters as more capable than the Union's own candidate. Schmidt's electoral and policy successes, however, were not matched in his relationship to his party, the Social Democrats. Specifically, he was unable to overcome and integrate the opposition of the SPD left and especially the Young Socialists. He also under-estimated the intensity of the opposition within his own party, and in the country as a whole, to nuclear energy.

Soon after the 1980 election victory Schmidt was once again confronted with opposition to his leadership by segments of the SPD. Budget cuts in social pro-grams, due in large part to the worsening economic situation, the planned deploy-ment of new middle-range nuclear missiles in Western Europe, and arms sales to Saudi Arabia were issues that prompted sharp criticism from the SPD left. The Schmidt government by 1981 also became a prime target for the peace movement—a loose collection of environmentalists, religious pacifists, and elements of the SPD left—which strongly opposed the NATO missile decision. The movement accused Schmidt of deferring to the alleged American military strategy of attempting to con-fine at least the first stages of a nuclear conflict to Europe and, specifically, to the Federal Republic. Schmidt rejected this charge, but the peace movement had gained significant support among SPD activists and became a force that seriously weakened the governing coalition.

On September 17, 1982, Helmut Schmidt lost his parliamentary majority when the Free Democratic party, the junior party in the governing coalition with the SPD since 1969, left the government. Two weeks later, in the first successful use of the constructive vote of no confidence procedure, Helmut Kohl became the Federal Re-public's sixth chancellor.

The "Unity Chancellor": Helmut Kohl

Helmut Kohl first became a significant figure on the German political scene in 1969 when he became chief executive of the state of the Rhineland-Palatinate (*Rheinland-Pfalz*). His success at the state level coincided with the decline of his party, the CDU, in national politics. After CDU/CSU defeats in 1969 and 1972, Kohl moved from his provincial power base, and in 1973 he assumed the leader-ship of a divided and weakened CDU. He is credited with initiating a thorough modernization and revitalization of the party's organization. In 1976, as the chan-cellor candidate of the CDU/CSU, he conducted a well-planned campaign that al-most toppled the Schmidt government.

Born in 1930, Kohl is the first chancellor who did not experience the Third Reich and World War II as an adult. Following the completion of his university stud-ies in the early 1950s, he began a political career. Like his predecessor, Helmut Schmidt, Kohl is a political pragmatist. Unlike Schmidt, he did not have, until the collapse of East Germany and the beginning of the unification movement in 1989–1990, the reputation as a crisis manager or innovative political leader. In con-trast to Schmidt, Kohl was an active party leader who carefully attended to the tasks of political fence-mending and coalition-building within the diverse Christian Democratic Union. This control of the party was a major factor in his political longevity.

The most difficult problem confronting the first Kohl government (1982–1987) was the economy. Like other West European states, Germany was slow to recover from the 1981–1983 recession. Cuts in social programs, tax incentives for business investment, and a general tax reform were the chief means he used to stimulate the economy. From 1983 to 1988 the economy did expand, albeit at a slow rate. And although inflation was reduced, unemployment remained high. Kohl's policies were a German version of supply-side economics, but he is generally identified with the moderate wing of the Christian Democrats, which supports both the market economy and an extensive welfare state.

In foreign affairs Kohl was a firm supporter of the Atlantic Alliance and the most pro-American chancellor since Adenauer. In spite of widespread protests and the opposition of the Social Democrats and the Greens, the Kohl government secured parliamentary approval for the stationing of new intermediate-range missiles in the Federal Republic in November 1983. This strong position against the peace movement was vindicated by the 1987 United States–Soviet treaty eliminating these middle-range nuclear missiles in Europe. Kohl's support for American policies, however, did not prevent his government in 1989 from entering into open diplomatic conflict with the United States over the question (now moot) of when and if a generation of short-range missiles should be developed and stationed in the Federal Republic.[42] More than any of his predecessors, Kohl attempted to appeal to patriotic symbols and national pride. Terms such as *Vaterland* (Fatherland) and *Nation* and an emphasis on post–World War II German history as an object of pride have been a frequent theme in Kohl's speeches. Although not denying the country's responsibility for the Third Reich, the Holocaust, and World War II, Kohl urged that Germans in general, and postwar generations in particular, develop a positive sense of German history. Germany, Kohl believed, has earned the right to be accepted as an equal in the Western community, and the past should no longer limit the capability of the Federal Republic to act.

This approach to Germany's past prompted Kohl in 1985 to invite then President Reagan to visit a German military cemetery as a symbolic gesture of reconciliation between the two countries. When it was discovered that the cemetery also contained the remains of SS soldiers, the visit was opposed by Jewish organizations, veterans groups, and many members of the American Congress. They urged Chancellor Kohl to propose an alternative. The visit provoked the sharpest sustained criticism that Kohl had faced since taking office. In Germany he was charged with sloppy planning and insensitivity to the horrors of the Nazi era. But two weeks before the visit, Kohl, speaking at the Bergen-Belsen concentration camp, clearly stated that "Germany bears historical responsibility for the crimes of the Nazi tyranny. This responsibility is reflected not least in never-ending shame."

Kohl and the Unification Process.   Kohl seized the initiative on the unification issue with a ten-point program for German unity that he announced in the parliament on November 28, 1989, less than three weeks after the opening of the Berlin Wall. Although many of his proposals, such as a network of treaties between the two states as a preliminary stage to a confederation, were overtaken by the rapid pace of events, his initiative established a pattern of decisive and timely action throughout 1990.

His crowning achievement occurred at a July 1990 summit meeting with Soviet President Gorbachev at the Soviet leader's summer retreat in the Caucasus. In exchange for German economic aid, a sharp reduction in the size of the German army, and a comprehensive treaty regulating the two nations' future economic, technical, and political relations, Gorbachev agreed that a unified Germany could remain in NATO; he further pledged that all 400,000 Soviet troops in East Germany would leave by 1994. This agreement earned Kohl the praise of even his harshest critics.

During the 1990 all-German election campaign, Kohl was at the zenith of his popularity, power, and influence both domestically and internationally. He promised Eastern Germans Western-style economic prosperity within five years and assured West Germans that unification could be financed without any tax increases. For the first time in the chancellor's many election campaigns, his popularity exceeded that of his party.

After the election, however, the Eastern German economy continued to deteriorate and Kohl had to concede that his prediction of a rapid economic upturn had been overly optimistic. With rising unemployment in the East, his support dropped. Then, in 1991, contrary to his campaign promise, he announced major tax increases to finance unification. This prompted a strong voter backlash in the West, and support for Kohl and the Christian Democrats in state elections and public opinion polls dropped sharply.

The 1992–1993 recession further weakened Kohl's standing with the voters. As in the past, there were calls for his resignation both from within and outside the government. The opposition's new candidate—the young, pragmatic Rudolf Scharping—outranked Kohl in most polls during this period. But by early 1994 the economy was reviving, and as the election approached, most German voters did not want a change in the chancellor's office. In October 1994, Kohl won his fourth straight national election—equaling the record of his idol, Konrad Adenauer.

1998: Kohl's Last Hurrah.   Following the 1994 victory it was widely expected that Kohl would step down sometime before the 1998 election in favor of his designated successor, Wolfgang Schäuble, the leader of the CDU in the Bundestag. But the chancellor hesitated and did not heed the warnings from within his own party and from his declining status in public opinion polls after 1994. Kohl believed that given the divisions within the Social Democratic party, he could probably win one more election. He believed that his 1998 opponent would be Oskar Lafontaine, whom he had soundly defeated in 1990.

When the Social Democrats decided in March 1998 to nominate Gerhard Schröder, Kohl and the Christian Democrats were slow to react. Record-high unemployment, the inability to pass major reform legislation, and the general perception that it was time for a change were major handicaps from which Kohl and his party could not recover. Helmut Kohl, who had led his party to a record four consecutive victories, suffered his worst defeat in 1998 as the CDU received only 35 percent of the vote. Europe's last great heavyweight had to make way for a new leader and the coming to power of a new generation.

The 1998 defeat will have little effect on history's assessment of his chancellorship. He succeeded in fulfilling the Basic Law's primary mandate: the unification of Germany in peace and freedom. This is a goal that had eluded his five predecessors. Equally important was his unrelenting commitment to the unification of Europe. Without his leadership the pace of European unity, especially the introduction of a common European currency, would have been much slower. He leaves to his successors a united Germany surrounded by neighbors who now share common political, economic, and social values. Whether his questionable fund-raising tactics, which are currently under investigation, will substantially damage this legacy remains to be seen.

Gerhard Schröder:
A New Chancellor for a New Century

The man who toppled Helmut Kohl, unlike any of his six predecessors, is fully a child of the Federal Republic. Born in 1944, he, of course, had no living memory of the Third Reich or World War II. Both his supporters and opponents have considered Schröder to be intensely ambitious and even ruthless in his pursuit of Germany's top job. Much of his drive can be traced to his impoverished childhood. He never knew his father, who was killed in World War II. His mother had to support five children on her meager earnings as a cleaning lady. Forced to leave school at the age of 14 to work as an apprentice salesman in a porcelain shop, Schröder was able to complete his university preparatory studies by taking night classes. In 1978, at the age of 33, he graduated with a law degree from Göttingen University.

While still a student, Schröder became active in the Social Democratic party and by the late 1970s was the leader of the Young Socialists, who were considered radical neo-Marxists by their more conservative elders in the party. In spite of his radical rhetoric Schröder was able to maintain good relations with all factions of the party and by the early 1980s he began to move toward the center. In 1990 he became the minister-president or governor of Lower Saxony, one of Germany's largest states. As governor he was very supportive of business interests. In spite of his state's high unemployment, he was reelected in March 1998. With this victory he became the SPD's chancellor candidate.

Schröder has pledged that his government's first task will be to reduce unemployment, which is about 11 percent of the work force. The cornerstone of this program is an "Alliance for Jobs," a combined business-labor-government effort that will include government subsidies for new entry-level positions. A loosening of Germany's rigid work rules will be another target of the Alliance. In foreign policy Schröder promises continuity in relations with the United States and the European Union. But he wants to strengthen the Federal Republic's ties with the Blair (British) government and move away from what he considered the Kohl government's overreliance on former Russian President Boris Yeltsin.

To accomplish these goals Schröder must have the support of his own party's traditional left wing and the SPD's coalition partners, the Greens. Many in Schröder's party are wary of his pro-business "new center" policies, fearing the dismantling of Germany's generous welfare state. The leader of the SPD left, Oskar Lafontaine, became finance minister in Schroder's government, but abruptly resigned in March 1999 after only five months in office. Lafontaine apparently was displeased that Schroeder had in fact decided to move his government into the center on domestic issues, that is, deep tax cuts for business, reductions in social programs, and the acceptance of a low-wage service in the work force. The Greens' radical or Fundamentalist faction (see Chapter 5) can also become a problem for the new chancellor. Some Greens have advocated a variety of ecological measures such as raising gasoline prices to about $10 a gallon and restricting Germans to one airplane vacation trip every five years. Neither proposal is popular with car- and travel-loving Germans.

With the March 1999 NATO attack on Serbia, Schroeder came under sharp criticism from the SPD Left and Fundamentalist Green factions. His refusal to support the deployment of ground troops in Kosovo was largely due to the opposition of these groups.

THE FEDERAL PRESIDENT

The framers of the Basic Law were determined to avoid the problems created by the dual executive of president and chancellor during the Weimar Republic and thus made the office of federal president clearly subordinate to the chancellor and parliament in the policymaking process. In contrast to the Weimar system, the president is not directly elected, but is chosen every five years by a federal assembly (*Bundesversammlung*) of all Bundestag deputies and an equal number of deputies from the various state parliaments. The president is the ceremonial head of state; he or she formally proposes the chancellor and the cabinet for election by the Bundestag; he or she signs all laws and must certify that they were passed in the prescribed manner; and he or she formally appoints and excuses national civil servants and federal judges. If the federal government and the Bundesrat request it, the federal president can declare a state of legislative emergency that would enable the government, but not the president, to rule by decree. In all these functions, however, the president is merely implementing the will of the government or parliament. The question of whether the president has the power to refuse to accept the recommendation of a chancellor for a particular cabinet appointment has never been legally resolved. Yet on those few occasions when the president has in various ways indicated his reservations or objections to a particular candidate, he has seldom been able to block the appointment.

The president does, however, have the right to be consulted and thoroughly informed about planned governmental actions. In the event of a parliamentary crisis, the president is expected to be a mediator and conciliator. Thus, in selecting candidates for this position, emphasis has been placed on personalities with fairly nonpartisan images, who evoke few strong negative feelings among the parties and whose backgrounds and personal styles would make them appropriate representatives of the Republic.

The first president, Theodor Heuss (1949–1959), had all these qualities. A former journalist and parliamentary deputy of the left liberals (Democratic party) during the Weimar Republic, he had played a major role in the founding of the Free Democratic party and in the drafting of the Basic Law. Heuss carefully avoided any partisanship during his two terms and was an effective symbol of the new, democratic state both at home and abroad. His successor, Heinrich Lübke (1959–1969), had been minister of agriculture in the Adenauer government and generally followed in the traditions established by Heuss. He became, however, a frequent target of media criticism for his occasional lapses into partisanship and his alleged participation as an architect in the construction of concentration camp buildings during the Third Reich. This latter charge was not substantiated, and Lübke steadfastly denied any involvement.

The third president of the Republic and the first Social Democrat was Gustav Heinemann, elected with the help of the Free Democrats in 1969. Heinemann was also the first president whose general political philosophy was clearly left of center. A CDU minister in the early Adenauer cabinets, he left the Christian Democrats and the government in 1950 over Adenauer's decision to rearm and founded a small party that advocated neutralism in foreign policy. In 1957 he joined the SPD and quickly rose to a prominent position within the party, and in 1966 he became minister of justice in the Grand Coalition. Unlike his two predecessors, he did not seek reelection in 1974, largely for reasons of age and health. During his tenure, he raised the prestige of the office and distinguished himself by his concern for the underprivileged in German society and by his support for the conciliatory foreign policy of the Federal Republic toward its Eastern neighbors.

In 1974, Walter Scheel became the Republic's fourth president and the second Free Democrat to hold the post. At the time of his election, Scheel was also at the height of his career as party leader and foreign minister. As president, Scheel explored briefly the possibilities of enlarging the power of the office. He delayed signing some legislation and refused to sign a few other bills on the grounds of their questionable constitutionality. He also attempted to challenge the authority of certain cabinet ministers to dismiss top ministerial aides.[43] His efforts were firmly blocked by the chancellor and the parliament, and there was little support for Scheel's exploration of the constitutional limits of his office.

The majority in the federal assembly held by the SPD and FDP at the time of Scheel's election in 1974 disappeared by 1979 as the coalition parties lost votes in various state elections. Unable to secure Christian Democratic support for his reelection, Scheel stepped down in 1979. His successor was Karl Carstens, a former chairman of the CDU's *Fraktion* and top-ranking civil servant in the foreign ministry and chancellor's office. Although he was from northern Germany, Carstens's conservative-nationalist image also made him acceptable to the Bavarians. In May 1979 Carstens was elected on a straight party vote by the federal assembly as the fifth president of the Republic. Revelations about his membership in the Nazi party while a young law student provoked strong criticism from some foreign countries, but it was not a significant factor in his election. Some SPD and FDP leaders questioned whether his partisan past would be a hindrance in the office, but after his election he took care to maintain a neutral political stance.

In 1984 Carstens declined to run for a second term. With an absolute majority in the federal assembly, the Christian Democrats nominated Richard von Weizsäcker as Carstens's successor. Von Weizsäcker, who had been the governing mayor of West Berlin since 1981, was widely regarded as an ideal choice. A lawyer by training, he had been a leading lay figure in the Protestant Church and a prominent member of the Christian Democrats' moderate wing. As a recognition of his nonpartisan image, the Social Democrats did not nominate their own candidate.

One of President von Weizsäcker's most notable achievements was his address on the fortieth anniversary of Nazi Germany's unconditional surrender, May 8, 1945. For the first time a major German political leader challenged the traditional explanation used by older, ordinary Germans that they "knew nothing" about the Holocaust:

> every German was able to experience what his Jewish compatriots had to suffer, ranging from plain apathy and hidden intolerance to outright hatred. Who could remain unsuspecting after the burning of the synagogues, the plundering, the stigmatization with the Star of David, the deprivation of rights, the ceaseless violation of human dignity? Whoever opened his eyes and ears and sought information could not fail to notice that Jews were being deported. . . . When the unspeakable truth of the Holocaust then became known, all too many of us claimed that they had not known anything about it or even suspected anything.[44]

This speech, which attracted worldwide attention, illustrates the capacity of the federal president to bring important questions that transcend party politics to the attention of the public.

After the collapse of the GDR, von Weizsäcker cautioned against a speedy unification, which would disregard the interests and feelings of the average East German. He criticized West German domination of the process and urged more tolerance to overcome the psychological wall that still separates the two regions. He also urged that Berlin replace Bonn as the political capital as soon as possible. His strong support for Berlin and his call for "political leadership" to resolve the capital city question played a major role in the government's decision to bring the issue to a vote in June 1991. The Kohl government had hoped to put off a final decision until the mid-1990s.

In 1994, after serving the maximum of two terms (ten years), von Weizsäcker was succeeded by Roman Herzog, president of the Federal Constitutional Court. Herzog was the personal choice of Chancellor Kohl, whose ruling coalition held a narrow majority of seats in the Federal Assembly. Herzog was not the first choice of the Christian Democrats. They had hoped to nominate someone from the former East Germany, but were unable to find a suitable candidate.

Herzog was seen as a solid but uninspiring candidate who would have difficulty measuring up to the standards set by von Weizsäcker. But during his tenure (1994–1999) Herzog became a strong advocate for change. In 1997 he strongly criticized the entire German political and economic establishment for its inability to make the reforms necessary for the country to compete in the twenty-first century. For Herzog this *Reformstau* or stalled reform was the responsibility of all major groups and institutions in the Republic—business, labor, government, the universities, churches. He implored them to abandon their attachment to the status quo and explore new ways of dealing with the problems of unemployment and the erosion of the social welfare system. Herzog also spoke out forcefully on the need for Germans to fulfill their responsibilities to victims of the Holocaust.

Herzog declined to run for a second term. In May 1999 Johannes Rau, the former minister-president of North Rhine–Westphalia and the SPD's chancellor candidate in 1987, was elected by the Federal Assembly as his predecessor. Rau is a veteran political leader who enjoys good relations with most of the major political parties and personalities. He is only the second Social Democrat to hold the post.

Summary of the Formal Lawmaking Process

PREPARLIAMENTARY STAGE

About three-fourths of all bills submitted to the parliament are conceived and drafted by the government. The impetus for such legislation, however, may come from outside—from interest groups, the governing coalition parties, parliamentary delegations, or programs. In some cases, a proposal from the parliamentary opposition may even find its way into a bill, as was the case with the revision of the tax system in 1988 and the 1992 abortion law. Some idea of the mix of ministerial bureaucracy, party, and parliament can be seen in the replies of two cabinet ministers to the question of where and how policy proposals originate. According to one minister:

> The overwhelming number of bills submitted by me can be traced to my and my ministry's conceptions and preparatory work. In one or another case, the suggestion to prepare a specific bill came from the coalition Fraktionen, but was limited to their suggestion for a ministerial initiative. The way in which such initiatives were then considered and formulated was left up to me.[45]

According to the other minister:

> The source of bills nearly always goes back to multiple impulses and demands, thus making a rare "monocausal" explanation. Parliamentary decisions, resolutions and electoral programs of parties, discussions among the public about long-range development trends or suddenly emerging problems, preparatory work in the ministries, the chancellor's decision about the government program and, last but not least, the personal interest of the minister produce the most diverse combinations, which often make it impossible subsequently to sort out the decisive factors for the origin of a law.[46]

During the ministerial drafting process, the rules of procedures in governmental departments (as discussed in Chapter 5) also allow civil servants to consult with the affected interest groups. This is done as a matter of course, and the interest group–state bureaucracy relationship is well established. However, in order to ostensibly simplify the consultation process, ministries are generally required to negotiate only with the leadership or national offices of these interest groups. In practice, this procedure contributes to the centralized, hierarchical character of both governmental and interest group bureaucracies.

If a policy area is the concern of more than one ministry, such as economics and finance or defense and foreign policy, interministerial negotiations take place. In cases of conflict due to overlapping responsibilities, the chancellor's office is also informed and, if necessary, mediates and resolves the dispute. This is consistent with the chancellor's responsibility for the overall direction of policy. Most bills requiring new or increased appropriations also are cleared with the finance ministry at the drafting stage. This planning and drafting stage, as Gerard Braunthal has found, involves in many cases a "protracted bargaining process among specialists and politicians" within the ministries and governing parties.[47] Extensive revisions are very common.

Following ministerial approval, the draft legislation is presented to the full cabinet for approval before its submission to parliament. Most internal (governmental) opposition to the legislation is resolved before formal discussion in the cabinet. Although most cabinets—especially since Adenauer—have pursued a consensual style of decision making, the chancellor in fact has veto power over any ministerial proposal; similarly, the support of the chancellor virtually ensures cabinet approval. This latter situation has rarely occurred, although there is some evidence that Adenauer at various times was in a minority position, especially over questions of foreign policy and rearmament during the 1950s.

In practice, however, the chancellor's power can be limited by the size of the government's parliamentary majority, his personal interest in the policy area, the demands of the coalition partner, and the internal pressures from his party and the state bureaucracy. Governments with a relatively small majority have had difficulty in getting their proposed legislation through the chamber. The first Brandt government (1969–1972), with a majority of only 12 (which dwindled to zero by 1972), was able to pass a relatively low 75 percent of its proposed legislation. After the 1972 election, which gave the SPD-FDP coalition a majority of about 50 seats, the government's success rate rose to 93 percent, the highest percentage since the third Adenauer government (1957–1961).

Chancellors such as Adenauer and Brandt had little interest in many domestic policy areas and were willing to exchange concessions in this area for support in foreign policy and defense matters. Brandt's indifference or even disdain for issues such as a liberalized abortion law—an issue of considerable importance to elements in the SPD—was a major factor in the long delay before its passage in 1974.

During their coalitions with the Free Democrats, both major parties had to make concessions to their junior partners. The Christian Democrats, especially after Adenauer's departure, were urged by the FDP to pursue a more dynamic foreign policy toward Eastern Europe and to take a less clerical position on issues such as church schools. In collaboration with the CDU's conservative business wing, the Free Democrats were also able to block several social welfare programs advocated by the Union's labor wing. From 1969 to 1982, the Free Democrats played a major role in the delay that plagued the SPD's commitment to internal reform in areas such as codetermination and the reform of vocational education. The SPD-Green government, which took office in 1998, is also divided on several domestic and foreign policy issues including nuclear energy and the use of German ground troops in NATO "out of area" operations.

PARLIAMENTARY STAGE

After cabinet approval, draft legislation is presented to the Bundesrat for a first reading. The Bundesrat at this point can approve, reject, or amend the bill. Regardless of Bundesrat action at this stage, however, the bill will be submitted to the Bundestag—for even if the Bundesrat rejects a bill, it can still be overridden by the Bundestag. In the Bundestag, the bill is discussed in the Fraktionen. At this point, party strategy and policy toward the bill are formally discussed and determined. The bill is then given its first reading, during which only introductory formal debate is held, with no amendments allowed. Referral to the appropriate committee follows this first reading.

Because the government parties have a majority in each committee, a bill is rarely returned to the floor with a negative report. Committees also cannot pigeonhole a bill. In many cases, however, after consideration of a bill the committee does propose amendments.

After the committee report, a second and more thorough debate takes place in the Bundestag. At this time, amendments to the bill are considered. House debate is led by specialists in the policy area who act as spokesmen (*Berichterstätter*) for the committee. If, after the second reading and debate, a bill is approved without amendment, the third and final reading follows immediately. If the bill has been amended and passed in the second reading, a waiting period of at least two days after the distribution of the revised bill to all deputies is observed before the final vote.

Following Bundestag action, the bill returns to the Bundesrat for a second reading. If the policy area involved requires Bundesrat approval and if the Bundesrat has vetoed the policy, the bill is dead. When the policy area is not one affecting the states (defense, for example), a Bundesrat veto can be overridden by a simple Bundestag majority. If the Bundesrat veto is by a majority of two-thirds or more, the veto must be defeated by a majority of two-thirds.

In most cases, as discussed earlier in this chapter, the Bundesrat objects to parts of a bill affecting the states, and these differences are then referred to a joint conference committee (*Vermittlungsausschuß*) for resolution. In some cases, Bundesrat objections are already incorporated in amendments introduced in the Bundestag. The report of the conference committee is then submitted to both houses for approval. Finally, the bill is examined for constitutionality by the chancellor's office, justice ministry, and president's office before being signed and promulgated by the president.

The entire process is executive-dominated, and our examination of the state bureaucracy in Chapter 8 should make this even more apparent. Nonetheless, there are instances when the government does meet resistance from its parliamentary delegations after the submission of legislative proposals. In most of these cases, interest groups disappointed in their preparliamentary bargaining with the ministries attempt to mobilize their parliamentary contacts for one last try at revision. In addition, the increasing politicization of the Bundesrat, the assertiveness of the Bundestag, and the demands from the new Eastern states may be indicative of even more difficulty for chancellor democracy in the future.

Notes

1. Michael Z. Wise, "Where the Past Haunts, Berlin Embraces the New," *New York Times,* June 7, 1998 (Internet edition).
2. A party must have a minimum of 5 percent of the total membership, currently 34 deputies, to receive *Fraktion* status. After the 1994 election the PDS, with 30 seats, did not qualify. It was then given "group" status. A group cannot make any procedural motions, but it can have members on every committee and can introduce legislation. Groups are allotted speaking time in proportion to their size. In 1998 the PDS did receive enough seats to achieve Fraktion status.
3. John D. Nagle, "Elite Transformations in a Pluralist Democracy: Occupational and Educational Backgrounds of Bundestag Members, 1949–1972" (manuscript, Syracuse University, 1974).
4. Adalbert Hess, "Berufstatistik der Mitglieder des 10. Deutschen Bundestages," *Zeitschrift für Parlamentsfragen* 14, no. 1 (December 1983): 487–489.
5. In the eleventh Bundestag (1987–1990) the committee that dealt with most civil service questions (Domestic Affairs) was composed largely (80 percent) of civil servants, and the informal subcommittee that specialized in civil service salaries was made up solely of civil servants.
6. Gerhard Loewenberg, *Parliament in the German Political System* (Ithaca: Cornell University Press, 1966), p. 46.
7. Ferdinand Müller-Rommel, "Interessengruppenvertretung im Deutschen Bundestag," in *US Kongreß und Deutscher Bundestag,* ed. Uwe Thaysen, Roger H. Davidson, Robert G. Livingston (Opladen: Westdeutscher Verlag, 1989), p. 305.
8. *Ibid.*
9. *Ibid.,* p. 309.
10. The opening of the Stasi files in early 1992 apparently revealed that individuals in these occupations were by no means immune from contacts with the secret police.
11. Peter Schindler, ed., *Datenhandbuch zur Geschichte des Deutschen Bundestages* (Bonn: Presse und Informationszentrum des Deutschen Bundestages, 1983).
12. Kurt Sontheimer, *Grundzüge des politischen Systems der Bundesrepublik Deutschland* (Munich: Piper Verlag, 1984), pp. 162–163.
13. Institut für Demoskopie surveys cited in Schindler, ed., *Datenhandbuch,* p. 1048.
14. Institut für Demoskopie surveys, Nos. 0040 (1951) and 4036 (1983).
15. Prior to 1990, the four delegates from Berlin had no voting power.
16. States with more than 6 million but fewer than 7 million residents receive five votes.
17. Heinz Laufer, "Der Bundesrat," *Aus Politik und Zeitgeschichte,* no. 4 (January 22, 1972): 50–52.

18. Karlheinz Neunreither, *Der Bundesrat zwischen Politik und Verwaltung* (Heidelberg: Quelle und Mayer Verlag, 1959), pp. 84–86.
19. Uwe Thaysen, *The Bundesrat, the Länder and German Federalism* (Washington, D.C.: American Institute for Contemporary German Studies, Johns Hopkins University, 1994), p. 9.
20. *Ibid.,* p. 2.
21. The proportion of bills over which the Bundesrat has an absolute veto rose from 41 percent in the first Bundestag (1949–1953) to 63 percent in the thirteenth Bundestag (1994–1998). See Hans-Georg Wehling, "The Bundesrat," *Publius 19,* no. 4 (Fall 1989): 57; Thaysen, *The Bundesrat,* p. 12; Eckhard Jesse, *Die Demokratie der Bundesrepublik Deutschland,* (Berlin: Landeszentrale für politische Bildung, 1998).
22. Peter Schindler, "Der Bundesrat in parteipolitischer Auseinandersetzung," *Zeitschrift für Parlamentsfragen 3,* no. 2 (June 1972): 148–149.
23. *Die Zeit,* June 28, 1974, p. 8
24. Ingo von Münch, "Der Bundesrat als Gegenregierung?" *Die Zeit,* no. 15 (April 5, 1974), p. 5.
25. Peter Pulzer, "Responsible Party Government and Stable Coalition: The Case of the German Federal Republic," *Political Studies 26* (June 1978): 181–208; and Karl Friedrich Fromme, *Gesetzgebung im Wiederstreit: Wer beherrscht den Bundesrat? Die Kontroverse 1969–1976* (Stuttgart: Bonn Aktuell Verlag, 1976).
26. This has not prevented opposition parties from attempting to dismiss individual cabinet ministers through no-confidence resolutions. Such resolutions have been introduced at various times since 1949. They have all been rejected, tabled, or withdrawn. This is a political tactic designed to embarrass the chancellor and the cabinet member. Even if a resolution against an individual minister passed, it would have no legal effect. For a discussion of these resolutions, see Peter Schindler, ed., *Datenhandbuch zur Geschichte des Deutschen Bundestages, 1949 bis 1982* (Bonn: Presse und Informationszentrum des Deutschen Bundestages, 1983), pp. 418–421.
27. F.F. Ridley, "Chancellor Government as a Political System and the German Constitution," *Parliamentary Affairs* 19, no. 4 (February 1966): 446–461; Kenneth Dyson, "The German Federal Chancellor's Office," *Political Quarterly* 45, no. 3 (July–September 1974): 364–371.
28. Gerard Braunthal, *The West German Legislative Process* (Ithaca, NY: Cornell University Press, 1972), pp. 112–134. For an excellent account of the development of the chancellor's office, see Ferdinand Müller-Rommel, "The Chancellor and His Staff," in *Adenauer to Kohl: The Development of the German Chancellorship,* ed. Stephen Padgett (London: Hurst and Company, 1993), pp. 106–126.
29. Rolf-Peter Lange, "Auslesestrukturen bei der Besetzung von Regierungsämtern," in *Parteiensystem in der Legitimationskrise,* ed. Jürgen Dittberner and Rolf Ebbighausen (Opladen: Westdeutscher Verlag, 1973), pp. 132–171.
30. Ferdinand Müller-Rommel, "Federal Republic of Germany," in *Cabinets in Western Europe,* ed. Jean Blondel and Ferdinand Müller-Rommel (London: Macmillan, 1988), p. 166.
31. Ferdinand Müller-Rommel, "Federal Republic of Germany."
32. H. Pierre Secher, "Controlling the New German Military Elite: The Political Role of the Parliamentary Defense Commissioner in the Federal Republic," *Proceedings of the American Philosophical Society 109,* no. 2 (April 1965): 63.
33. Public opinion surveys generally find that the military is considered a rather unimportant institution compared to the parliament, the chancellor, the courts, and the federal bank. See Elisabeth Noelle-Neumann, ed., *The Germans: Public Opinion Polls, 1967–1980* (Westport, CT: Greenwood Press, 1981), p. 188.
34. The German figure, however, is actually higher than that found in some other European countries such as Italy (28 percent) and Belgium (25 percent). Survey data drawn

from the International Values Study cited in Elisabeth Noelle-Neumann and Renate Köcher, *Die verletzte Nation* (Stuttgart: Deutsche Verlags-Anstalt, 1987), p. 61. A 1985 study also found a low (33 percent) willingness to fight among Germans. *Eurobarometer,* no. 24 (December 1985): 26.

35. Peter Joachim Lapp, "Der Preis der Einheit: Kapitulation und Auflösung," *Das Parlament,* no. 24 (June 17, 1994), p. 16. See also Peter Schneider, "Die neuen Kameraden," *Der Spiegel,* no. 24 (June 13, 1994), pp. 74ff. There was widespread opposition in the West German army to accepting any former NVA personnel, especially officers, into the service. Over 90 percent of the NVA officer corps had been members of the Communist party, and their commitment to serving a democratic state was suspect. Prior to the 1990 unification, all East German generals had been required to resign or be demoted. None chose the latter course.

36. *Der Spiegel,* no. 3 (January 18, 1999); Eckhard Jesse, *Die Demokratie der Bundesrepublik Deutschland* (Berlin: Landeszentrale für politische Bildung, 1997), p. 257.

37. When Globke came under heavy criticism for his activity during the Third Reich (he wrote the legal commentaries to the infamous Nuremberg laws, which legalized persecution of Jews), Adenauer refused to dismiss his most important aide.

38. Kurt Sontheimer, *The West German Political System* (New York: Praeger, 1973), p. 131.

39. Karl-Dietrich Bracher, *The German Dictatorship* (New York: Praeger, 1973), pp. 499–500.

40. Kurt Sontheimer, *The West German Political System,* p. 131.

41. Klaus Bölling, *Republic in Suspense* (New York: Praeger, 1965), p. 74

42. The Kohl government's opposition to any modernization of the short-range missiles was based in part on its experiences with the medium-range weapons issue in the early 1980s. The government had no interest in another conflict with Germany's peace movement. In this sense the message of the movement had finally reached, albeit belatedly, the inner councils of the government.

43. "Die Kunst, bis an die Grenze zu gehen," *Der Spiegel,* no. 46 (November 15, 1976), pp. 30–34. See also Kurt Becker, "Wieviel Macht soll der Bundespräsident haben?" *Die Zeit,* no. 47 (November 19, 1976), p. 3.

44. For key excerpts from von Weizsäcker's speech, see *New York Times,* May 9, 1985, p. A20.

45. Cited in Gerard Braunthal, "The Policy Function of the German Social Democratic Party," *Comparative Politics 9,* no. 2 (January 1977): 143.

46. *Ibid.*

47. Braunthal, *West German Legislative Process,* p. 231.

8 Policymaking Institutions II: Administration, Semipublic Institutions, and Courts

The policy process neither begins nor ends with the formal decision making of government and parliament that we examined in the preceding chapter. The implementation and adjudication of policy decisions are also an integral part of government. In modern, developed political systems, these functions are largely the responsibility of the state's administration, courts, and semipublic institutions. Our concern in this chapter is with these institutions and their role in the policy process.

Although Germany did not invent bureaucracy or courts, it certainly contributed to their refinement and development. The Prussian civil service of the Hohenzollern emperors became a model of efficiency, dedication, and incorruptibility adopted not only throughout the Reich but in other countries as well. The German judiciary and the massive codification of civil and criminal law, completed at the turn of the century, influenced legal developments in such diverse settings as Greece, Korea, and Japan.

During the past century, specific governments and regimes have come and gone, but the civil service and judiciary have remained essentially unchanged in structure and procedures. It is little wonder that Germans at both elite and mass levels have had more confidence in dealing with their bureaucracy and courts than with other branches of government.[1] The legalistic-bureaucratic mentality attributed to the political culture is in part a result of the far greater stability of these institutions, and hence, the more extensive experiences Germans have had with them.

The Federal Republic also has an extensive network of semipublic agencies that are either independent of both national and state governments or have their own separate administrative structures. These institutions—most notably the Federal Bank (*Bundesbank*),which in 1999 became part of the European Central Bank system, the social security and health systems, and the Federal Labor Institute—play key roles in economic, social, and welfare policymaking and implementation. The unification process brought forth still another semipublic institution, the *Treuhandanstalt,* or

Trusteeship Authority, which became the single most important economic institution in the former East Germany. From 1990 to 1994 the Treuhand was the world's largest holding company. It controlled approximately 14,000 formerly state-owned enterprises, thousands of small businesses (restaurants and shops), 30 percent of the farmland, and two-thirds of the forests in the former East Germany. These enterprises at one time employed almost 9 million people. The origins and development of this institution, which was not directly controlled by the central government, can also reveal much about the semipublic institutions.

DEVELOPMENT OF THE GERMAN ADMINISTRATIVE AND JUDICIAL SYSTEM

The performance of the courts and state bureaucracy, defined in a narrow technical sense of getting the job done, has been good. However, the commitment of the bureaucracy and the judiciary to the values and processes of liberal democracy has been less than satisfactory. During the Weimar Republic, both institutions were at best ambivalent toward and at worst hostile to the new regime. Given their monarchical origins and the nationalist, upper-class character of their personnel, together with the association of the Weimar Republic with military defeat and foreign humiliation, these orientations should not be surprising. During the Third Reich, whatever independence and sense of integrity the judiciary and bureaucracy had were soon lost as both became tools of the dictatorship. Arnold Brecht, himself a former high-ranking civil servant in Prussia until he was driven out by the Nazis, observed:

> By the end of the Hitler era the German civil service had become a worldwide epithet for irresponsible servility, for turncoat opportunism, for bureaucratic self-preservation and for an utterly undemocratic type of authoritarianism. Its renowned incorruptibility had been shown to have an unexpected limit. While its members would not be bribed individually, as a group they had surrendered to the corruption of their work by the governing party. Gone with the storm was the admiration of the world.[2]

After 1945 the Western Allies intended to purge both institutions of Nazi party members and sympathizers and reorganize them to facilitate their democratization. Yet the occupation authorities soon found that the dismissal of all party members from the bureaucracy and judiciary would have brought administration to a standstill.

Thus, although Nazis were removed from top-level leadership positions and replaced by known antifascist or "clean" civil servants, the middle and lower levels of the civil service remained essentially intact and were transferred to the various local and state governments being formed by the military occupation. In all, about 53,000 civil servants were dismissed for party membership in the immediate postwar period, but only about 1,000 were permanently excluded from any future employment.[3] In 1951, after the restoration of partial sovereignty to the Federal Republic, a

Reinstatement Act gave even most of the dismissed party members full pension credits for service during the Third Reich and reemployment in civil service. The result was that by the early 1950s, 40 to 80 percent of officials in many departments were former party members.[4]

A similar development took place in the judiciary. Initially all courts were closed, and all Nazi party courts and special tribunals were abolished. Only those courts then devoid of Nazi influence and personnel and sanctioned by occupation authorities were reopened. At first, justice practically came to a standstill. By 1946, however, the regular system was functioning much as it had before the Nazi seizure of power.[5]

The elimination of Nazi party members from the judiciary was never accomplished. The problem was that the occupation authorities soon found that the great majority of all judicial officials, judges, and prosecutors had been in the party. Each case was decided on an individual basis, and distinctions were made between fellow travelers of varying degrees and committed Nazis. The occupation authorities, Karl Loewenstein reports, also discovered many non-Nazi judges seeking to protect colleagues who had been only nominal party members.[6] In spite of party membership, "if a man was a good judge, his redemption and readmission to the depleted ranks were made easy. The judicial caste had not failed its members."[7] At most, about 2,000 judicial officials lost their jobs, and only a few fanatics were permanently disqualified.

The abandonment for all practical purposes of the denazification and democratization of the civil service and judiciary was due to the Allies' desire to return to stability and normality as soon as possible. Countering the perceived Soviet threat to Western Europe, which heightened after the fall of Czechoslovakia and the Berlin Blockade in 1948, became more important than major internal reform in the Western zones.

Besides the absence of major personnel changes at the grass-roots level, the traditional legal and administrative structure of the German state was for the most part maintained. Apart from the changing of state boundaries and the creation of several new states, city, county, and village boundaries were retained or restored to their pre-1933 form.

Denazification could also be abandoned with little short-run risk because the great majority of former party members was more than willing to accept the rule of the new masters. Very few had actually been committed party members, and many of these had learned their lesson and were hardly inclined to subvert the new state. But neither could this generation of civil servants and judges be expected to show a genuine commitment to the ideals of liberty, equality, and the democratic process. The reform of the state administration was postponed, and it is a task still confronting the Republic—fifty years later.

STATE ADMINISTRATION

Structure

The German civil servant may work at one of several governmental levels: national, state, regional, district, county, or local. In spite of the decentralized structure of the state, civil servants generally share a common background and training, and they work within a similarly structured bureaucratic framework. The occasional coordination and integration of these multiple governmental layers is in part the result of this common training and administrative framework.

German administrative units are very hierarchical but not centralized. The bureaucratic pyramid is very steep, but there is little actual direct control from the top, of the activities in the middle and at the base.

At the national level there are sixteen federal ministries, ranging in size from the Ministry of Finance, with about 3,000 employees, to the Ministry for the Family, with 325 employees. All ministries have a common structure, and any doubt as to what is meant by the term hierarchical structure should be dispelled by Table 8.1, which shows one typical ministry—economics.

Ministries are divided into four levels: executive (the minister and the state secretaries), departments, subdepartments, and sections (bureaus). The ministry's personnel are classified into five groups: (1) political officials, (2) higher service, (3) elevated, upper-middle service, (4) intermediate service, and (5) simple, or lower-level service. Also within groups 2 to 5, but usually in the lower three levels, a public employee can be classified as a *Beamter* (official) with lifetime tenure, a white-collar employee, or a manual worker. Almost all civil servants at the top two levels are officials, whereas most of those in the intermediate and lower-level service are either white-collar employees or manual workers. The elevated service, group 3, is about equally divided between Beamte and white-collar workers.

Within each organizational level, however, different types of personnel with varying ranks, job titles, and responsibilities can be found. Beginning at the top of Table 8.1, we see that the minister's two state secretaries and the eight department heads are all "political" civil servants. Thus, although they are the highest-ranking employees in the ministry, they can be removed, transferred, or pensioned by the minister, if necessary.[8] In spite of their formal political status, most state secretaries and ministerial directors (the rank of most department heads) are longtime tenured civil servants. If they are not retained by the minister, they must by law be transferred to another position suitable to their status. If Germany had an administrative class or *grands corps* of civil servants, as in Britain and France, they would be at this level. But there are no graduates of elite schools whose members are distributed throughout the various ministries.

Although they function at two different organizational levels, the subdepartment heads (rank: ministerial dirigent, or councilor) and the section, or bureau, chiefs are part of the higher service. They all have academic training and decision-making responsibilities within their bureaus or subdepartments and are personally and legally responsible for decisions that bear their signatures. The section assistants constitute the lowest group in the higher-level service. These are comparable to junior executive positions. Their titles vary depending on the length of their service and the size of their section.

The elevated service is composed largely of caseworkers, or *Sachbearbeiter.* Because the higher service (section assistants to state secretaries) requires an academic degree, few caseworkers will ever enter it, even though their experience and job knowledge may make them more qualified than some of their superiors. The

TABLE 8.1 Hierarchical structure of the ministry of economics

Organizational Position	Employees	Service Group	Title
State secretaries	2	Political official	State secretary
Department heads	8	Political official	Ministerial director
Subdepartment heads	34	Higher service	Ministerial councilor
Section heads	175	Higher service	Varies from senior governmental councilor to ministerial councilor
Section assistants	460	Higher service	Varies from governmental councilor to governmental director
Officials	(362)		
White-collar workers	(98)		
Caseworkers	615	Elevated service	Varies from governmental inspector to senior official councilor
Officials	(405)		
White-collar workers	(210)		
Clerical and secretarial staff	822	Intermediate service	Varies from governmental assistant to official inspector
Officials	(64)		
White-collar workers	(758)		
Custodians, messengers, chauffeurs, copy machine operators	280	Simple, or low-level, service	Varies from office assistant to senior office master
Officials	(71)		
White-collar workers	(82)		
Manual workers	(127)		
	Number	Percentage	
Officials	1091	46	
White-collar workers	1148	49	
Manual workers	127	5	
	2366	100	

intermediate-level service is made up of clerical and secretarial staff and comprises about 35 percent of most ministries' total personnel. At the bottom of the organizational ladder are those in the simple service (messengers, copy machine operators, drivers, custodians).

Thus about 30 percent of a typical ministry's staff have executive or junior executive positions; another 25 percent are caseworkers; and the remaining 45 percent have clerical, secretarial, or custodial functions. The key unit is the section, or bureau, and the key personnel are the section heads (*Referenten*). Each section is assigned responsibility for a particular policy area. The development, initiation, and supervision of ministerial policy is centered in these sections.

They are the powerhouses of German administration; as one frustrated reformer observed, the section heads are the "princes" of the policymaking process within the ministries.[9]

The average section is small, with only three to seven members: a section head, one or two assistants, caseworkers, and clerical personnel. Overall there are about 2,000 such sections at the national level. To a large extent, national policy, as formulated in the ministries, is the sum of what these 2,000 parts produce.

Critics of Germany's administration have focused on this hierarchical yet decentralized structure. It is, they contend, highly fragmented, and discourages comprehensive policy planning or major reform initiatives that require extensive interdepartmental, interministerial, or federal-state cooperation: Small sections tend to work best with small problems.[10] Because the top political officials in each ministry have so little staff, they cannot in practice exercise the control they have in theory. Expertise is concentrated at the bottom, in the sections.

The small size of each section and the practice of making the section head personally and legally responsible for the section's decisions make success or failure highly visible. Promotion is related to success. Hence sections tend to concentrate on limited, short-run projects that will, in effect, yield only minor modifications in an already existing policy but that will be judged successful by superiors who approve of the existing policy. Risky projects are avoided in part because they exceed a section's limited capacity but also because their failure can be easily attributed to specific individuals.

At the ministerial stage of policy development, a complex process of bargaining and negotiation takes place among the experts at the base, the section head, the department and subdepartment chiefs, and the executive (minister and state secretary). The influence of outside forces—such as interest groups, parties, and consultants—is most directly felt at the executive and departmental levels. The sections are relatively insulated and secure in the knowledge that they have as much, if not more, expertise as anyone else in the house, even with the outside specialists whom the executive may call in. Shoring up the top to contend with the princes in the sections is, according to many students of the system, its most pressing need.[11] Political leadership is supposed to initiate, oversee, coordinate, and integrate policy programs, but it does not have the necessary resources. The problem is not an unwillingness of the middle and lower levels to respond, but an inability of political leadership to formulate and operationalize policy goals because of a lack of staff and planning capability. The problems of fragmentation and hierarchy at the national level are compounded by similar structural frameworks at the state and local levels.

Personnel

When the Federal Republic was established in 1949, many of its first civil servants came directly from either the unified (American, British, and French zones) Economics Administration in Frankfurt or the *Länder* bureaucracies. Early coordination between the central government and the states was thus facilitated by the common background and training of civil servants at both levels. From the beginning, the Bonn Republic had a well-trained, relatively intact bureaucracy in its service.

TABLE 8.2   Distribution of public employees by governmental level and rank (in percentages)

Level	Rank			
	Officials	White-collar Employees	Manual Workers	Total
National	10	6	17	9
State	78	46	27	56
Local	12	48	56	35

Source: Federal Statistical Office.

Today about 16 percent of the German work force is employed by government (excluding military personnel). This is very similar to the proportion of public employees in the United States (16 percent) and Great Britain (15 percent) and considerably smaller than the public sector in France (24 percent) or Sweden (33 percent). Moreover, the 1995 privatization of the post and the telecommunication systems and the partial privatization of the railroads has decreased the number of public employees by almost one million. Only about 40 percent of public employees have tenured civil servant status, and about 10 percent now work at the federal level. As Table 8.2 shows, the national government employs 10 percent of all Beamte, as compared to 78 percent for the Länder and 12 percent for local government. Moreover, most of the national civil servants are not employed in the federal ministries, but in various offices (tax administration, weather service, air traffic control, economic agencies). Only about 25,000 civil servants are directly employed in the federal ministries. Moreover, as we have seen, most of these are not in policymaking positions. Considering the 2,000 section chiefs and their assistants as policymakers, and adding subdepartment and department heads, the total number of civil servants with policymaking initiatives is about 3,000. All others are administrators in the strict sense of the term: They carry out the decisions of others.

German public officials at all levels are by law and custom a special group with unique privileges and obligations. The civil servants are expected to be loyal and obedient to the state and their superiors and willing to adjust their private lives to the demands of the service. In exchange for this commitment to the state, officials may receive lifetime tenure and salaries and benefits that enable them and their families to maintain a lifestyle commensurate with their status. In short, for loyal and correct service, the Beamte receive a guarantee of lifelong security. Other occupational groups must take their chances in the free-market economy, but the civil servants are risk-free. The postwar restoration of this privileged status, which has its origins in the age of monarchy, was opposed by American occupation authorities and the Social Democrats. Nonetheless, civil servants, through energetic and effective lobbying, were able to secure the restoration of the service to its traditional position.[12]

The conception of the civil servant as an official with a special and privileged relationship to the private citizen has certainly changed since 1949. The modern executive, unlike those during previous regimes, is now more dependent on social and political forces, specifically political parties, than on a politically independent "supreme authority." Yet the fact that Germans have traditionally viewed the state as an institution above and superior to society still persists to some degree and gives powerful support to the acts of the German bureaucrat.

Recruitment.   Recruitment to the service is closely tied to the educational system, with each level having specific educational requirements. The higher level, still the monopoly of the university-educated, was once even more restricted in that a legal education was required. Today lawyers still dominate the upper ranks, and surveys have shown that they remain the most privileged of the privileged.[13]

Although the constitution (Article 36) calls for higher-level national civil servants to be selected from all constituent states on a proportionate basis, some regions are disproportionately represented at the top of the federal bureaucratic pyramid. One study found that 36 percent of all high-level civil servants in office from 1949 to 1984 had come from the then East Germany (that is, they had fled after 1945), the "lost" provinces east of the Oder-Neisse line, or Berlin. These areas were historically part of Prussia, or Prussian-dominated. Generally, northern Germans were far more likely to be higher-level civil servants than were southern Germans (from Baden-Württemberg, Bavaria).[14] The typical high-level German civil servant is male, the son of a civil servant, Protestant, from northern Germany or "Prussia," and a lawyer. Although Germany has no specific elite school (such as the French Ecole Nationale d'Administration) that produces a large percentage of high-level civil servants, the universities of Frankfurt, München, Tübingen, and Hamburg are very well represented in the senior bureaucracy.

Entrance into the service, especially at higher and elevated levels, is normally limited to young candidates who are expected to make a long-term if not lifetime commitment. Most candidates must pass entrance examinations that, like those in most other European countries, test not for ability in specific positions but for general career aptitude. After admittance to the service, there is a probationary period of two to three years, during which systematic in-service training is given before a final examination and eligibility for the coveted status of *Beamter auf Lebenszeit* (public official for life).

These procedures apply to all public positions that have civil service status. Sharp distinctions are made within the service between those with Beamte status and those without (manual workers and white-collar employees), as well as between the career civil servant and the outsider. If we add these features of the recruitment process to the hierarchical structure described earlier, we have a further explanation for the absence of major programs of innovation emanating from the established bureaucracy. The still-dominant influence of lawyers in the higher service and the pervasive influence of legal norms and practices do, however, aid in the integration of local, state, and federal bureaucracies. Practices and procedures within the bureaucracy are explicitly prescribed both in law and in the Common Code of Administrative Procedure, which is a revised version of a code from the 1920s. This document—part office manual, part code of etiquette—is still used in some form in most German governmental offices.

Attitudes and Values.   Given the background, recruitment, and structural environment of German civil servants, one should not be surprised that surveys have found them to be a status-conscious, somewhat cautious group of people with nonetheless a firm commitment to the Republic and to the values and processes of liberal democracy. One study of students' career plans found that those planning to enter the state bureaucracy deviated from average students in their emphasis on "the occupational values of job security, old age security, clearly structured tasks, and well-circumscribed demands on one's abilities and time."[15] The more independent, ambitious, and achievement-oriented students were less interested in a civil service career. Not unexpectedly, bureaucrats are also very promotion-oriented, and most feel that special efforts are necessary to merit promotion.[16]

The civil servant's perception of the political character of the job, however, has increased. In a comparative study of top administrators (department heads), German respondents were found to be as (1) equally conscious of the ways in which democratic politics affect their work and, conversely, of the ways in which their work affects the stability and effectiveness of the postwar democracy, as are civil servants in Britain, and (2) more aware than Italian bureaucrats.[17] A study of assistant section heads (the lowest or beginning level of the higher service) in the Economics Ministry found that most recognized and accepted the political character of their job; 67 percent perceived that they were involved "in politics" and were not merely administering the laws as "neutral" agents of a state above society, parties, and parliament.[18]

This commitment to democratic principles has been especially strong among younger civil servants, and there is somewhat of a generation gap in the area of political values. Younger civil servants were usually more likely to see their activity within a political context, to be less authoritarian and more personally committed to democratic party politics, and to support greater parliamentary control over the bureaucracy. Even among older age groups, however, there is little doubt that the civil service of the Federal Republic, in contrast to that of the Weimar Republic, is committed to the political system it serves.

The civil service has also adapted to a variety of political masters since 1949 and has provided a strong element of continuity. Contrary to expectations, after twenty years of Christian Democratic rule the civil service did not attempt any sabotage of Social-Liberal reforms after 1969. That many of the SPD's domestic reform programs between 1969 and 1982 did not become reality is usually attributed to factors over which the bureaucracy has little or no control: disagreements within and between the parties in the governing coalition, lack of adequate financial resources, and inadequate political leadership. The civil service has also received high marks for its work during and since the unification process.[19]

Pressures for Reform

Nonetheless the state bureaucracy and its role in the policymaking process have come under increasing criticism in recent years. Much of this criticism focuses on its inability to adapt to new policy demands and developments, especially where major innovations are needed: economic development, transportation, land use, health care, and education. Although it has served the Republic well in the reconstruction phase of the postwar period, it has not been able, the critics charge, given its present structure and mode of operation, to respond to the new, more complicated policy needs of the future.[20]

Specific recommendations for change have centered on:

1. the size of the administration, in terms of both the number of public employees and the number of administrative units
2. the outmoded hierarchy and reward system
3. the privatization of public services and state-run enterprises

The Size of the Administration and the Number of Units.   Within a physical space about half the size of Texas are a national government, 16 states, 45 governmental districts, 426 counties, 129 cities (independent from county government), and about 14,600 local communities. The division of labor among these units, the coordination of administrative activity, and the relationship between their size and responsibilities are insufficiently defined. Given this number of administrative units, it is not surprising that although the number of Germans gainfully employed in the private sector has remained relatively constant since 1960, the number of public employees rose by 62 percent between 1971 and 1990.

With unification the Federal Republic inherited a bloated East German bureaucracy that had been thoroughly controlled by the Socialist Unity (Communist) party. Most of the 1.2 million public employees in the former East Germany were put on probationary status, and eventually about 300,000 become permanent pubic employees. In 1991 the Federal Constitutional Court upheld the provisions of the intra-German Unity Treaty of 1990, which allows the dismissal of public employees in the Eastern region because of their support for the Communist dictatorship or in order to establish a "rational effective administration" in the new states.

Hierarchy and Reward System.   The strict distinctions of higher, elevated, intermediate, and low or simple service levels; the privileges of lifetime tenure and generous pensions; and the aversion to outside experts are expensive and outmoded and have increasingly little relationship to the actual work of administration. Much of the work done by academically trained higher-level civil servants could be done just as well by caseworkers at a lower level. In a 1997 survey 47 percent of the adult population agreed that the Beamte could be replaced by white-collar employees; only 29 percent wanted the present system retained.[21] In some states pension costs for Beamte equal the salary costs of in-service personnel. Some of the poorer states, such as the Saar, spend almost all their revenue for personnel and are dependent on federal grants for capital investment.

Privatization.   The current discontent with big bureaucratic government so noticeable in the United States and Britain has not escaped the Federal Republic. The state-run postal service, banks, telephone system, railroads, and the national airline,

Lufthansa, have been or are in the process of being partially or totally privatized. The postal system has been divided into three independent units: (1) letters and packages, (2) postal savings banks, and (3) telephone and telecommunications (*Telekom*). All three are eventually to be run as private enterprises with no government subsidies. Many of the employees of these enterprises have civil service status and have opposed any attempts to change in the name of free enterprise or sound business principles.

The Kohl government proposed legislation that would phase out civil service ranks in the newly privatized enterprises. The state's near monopoly of the job placement process through the Federal Labor Institute (see below) was also abandoned in 1994. Plans for the privatization of many functions now performed by local or state governments (e.g., garbage collection, libraries, and recreational centers) have also drawn the wrath of public employees and their unions, but the process of privatization and downsizing the bureaucracy will continue under the Schröder government elected in 1998.

SEMIPUBLIC INSTITUTIONS

Among the semipublic institutions, the German social security and health systems, like the bureaucracy and courts, have survived the frequent and sudden regime changes of the past century. Both were established in the 1880s by the conservative Chancellor Otto von Bismarck, who sought to ensure that the growing working class would support the existing monarchical regime and not the Socialists. The Federal Labor Institute (*Bundesanstalt für Arbeit*), located in Nuremberg, administers a nationwide network of employment offices first established during the Weimar Republic that reemerged relatively intact after 1949. The Bundesbank in Frankfurt, which has been primarily responsible for monetary policy and now represents German interests in the European Central Banks, is a postwar creation, although it can trace its origins to the Reichsbank of the Hohenzollern Empire. These institutions assume functions performed by national governments in centralized systems such as Britain and France. The East German Trusteeship Authority and its successor organizations have been a major economic force in the Eastern Länder. Even though they are nominally under the supervision of the national Finance Ministry, like the other semipublic bodies, they have substantial independence from the federal government. These semipublic institutions lessen the total political load carried by the national government, but they also reduce its strength. Their distance from the national and state governments has also generally shielded them from the conflicts of partisan politics.[22]

The Social Security and Health Systems

The German welfare state is one of the most generous and comprehensive in the world. Expenditures for health care, pensions, industrial accident compensation, child support, public housing, veterans' support, and (since 1995) long-term nursing care insurance consume about 35 percent of the country's Gross Domestic Product. It also provides Germans with over one-fourth of their disposable income. The pension and health care programs are financed largely through equal employer and employee contributions. The new long-term nursing care program, however, is intended to be financed almost entirely by employee contributions (increased payroll taxes and a reduction in the number of paid holidays). The costs of other programs (e.g., child support, housing and rent subsidies, and welfare) are taken from general tax revenue. Employers must pay the costs of the accident insurance program. Yet the administration of these huge programs is not carried out by either the national or state governments but by more than 1,800 social security and health funds located throughout the country.

The health, or "sickness," funds cover about 90 percent of the population. They are organized by economic sector (business, agriculture, professions), occupational group, and geographic area. The social security (pension and accident) programs insure about 43 million adults.

Although dating from the late nineteenth century, the programs have undergone extensive changes since the founding of the Federal Republic. The governing boards of all the funds are now based on the principle of parity representation for the various business, professional, and labor interests most concerned with the programs. After 1949 the left, or labor, wing of the ruling Christian Democratic Union, working with the trade unions and the opposition Social Democrats and enjoying the support of Chancellor Adenauer, was able to convince business interests that the confrontational class politics of the Weimar Republic should be replaced with a new emphasis on "social partnership." This required concessions from both business and labor. The trade unions gave up their majority control of the health funds, and employers did the same for the pension and accident insurance programs. Although the officials of the funds are nominally elected by their millions of members, the turnout at *Sozialwahlen* (social welfare program elections) is very low, and the slates or candidates presented by the labor unions and business and professional associations are rarely contested.

The administrative independence of the funds is limited by federal law. For example, the size of pension payments and the taxes to pay for them are determined by the parliament. The funds do, however, have considerable discretion in setting the fee structure for physicians, the construction and management of hospitals, and the investment for pension fund capital. The concept of social partnership thus extends to the state as well. The funds, according to one authority, are "political shock absorbers," connecting "state with society because they leave it to the major economic interest groups to mediate the state's administration of major social welfare programs."[23]

The postwar emphasis on consensus and social partnership is seen most clearly in the landmark 1957 reform of the pension system. Previous pension legislation based the size of payments largely on the individual's contributions. The 1957 law, although retaining some elements of individual insurance, linked increases in pension payments, with some time lag, to increases in the overall national wage level.

This dynamic feature enabled all pensioners, regardless of their individual contributions, to share directly in the expanding national economy. It was also expected that these pension increases would have a stabilizing, countercyclical effect. That is, in periods of rapidly rising wages the pension increases would be relatively lower than wages, reflecting the previous three-year average; but in periods of modest wage hikes the pensioners would receive increases reflecting the previous prosperity. The 1957 law was a political compromise. Conservative business interests and the Christian Democrats accepted its dynamic provisions (i.e., indexing pensions to the national economy), and the labor unions and the Social Democrats abandoned their preference for a more uniform, egalitarian system. By 1990 the average pension payment amounted to about 70 percent of the employee's preretirement income, as compared to only 18 percent for the first recipients in 1891.[24] The system now combines elements of individual insurance with collective welfare. In recent years, however, this postwar consensus on the pension and health systems has been strained by budgetary cutbacks, rising unemployment, and the costs of integrating the former East Germany into the market economy.

The costs of pensions to retired East Germans, for example, is far higher than the amounts they pay into the system. The difference is made up by working West Germans. In 1999 the West German part of the pension fund had a surplus of about $15 billion while the East German portion ran a deficit of about $9 billion. Since unification these transfers for pensions have totaled about $62 billion.[25] Germans, like their neighbors in other West European societies, are also living longer, but retiring earlier. This means that there are ever fewer contributors paying for ever more recipients.

In response to this crisis, the Schröder government in 1999, like the Kohl government before it, proposed limiting pension increases until 2002 to the rise in the cost of living instead of the average annual wage increase. This would mean a de facto cut in the average pension from about 70 percent of the average wage of working Germans to 65 percent. While they were the opposition Schröder's Social Democrats opposed such a plan, but since returning to power they have also had to deal with these harsh demographic and economic realities. This proposal to, in effect, cut pensions for two years has provoked strong opposition from the trade unions, pensioner associations, the churches, and other social welfare interest groups. Many of these groups supported Schröder in 1998 with the expectation that his government would preserve the existing system and not cut benefits.

The Federal Labor Institute

The Federal Labor Institute is a semipublic institution that is assigned primary responsibility for organizing the labor market (i.e., bringing jobs and job seekers together) and for administering the system of unemployment insurance. The institute also (1) administers programs financed from unemployment insurance revenues that retrain workers, and (2) supplements the income of those put on a reduced work week. In its programs the institute must give special attention to the elderly, women, the handicapped, the long-term unemployed, and other special groups such as seasonal workers. The institute, which was established in 1952, is under the supervision but not the direct control of the Labor Ministry. It is governed by a president, an executive committee, and a supervisory board, which has representatives from the trade unions, employers, and federal and state officials. The major guidelines determining labor policy are developed in Nuremberg and are administered by branch, local, and regional offices. Most of the unemployment compensation programs are financed by equal employer and employee contributions, which amount to about 3 percent of a worker's gross income. If the unemployment level is high, however, the federal government must subsidize the institute. Thus in certain circumstances the institute can be financially dependent on the federal government.

As in the case of the pension and health systems, business and labor representatives are closely involved in the work of the institute's employment offices through their membership on the institute's local, regional, and national administrative committees. The members of these committees are proposed by the trade unions, business associations, the federal government, and local government authorities. The Institute has almost 100,000 employees at its headquarters in Nuremberg and at almost 200 branch offices and 650 counseling centers. The Institute is also responsible for overseeing the vocational education system, which supports over 1.6 million apprentices. The Institute still has a legal monopoly on career counseling and is the largest employer of psychologists in the country.

The independence of the Institute was enhanced during the twenty-year tenure of its former president, Josef Stingl. Although he was a member of the conservative Christian Social Union, the Bavarian affiliate of the Christian Democrats, Stingl enjoyed the support of the trade unions and remained in office during the Social-Liberal era (1969–1982). Through skillful use of the media, he established himself in the view of many citizens as the preeminent authority on the unemployment problem and was relatively immune from criticism from the national government. His monthly reports from Nuremberg became media events as Stingl, armed with graphs and charts, would lecture the nation, including his superiors in Bonn, on the severity of the unemployment problem.

Unification and the resultant mass unemployment in the East have severely taxed the resources of the Institute. From 1989 to 1999 its annual budget increased from about $24 billion to $84 billion. Currently about half of the Institute's unemployment payments go to the East, although the population in this region comprises only about 20 percent of the country's total. Thus the Institute is also transferring large amounts of insurance premiums paid by Westerners to the East. But in 1993, when the West was in a recession, total income was insufficient to cover all claims and the government had to subsidize the Institute with borrowed funds. Between 1991 and 1999 national government subsidies to cover the Institute's shortfall totaled about $140 billion.[26]

Since 1994 the near-monopoly of the Federal Institute has been broken. Commercial agencies are now allowed to place employees in all available positions; previously they were restricted to placing managers, artists, and models. The new firms may charge for finding employees, but they may not take fees from individuals using their services to find employment (i.e., the costs are paid by the employer). Approximately 2,000 private employment agencies have opened since the 1994 law went into effect.

The Bundesbank

The Bundesbank is the German national bank, roughly equivalent to the American Federal Reserve or the Bank of England. It is the institution chiefly responsible for monetary policy and hence price stability. According to one study,

> The distinctive element in the Bundesbank ethos is a refusal to compromise on inflation. "There is no such thing as a little bit of inflation," Bundesbank officials like to say; and the Bundesbank view has been constant on this issue. Even single-digit inflation destroys a currency's value over the medium term and gradually destroys the economy as a whole.[27]

No central bank in the world has guarded the value of its currency as carefully as the Bundesbank has protected the Deutsche Mark (DM). The bank is legally independent of the federal government, the states, and private interest groups. Its autonomy is greater than that of its counterparts in Britain, France, Japan, Sweden, and even the United States.

Since 1982 the bank has also been directly involved in reducing the national government's deficits by transferring a portion of its profits from foreign exchange transactions to the national treasury. In 1997 these transfers reduced the federal deficit by about $16 billion.

The power and independence of the bank reflect the strong concern about inflation held by all Germans. Twice in this century, following each world war, Germany experienced disastrous inflations that wiped out the savings of millions of citizens. Determined to keep monetary policy out of the reach of politicians, West Germany's postwar leaders did not make the bank subject to any national ministry or to the general supervision of the chancellor under his guideline power (see Chapter 7). Nor is it accountable to the parliament. According to its 1957 constitution, the bank is obligated to support the government's overall economic policy; but this applies only as long as government policy, in the judgment of the bank's leadership, does not conflict with the bank's prime mission: the safeguarding of the currency. If a bank decision is opposed by the federal government, the government can delay implementation of the decision for only two weeks.

The bank is governed by two executive bodies, a directorate and a central bank council. Members of the directorate are appointed to eight-year terms by the federal president on the recommendation of the federal government. The central council mainly represents the interests of the regional branches of the bank. It is largely controlled by the regional bank presidents, who are appointed by the Bundesrat on the recommendation of the respective state governments. Thus the directorate has a more national perspective, whereas the bank council tends to reflect state or regional interests. Since unification, the bank has also established regional offices throughout the new Eastern states.

The bank has not become a partisan political institution. Although the CDU was in power at the national level from 1982 to 1998, there was not a single CDU supporter among the directorate's seven members until 1989. The current chief executive officer is the first Christian Democrat to hold the post; his predecessors, under Christian Democratic governments in Bonn, have included independents and Social Democrats. In recommending appointments to the directorate, the government has usually selected individuals who are acceptable to the banking community and generally in agreement with the main economic policy objectives of the government. Once appointed for eight-year terms, however, the directors have tended to be independent. After a careful analysis of central bank policy in Germany, France, and Italy from 1973 to 1985, John Goodman found no evidence that the Bundesbank, in contrast to its counterparts in France and Italy, had manipulated German monetary policy for electoral purposes before the national elections of 1976 through 1983. He adds, however, that this finding does not reflect the absence of government interest in the setting of monetary policy. Indeed, the chancellor and his ministers were quite conscious of the effects of monetary policy both on the economy and on their prospects for reelection. But their influence over the course of monetary policy was limited by the independent status of the German central bank.[28]

The bank has not hesitated to criticize the government when it considers the government's economic policies a threat to monetary and price stability. In the late 1970s the Bundesbank initially opposed Chancellor Schmidt's plan to create a European Monetary System (EMS), which linked the Deutsche Mark to the currencies of several other European Community nations. The bank feared for the stability of the Deutsche Mark in a system where it was tied to the weaker currencies of countries with high inflation, such as France and Italy. Chancellor Schmidt was able, however, finally to convince the bank that the advantages of the EMS—such as decoupling European currencies from the unstable dollar—outweighed the potential disadvantages of rising inflation. In practice, the EMS did not restrict German monetary policy or the bank's independence.[29] On the contrary, in the view of many of Germany's neighbors, the EMS imposed German anti-inflationary discipline on its participants and promoted German trade.

In 1981–1982, Karl Otto Pöhl, then president of the bank, clashed with Chancellor Schmidt over interest rates. Schmidt wanted lower rates to help take the Federal Republic out of a recession; Pöhl, supported by the bank, saw inflation as a larger danger than sluggish growth and unemployment. Schmidt later blamed the bank for the collapse of his government in September 1982.[30]

The bank became a major factor in the 1987 conflict between the United States and the Federal Republic over international economic policy. The Reagan administration urged the Germans, as one of the world's major trading nations, to speed up their economy in order to increase the demand for U.S. goods and reduce the U.S. trade deficit. Given the Federal Republic's high unemployment, low inflation, and slow growth rate, Washington argued, there was ample room for Germany to expand its economy through lower interest rates, tax cuts, and increased government spending. Although the Kohl government could and did cut taxes and increase spending, it had little control over interest rates, which fell largely within the domain of the Bundesbank. The bank downplayed Germany's economic influence, pointing instead to the U.S. budget deficit as the primary cause of the American trade imbalance and falling dollar.[31]

This German-American impasse became a major factor in the international financial crisis that began with the plunge of the New York stock market in October 1987. In the week preceding the October crash, the Bundesbank actually increased one of its key interest rates; meanwhile James Baker, U.S. Treasury Secretary at the time, warned the Germans that unless they stopped raising rates and restraining their economy, the United States would take no steps to prevent a drastic decline in the value of the dollar.

Responding to pressure from the Kohl government, the international financial community, and major German business interests, the bank finally lowered rates on four types of loans within six weeks after the New York stock market crisis. Until the stock market drop, however, the bank's central council was divided over the question of whether to give first priority to keeping inflation low or stimulating the economy. The council's faction for low inflation (composed largely of regional bankers, who were less concerned about international factors and more about the effects of inflation on their institutions) held the upper hand. However, the sharp drop in the dollar and stock prices increased the influence of the bank's growth faction, which was led by Otto Pöhl, then the president.[32] This incident clearly shows the limitations placed on the national government by the power of the semipublic institutions. The American disagreement was not with the government, but with the unofficial "fourth" branch, the Bundesbank.

The Bank and German Unification.   In 1989 the bank initially opposed the Kohl government's plan for a 1-to-1 exchange rate for East German marks. The bank— and especially Pöhl—considered the currency exchange "fantastic" in the sense of having little to do with reality; on the free market East Germany's currency had about one-fifth to one-sixth the value of the West German mark. The bank's opposition eventually led the government to limit the 1-to-1 rate to personal savings under 4,000 East Marks. Above that level, the exchange rate would still be a very generous 2 to 1. The bank reluctantly accepted the government's plan as a political necessity, which still made little economic sense. The resulting 20 percent increase in the money supply was met by only a 6 percent increase in gross national product due to the merger of the two economies. The relatively high inflation rate of over 4 percent in 1992 was related in part to this decision. Upon his retirement in 1991, Pöhl delivered a parting shot to the Kohl government by attributing the slow pace of East German economic recovery and skyrocketing unemployment to the exchange rate policy.

The Bank and European Unification.   In 1997 Germany's efforts to meet the criteria for membership in the currency union led to increases in interest rates and a major conflict between the Kohl government and the bank. The government attempted to reduce the budget deficit by revaluing the nation's gold reserves. The move was strongly criticized by the Bundesbank as an accounting trick that would undermine the independence of the bank and public confidence in the currency union. While such creative bookkeeping was also used by other countries, the Germans had insisted on strict adherence to the provisions of the Maastrict Treaty establishing the bank. The controversy drew international attention and an embarrassed Kohl government eventually backed down.

In 1999 the Bundesbank began to cede many of its powers to the new European Central Bank, which is also located in Frankfurt. The Bundesbank will become one of the regional banks in "Euroland," the eleven nations that have agreed to phase out their national currencies and replace them with the Euro, the common European currency. The common currency means the end of the Deutsche Mark by 2002. Although most Germans have consistently supported the economic and political integration of postwar Europe, the prospect of actually losing the mark has provoked some concern in public opinion.[33] The bank, together with the federal government, did lobby successfully for Frankfurt as the seat of the planned European central bank. This will allay some German fears about the future value of their Europeanized currency.

While the Bundesbank will formally only be one of eleven regional units of the European Central Bank, the size and weight of the German economy in Euroland, not to mention the Bank's physical proximity to the European Central Bank, ensure that it will be an influential voice in the councils of the new central bank. Indeed, the Bundesbank's "footprint" is very visible in the European Central Bank. Many observers in fact consider the European bank to be a German creation in the sense that it is committed to the strong anti-inflationary policies of the Bundesbank.

The Trusteeship Authority (Treuhand)

The Trusteeship Authority (Treuhand), the agency charged with privatizing the state-owned economy of the former East Germany, was established in March 1990 by the last communist government only days before the East's first free election.[34] Staffed largely by holdovers from the former communist regime, the agency did little more than offer minority holdings in old Eastern firms to Western companies. It made little if any progress in closing down unprofitable firms or modernizing those with a chance to compete successfully in the free market. Initially it was given over $10 billion by West Germany to keep the state-owned companies afloat during the beginning of free-market competition. But the companies in the first month alone applied for about $9 billion in aid, and the Treuhand, in classic socialist fashion, gave each firm the same proportion of its claim (41 percent) regardless of the company's chances to survive in the free market.

In June 1990 the Treuhand came largely under West German control. Its second director, Detlev-Karsten Rohwedder, the former head of a major chemical firm, had the reputation of salvaging troubled companies. The authority was given the task of either (1) transforming East Germany's 14,000 industrial companies, all state-owned, into private corporations able to compete in a free market, or (2) closing them down.[35] In some cases the authority could pursue a third course: modernize an efficient state-owned company with the goal of selling it to a private owner. The Treuhand was to be largely self-financing. The sale of efficient state properties would provide funds for the modernization of less viable firms and ease the burden for those enterprises that would be closed.

The Treuhand was an independent public corporation under the general supervision of the Federal Finance Ministry in Bonn. It was led by a president (appointed by the chancellor), a nine-member executive, and an administrative council. The Treuhand was essentially required to perform a sort of triage over the 14,000 enterprises with 9 million employees that it controls: (1) state-owned firms that could attract buyers at the right price were to be sold; (2) enterprises that could not be sold because they were hopelessly inefficient and outmoded were to be closed; however, some benefits to workers—retraining courses, early retirement, severance payments—were to be financed in part by the proceeds from the sales of healthy firms; and (3) with funds borrowed from the government and with capital generated by the sale of healthy firms, some companies were to be restructured, downsized, or modernized so that they could become competitive in the free market.

The Treuhand experienced major difficulties in carrying out its mission. There were too many weak firms, and it became politically difficult to close them all. Many firms lacked capital and efficient organization; they were overstaffed, produced goods of poor quality, and were hindered by poor infrastructure.

The agency did not lack for critics. Its selling strategy focused heavily on searching for West German buyers or merger partners. The result, according to one authority, was that "unification has led mainly to market extensions of West German firms into East Germany." By emphasizing largely sales to or mergers with West German firms, "the THA forfeited the opportunity of establishing a more competitive market structure in many of East Germany's industries and of preventing the take-over of the economically profitable firms in the East through mostly West German companies."[36]

Thus in the East the Treuhand is still denounced as a job killer, which sold valuable property at fire sale prices. In the West it was attacked by business interests for not closing plants quickly enough or for not promptly accepting Western offers to buy. Tragedy struck the agency in March 1991 when its director, Detlev-Karsten Rohwedder, was assassinated by terrorists at his home in West Germany.

The Treuhand under its new director, Birgit Breuel, pushed ahead with privatization and became less concerned with modernizing industrial properties before selling them. The privatization work of the Treuhand largely ended in December 1994. But the agency, now renamed the Federal Institute for Unification Related Special Projects, will continue to manage large tracts of real estate and farmland, monitor the over 85,000 contracts it concluded with foreign and domestic corporations, and administer the several large firms it has been unable to sell.

The bottom line for the Institute's privatization work is as follows:

1. Approximately two-thirds of the 14,000 enterprises were either sold to private owners or turned over to state and local governments. The remaining 3,600 businesses were shut down.

2. The Treuhand received commitments from the new owners to invest about DM 207 billion ($140 billion) in the enterprises and to create or save 1.5 million jobs.

3. The Treuhand's work will eventually cost the German taxpayer about DM 275 billion ($180 billion).[37]

Initial expectations that the sale of these properties would produce a net profit proved to be overly optimistic.[38]

Even though the privatization phase has been largely completed, the agency is expected to continue to operate for at least another decade. Its successor management organizations will have over 3,000 employees.[39] Like other semi-public institutions, it has insulated the national government from direct criticism while being nominally under its control. As a state holding company, it has also been relatively free of parliamentary supervision.[40]

THE JUDICIARY AND THE COURT SYSTEM

Contributing to the complexity and organized character of German social, economic, and political life are the courts and the judiciary, which play a major role in regulating the entire process. One observer has pointed out, "There is hardly an area of human relations in Germany, untouched by some rule, order or regulation."[41] For example, the opening and closing hours of shops and stores and the nighttime working hours of bakers are fixed by law. Donald Kommers has even found a Bavarian ordinance that requires parents to keep their children quiet each afternoon between 1 and 3 P.M.[42]

Whether Germans are simply more inclined to settle their disputes by legal means rather than through informal negotiations and bargaining or whether it is because of the relatively extensive court system available to them, they are a very law- and court-minded people.

The Character of German Law

Like that of most of its Western European neighbors, German law was fundamentally influenced by the Roman legal codes introduced by Italian jurists during the Middle Ages and by the Napoleonic Code enforced in the Rhineland during the French occupation in the nineteenth century. After the founding of the empire in 1871, the civil and criminal codes were reorganized and in some cases rewritten by teams of legal scholars. This massive work was completed by the turn of the century. Although relatively few changes have been made in the civil code since then, the criminal code since the early 1950s has been in a process of major revision.

These codes form the basis of Germany's unified legal system. Although political institutions are decentralized and fragmented, German law is the same in all states of the federation. Thus unlike the situation under American federalism, laws regarding such matters as bankruptcy, divorce, criminal offenses, and extradition do not vary from state to state.

The codified character of German law also means that unlike in countries using the Anglo-American legal system, there is little judge-made, or common, law. The judge in a codified system (in theory at least) is only to administer and apply the codes, fitting the particular case to the existing body of law as found in them. The German judge may not set precedents and thus make law, but must be only a neutral administrator of the existing codes. According to this theory, judges do not have to make law; all the law that is needed is already in the codes. This conviction, that the judge is not an independent actor in the judicial process but merely an administrator, lies at the base of the still-dominant philosophy of legal positivism, or analytical jurisprudence. Legal positivism contends that existing general law as found in the codes sufficiently encompasses all the rights and duties of citizens. In other words, judicial review is not necessary. The law supposedly offers the citizen the best protection against the arbitrary exercise of power by political authorities. Politics, according to this philosophy, must be kept strictly distinct from law.

Although in theory the judges are neutral administrators, according to the rules of procedure they are not disinterested referees or umpires of court proceedings. They are expected to take an active role in fitting the law to the facts of the particular case and in ensuring that all relevant facts become known. Court observers accustomed to the Anglo-American system would be surprised by the active, inquisitorial posture assumed by German judges. At times they seem to be working with the prosecution against the defendant. But if one assumes, as the German legal system does, that it is the duty of all participants to discern the truth or facts of the case in order to ensure a just application of the law, this activist orientation of the judge is to be expected. Unlike the Anglo-American system, the process is not one of advocacy, with defense and prosecution each presenting their side of the case as forcefully and persuasively as possible, and with the judge or jury making the final decision. It is more inquisitorial, with all participants—defense, prosecution, and judge—expected to join together in a mutual search for the truth, the real facts of the case.

Many critics of the German legal system have focused on this legal philosophy as the root cause of the judiciary's scandalous behavior during the Third Reich. By claiming to be only neutral administrators of the law, judges disclaimed any responsibility for judging the contents of the laws they were to administer. According to legal positivism, the judge is a "cog in the wheel of judicial administration, unmoved by feeling or even conscience."[43]

This philosophy also grants no legitimacy to any other type of law, such as natural or common law, that does not emanate from the sovereign state through its official representatives. Thus the state is the only source of law. In this sense, positivism is quite supportive of the statist mentality—that is, the setting of state above society—attributed by many to the German political culture of the past.

The Judiciary

Socialization and Recruitment.   In Germany, as in other continental European states, there traditionally has been a close relationship between the court system and the state bureaucracy. Nearly all judges—with the exception of those in specialized courts and the relatively few (about 900 out of 15,000) at the federal level—are appointed by the state ministers of justice. They are civil servants with roughly the same salaries, rank, tenure, and promotion structures as the Beamte in the higher service. Indeed, during the empire and the Weimar Republic, judges were not distinguished at all from higher-level civil servants. In the Federal Republic, however, a separate set of regulations for judges was introduced, designed to ensure judicial independence. Nonetheless, structurally at least, the judge remains very much a part of the bureaucratic hierarchy. Starting at the lowest level (the local courts), a judge is promoted on the basis of recommendations from superiors. Independence and individual initiative are not encouraged by this system.

A German judge, unlike many of her or his American counterparts, has in most cases chosen a lifetime career and does not enter private practice and rarely even goes into the prosecuting end of judicial administration. There is a relatively strict separation between bench and bar. After about four years of legal study, all prospective lawyers and judges take a state examination. Upon passing this test, the student becomes a *Referendar,* a sort of apprentice or junior jurist, and begins a two-and-a-half-year period of training in ordinary courts, in administrative courts, as an attorney, and in the office of a public prosecutor—thus gaining experience in all major areas of the profession. After this practical experience, prospective jurists must take a second state examination that, if passed, qualifies them to practice law. At this point (around age 27 to 32) the candidates must make career decisions: private practice, a business or corporation career, civil service, or the judiciary. Those who enter private practice as attorneys or who work for corporations (about 50 percent of the total) can and do switch from job to job; but those who enter state service must commit themselves to the judiciary, the prosecutor's office, or the regular civil service. Those who embark on a judicial career must go through an additional three-year probationary period before receiving lifetime tenure as a judge and beginning the ascent up the career ladder. Once committed, the German judge has little contact with other lawyers not in the judicial track, with the possible exception of those in the prosecutor's office.

Judges come from predominantly middle-class or upper-middle-class backgrounds. One study found that about half of all judges come from the top 5 percent of the population in terms of socioeconomic background; only about 6 percent of the judiciary come from working-class families, although the working class constitutes about 40 percent of the population.[44]

Attitudes and Values.   Taken together, the socioeconomic background, recruitment, and professional socialization of judges would seem to make for a rather conservative group oriented toward the status quo. In the sense of supporting the status quo (i.e., a middle-class liberal Republic), the judges are conservative. Opposition to the values of liberal democracy, much less hostility to the Republic à la Weimar, are hardly to be found, at least not in studies of judges' attitudes and values. In one extensive study based on a representative sample of federal and state judges, it was found that all but 5 percent supported one or more of the mainstream, democratic political parties.[45] Almost 40 percent of the judges sampled in another study said they would personally participate in a political demonstration if they were in agreement with its goals.[46]

In more specific policy areas, judges have tended to take a mildly center-right position. Over 40 percent of the sample, for example, said they would support an employer lockout during a labor dispute, yet only 15 percent thought striking workers would be justified in preventing nonstrikers from entering the factory. Although 52 percent saw a danger to the Republic from the radical left, only 16 percent viewed extreme right-wing groups as a current danger. Almost 80 percent of the judges approved of the "education of the young in such a manner that they adapt to the existing order," and a solid 60 percent also supported the "classless comprehensive school."[47]

Judges and Justice in Eastern Germany

Following unification the Federal Republic's legal system went into force throughout the five new Eastern Länder. But neither the existing court structure nor the judges themselves were in any way comparable to the West German system. For the East German communists, law and judges were both subordinate to party control. The rule of law and an independent judiciary meant little in the one-party "dictatorship of the proletariat."

The great majority of the former judges and prosecutors had been members of the Communist party. Their decisions included many scandalous political trials reminiscent of an earlier era. East Germans were sentenced to prison terms for wearing a white bow in their lapel as a sign that they had applied to leave the country. In 1989 a young East German received a two-and-a-half-year prison term because he attempted to hand a visiting West German leader a note appealing for help. Another East German was given a ten-year sentence for talking to West German television correspondents. But the most outrageous judicial acts involved citizens who were trying to flee the country. In some cases they were forced to give up their children, who were then adopted by parents loyal to the regime. West German authorities estimate that at least half of all East German judges and prosecutors were incriminated by evidence maintained at a West German center that monitored human rights abuses in the former GDR. The center has documented over 40,000 cases of East German maltreatment of its citizens.

Most ministries of justice in the new Eastern states are still largely staffed at the top by West German jurists. Retired judges from West Germany and recent graduates from West German law schools are also filling the gap. After unification in 1990 about two-thirds of the former GDR's 1,500 judges and prosecutors were given probationary appointments. By 1998 about 400 of this group had been given permanent civil service tenure, and the remaining 600 had been dismissed or had resigned.[48] Thus of the original 1,500 East German jurists, less than a fourth were deemed qualified to serve in the new democratic system. This relatively thoroughgoing purge of the communist legal system is in sharp contrast to the "denazification" of the West

German judiciary after 1945.[49] Eventually, the graduates of the law schools established in the Eastern states will assume leadership positions in the regional and national judiciary.

Court Structure

In addition to a unified body of law, all regular courts follow the same rules of procedure. However, the structure of the courts is decentralized. Unlike in the United States, there is no separate system of federal and state courts. With the exception of the seven national high courts of appeal, all regular tribunals are state courts; and although national law outlines the basic organization of the judiciary, the courts are established and administered by state statutes. The other significant characteristics of the German structures are the collegial nature of most tribunals and the extensive system of specialized courts.

Regular (civil and criminal) courts are organized on four levels: local, district, appellate, and federal. Roughly 700 local courts (*Amtsgerichte*) are usually staffed by a single judge (in criminal cases the judge is assisted by two lay judges chosen randomly from local citizens) and are located in most small- to medium-sized towns. Local courts have jurisdiction over minor civil matters and petty criminal offenses and also perform some administrative functions (bankruptcy supervision, administering estates, appointing guardians). At the next level are 116 district courts. These are appellate courts for the Amtsgerichte, but they also have original jurisdiction over most major civil and criminal matters. All district court cases are tried by panels of three to five judges. There are several panels at this level, and each tends to specialize in different types of cases. The final court of appeal below the national level is the *Oberlandesgericht* (state appellate court). These courts take cases only on appeal, with the exception of cases involving treason and anticonstitutional activity. In Germany, an appeal involves both a reexamination of the facts in a case and its procedural and legal aspects. These courts are also divided into panels of three to five judges, with each panel specializing in different types of cases. The final appellate court in the regular system is the federal appeals court at Karlsruhe (not to be confused with the Federal Constitutional Court, discussed later, which is also located at Karlsruhe). This is a very large tribunal with over a hundred judges divided into over twenty panels or senates (see Table 8.3).

The specialized court system is also decentralized. Courts dealing with administrative, social welfare, and labor matters operate at three levels—district, appellate, and national—with the national court serving as the final court of appeal. Specialized courts dealing with fiscal and tax matters operate only at the state and national levels.

In their respective areas, these courts dispense relatively speedy and inexpensive justice. If a citizen or a group feels that any state official or agency has acted illegally or arbitrarily, the case goes to an administrative court. Recently this system has been the major recourse for opponents of nuclear power.[50] The regular court system does not allow class action (*Verbandsklage*) suits, and grants standing to an environmental group only when its rights and those of its members are directly af-

TABLE 8.3   The German court structure and judiciary

Court	Number	Number of Judges
Regular courts*	849	15,649
Local	(707)	
District	(116)	
Appellate	(26)	
Specialized courts (state control)	279	5,320
Administrative courts	(52)	
Social courts	(69)	
Labor courts	(123)	
Fiscal courts	(35)	
State-level constitutional courts	13	140
Federal (national) courts	7	485
Federal appeals court		
Federal administrative court		
Federal labor court		
Federal social court		
Federal fiscal (finance) court		
Federal patent court		
Federal constitutional court		
Totals	1,148	21,594

*Civil and Criminal cases.

Source: Statistisches Bundesamt, *Datenreport 1997*, Bonn: Bundeszentrale für Politische Bildung, pp. 226, 229.

fected. However, the numerous permits and procedures required for the construction of a nuclear plant offer these groups an opportunity to challenge the government in the administrative courts on a variety of technical legal grounds.

Administrative courts have ruled that safety must take precedence over economic and technical questions in the construction of nuclear plants; several plants have been closed by administrative court rulings.

Specific disputes involving the social security, health, or welfare systems are heard in a "social" court. Similarly, labor-management problems, usually involving issues arising from collective bargaining agreements, are addressed in labor courts. In the specialized courts, professional judges sit with lay members; in the case of labor courts, for example, these lay members are selected by employers and employees.

Thus these institutions adjudicate matters that would be resolved either out of court or in the nonspecialized regular courts in the United States or Britain. To an extent, the readiness of Germans to go to court is due to the fact that there are so many available. Their presence also encourages the cautious, legalistic approach to administration so characteristic of the bureaucracy. Knowing that their mistakes may quickly find them in some court makes civil servants more concerned about the legal correctness of their actions and less concerned about the political implications of such actions.

Judicial Review and the Federal Constitutional Court

All courts and judges are engaged in politics, but a court is most political when it strikes down the acts of other governmental bodies, usually those of the executive or the legislature. In the continental legal tradition, judicial review (the authority of courts to nullify legislative or executive acts on constitutional grounds) has been an alien concept. It has been regarded as an undemocratic infringement on the right of popular sovereignty (1) as expressed in parliamentary acts, or (2) as contradictory to the principles of legal positivism that assign only an administrative role to judges. Although the practice of constitutional review, whereby courts resolved disputes between different levels of government or determined the validity of constitutional amendments, had some historic precedent in Germany, the acceptance of judicial review is essentially a twentieth-century and specifically postwar development.[51]

The framers of the Basic Law, desiring to check and balance governmental authority, were in general agreement on granting the courts the power of judicial review and on establishing a specific national court as the final arbiter in constitutional questions. American occupation authorities, with the U.S. Supreme Court in mind, also supported such an institution.

The result was Articles 93 and 94 of the Basic Law, which established the constitutional court, assigned its competency and jurisdiction, and defined its composition. The court was a new addition to the postwar legal system and has become the most political of all German courts. It is assigned the functions of judicial review, adjudication of disputes between state and federal political institutions, protection of individual civil rights as guaranteed in the constitution, and responsibility for protecting the constitutional and democratic order against groups and individuals seeking to overthrow it. In the latter area, the constitutional court has the right to ban such groups and their activities. These powers make the court unique in German judicial history.

The constitutional court is also distinct from other courts in organization and composition. Unlike state and national courts, which are administratively dependent on their respective justice ministers, the constitutional court is administratively independent. It hires, fires, and supervises all its employees, and justices are exempt from the administrative rules and regulations applicable to their colleagues on state and federal courts. Indeed, not even the parliament can impeach a constitutional court justice; only the federal president, upon a motion from the court itself, can remove a justice.[52] The court is financially autonomous. Like the two houses of parliament, it draws up its own budget, negotiating directly with the Finance Ministry and the parliament's judiciary committees.

The unique position of the constitutional court and its explicitly political character is most apparent in the selection of its members. Half of the sixteen judges are selected by the Bundesrat (the upper house), and half by the Bundestag (the lower house); in each case a candidate must have at least a two-thirds majority. These selection provisions ensure that both state and party/political factors play an important role and that they further enhance the unique character of the court. The Bundestag's candidates are nominated by a special judicial selection committee, an elite group composed of leading members of all parties in proportion to their strength in the chamber. The Bundestag parties attempt to influence the appointment of judges by presenting lists of candidates to the committee, although legally they cannot instruct their members on the committee how to vote. The Bundesrat's eight appointees are elected in a bloc vote from nominees proposed by its judiciary committee. Because the two houses cannot nominate the same judges, there is an ad hoc conference committee that coordinates the process. In the Bundesrat, as discussed in Chapter 7, each state's delegation votes *en bloc* on instructions from its government. This ensures that state governments have a direct influence on the selection process; moreover, interstate bargaining over nominees is quite common—especially over appointees to the court's second chamber, which hears most states' rights cases.

It is not difficult for knowledgeable students of the constitutional court to determine how each appointee got the job. Although there is considerable open political "horse trading" and occasional conflicts in the selection process, the quality of appointees has been high.[53] The Bundesrat has usually preferred high-level civil servants with excellent records in state administration. The lower house tends to nominate active politicians and judges from other federal courts. Both houses have recently drawn more candidates from their own ranks, that is, state justice ministers and leading members of the judicial selection committee. Membership on the court is regarded as a very prestigious appointment, and the quality of candidates is indicative of the status this institution has in the political system. Its strong penetration by state governments and parties also sets it apart from the traditional judiciary and makes it clearly a child of the Republic.

The constitutional court's sixteen members are divided into two senates, or chambers. Election is to a specific chamber, and members may not transfer. Each senate is administratively separate from the other and has its own areas of specialization. The first senate's jurisdiction includes all cases dealing with basic liberties covered by Articles 1 to 20 of the Basic Law and constitutional complaints involving these articles. The second senate is responsible for constitutional conflicts between different levels of government (federal-state, state-state) as well as a variety of specific political matters (political parties, election disputes, anticonstitutional activity, international law disputes).

Decisions.   In its forty-year history, the constitutional court has made its mark as an independent guardian of the democratic constitution, a protector of human rights, and an adjudicator of German federalism. By the early 1990s it had interpreted over half of the constitution's 151 articles in over 2,100 cases, and in almost 800 of these cases involving the constitutionality of legislation, it had invalidated federal and state laws or regulations.[54] In its early decisions such as the Southwest case (1951), a dispute over state boundaries comparable to the landmark American cases of *Marbury v. Madison* and *McCulloch v. Maryland,* the constitutional court established its authority as the supreme source of constitutional interpretation, clearly departed from legal positivism in granting legitimacy to certain higher or natural-law values, and set forth fundamental principles (e.g., federalism, democracy, and the rule of law) that are superior to all other constitutional or legal provisions.

More than any other postwar institution, the constitutional court has enunciated the view that the Federal Republic is a militant democracy whose democratic political parties are the chief instrument for the translation of public opinion into public policy. The concept of the party state, discussed in Chapter 5, owes much to the opinions of the court. The controversial banning of the Communist and neo-Nazi *Sozialistische Reichspartei* in the 1950s was also an expression of this concept of militant democracy.

Nor has the court shirked conflict with the government and top executive leadership. When Adenauer attempted to form a second television network that would have been under national control, the court, responding to state claims that such a network violated the reserved rights of the Länder to govern their own cultural affairs, struck down the legislation. The cries of protest from the chancellor's office left little doubt that the court was doing its job.

In other significant political decisions, the court upheld the landmark 1970 treaties with the Soviet Union and Poland, struck down the abortion law passed by the Social-Liberal government in 1974, ordered major changes in the 1983 census law, threw out the government's electoral law for the 1990 federal election, and ruled that citizens whose property had been confiscated during the 1945–1949 Soviet military occupation of the former East Germany are not entitled to the return of their property but may receive monetary compensation. The 1990 Unity Treaty between the two German states did not allow for the return of property seized during that period, and in 1991 the court ruled that the provisions of the treaty were indeed constitutional.[55]

In 1993 the court struck down yet another abortion law that had been passed in response to the differing West and East German laws (see Chapter 2). In 1995, in a controversial unification decision, the court ruled that top East German spies could not be tried in a unified Germany if they had done their work exclusively from the territory of the former East Germany against the former West Germany. The ruling amounted to a virtual amnesty for the top leadership of the GDR intelligence agencies. However, East German spies formerly operating within West Germany (in many cases on orders from the top GDR agency leaders) can be prosecuted. The ruling drew sharp criticism from East German civil rights groups that want the Federal Republic to bring their former oppressors to justice.

Later in 1995 the court was again at the center of a storm of controversy when it struck down a Bavarian school ordinance mandating that each classroom be equipped with a crucifix. The court ruled that the regulation, which in effect required all children to learn "under the cross," violated constitutional guarantees of religious freedom and the neutrality of the state in religious questions (Article 4). The decision was immediately denounced by Catholic Church officials and the Bavarian government as an unwarranted intrusion into the state's deeply rooted cultural traditions and a violation of Bavaria's right to run its own schools. Some Bavarian leaders called for a boycott of the ruling. Chancellor Kohl also criticized the court's decision. In 1998 the court ruled that Bavaria's abortion regulations violated the constitution. The ruling sharply limited the rights of states to pass regulations and legislation that conflict with federal law. In the Bavarian case, the state administration had attempted to restrict the freedom-of-choice components of the national abortion law. Also in 1998, the Court ruled that Germany's entrance into the European Monetary System was constitutional.

In 1999 the Court in a spectacular decision ruled that the existing tax laws for child-care expenses were unconstitutional because they allowed single parents to deduct more than married parents. The existing law assumed that "intact" families would spend less for child care than single parents. The Court ruled that the law violated the equal protection provisions of the Constitution as well as Article 6, which obligates the state to protect and promote the family. The decision, however, if implemented, will cost the federal treasury about $13.5 billion in reduced revenues and would wreak havoc on the government's plan to reduce taxes.

Thus, like those of its American counterpart, the constitutional court's decisions have often provoked sharp reactions from political leaders, and charges have been made that the court has failed to exercise judicial restraint and has attempted to usurp legislative functions. To students of judicial review, especially as practiced by the U.S. Supreme Court, these charges are very familiar. Although disputes about court decisions are usually couched in legal terms, both supporters and critics of the court's decisions have ample political reasons for their positions. In other words, it all depends on whose ox is gored. Public support for the court is strong. Surveys generally find that Germans have more trust in the court than in any other public institution.[56] There is no doubt that the court has become a legitimate component of the political system, and that its decisions have been accepted and complied with by both winners and losers.[57]

Reform of the Legal System and Judiciary

Perhaps with the example of the constitutional court in mind, a growing number of judges and legal scholars have advocated a thorough reform of the judiciary and the legal codes. The issue is not, as during the immediate postwar years, the commitment of judges to the principles of the Republic, but the rigidity and conservatism of the court structure (and some judges) as well as the outmoded and irrelevant character of many provisions of the nineteenth-century civil and criminal codes.

Numerous proposals for reform of the legal profession and especially the judiciary have been made. Most have focused on changes in legal education and the replacement of the still-dominant philosophy of positivism with one that stresses judicial independence and makes the judges consciously "internalize" those democratic values which, according to the constitution, are to determine social, economic, and political life."[58] The judge is to be aware of the political character of his or her activity and to recognize her or his individual responsibility, not to the bureaucratic hierarchy but to the constitution. This concept of the political judge is still controversial in the Federal Republic, and the changes in judicial values that it assumes will take far longer than the revision of the codes.

SUMMARY AND CONCLUSION

The administrative and judicial institutions of the Federal Republic have provided an important element of continuity between the postwar democracy and earlier political systems. As in the past, they have adapted to new political events and situations with few difficulties. The unification process of 1989–1990 was also an impressive achievement for the West German civil service; it belies the notion that bureaucracies cannot respond quickly and efficiently to new situations. Moreover, the process of generational change has produced younger civil servants and lawyers who are committed to democratic principles and ideals.

During the reconstruction phase of the postwar period (from 1945 to about 1965) these institutions, faced with straightforward, relatively routine policy tasks, performed well. However, their ability to adapt to the new quantitative and qualitative demands of modern policymaking has been seriously questioned in recent years. It is the fragmented, decentralized, ad hoc character of policymaking and administration that concerns many students of German governmental institutions.

On the other hand, when one considers the circumstances of the Republic's founding, the pressures of Allied military occupiers, and the experiences with the centralized, "efficient" Third Reich, the current structure does not seem inefficient or irrational, at least to many foreign observers. Where some see fragmentation, others see pluralism; and there is little doubt that postwar decentralization has provided many opportunities for practicing the art of compromise and bargaining, which are essential to conflict management in a modern democracy. Also, some planners and reformers want a stronger, centralized political system that would be far more committed to basic social and economic change than most Germans seem to prefer. The construction, then, of a synthesis of the legitimate demands of reformist and traditionalist administrative and judicial interests has now become a major task for the political system.

Notes

1. Gabriel Almond and Sidney Verba, *The Civic Culture* (Princeton, NJ: Princeton University Press, 1963), pp. 189ff.

2. Arnold Brecht, "Personnel Management," in *Governing Postwar Germany,* ed. Edward H. Litchfield (Ithaca, NY: Cornell University Press, 1953), p. 264.

3. *Ibid.,* p. 267.

4. *Ibid.,* p. 268.

5. Karl Loewenstein, "Justice," in *Governing Postwar Germany,* pp. 236–262.

6. *Ibid.,* p. 248.

7. *Ibid.,* p. 245.

8. Following the 1969 and 1982 changes of government, approximately one-half of the government's state secretaries and one-third of the department heads were removed for political reasons and either pensioned or reassigned elsewhere in the state administration. Hans-Ulrich Derlien, "Repercussions of Government Change on the Career Civil Service in West Germany: The Cases of 1969 and 1982," *Governance* 1 (1988): 50–78. The replacement rate for the 1998 change of government appears to be higher, but this is distorted by the civil servants who have chosen to retire instead of moving to Berlin.

9. Reimut Jochimsen, "Integriertes System," *Bulletin: Presse-und Informationsamt der Bundesregierung,* no. 97 (July 16, 1970): 953.

10. Renate Mayntz and Fritz W. Scharpf, *Policymaking in the German Federal Bureaucracy* (New York, Amsterdam: Elsevier, 1975), pp. 69–76.

11. *Ibid.,* pp. 77 ff.

12. Werner Thieme, "Das Stiefkind des Staates," *Die Zeit,* no. 38 (September 18, 1970), p. 60.

13. Gerhard Brinkmann, "Die Diskriminierung der Nicht-Juristen im allgemeinen höheren Verwaltungsdienst der Bundesrepublik Deutschland," *Zeitschrift für die gesamte Staatswissenschaft* 129 (1973): 150–167; and Bärbel Steinkemper, *Klassische und politische Bürokraten in der Ministerialverwaltung der Bundesrepublik Deutschland* (Cologne: Carl Heymanns Verlag, 1974), p. 20. A recent comparative study found that over 60 percent of top German civil servants were lawyers, as compared to approximately 20 percent of high-ranking American bureaucrats. Joel D. Aberbach, et al., "American and German Federal Executives: Technocratic and Political Attitudes," *International Social Science Journal,* no. 123 (February 1990): 7.

14. Jürgen Plöhn and Winfried Steffani, "Bund und Länder in der Bundesrepublik Deutschland," in *Handbuch der deutschen Länder,* 2nd edition, ed. Jürgen Hartmann (Bonn: Bundeszentrale für politische Bildung, 1994), pp. 33–48.

15. Mayntz and Scharpf, *Policymaking,* pp. 53 ff.

16. Niklas Luhmann and Renate Mayntz, *Personal im öffentlichen Dienst* (Baden-Baden: Nomos Verlagsanstalt, 1973), pp. 56 ff.

17. Robert D. Putnam, "The Political Attitudes of Senior Civil Servants in Western Europe: A Preliminary Report," *British Journal of Political Science 3* (1973): 257–290.

18. Eberhard Moths and Monika Wulf-Mathies, *Des Bürgers teuere Diener* (Karlsruhe: Verlag C.F. Mueller, 1973), p. 59.

19. For a comprehensive account of the professional civil service and the unification process, see Wolfgang Seibel, et al. (eds.), *Verwaltungsreform und Verwaltungspolitik im Prozeß der deutschen Einigung* (Baden-Baden: Nomos Verlagsgesellschaft, 1993).

20. In 1991 some officials in the Post and Transport ministries of the Kohl government proposed the abolition of career civil service status for employees of the Federal Railroad and Post Office. As in other Western European societies, the privatization of some government services is also well underway.

21. Elisabeth Noelle-Neumann and Renate Köcher, *Jahrbuch der Demoskopie, Vol. X,* Munich, Allensbach: K.G. Saur Verlag, 1997, p. 741.

22. Peter J. Katzenstein, *Policy and Politics in West Germany: The Growth of a Semi-Sovereign State* (Philadelphia: Temple University Press, 1987), Chapter 1.

23. *Ibid.,* p. 58.

24. Pension fund statistics cited in *Der Bürger im Staat* 41, no. 1 (March 1991): 22.
25. Volker Meinhardt, "Weiterhin hohe Transfers an die ostdeutschen Sozialversich-erungsträger," *Wochenbericht* No. 45, Deutsches Institut für Wirtschaft, Berlin (1999), p. 6.
26. DIW, *Wochenbericht* No. 45 (1999), p. 6.
27. Ellen Kennedy, The Bundesbank (New York: Council on Foreign Relations Press, 1991), p. 8.
28. John B. Goodman, "Monetary Politics in France, Italy and Germany: 1973–1985." Un-published paper, Graduate School of Business Administration, Harvard University, Sep-tember 1987, p. 23.
29. *Ibid.,* p. 12.
30. Kennedy, *The Bundesbank,* pp. 99ff.
31. *New York Times,* November 19, 1987, p. D8; December 3, 1987, p. D2.
32. *New York Times,* October 30, 1987, p. D7; November 5, 1987, p. D1.
33. Forschungsgruppe Wahlen, *Politbarometer,* No. 9 (September 1998), p. 3.
34. Before the Treuhand law went into effect, several state-owned firms and properties were converted into private corporations by their former managers. In many cases for-mer Stasi and other high-ranking party officials were involved. Large plots of prime commercial land, previously the property of the state, were the major assets of these new corporations. The land and buildings are now being rented to legitimate firms. The rental income ensures the stockholders (i.e., former Stasi officials) a comfortable income requiring no special expertise. Because these transactions took place before the Treuhand law went into effect, it is difficult for the Treuhand to receive the hold-ings. West German law does not recognize "the people-owned property" as defined in the former GDR. Hence the action of the former Communists—that is, turning state-run property into private enterprises—does not technically violate any West German law. The knowledge that many Stasi and party stalwarts are profiting from the collapse of the Communist regime is a source of substantial discontent among citizens of the former GDR.
35. This figure does not include over 20,000 small businesses, hotels, restaurants, and drug-stores that the Treuhand also controlled. In addition, the agency had to privatize about 30 percent of the farmland in the former East Germany.
36. Helmar Drost, "The Great Depression in East Germany: The Effects of Unification on East Germany's Economy," *East European Politics and Society 7,* no. 3 (Fall 1993), 470.
37. *Frankfurter Allgemeine Zeitung,* December 31, 1994, p. 13.
38. The late, former head of the agency, Detlev-Karsten Rohwedder, once estimated that "*der ganze Salat* [the whole shebang] was worth about DM 300 billion ($200 billion)." This very inaccurate estimate illustrates the difficulty that even experienced Westerners had in determining the real value of property in socialist economies.
39. For an account of the new organization of the Treuhand, see *Frankfurter Allgemeine Zeitung,* December 29, 1994, p. 10.
40. The parliament, however, must approve any extensions of the agency's credit line. In 1992, only 40 percent of the Treuhand's expenses were covered by its income of about $10 billion. *Der Spiegel,* no. 17 (April 20, 1992), pp. 160–161. See also Peter Christ and Ralf Neubauer, *Kolonie im eigenen Land. Die Treuhand, Bonn und die Wirtschaftskatas-trophe der fünf neuen Länder* (Berlin: Rowohlt Berlin Verlag, 1991).
41. Donald P. Kommers, *Judicial Politics in West Germany* (Beverly Hills and London: Sage Publications, 1976), p. 50. See also Donald P. Kommers, *The Constitutional Jurispru-dence of the Federal Republic of Germany* (Durham, NC: Duke University Press, 1989).
42. Kommers, *Judicial Politics,* p. 34.
43. Kommers, *Judicial Politics,* p. 44.
44. Theo Rasehorn, "Die dritte Gewalt in der zweiten Republik," *Aus Politik und Zeit-geschichte,* no. 39 (September 27, 1975): 5.

45. Manfred Riegel, "Political Attitudes and Perceptions of the Political System by Judges in West Germany." Paper, IX World Congress of the International Political Science Association, Montreal, 1973, p. 2a.

46. Ursula Hoffmann-Lange, "Eliteforschung in der Bundesrepublik Deutschland," *Aus Politik und Zeitgeschichte,* no. 47 (November 26, 1983): 14.

47. Riegel, "Political Attitudes and Perceptions of the Political System by Judges in West Germany," p. 2a.

48. There were strong regional variations in the examination process. Only a handful of East German jurists passed muster in Berlin (4) or the states of Saxony (7) or Mecklenburg-West Pomerania (19), but 135 judges and prosecutors in the small state of Saxony-Anhalt made the grade. *Frankfurter Allgemeine Zeitung,* June 10, 1994, p. 4.

49. Several top former GDR judges and prosecutors have been convicted of human rights violations and of disregarding even the GDR's laws when it was politically expedient to do so. In 1994, for example, a former judge of the East German supreme court was sentenced to almost four years in prison for unjustly sentencing two East Germans to death. *Frankfurter Allgemeine Zeitung,* June 18, 1994, p. 4. Between 1990 and 1998 judicial authorities in the new Eastern states initiated about 22,500 investigations into human rights abuses, judicial misconduct, and criminal acts (mainly fraud and misuse of government funds) committed by DDR authorities. These investigations led to 877 indictments and 211 convictions; about 1,000 investigations are still underway. The most convictions (78) occurred with police and border guards. Over 100 indictments against DDR judges and prosecutors yielded only 16 convictions. About 60 Stasi officials were indicted and 12 convicted. About 80 former GDR officials were convicted of economic crimes connected with the unification process. German judicial officials consider this work largely completed and anticipate no major new investigations. Karl-Heinz Baum, "Justiz will Akten schließen," *Frankfurter Rundschau,* November 6, 1998 (Internet edition).

50. Dorothy Nelkin and Michael Pollak, "French and German Courts on Nuclear Power," *Bulletin of the Atomic Scientists,* May 1980, p. 37. It has also been suggested that administrative court judges are more likely to be concerned with citizens' rights against the state (rather than the "general" interest) than are their counterparts in the regular court system. Some of the younger administrative court judges were also part of the student protest movement of the 1960s. According to a leading environmental lawyer, "Judges with a left ideology will usually try to find a job in the administrative rather than the civil courts." Cited in Nelkin and Pollak, "French and German Courts," p. 41.

51. Kommers, *Judicial Politics,* p. 29. During the Weimar Republic the *Reichsgericht* (the highest general court in the Weimar system), capitalizing on the ambiguity of the constitution in this area, did in fact strike down legislation on constitutional grounds, especially between 1921 and 1929. Most state courts at this time also accepted judicial review in theory, although they rarely used it to nullify legislative acts. Thus there was some tradition, albeit fragmentary, for this principle.

52. Kommers, *Judicial Politics,* p. 85.

53. *Ibid.,* pp. 120–144.

54. In approximately 300 cases the court ordered a revision of the unconstitutional legislation. By early 1991 it had upheld the constitutionality of about 1,400 federal or state laws and regulations. Court statistics cited in *Das Parlament,* no. 36 (August 30, 1991), 4.

55. The court did not rule out subsequent action by the government and parliament (1) to compensate those citizens whose property was confiscated by the communists from 1945 to 1949, or even (2) to return the property if it was in public ownership and still intact. *Frankfurter Allgemeine Zeitung,* September 2, 1994, p. 8.

56. For data from a 1994 study see General Social Survey (ALLBUS), 1994, pp. 104–123.

57. The success of the constitutional court is related, of course, to the performance of the overall system of which it is a part. Because the judges are selected by legislative institutions, political and ideological considerations have played a role. However, the dominant

political parties have shared a consensus on the basic values, norms, and institutions of the Republic, including the types of people who are to serve on the court. A breakdown in this consensus would also over time undermine the court's representativeness and legitimacy. See Nevil Johnson, "The Interdependence of Law and Politics: Judges and the Constitution in West Germany," *West European Politics 5,* no. 3 (July 1982): 249, for a discussion of this point.

58. Rudolf Wassermann, "Zur politischen Funktion der Rechtssprechung," *Aus Politik und Zeitgeschichte,* no. 47 (November 23, 1974): 3. For more recent criticisms see Kommers, *The Constitutional Jurisprudence of the Federal Republic of Germany.*

9 | Subnational Units: Federalism and Local Government

The federal structure of the Republic, which corresponds to German political tradition as well as to the wishes of postwar Allied military occupiers, ensures that the formulation and implementation of policy, together with the recruitment of political leaders, are not concentrated at the national level. In 1990, prior to the formal unification of East and West, the once rigidly centralized German Democratic Republic was reconstituted as a federal state with five new states joining the eleven from West Germany, a further testimony to the strength of the federal idea in Germany's political tradition. More than any other major West European state, the Federal Republic has decentralized and fragmented political power. Indeed, as discussed in the preceding chapter, many experts contend that power and authority are too decentralized and compartmentalized.[1] In contrast to Britain, France, Italy, and other states, the devolution of power is really not an issue in Germany; more important is its consolidation. Germany's membership in the European Union has also complicated the relationship between the national government and the constituent states.

THE DEVELOPMENT OF GERMAN FEDERALISM

The German Reich founded in 1871 was composed of twenty-five historic German states, which voluntarily entered into a federation. These entities, however, were grossly unequal in size and population. Seventeen of them combined made up less than 1 percent of the total area of the Reich and less than 10 percent of the total population. Prussia was by far the largest unit in the federation, accounting for two-thirds of its area and population.

The unity of this newly formed Reich was tenuous. Some of the member states had, in fact, been forced into the federation by a combination of military defeat at the hands of Prussia and the power politics practiced with consummate skill

by Bismarck.[2] The remarkable industrial and economic growth that followed unification temporarily stilled opposition to Prussian dominance and reduced particularistic sentiment. Germany's defeat in World War I, coupled with the political,
social, and economic unrest that plagued the postwar Weimar Republic, brought
forth a variety of individuals and groups in areas such as Bavaria and the
Rhineland that demanded the end of the centralized Reich and the restoration of
full sovereignty to the constituent states. In some cases, foreign governments (especially that of France) aided the forces of particularism. The Nazis, who ironically in their early years found common ground with the separatists in their
opposition to the Republic, abolished state government and imposed a centralized
administration on the Third Reich.

The destruction of the Nazi system and postwar military occupation returned
the forces of decentralization to a dominant position. All Germany's conquerors
wanted a decentralized postwar Germany in some form. The French would have
preferred a completely dismantled Reich composed of several independent states,
none of which would be powerful enough ever to threaten France again. The
American occupiers, having considerable experience with federal structures,
urged an American-type system. The British, although more centrist than the
Americans or French, also envisioned a decentralized postwar Germany. Among
the Germans, opposition to a strong federal system was mostly limited to the SPD
and to those Christian Democrats in the Soviet zone, which incorporated what remained of postwar Prussia.

With the emerging Cold War and division of Germany, the influence of centrist
elements waned still further; and by 1949 there was little significant West German
opposition to plans for a decentralized state. Indeed, Western occupiers could count
on German support for federalism in their occupation zones because the zones included the historically most particularistic and anti-Prussian segments of the former
Reich: Bavaria, the Rhineland, the province of Hanover, and the Hanseatic cities of
Hamburg and Bremen. The framers of the Basic Law were also largely state-level or
former Weimar politicians, who since 1946 had to renew their political careers at the
state level. Thus the delegates to the parliamentary council were a very states'
rights–oriented group.

The Basic Law ensures the states' substantial influence in three ways:

1. Through powers reserved to them (education, police and internal security, administration of justice, supervision of the mass communications
   media)
2. Through their responsibility for the administering of federal law, including the collection of most taxes
3. Through their direct representation in the parliament (the Bundesrat)

Since 1969 the states are also equal participants with the federal government in certain joint tasks enumerated by Articles 91a and 91b of the Basic Law: higher education, regional economic development, and agricultural reform. Thus, in addition to
their own reserved powers, the states have either direct or indirect influence on all

national legislation. In only a few policy areas, such as defense and foreign affairs, does the national government not have to consider the views of the states in either the making or the implementation of policy. A series of constitutional amendments passed in 1994 is also designed to ensure state influence at the European level. The states are concerned that the national government respect their authority and prerogatives when negotiating in the European Union.

STATE-LEVEL POLITICS

Unity and Diversity among German States

The sixteen states differ in tradition, size, population, and socioeconomic resources. In the "old" Federal Republic (i.e., before unification), only three of the states—Bavaria and the two city states of Hamburg and Bremen—existed as separate political entities before 1945. The remaining *Länder* were created by Allied occupiers, in many cases to the consternation of tradition-conscious Germans. In the American zone, two new states, Hesse and Baden-Württemberg, were formed.[3] In the French zone, on the left bank of the Rhine, another new state, the Rhineland-Palatinate, was created from territories that had earlier been provinces of Prussia, Bavaria, and Hesse. In the north, some previously independent areas and still more Prussian provinces were rearranged by the British to make the two new states of Schleswig-Holstein and Lower Saxony. In 1957 the Saar region, which had been under French control since 1945, returned to Germany after a plebiscite and became the tenth Land. Finally, West Berlin, whose status as a Land was disputed by the GDR and the Federal Republic, as well as by the Western powers and the former Soviet Union until the 1990 unification, existed de facto as a state after 1949. On October 3, 1990, Berlin's division ended and the city, East and West, is now a full-fledged member of the federation.

The five new East German states have also had a checkered postwar history. Three of the states—Mecklenburg–West Pomerania, Saxony, and Thuringia—had existed as separate political entities before World War II. The Soviet occupation authorities created a new state, Saxony-Anhalt, from parts of Saxony and Thuringia. The state of Brandenburg, which surrounds Berlin, constitutes the remains of the prewar Prussia, which was dissolved after World War II. But in 1952, only three years after the formation of the German Democratic Republic, all five states were abolished and replaced with fifteen administrative districts. East Germany's first (and last) freely elected government reestablished the five states prior to the October 1990 unification.

The Big Four

The four largest states in area and population are North Rhine–Westphalia, Bavaria, Baden-Württemberg, and Lower Saxony. Of these North Rhine–Westphalia is by far the most populous. Over 22 percent of Germany's 82 million inhabitants live in this state, which incorporates the Rhine-Ruhr region. Politics in this Land have been competitive since 1946, with relatively close elections and alternations of government and opposition parties. Since the mid-1980s, however, the Social Democrats have been the dominant party; they govern in coalition with the Greens.

The largest state in area and second largest in population is Bavaria. Left intact after the war, Bavaria is without question the most particularistic of the states. If there are any American-style states' rights advocates left in the Federal Republic, they are in this heavily Catholic, tradition-conscious region that has been marching to a slightly different beat from the rest of Germany since long before the Federal Republic. Bavaria entered the Bismarckian Reich in 1871 only after receiving special concessions (its own beer tax among them), and it was a hotbed of separatist and extremist sentiment during the Weimar Republic. It was the only Land that did not ratify the Basic Law in 1949, although the Bavarians acceded to the will of the other states and did finally join the Federal Republic. Bavaria thus rejected the Basic Law but also rejected its own exclusion from "the common German destiny" (*deutsche Schicksalsgemeinschaft*), that is, Bavaria joined but with little enthusiasm.

In spite of their particularist traditions and strong support of federalism, the Bavarians (and especially the ideologically committed among them in the Christian Social Union) in many ways consider themselves the guardians of the German nationalist tradition in an increasingly cosmopolitan and integrated Western Europe. Following unification in 1990, Bavaria went before the court again in an effort to stop the Kohl government from accepting the Oder-Neisse line as the legitimate border between Germany and Poland. Its leaders have been among the most prominent opponents of the Euro, the common European currency introduced in eleven countries in 1999. Bavaria is a strong one party–dominant state. The Christian Social Union (CSU) has been the strongest single party in all but one of twelve postwar state elections and has governed either alone or in coalition for all but four years since 1946.

The third largest Land in population, with 10 million inhabitants, is the southwestern state of Baden-Württemberg. More religiously balanced than Bavaria, its politics have usually been controlled by center-right parties, most often the CDU in coalition with the Free Democrats. Grand Coalitions between the CDU and SPD, however, have also governed at various times. From 1969 to 1988 the CDU governed alone. Currently the Christian Democrats rule in a coalition with the Free Democrats. Overall, then, it has been a more competitive state than Bavaria.

Lower Saxony is the fourth most populous state and the third largest in area. A heavily Protestant (80 percent) Land with a high concentration of former refugees and a strong rural component to its economy, Lower Saxony has had generally competitive party politics in the postwar period. After fourteen years in opposition, the Social Democrats returned to power in 1990 with the help of the Greens, and since 1994 have governed alone. The current chancellor, Gerhard Schröder, was the chief executive of this state from 1990 to 1998.

The remaining six states from the "old" West Germany—Hesse, the Rhineland-Palatinate, the Saar, Schleswig-Holstein, Hamburg, and Bremen—all have fewer than 7 million inhabitants. Both Schleswig-Holstein and the Rhineland have significant rural, small-town populations and are two of the poorest states from the standpoint of per capita income. The CDU has frequently dominated state politics in both, usually in coalition with the Free Democrats. But in 1988 the Social Democrats for the first time in their history won an absolute majority in Schleswig-Holstein. They were reelected in 1996. In 1991 the voters in the Rhineland-Palatinate, Helmut Kohl's home state, also made the Social Democrats the largest party; and it governs, in coalition with the Free Democrats, for the first time in the state's history. Hesse is a heavily industrialized Protestant Land with some Catholic enclaves. It has generally been an SPD stronghold, but in 1999, only a few months after the national election, which brought the Social Democrats and Greens to power, the Christian Democrats and Free Democrats won a surprise victory. The city states of Hamburg and Bremen, both largely Protestant, have been governed mainly by the Social Democrats, in frequent coalition with the middle-class Free Democrats and, in recent years, the Greens.

Hamburg is the richest state in the federation. The city has profited mightily from unification. It is the main port of entry for the many goods now imported into the East. The Elbe, Germany's "blue-collar" river, flows into the Baltic Sea at Hamburg, and the river is once again open for business. In 1998 Hamburg, measured by per capita gross national product, also became the richest city in Europe. The Saarland, one of the smallest states, is primarily an industrial area with a large Catholic population. Until the mid-1980s this state was controlled by the Christian Democrats. At the next three elections, however, the Social Democrats, led by Oskar Lafontaine, won an absolute majority. In 1999 the Christian Democrats returned to power.

The New East German States

The five new additions to the federation are relatively small. The largest Land, Saxony, with about 5 million residents, is only the sixth largest of the sixteen states. Saxony is also the major industrial center of the former East Germany, accounting for about 35 percent of the area's gross national product. Before 1933 Saxony was a stronghold of the Social Democrats, but the Christian Democrats won an absolute majority at the state's first free election in 1990 and were reelected in 1994 and 1999. The strip-mining of lignite, an outmoded chemical industry, and decades of neglect have left the state with massive environmental problems.

The other four states are smaller and less industrialized than Saxony. Its neighbor, Saxony-Anhalt, has the shortest history as an independent political entity. The state, which contains some of Germany's most fertile farmland, is governed by the Social Democrats in a minority government tolerated by the Party of Democratic Socialism (PDS), the successor to the ruling Communist party of the former East Germany. Thuringia, with 2.6 million inhabitants, has a more mixed economy than Saxony or Saxony-Anhalt. It was the center of the former GDR's high-tech microelectronics industry. The state is governed currently by the Christian Democrats. Because of its proximity to the Western states, Thuringia has had the highest growth rate of any East German region. About 100,000 Thuringians commute daily to jobs in Hesse and Bavaria.[4] Brandenburg is a sparsely populated Land in the northeast. Until 1920 Berlin was a province of Brandenburg; the city lies within its borders. From 1990 to 1999 Brandenburg was the sole stronghold of the Social Democrats in

TABLE 9.1   The Länder of the Federal Republic

Land	1998 Pop. (millions)	Area (000 sq. km.)	Pop. (per sq. km.)	Gross National Product Total ($billions)	Gross National Product Proportion of Total	Gross National Product Per Capita ($thousand)*
North Rhine-Westphalia	18.0	34.1	527	698.0	22.8	28,943
Bavaria	12.0	70.6	170	526.0	17.2	32,713
Baden-Württemberg	10.4	35.8	291	449.0	14.7	32,174
Lower Saxony	7.8	47.6	165	279.0	9.1	26,726
Hesse	6.0	21.1	286	306.0	10.0	38,065
Saxony	4.5	18.4	246	84.0	2.7	15,827
Berlin	3.4	0.9	3846	123.0	4.0	28,374
Rhineland-Palatinate	4.0	19.8	202	134.0	4.4	25,777
Saxony-Anhalt	2.7	20.4	132	48.0	1.6	15,623
Schleswig-Holstein	2.8	15.8	175	98.0	3.2	27,112
Brandenburg	2.6	29.5	87	50.0	1.6	16,759
Thuringia	2.5	16.2	153	44.0	1.4	15,502
Mecklenburg-West Pomerania	1.8	23.2	78	32.0	1.0	14,975
Hamburg	1.7	0.8	2257	119.0	3.9	52,574
Saarland	1.1	2.6	421	39.0	1.3	26,359
Bremen	0.7	0.4	1667	35.0	1.1	38,750
Total	82.1	357.2	230	3064	100.0	27,265

*DM 1.50 equal $1.00

**Local Alternative Party

Source: Federal Statistical Office (Wiesbaden).

the Eastern states. Since the 1999 state election, the SPD has had to share power with the Christian Democrats.

The smallest of the new states in population, with fewer than 2 million residents, is the coastal Land of Mecklenburg-West Pomerania. Although composing 2.3 percent of the country's population, it contributes less than 1 percent to the country's GNP. Since unification over 80,000 residents have left the Land. This region is primarily agricultural, but it has a shipbuilding industry that could become

		Work Force			
% Foreign Residents (1998)	% Agriculture (1998)	% Unemployment (1999)	% Roman Catholic	2000 Governing Party or Coalition	Capital
8	2	9.0	51	SPD-GREEN	Düsseldorf
9	4	7.9	69	CSU	Munich
12	3	7.1	46	CDU-FDP	Stuttgart
6	4	11.5	19	SPD	Hanover
14	2	9.1	33	CDU-FDP	Wiesbaden
2	3	18.9	5	CDU	Dresden
14	1	16.3	11	CDU-SPD	
8	3	9.2	55	SPD-FDP	Mainz
2	4	21.8	8	SPD	Magdeburg
5	3	10.7	6	SPD-GREEN	Kiel
2	5	18.3	5	SPD-CDU	Potsdam
1	4	17.0	9	CDU	Erfurt
1	6	20.1	5	SPD-PDS	Schwerin
18	1	11.2	8	SPD-GREEN	
7	0	11.4	73	CDU	Saarbrücken
12	0	15.2	10	SPD-CDU	Bremen
9	3	11.6	36		

competitive in the international marketplace. In 1998 a coalition between the Social Democrats (SPD) and the Party of Democratic Socialism (PDS) formed a new state government. It marked the first time since unification that the PDS, the successor to the former ruling Communist party of East Germany, had acquired governmental responsibility at the state level. Many Christian Democrats sharply criticized the Social Democrats for aligning with what they considered an antidemocratic party. This government will be closely watched to determine whether the PDS has overcome its communist heritage and is indeed committed to the democratic political process.

All these new states are poor. Per capita gross national product is only about 60 percent of the level in West Germany. Tax revenues cover less than one-half of the states' expenditures, which have already been cut to the bone. The new states are still in the process of developing a civil service, educational system, and court structure that conform to Western standards and the constitution.

As Table 9.1 shows, the sixteen states range in population from Bremen, with fewer than 1 million inhabitants, to North Rhine–Westphalia, with a population of 18 million. Their areas range from Bavaria's 70,600 square kilometers to Hamburg and Bremen's combined 120 square kilometers. Per capita GNP ranges from only $14,975 in Mecklenburg–West Pomerania (the other former GDR states are only slightly better off) to over $52,000 in Hamburg. Politically, the Social Democrats have been the strongest party in Hesse, Hamburg, Bremen, and Berlin; the CDU/CSU has done best in Bavaria, Baden-Württemberg, Schleswig-Holstein, the Rhineland-Palatinate, and the Saarland. Competitive party politics have been most prevalent in Lower Saxony and, at least until the 1980s, North Rhine–Westphalia.

Since the late 1970s, the southern states of Baden-Württemberg and Bavaria, Germany's version of the "Sun Belt," have experienced more economic growth and less unemployment than the northern states. Most of Germany's microelectronics, robotics, and aerospace industries are in the southern states, whereas the declining coal, steel, textile, and shipbuilding sectors of the economy are concentrated in the north. By 1999 unemployment in the south averaged about 7 percent, as compared to about 11 percent in northern states such as Lower Saxony and North Rhine–Westphalia.

THE CONSTITUTIONAL STRUCTURE OF THE STATES

The Basic Law requires that the "constitutional order in the Länder conform to the principles of republican, democratic, and social government based on the rule of law" (Article 28, paragraph 1). The specific form of government, including the questions of whether the legislature is to be bicameral or unicameral and the executive directly or indirectly elected, is left to the discretion of the states. All states have unicameral legislatures with an executive (minister-president and cabinet) responsible to it. Most states have also adopted the personalized proportional electoral law described in Chapter 6. State-level cabinets are composed of eight to twelve ministers. In addition to the classic ministries of finance, education, health, justice, and internal affairs, each state has several ministries whose activities reflect the state's special characteristics (e.g., the Rhineland-Palatinate's wine ministry, Hamburg and Bremen's harbors ministry).

Coalition governments have been as common in the states as they have at the national level. Until the mid-1960s, coalition alignments, especially in the larger states, were usually similar to those at the national level. This ensured that the national government would have adequate support for its program in the Bundesrat. The practice was an example of the integrating effects that political parties can have in a federal system. It began in the 1950s when Adenauer sought to compel all CDU state parties to leave coalitions with the Socialists and conform to the federal pattern of governing alone, if possible, or with other middle-class parties.[5] By the end of the decade, all state governments were controlled by either the CDU and its allies or the Social Democrats.

The waning of Adenauer's influence, CDU/CSU intraparty conflicts, and the greater acceptability of the SPD as a partner to the Free Democrats, and in some cases the Union itself, led to the breakdown of this pattern in the early 1960s. After the formation of the Grand Coalition in 1966, almost all types of party alignments possible could be found in the states. There were Grand Coalitions (SPD-CDU) in Baden-Württemberg and Lower Saxony; CDU/CSU–FDP alignments in Schleswig-Holstein, the Rhineland-Palatinate, and the Saar; SPD-FDP coalitions in North Rhine–Westphalia, Hamburg, and Bremen; and single-party governments in Bavaria (CSU) and Hesse (SPD). After the formation of the national SPD-FDP coalition in 1969, coalition governments at the state level again became consistent with the Bonn pattern: Either the SPD-FDP governed in coalition (Hesse, Hamburg, Bremen, Lower Saxony, North Rhine–Westphalia), or the Christian Democrats ruled alone (Bavaria, Rhineland-Palatinate, the Saar, Baden-Württemberg, Schleswig-Holstein). After 1976, however, a mixed pattern returned as the Christian Democrats and Free Democrats formed coalition governments in Lower Saxony and the Saar.

The return of the Christian Democrats to power in Bonn in 1982 was not followed by any major changes in the partisan composition of state governments consistent with the national CDU/FDP. Following the 1990 and 1994 post-unification national elections, there was also no discernible pattern in state-level coalitions. Although the Free Democrats governed with the Christian Democrats in Bonn, they were aligned with the Social Democrats in the Rhineland-Palatinate, and in the new East German state of Brandenburg until 1994. The two largest parties were also in a Grand Coalition in Berlin and Baden-Württemberg, and since 1995, Bremen. Between 1990 and 1998 the Free Democrats disappeared from the parliaments in twelve of the sixteen states, thus depriving both major parties of a traditional coalition partner. The Christian Democrats in these states are now in an especially difficult situation. They could form Grand Coalitions with the Social Democrats or break new ground and take the Greens, a party they once denounced as a radical left-wing sect, as a coalition partner.

State-Level Party Systems

The simplification of the national party system, discussed in Chapter 5, has been paralleled at the state level. During the early postwar years and into the 1950s, small regional parties played an important role in several states, principally Lower Saxony (the Refugee party and the German party), Bavaria (the Bavarian party) and North Rhine–Westphalia (the Center party). Their disappearance by the early 1960s reduced the particularistic or regional component and intensified the nationalization of state politics. Nonetheless, it is still easier for new parties to test the water and make a national impact by first concentrating on the state level. This was the strategy pursued by the right-wing National Democratic party (NPD) during the 1960s. By gaining representation in state parliaments, the party secured a foothold and received nationwide attention far sooner than if it had concentrated on national elections. Even in this case, the substance and direction of the party's appeal were national, and the NPD's defeat in the 1969 election also ended its string of successes in state elections. A similar strategy was followed by the Greens in the 1980s. In two states, Bremen and Baden-Württemberg, the party cleared the 5 percent hurdle and suddenly became a national political phenomenon. Since 1990 the Party of Democratic Socialism has succeeded in establishing itself as a regional party supported above all by those East Germans who are disappointed with unification.

State-level party systems also increase the sociological and ideological diversity of the national parties. For example, the impetus for the transformation of the SPD during the late 1950s came from those SPD state organizations that were in power. Indeed, the SPD was able to endure twenty years (1949–1969) of national opposition without becoming a radical, extremist sect, partly because it held power in several states where it had to deal with concrete policy problems. In this sense, state-level politics kept the SPD in the mainstream of national political life. In the case of the CDU/CSU, the federal system increased the national influence of the Union's right wing by providing it with a power base in Bavaria. In a unitary system, the Bavarian component of the party would have far less impact on the national organization than it now has under a federal system.

Electoral Politics in the States

Since the early 1960s, state elections, especially in the larger Länder, have increasingly become indicators or tests of the electorate's mood toward national parties, leaders, and issues. They can also have a direct effect on national politics by altering the party alignment in the Bundesrat.

As in congressional elections in the United States and by-elections in Great Britain, the party or parties in power at the national level generally lose support in state elections, which are usually held in off years. The results of state elections can also have an effect on the stability of the national governing coalition and its leadership. The resignation of Willy Brandt in 1974 was related to poor SPD showings in state elections after 1972. The collapse of the Schmidt government in 1982 was preceded by losses in state elections. In 1999, just four months after the stunning victory of the SPD and the Greens at the 1998 national election, the two parties lost a state election in Hesse. The defeat in Hesse, which was due largely to the national government's proposed changes in the citizenship laws, meant that the Schröder government no longer had a majority of votes in the Bundesrat (Federal Council). Thus changes at the state level can have a direct and immediate impact on national politics. All major transfers of power at the national level since 1949 have in fact been presaged by developments in state-level politics.

These consequences of state elections are largely the result of campaign strategies adopted by the parties, which have increasingly used state polls as tests of current support for national policies. The state election of 1998 in Lower Saxony was the critical test for Gerhard Schröder's chancellor candidacy. His success at that election made him the SPD's national candidate. The 1986 state election in Lower Saxony was widely considered a test election for the 1987 national vote. When the SPD failed to win in this state, its standings in the national polls dropped. The infusion of national personalities and issues into state campaigns may also explain the relatively high turnout in these elections, which has averaged about 70 percent since the early 1950s. In some cases, a party may not want to "nationalize" a state election because of unfavorable national conditions. Chancellor Schmidt, for example, expecting the SPD to lose votes because of the Brandt crisis, tried to stay out of state campaigns after his accession to the chancellorship. Because of Chancellor Kohl's declining popularity, the Christian Democrats in 1986 and early 1989 sought to reduce his role in state campaigns. Nonetheless, the opposition may well compel national leaders to come out and fight the electoral battle in the provinces. Thus, in spite of the occasional presence of genuine state factors in elections, they have increasingly become part of the national political struggle.

Leaders and Policies

The style of state *Ministerpräsidenten* has ranged from the strong father figure to a low-key bureaucratic approach. The postwar leaders of Hesse, Hamburg, and Bremen, and the former chief executive of Bavaria, are representative of the father-figure type. Most minister-presidents, however, have been relatively colorless administrators with extensive careers in local and state party organizations as their most common background characteristic.

Four of the Republic's seven chancellors (Kiesinger, Brandt, Kohl, and Schröder) were state chief executives before assuming the top spot in Bonn. The current chancellor, Gerhard Schröder, was minister-president of Lower Saxony. The SPD's chancellor candidates in 1987 (Johannes Rau), 1990 (Oskar Lafontaine), and 1994 (Rudolf Scharping) have all been state-level chief executives. The current leader of Bavaria, Edmund Stoiber, is a strong contender for the chancellor candidacy of the CDU/CSU in 2002. Leadership experience at the state level, as opposed to parliamentary experience at the national level, may become more common for future chancellor candidates.

The major issues of state politics tend to focus on those areas for which the states have primary responsibility: education, police and law enforcement, environmental questions, the supervision of radio and television, and the organization and regulation of the bureaucracy. The remainder of state activity tends to be rather routine administration of policies formulated at the national level, albeit with state input.

The states have varied considerably in their treatment of educational matters. During the 1950s and 1960s, the issue of separate schools for Protestant and Catholic children was a major problem in those states with large Catholic populations. The reform of secondary and university-level education has also varied, with CDU/CSU states such as Bavaria and the Rhineland-Palatinate being decidedly less enthusiastic about the comprehensive school and democratized universities than are SPD states such as Hesse and North Rhine–Westphalia. Also, as discussed in Chapter 4, the issue of radicals in public employment has been treated differently in conservative CDU states than in liberal SPD regions.

A clearer picture of state policy activities and the federal-state division of labor is provided by Table 9.2, which shows the expenditures of state and national governments by policy areas. Although the national government has almost sole responsibility for defense, internal security (police) is primarily a state function. In the area of social welfare, the national government spends about four times as much as the states. Education has clearly been the prerogative of the states, and it still consumes

TABLE 9.2   Expenditures of state and national governments by policy area (in percentages)

Policy Area	National	State
	Level	
	National	State
Social security, health, and welfare	33	8
Defense	19	—
Education	5	31
Police and administration of justice	1	10
General administration	4	6
Grants and other transfer payments	10	17
Transportation and communication	8	5
Housing	1	5
Energy and water resources	3	3
Economic enterprises	3	3
Agriculture	1	2
Debt service	12	10
Total	100	100

Source: *Statistisches Jahrbuch, 1990*, pp. 446–447.

about one-third of all expenditures. Nonetheless, federal efforts to gain a foothold in the education area are evident by the $22 billion Bonn spent in 1998. Both levels are also the dispensers of public largesse to other levels of government. In the case of the states, about one of every five marks goes to local government in the form of grants. The grants of the federal government (10 percent of expenditures) go largely to the states, but local communities are also the recipients of some national grants.

Federal-State Integration: Revenue Sharing

The Basic Law commits the Federal Republic to the maintenance of a "unity of living standards" for the various states of the federation. This is accomplished largely through money. Financial relations between the states and the federal government are very complex. They involve the following:

1. Vertical equalization (federal payments to poorer states)
2. The sharing of common tax revenues between the states and federal government
3. Horizontal equalization (payments to poorer states by richer ones)
4. Intergovernmental grants and subsidies for various special and joint projects, as well as federal payments to the states to defray the costs of administering federal law

German revenue sharing, especially on the federal government's part, has been designed to consolidate the structure and process of policymaking. Although the federal government receives about 55 percent of all tax revenues, it is responsible for only about 45 percent of all public expenditures, including national defense. The states and local communities, on the other hand, spend more than they receive in taxes, with the federal government making up most of the difference. This financial leverage has enabled the national government to effect some coordination in areas such as education, regional economic development, and social welfare programs.

The states, however, have steadily struggled for a larger piece of the tax pie and hence greater independence from the national government. At present, the states receive about one-third of the largest source of tax revenue, the individual and corporate income tax (division: 48 percent to Bonn, 34 percent to the states, 12 percent to the cities, and the remainder to the European Union). Since 1995 the states' share of the second-largest money raiser, the value-added tax, has increased from 37 percent to 44 percent (see Table 9.3 for information about sources of tax revenues). The federal government receives about 95 percent of its income from taxes, but taxes account for only 70 percent of state revenues; the difference of 25 percent is, in a sense, the margin of state dependency on the national government. For the national government, on the other hand, it is a means of facilitating integration and consolidation. Neither side is satisfied with the arrangement, and the struggle over the distribution of tax revenues continues.

TABLE 9.3   Sources of tax revenues by governmental level (in percentages)

Source	Level		
	National	**State**	**Local**
Individual and corporate income taxes	36	58	40
Value-added tax	29	26	—
Gewerbesteuer	—	—	42
Oil and gasoline tax	15	—	—
Tobacco	9	—	—
Automobile tax	—	8	—
Capital and inheritance tax	—	5	—
Custom duties	3	—	—
Liquor and beer tax	4	2	—
"Bagatelle" taxes (coffee, sugar, dogs, amusement)	1	—	1
Payroll tax	—	—	7
Property tax	—	—	9
Other	3	1	1
Total	100	100	100

Source: *Statistisches Jahrbuch, 1990,* pp. 444–445.

Until 1995 these revenue-sharing provisions were suspended for the new East German states. The old states, fearing a large drain on their treasuries, insisted that the new states would have to experience a substantial economic revival before these sections of the constitution could take effect. In exchange, the old states agreed to underwrite partially the "German Unity Fund," a bond issue to finance economic development in the new regions. In 1993 a "Solidarity Pact" was passed by the national parliament that restructured the distribution of tax revenues between local, state, and national governments and in 1995 brought the new states into the revenue-sharing system.

These new programs, however, have placed an added burden on Germany's richer states, such as Baden-Württemberg and Bavaria. Both have been major contributors to horizontal revenue-sharing. From 1970 to 1994 Baden-Württemberg alone paid about $25 billion into revenue sharing, almost half of the national total. Not surprisingly, together with Bavaria, the Baden-Württemberg government has frequently complained about revenue sharing and challenged its constitutionality. Critics of the program argue that it penalizes the efficient, productive states and rewards states like the Saarland with its outmoded rust-belt economy. It also hinders any chance of reducing the number of states in the federal system.

THE FUTURE OF FEDERALISM

On balance, one can say that the federal system has worked well since 1949. The data presented in Figure 9.1 also show that over a recent forty-year period, federalism has gained the support of the great majority of Germans. In 1952 over 50 percent of the adult population thought that the elimination of the states was a good idea. Only 20 percent of the population at that time favored the federal system of states. By 1992, however, support for federalism had grown to over 70 percent. In 1992 East Germans, when asked their opinion of federalism for the first time, were actually slightly more supportive (74 percent to 72 percent) than their West German counterparts. Forty years of communist centralization had apparently convinced them of the value of federalism.

Federalism is not without its problems. The states have jealously guarded their independence and have opposed many long-overdue administrative reforms, fearing a loss of power and funds. In the "joint projects" program dealing with higher education, regional economic development, and health care, they opposed giving the national government any significant coordinating authority, but conceded it only as a planning function. They have also opposed increased authority for the national government on questions of water and air pollution. Thus, for example, the national government is being held responsible by neighboring countries such as Switzerland and the Netherlands for the pollution of the Rhine River; but because of federalism, the national government's power to make and enforce stricter pollution control laws, without the consent of the states, is limited.[6]

The weakness of the federal system was also noticeable in the inability of the police to apprehend many terrorists responsible for robberies, kidnappings, and murders that plagued the Federal Republic for over two decades. Since the end of the Cold War Germany has also become a target country for organized crime groups from Eastern Europe and the former Soviet Union. Terrorism and crime are national

FIGURE 9.1   Attitudes toward federalism, 1952–1992

Question: What would you say if all state parliaments and governments were dissolved and the laws as well as political decisions would all come from Bonn? How do you feel about this proposal? Positive attitude toward federalism = states should not be abolished; negative attitude toward federalism = yes, dissolve the states—all decisions should come from Bonn.

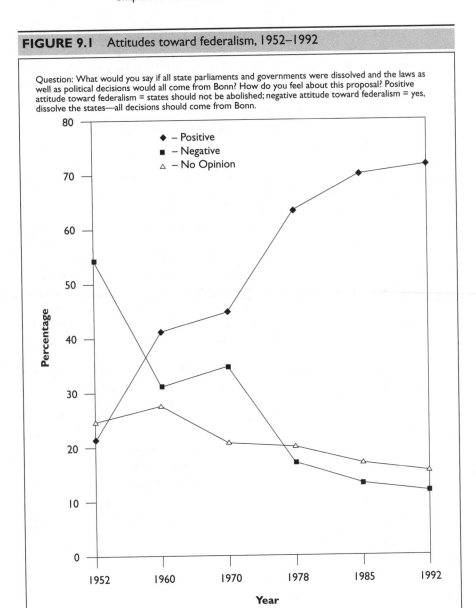

Source: Institut für Demoskopie, *Jahrbuch der Öffentlichen Meinung,* Vol. IX, 1984–1992 (Munich, New York: K.G. Saur Verlag, 1993), p. 654.

problems, but the structure of law enforcement—largely as a consequence of experiences with the centralized Nazi police state—is very decentralized. Police powers are largely reserved to the states, which have been reluctant to concede any major responsibility to the federal government. Because terrorists and organized crime do not respect state boundaries, the inadequate coordination and communication (1) among the states and (2) between them and the federal government is a major factor in Germany's fight against terrorism and organized crime. In the case of terrorism, only after national law enforcement agencies, such as the Federal Criminal Office and the Office for the Protection of the Constitution, were strengthened was significant progress in the apprehension of terrorists made.

Finally, by insisting on a greater role in the European Union, the states have reduced the capacity of Germany to speak with a single voice in the councils of Europe. This may be comforting to Germany's neighbors, but it probably reduces the Federal Republic's effectiveness in the European Union. Before committing Germany to any major European initiative, the national government must consult with the states.

One solution to these problems might be the consolidation of the federal system through a reduction in the number of states from the present sixteen to seven or eight units of roughly equal size, population, and economic resources. Such a federal structure would greatly reduce, if not eliminate, the poor state–rich state problem and hence the need for the national government and the richer states to pay subsidies or equalization money to the poorer states. Realignment and consolidation would also end the veto power now enjoyed by even the smallest state in many federal-state undertakings. Fewer but stronger states, however, would probably increase the assertiveness of the Bundesrat. The adoption of any realignment would require the approval of both the Bundestag and the Bundesrat; thus, without bipartisan support, realignment would be very difficult. However, the addition of the five new East German states has once again focused attention on this problem.

Federalism and specifically the ability of the states to block national legislation led some critics in the late 1990s to call for a drastic overhaul of the federal system. The immediate problem was the weak economy and the inability of the Kohl government to pass in 1997 its much-heralded pro-business tax reform legislation. In the wake of the failed reform, one representative of a major business interest group, the *Bund der Deutschen Industrie* (BDI), even called for reducing the power of the states through constitutional amendments and ending the practice of revenue sharing. Plans for realigning and reducing the number of states were also resurrected. Clearly, the traditional federal system is under stress and must demonstrate that it can adapt to the demands of economic globalization and increased European integration.

European Unity and German Federalism

European unity poses particular problems for the Federal Republic, the only large federal state in the European Union. The increasing delegation of national autonomy to the organs of the European Union called for in the 1986 Single European Act, with its goal of an open internal European market by 1992, has further complicated the future of German federalism. For example, in order to meet the regulations of the European Union, the national government is seeking more powers in education and over the mass media, areas in which the states have been autonomous. Because Germany (until the recent addition of Austria) has been the only federal state in the European Union, the German Länder have received little sympathy from other European countries. Ironically, in a federal or united Europe the German states may lose autonomy to the national government. The states are already charging that Germany's European commitments have hurt their budgets for housing, local transportation, and economic development. It appears, according to one authority, "that the . . . costs attributed to the expansion of the European Community will be paid primarily by the states."[7]

The states want to be consulted on questions of European unity that affect them. In the absence of consultation, the states, through their representatives in the Bundesrat, could veto treaties dealing with European unity that the central government negotiates. For the Länder, many European issues such as the standardization of educational systems are no longer "foreign" policy, but important domestic problems.

To meet these concerns of the states, in late 1992 a series of constitutional amendments was passed that explicitly grants the states the right to veto, via the Bundesrat, any commitments the Federal Republic may make to the European Union. The most important provisions are found in the constitution's new Article 23 (see Appendix). Section Four of this article calls for the national government to involve the Bundesrat in European decision making "insofar as it would have to be involved in a corresponding internal measure or insofar as the Länder would be internally responsible." Thus for the states, policymaking in the European Union is not foreign policy, which is still solely the prerogative of the national government. It is now constitutionally impossible for the national government to make any major decision involving the European Union without the approval of the Länder.

LOCAL GOVERNMENT

Germany has a long tradition of local self-government. Many cities proudly trace their independence to the Middle Ages, before the establishment of the nation-state. Although the consolidation of monarchical rule, especially in Prussia, later reduced the autonomy of cities, the reforms of Freiherr vom Stein, which followed Napoleon's defeat of Prussia, revived local independence. The Weimar Constitution also gave all communities the right of self-government.

During the Weimar Republic three types of local self-government were common:

1. A single council system fusing both legislative and executive functions (most prevalent in southern Germany)

2. A strong mayor form in which an elected council appointed a mayor with long tenure to perform executive functions—for example, Konrad Adenauer, mayor of Cologne from 1917 to 1933

3. A bicameral municipal council according to which the lower house, directly elected, invested executive power in a board of magistrates, which served as the upper chamber.[8]

Local elections and self-government were abolished by the Nazis in the Municipal Government Act of 1935, and thereafter all local officials were appointed by higher-level Nazi party or governmental agencies. Committed to a grass-roots approach to postwar democratization, Allied occupation powers restored and actually strengthened local self-government after 1945. The Basic Law (Article 28) guarantees local communities "the right to regulate under their own responsibility all the affairs of the local community within the limits set by law."

Structures and Functions

There are approximately 14,600 local communities (*Gemeinden*) in the Federal Republic, ranging in size from towns and villages of less than 2,000 inhabitants to large cities (*Großstädte*) of 1 million or more. Until the 1960s in West Germany, the number of local communities approached 30,000, but local government reform in many states has consolidated most units with fewer than 8,000 inhabitants. In the East the consolidation process is proceeding at a slow pace. About 20 percent of Easterners still live in towns and villages of less than 2,000 inhabitants as compared to only 6 percent in the West.[9]

Generally there are four types of local government, but all have an elected council (*Stadtrat* or *Gemeinderat*) in common.[10] Within each state, local government structures are uniform: In Lower Saxony, Hesse, and North Rhine–Westphalia, this council delegates executive and administrative authority to an appointed city manager (*Stadtdirektor*). In Schleswig-Holstein this executive is collegial. The Rhineland-Palatinate has a dominant mayor system with the mayor being responsible to the council. In Bavaria and Baden-Württemberg, the council has both executive and legislative functions but shares executive responsibility with a directly elected mayor. Elections to these councils, which range in size from about six to as many as seventy-five members, usually take place every four years.

The primary organs of county (*Kreis*) governments are an elected council (*Kreistag*) and an executive official, the *Landrat,* chosen by the council (except in Bavaria, where the executives are directly elected). Only ninety-eight cities are *kreisfrei,* that is, not within the jurisdiction of a county. The Landrat is a type of county manager supervising local administration, especially those local activities performed on behalf of the state government. If a local community within a county disagrees with county policies, it can challenge them in the administrative or constitutional court. The character of local-state relations is determined by each state's local government constitution (*Gemeindeverfassung*).

Generally, local politics tend to be more focused on individual personalities than those at the state or national levels. People know more about local problems, feel they have some influence, and are more likely to vote in local elections because of the candidate's personality rather than his or her party label. About 80 percent of voters in local elections, for example, report that they personally know the candidate they supported. The occupational prestige of the local candidates is another major factor in local elections. One 1994 study in the state of Baden-Württemberg concluded that "medical doctors, above all gynecologists, are guaranteed winners." Lawyers, tax consultants, architects, police officers (especially detectives), and well-known local merchants also do very well in these elections.[11]

The belief that local government is largely a matter of nonpolitical administration and hence not appropriate for party politics is widespread. As a concession to this attitude, political parties frequently nominate well-known local figures who are not party members. Most candidates try to deemphasize their party affiliations and stress their concern for the particular community. The small size of most localities also enables personal relationships to remain determinants of political relationships. In local elections, the national parties must sometimes compete with two types of local voter groups: relatively stable local *Rathaus* (city hall) parties with a formal program and organization; and more loosely structured voter groups that are formed for specific elections and then disband. In some states these local *antiparties* (Citizen Unions, Free Voters Associations) have secured over 40 percent of the vote.

In spite of the partisan structure of local elections, especially in large cities, there is little evidence to suggest that major policy differences in German cities are the result of party/political factors. Rhetorically the parties do differ in their approaches to local government. The SPD supports a so-called municipal socialism with publicly owned utilities, hospitals, and cultural centers over private control of such institutions. The SPD has also advocated municipal control of land and large housing projects, whereas—in theory at least—the Christian Democrats have supported individual property and home ownership. Studies that have attempted to relate policy outputs in fields such as housing and education to local party control have found few differences that could be explained by party/political factors.

There are two types of local government functions: the so-called compulsory responsibilities (e.g., schools, fire protection, streets, and sanitation), and the transferred responsibilities, activities carried out for the Länder or national government (e.g., tax collection, health care, and housing). In spite of administrative reforms that reduced the number of communities, many are still too small to carry out these responsibilities independently. County government and regional local associations with pooled resources assume many of these functions. Regional associations of local communities are a relatively recent innovation and have been assigned an important role in plans for regional economic development.

Although local self-government is constitutionally guaranteed, this independence is considerably limited by local dependence on federal and, especially, state grants as well as tax revenues from industrial enterprises. Only about one-third of local government revenue comes from taxes—mainly its share of the income tax (12 percent) and the *Gewerbesteuer,* a tax on the production and capital investment of commercial and industrial firms. Property taxes, a major source of local government revenue in the United States, account for only about 9 percent of tax revenue for German communities. The low return on property levies is primarily a result of assessment rates that are kept artificially low by federal law for reasons of social policy. Also, large proportions of land located in the communities—such as public housing projects, defense installations, and other government-owned property—are tax-exempt.

Besides taxes and grants, the fees charged by the cities for their services (water, electricity, public transportation, gas, refuse collection) constitute another major source of local government revenue. Generally, German cities offer a broader range of services than do their American counterparts: publicly owned utilities, public transportation, city-run banks, markets, breweries, and an extensive range of cultural activities (operas, repertory theater, orchestras, festivals, adult education). The latter services are heavily subsidized by local, state, and federal governments. Admission prices to the opera, for example, cover less than half the costs.[12]

THE URBAN CRISIS, GERMAN-STYLE

Like local communities in other advanced industrial societies, German local government is heavily indebted, is facing rising demands for goods and services, in many areas is structurally outmoded, and is burdened by a heavy concentration of foreign residents. The condition of West German cities, however, is far better than that of cities in the former East Germany.

Mounting Financial Deficits

Although the cities' share of tax revenues has increased in recent years, their expenditures, especially for personnel and construction costs, continue to increase at a faster rate than their revenues. The total debt of West German cities in 1995 was over $100 billion. Two-thirds of all local government investment is done with borrowed money, and about one-third of local tax revenues is consumed by debt service. East German cities were formerly completely dependent on financial allotments from the central government in East Berlin. Although they now have the legal authority to levy taxes, they must first develop a functioning local administration that can collect the revenues.

The increased demand for more and better public services and their increased cost, coupled with an inadequate tax distribution system, are largely responsible for these financial problems. Yet poor planning and accounting procedures on the part of local government are also involved. Cost overruns on major urban projects such as cultural centers and subways are common. There is hardly a major German city that has not had its share of scandals over the financing of major construction projects.

Long periods of one-party domination of many large cities and the right of city employees to hold legislative positions have produced a political style in some urban areas not unlike the party machine politics once characteristic of most large American cities. In Berlin during the 1970s, for example, the SPD party organization and the SPD-controlled city administration became so interlocked that it was difficult to separate the two. Approximately two-thirds of the SPD's delegation in the Berlin parliament were employees of the city, and almost 90 percent of the parliament's internal affairs committee, which plays a key role in salary and wage determination, were themselves city employees. This *Verfilzung* (literally, "entanglement") of governmental bureaucracy and party is one reason why local governments have been the least likely to hold the line against the wage demands of public officials.

Urban Transport

European cities were never built for automobiles, nor did the planners of cities rebuilt after the war plan for the massively motorized society that was to emerge in the 1960s. After attempting to construct streets and freeways to accommodate cars, most urban planners believe it is financially and ecologically impossible for the city and the automobile to coexist. The historical core of many cities already is badly damaged, and streets remain jammed and parking facilities inadequate. These conditions leave mass public transport as the only alternative. To make this appealing to the car-loving Germans, however, will require new capital that the cities simply do not have.

Housing and Land Use

Existing zoning regulations and the postwar commitment to a free-market economy encouraged widespread urban land speculation, and a booming economy meant that highly profitable projects such as office buildings and apartment houses received priority over parks, playgrounds, and low-cost public housing. City governments, greatly dependent on the Gewerbesteuer for revenue, were forced into competition for new industry. By catering to industry, cities also neglected public services such as schools, hospitals, homes for the elderly, and the environment. In Hanover, for example, to secure a large IBM assembly plant, the city developed large tracts of prime park and recreational land at public expense, which was then offered to the firm as a plant site. When IBM later pulled out of the deal, the pitfalls of catering to private interests became painfully apparent to the community.

In many large German cities the shortage of affordable housing has become acute during recent years. The high price of land and soaring interest rates have reduced new construction. Programs for government-subsidized public housing were cut back by the Kohl government. Access to existing low-cost housing favored older families who already had been in public housing or on waiting lists. Young people moving into the cities had to face the high rents in private housing. In some cities, however, groups of homeless citizens simply occupied vacant houses and apartment buildings. This squatters' movement has also been accompanied by frequent demonstrations and in some cases clashes with police. One such incident in Berlin in 1990 led to the collapse of the SPD-Green city government and played a key role in the SPD's defeat at the city's parliamentary election later in the year. Urban squatters have also been subject to mass arrests, with some accompanying violence, in Hamburg. Some local authorities have justified this hard-line approach by alleging a link between the urban squatters and the terrorist scene.

These problems are to a great extent the result of inadequate urban and regional planning in the postwar period. German urban policymakers understandably wanted to rebuild as quickly as possible; comprehensive long-range planning was not a priority. The emergence of urban citizen initiative groups, discussed in Chapter 4, illustrates the extent to which established local political institutions have been unable to meet the more sophisticated demands for change they now face.

Foreign Residents

Germany's immigration problem, discussed in Chapter 4, is also an urban problem. Most of the country's 8 million foreign residents have settled in Western urban centers such as Frankfurt, Stuttgart, Munich, and Hamburg, and in West Berlin. The proportion of foreigners in these cities is almost three times the national average. This clustering of immigrant populations in urban areas means added costs and burdens for local government. Providing adequate housing and education for foreign residents are the most pressing problems. The cities have also had to accept and provide for the hundreds of thousands of asylum-seekers that have come to Germany from the former Yugoslavia and other world trouble spots. Local governments in many cases have done more to integrate foreign residents than the state and national governments. The cities pioneered foreign resident advisory councils and local foreign resident assemblies, which give foreign populations some voice in local politics.

The Urban Crisis in Eastern Germany.   Local government in the former German Democratic Republic had little independent power. Control at the local level was in the hands of the Communist party organization, specifically the first secretary of the party. Government merely carried out the dictates of the center or took on those assignments the party assigned to it. Many local government officials were merely party hacks or members of the puppet parties aligned with the Communists in the so-called National Front. Hence the first task for local government after unification was to recruit competent officials who could be trained in the new democratic procedures. Thousands of West German civil servants were sent to the East to help in the construction of a democratic civil service at the local level. Many incumbent officeholders were dismissed for their past involvement with the communist system, especially those who worked for the secret police (the *Stasi*) as informers. Other holdovers from the communist system remained on the job in a probationary status. They will be given a chance to demonstrate their competency and commitment to the new democratic system.

The West German imports and their East German colleagues face a myriad of problems.

1. Most towns and cities are heavily in debt and are dependent on grants from state governments and the national government. Although their dependency on these transfer payments declined from 78 percent in 1991 to 54 percent by 1998, East German cities are still far from the West German level of 27 percent.[13]

2. The large cities in the East, i.e., those over 100,000, have lost about 12 percent of their population since 1990 as compared to about 5 percent for the entire region.[14] This population loss lowers the tax base and increases the financial problems of local government.

3. Under communism the local administration was bloated. Even by 1994 there were still 60 local government employees for each 1,000 residents in the East as compared to 40 for each 1,000 residents in the West. Thus hundreds of thousands of local government jobs still have to be eliminated, which will save local government about $15 billion annually in salary expenses.[15]

4. The inner core of most East German cities was woefully neglected by the Communists.[16] Instead of renovating existing housing in the inner cities, the Communist regime built new settlements on the outskirts.[17] Now, giant concrete silos, all identical, dot the landscape. These new communities have little or no social identity. Shops, recreational facilities, children's play areas, and adequate parking facilities were not a priority in the regime's housing plans. Moreover, apartment houses were built from prefabricated concrete panels. Workers for the most part simply stacked the parts on top of each other. The quality of construction was poor. Almost 20 percent of all new housing built since 1981 is already in need of repair. Some Western experts propose tearing down much of this housing, which was based on procedures imported from the former Soviet Union.

5. Much of the infrastructure of most East German cities (i.e., the roads, sewer systems, waste treatment plants, and water systems) dates from the pre–World War II era and is in dire need of repair or complete replacement. The city of Dresden, for example, the third largest in the former East Germany, had been discharging much of its industrial and residential sewage untreated into the Elbe River since 1987, when the city's eighty-year-old sewage treatment facility stopped operating because of a flood.

6. Local governments in the East must attempt to balance the need for economic growth in urban areas with the need for environmental protection and preservation of the cities' architectural past. Will the cities' financial problems cause them to allow unrestrained development? Will some of the same mistakes made in the West after 1945 be repeated now in the East? East Germany's local policymakers are wrestling with these problems under severe constraints of time and money.

SUMMARY AND CONCLUSION

German federalism and local self-government are largely the expression of a historically rooted particularism and the disastrous experiences with the centralized Third Reich. Like the Basic Law of which they are a part, these structures are primarily oriented to the past and the avoidance of the errors of former regimes. Their future utility is now a topic of serious political debate. At issue is not the abolition of the federal system or local self-government, but their modernization. This involves at a minimum the consolidation and realignment of state and local units, their support for more cooperative policy programs with the national government, and their acceptance of a greater federal role in areas traditionally reserved to them: education, economic development, police, administration of justice, the protection of the environment.

In many areas federalism has been a positive force in the Republic's postwar development. It has enhanced the internal diversity of the political parties, has provided at times an opportunity for policy innovation, and has enabled the national government to avoid the disadvantages of a large centralized bureaucracy.[18] There was no hesitation or opposition when the tightly centralized German Democratic Republic restored federalism prior to unification. But Germany today, even with the addition of the former East Germany, is a far more integrated society than any of its predecessors, and it now confronts policy problems that are more complex and national in scope. The popular support that the Republic enjoys is in large part the result of its performance. The question is whether this performance level can be maintained in the future with the structures and processes of the past.

Notes

1. Fritz W. Scharpf, "Politische Durchsetzbarkeit Innerer Reformen im Pluralistisch-Demokratischen Gemeinwesen der Bundesrepublik" (Berlin: International Institute for Management, 1973), pp. 33ff. Unification has also prompted a new discussion about the

viability of the current federal structure. See "The New Federalists," *The Economist* (October 6, 1990), pp. 54–55.

2. Rudolf Hrbek, "Das Problem der Neugliederung des Bundesgebiets," *Aus Politik und Zeitgeschichte,* no. 46 (November 13, 1971): 3–12.

3. Between 1946 and 1951 Baden-Württemberg was divided into three separate units that were merged after a plebiscite.

4. Ralf Neubauer, "Magnet in der Mitte," *Die Zeit,* no. 42 (October 14, 1994), p. 30.

5. Arnold J. Heidenheimer, "Federalism and the Party System: The Case of West Germany," *American Political Science Review 52* (1958): 808–828.

6. It must be noted, however, that other countries, such as Switzerland and France, also bear considerable responsibility for the condition of the river because of their discharge of wastes into the river.

7. Hartmut Klatt, "Forty Years of German Federalism: Past Trends and New Developments," *Publius 19,* no. 4 (Fall 1989): 202.

8. Linda L. Dolive, "Electoral Politics at the Local Level in the German Federal Republic" (Ph.D. dissertation, University of Florida, 1972), p. 29.

9. Statistisches Bundesamt, *Datenreport 1997* (Bonn: Bundeszentrale für politische Bildung, 1997), p. 25.

10. A rarely cited provision of the constitution (Article 28) does permit local communities to be governed by citizen assemblies (town meetings) instead of by elected, representative bodies. Few if any communities, however, have made use of this form of direct democracy at the local level. Referenda are also permitted in most states.

11. The study was conducted by Professor Hans-Georg Wehling of Tübingen University and is discussed in the *Frankfurter Allgemeine Zeitung,* September 17, 1994, p. 4.

12. *Kulturchronik,* no. 3 (March 1991): 19.

13. Heinz Sahner, "Zur Entwicklung ostdeutscher Städte nach der Wende: nicht nur 'dem Tod von der Schippe gesprungen,'" *Aus Politik und Zeitgeschichte,* no. 5 (January 31, 1999), p. 33.

14. Sahner, "Zur Stadtentwicklung," p. 30.

15. *Frankfurter Allgemeine Zeitung,* October 28, 1993, p. 4; Sahner, "Zur Entwicklung . . . ," p. 33.

16. About three-fourths of the apartment buildings in Leipzig's inner city, for example, were in dire need of repair. An additional 10 percent were uninhabitable. Carola Scholz and Werner Heinz, "Stadtentwicklung in den neuen Bundesländern: Der Sonderfall Leipzig," *Aus Politik und Zeitgeschichte,* no. 11 (March 17, 1995): 17.

17. Jürgen Rostock, "Zum Wohnungs und Städtebau in den ostdeutschen Ländern," *Aus Politik und Zeitgeschichte,* no. 29 (July 12, 1991): 41–50.

18. In a study of nuclear energy policy in France and Germany, Dorothy Nelkin and Michael Pollak found that Germany's decentralized political/administrative structure, in contrast to French centralization, was a major factor in the relatively greater success of the German anti-nuclear movement. In Germany "intragovernmental conflicts are inevitable—between, for example, regional and national governments, or between environmental agencies and the ministry of economics. The anti-nuclear movement increased its own influence by exacerbating such intra-administrative conflicts." Dorothy Nelkin and Michael Pollak, *The Atom Besieged* (Cambridge, MA.: MIT Press, 1981), p. 182.

CHAPTER

10 Conclusion: The Unified German Polity Faces the Future

n 1999 the Federal Republic celebrated its fiftieth anniversary. Never before in German history has a liberal republic functioned as successfully or endured as long as the system we have examined in the preceding chapters. Within a constitutional framework rather hastily constructed in 1948 and 1949, Germany has become a legitimate, dynamic democracy. The success of this system since 1949 has proved a powerful magnet that attracted the attention and eventually the allegiance of the millions of Germans living in the former German Democratic Republic (GDR). The performance of the Federal Republic—its ability to give its citizens more freedom, prosperity, and peace with its neighbors than any other regime before it—proved an insurmountable obstacle to the attempts of the communist leadership in the GDR to create a separate East German identity. With unification in October 1990 the Federal Republic thus achieved what in 1949 was its foremost policy goal: the unification of Germany in peace and freedom.

The political, cultural, economic, and social integration of the former GDR into the Federal Republic, the bringing together of the divided nation, remains a critical challenge confronting the German polity as it enters the twenty-first century. What happened on October 3, 1990? Was the old Federal Republic simply enlarged by the addition of 16 million new citizens? Or was a new state created from the merger of two independent states? Will Germany now turn more toward Eastern Europe, reasserting its traditional economic and political role in this region? Will its role in Western Europe and within the European Union change? Do Germany's neighbors have anything to fear from a unified Federal Republic? These questions are now being debated by Germans themselves. The issues and related problems will make up much of the substance of German politics in the years ahead. This chapter will examine some of these questions.

A NEW CONSTITUTION AND A NEW STATE?

As we discussed in Chapter 1, unification took place largely on West German terms via Article 23 of the Bonn Constitution, which allows other German Länder to join the federation much as states once joined the United States. After reconstituting itself into five states, the German Democratic Republic ceased to exist as a sovereign political entity on October 3, 1990. From a legal or constitutional perspective, the Federal Republic in 1990 was simply enlarged by the addition of the five new *Länder.* Unification was thus not a merger of two independent entities, but rather a "friendly buyout" by West Germany.

Many East German dissidents, who played such a critical role in bringing down the communist regime, regretted the rapid unification process. They had hoped to find a third way between West German capitalism and East German socialism. They had envisioned a gradual unification process, with East Germany retaining some of what they considered to be the positive aspects of the country's forty-year history: women's rights, full employment, low cost housing, and day care.[1] These East Germans and some West Germans, particularly in the Social Democratic and Green parties, preferred that unification take place in accordance with Article 146 of the Basic Law, which would have allowed for an entirely new constitution, requiring approval by the entire electorate in a referendum; the current basic Law was ratified only by the West German state legislatures. Yet the rapid course of events and the support of East Germans for the Christian Democrats under Helmut Kohl left the governing parties with little enthusiasm for unification via Article 146.

In the final August 1990 unification treaty between the two German states, there is a provision (Article 5) enabling the parliament to examine within two years whether constitutional changes with reference to "strengthening the federal structure and the goals of the state" are necessary. In May 1991 the Bundestag took up this question for the first time. Not surprisingly, the government and opposition differed on whether and how much the existing constitution should be changed. The governing coalition (Christian Democrats and Free Democrats) supported only a "constitutional committee" to "modernize" the current Basic Law by making changes, but stopping short of a new constitution. The committee would be composed of thirty-two members: sixteen each from the Bundestag and the Bundesrat. This constitutional committee, according to the governing CDU/CSU and FDP would consider such questions as the right of foreigners to vote in local elections, the role of the Länder in the European Union, and German military participation in United Nations operations. German law does not give the franchise to foreign residents from non-European Union countries, and it was not until 1994 that the Constitutional Court ruled that military forces could be active outside of NATO territory.

The Social Democrats and the Greens, however, wanted a "constitutional council," which would develop the current Basic Law into a permanent constitution for the newly unified country. The council would have 120 members equally divided by gender and elected by the Federal Assembly, the same body that elects the federal president (see Chapter 7). In addition to members of parliament, the SPD council would have representatives of the citizens' movement in the former GDR and "leading personalities" from all areas of public life. The SPD supported a new constitution, based on the Basic Law, that would contain provisions making environmental protection, the right to a job, decent housing, equal rights for women, a prohibition against the export of arms, and the rejection of atomic, biological, and chemical weapons (ABC) for the armed forces formal goals of the state, thus obligating all governments, regardless of party composition, to support them. This constitution would be presented to the people via a referendum as called for in Article 146 of the Basic Law.

After extensive bargaining, a "Joint Constitutional Commission" composed of 64 members (32 each from the *Bundestag* and the *Bundesrat*) was established. The Commission was co-chaired by a former member of Chancellor Kohl's government and the SPD mayor of Hamburg. Largely ignored by the mass media and much of the public, the Commission held 25 meetings, considered 75 proposed changes that covered about half of the current constitution's 146 articles, and received over 800,000 petitions from concerned groups and individual citizens.

In the end, however, all this effort produced very few changes. The representatives from the governing parties, CDU and FDP, were able to block most of the major proposals of the Social Democrats and Greens: the inclusion of social-economic rights as goals of the state, the introduction of direct democracy components such as referendum and recall, the right of non-European Union foreigners to vote in local elections, improvement of children's rights, and the legal recognition of same-sex relationships. The Commission did agree on the need to strengthen the federal dimension of the constitution. In Article 28 the Länder were given more control over legislative proposals, the powers of the Bundesrat were increased, and the independence of the state and local communities was emphasized. If the legislatures of the affected states agreed on a realignment and if the citizens approved this agreement in a referendum, the realignment would not require a constitutional amendment.

The Commission also agreed on two amendments to Article 3 on gender equality and the handicapped, an amendment to Article 20 declaring the state's commitment to environmental protection, one amendment on local self-government and several alterations in the legislative powers of the Länder and the national government.

In June 1994, after the most extensive debate on the constitution since 1949, the Bundestag passed these amendments. But thus far they have failed to gain the approval of the Bundesrat. The Länder have objected to the proposed changes in the states' legislative powers. Thus the entire process of constitutional review is once again stalled.

This constitutional discussion reflects not only the problem of integrating East Germans into the larger political community, but also the presence of contending conceptions of democracy in the Federal Republic. The Christian Democrats and Free Democrats see democracy largely as a set of political and governmental procedures such as political equality ("one-person, one-vote") and civil rights and liberties, with the emphasis on limited governmental interference in socioeconomic affairs. They contend that the current Basic Law established and supports only this limited version of democracy. The CDU/CSU view the democratic state as largely realized and argue that the foremost goal of any government now must be to maintain and defend it against those who advocate more governmental control over the economy. Some Christian Democrats have indeed suggested that the Basic Law condones only a capitalist market economy and that to oppose the Republic's current

TABLE 10.1   The government's economic role: East-West Germany, 1996

	"Definitely the Government's Responsibility" (% respondents)		
	East	West	Difference
Full employment	57	28	29
Keep prices under control	43	23	20
Health care	66	51	15
Maintain the living standards of the elderly	64	48	16
Decent standard of living for the unemployed	38	17	21
Reduce income differences between rich and poor	48	25	23
Adequate housing for all	38	20	18

Source: ALLBUS 1996 survey. Study no. 2800, Zentralarchiv für empirische Sozialforschung, Cologne.

economic system, which is based on free enterprise and private property, is to oppose the Republic itself.

The Social Democrats and the Greens support a more substantive conception of democracy. They contend that because of the inequalities in wealth, status, and power in the Republic, the Basic Law is far from realized. They suggest that the best means of both maintaining the democratic political order and fully realizing its potential is through social and economic reforms largely in the direction of more social equality and economic security, which will in turn extend more genuine freedom to more citizens. They reject the position that the constitution ordains any particular economic system; they argue that it requires policies aiming at social and economic reform.

Most East Germans seem to support this Social Democratic-Green conception of democracy. As Table 10.1 shows, solid majorities of East Germans strongly favor government control of health care and state policy to create jobs. Substantially more East Germans than West Germans also favor government control of wages, support for industry, the protection of jobs, and the reduction of the work week. Forty-plus years of a social market economy in the West and a state-controlled planned economy in the East have had an impact on what East and West Germans expect of government.

POLICY ISSUES AND PROCESSES: TRENDS AND PROSPECTS

As the preceding chapters have shown, the Federal Republic is a complex political system characterized by the presence of several power centers. The national executive with its control over the civil service initiates the broad outlines of policy, but it cannot secure the approval of its policy proposals or their implementation without at least the tacit support of other actors in the political system: the major interest groups, the extraparliamentary organizations of the governing parties, the back-benchers in the legislature, the states, the semipublic institutions such as the Bundesbank, and even the opposition party when it has a majority of the delegates in the Bundesrat. Strong opposition by any of these actors will greatly hinder the efforts of the government and chancellor to determine the main guidelines of policy. Successful policymaking must be accomplished within the framework of the politico-economic consensus that has emerged since 1949. This means that the system resists any efforts at introducing major innovations within a relatively short time. Change tends to be gradual and incremental, and rarely will it have a redistributive effect. The issue of codetermination, for example, has been a policy problem throughout most of the Republic's history. Codetermination—the right of workers and other employees to share in a firm's decision-making process through equal representation on its supervisory board—was a key element in the SPD program in 1969 when it became the major partner in a coalition with the FDP, and again in 1972 when the coalition secured a comfortable parliamentary majority. In spite of these favorable political conditions, the new codetermination law that finally went into effect in 1976 did not give a firm's workers parity with capital and management. Attempts to make major changes in the tax system have also been stymied, at times by the opposition of the pro-business Free Democratic party, but also through the efforts of well-organized interest groups that have extensive contacts with governmental ministries, or as in 1997, through a veto of the government's program in the Bundesrat, the second house of parliament. As we discussed in Chapter 2, the burden of financing unification has thus far not been shouldered by the most affluent segments of society, but rather has been carried by middle- and lower-income groups.

For most of the past fifty years this consensus-oriented political leadership and policy process style has worked well. Inflation has been low and until the 1990s unemployment was also well below the level of other European countries. At the same time, the social welfare system (pensions, health insurance) has helped to maintain a high level of demand. In comparison to its neighbors, Germany has also ranked high in capital investment, which has provided an adequate number of new jobs. The disastrous experience with inflation in the 1920s and the real economic gains in the postwar period have made all parties sensitive and responsive to inflationary problems.

Policy Issues: The Future of the Welfare State

The extensive welfare state has also been part of this consensus style of governing. The constitution states that the Federal Republic is a *sozialer* state, or state obligated to establish and maintain basic social welfare rights. Thus governmental policies designed to provide full employment, education, housing, child support payments, social security, and health care have not been, for the most part, matters of partisan conflict over the issue of whether the government should be involved in these areas, but rather the *extent* of governmental activity. Partisan debates about these issues have tended to revolve around problems of detail and administration.

Germans have had "cradle-to-grave" security. All of life's core risks are covered in this system: sickness (including since January 1, 1995, long-term nursing care) accident, disability, unemployment, and retirement. The social welfare program also provides housing subsidies for low-income families and direct cash payments to all parents and guardians to defray some of the costs of raising children. Even a university education is tuition-free, with government grants and loans available to cover living costs. Few countries in the world offer such a comprehensive and generous system of social welfare. The system is also very expensive. In 1999 the total cost for these programs was about $800 billion. Germans pay over 46 percent of their income in taxes, as compared to about 32 percent for Americans. The biggest share of the social welfare budget goes to the pension and health insurance programs, which are financed by employer and employee contributions (see Chapter 8). On the employer side, these "fringe benefits" now make up almost 45 percent of labor costs. Additional fringe benefits (which also usually include additional cash payments for vacations and Christmas holidays), coupled with high wages and salaries, make labor costs in Germany among the highest in the world.[2] The high labor costs are also responsible for the reluctance of employers to hire new workers and for the high costs of Germany's goods and services in the international marketplace.

Voters and policymakers alike must wrestle with the question of whether this system has now reached a level at which it endangers the long-term health and competitiveness of the economy. By 1998 almost 50 percent more was being spent on social welfare programs than on investments in new plants and equipment. Present consumption now exceeds by a wide margin the investments that create the jobs of the future. The price/performance ratio (i.e., the relationship between the price of a product and its functional value) has dropped in recent years for many German products, most notably automobiles and machine tools.

Increasingly, market share is being lost to newly industrialized countries such as Korea that offer low prices and good quality. Since the end of the Cold War the problem has actually worsened. Eastern neighbors such as Poland, Hungary, and the Czech Republic offer a well-trained labor force at a fraction of the cost of German labor. Numerous German firms are relocating their production facilities to take advantage of these lower labor costs.

The political system has been slow to respond to these new realities. The globalization of the modern economy and the rapid and free flow of capital to the most promising markets and labor sources have challenged this German system of a "social market economy." By 1999 Germany had Europe's highest wages, the shortest work week, the highest corporate taxes, the oldest students, and the youngest pensioners.

Unification has added new burdens to this struggling "social market economy." The West German pension system in 1991 was applied to the new Eastern states. By the late 1990s Eastern pensions were almost at the West German level. But Eastern contributions fell far short of those paid by workers in the West. The difference has been made up out of general revenue. At present, the once self-supporting pension system is dependent on general revenue for about 20 percent of it expenditures; that is, contributions account for only 80 percent of disbursements. The welfare system also includes large subsidies to well-organized occupational groups such as farmers and coal miners. Since 1970 national and state governments have spent over $125 billion to subsidize a declining and inefficient coal mining industry. By 1998 these subsidies amounted to about $60,000 annually for each of Germany's 85,000 remaining coal miners. The result: German coal costs about four times more than the world market price. Agricultural subsidies add about $1,000 to the average German's annual food bill. These resources could be better spent in supporting education or hi-tech research and development.

Beginning in the 1980s, both the Social Democratic governments of Helmut Schmidt and the Christian Democratic coalition of Helmut Kohl, responding to the sluggish economy and reduced state revenues, began to make significant cuts in the extensive social welfare system. First introduced in 1957, the dynamic pension system, which linked pension increases to wage and salary increases in the working population, was trimmed. Pension increases are now only indirectly connected to net wage and salary gains. Moreover, since 1984, retirees must pay a portion of the costs of their health insurance. In 1996 the Kohl government also reduced future pension payments for many workers.

The generous health insurance program has also encountered major fiscal problems. Since 1983, hospital patients must pay part of the costs of their stays. Prescription drugs under the system are no longer free. In the early 1990s extensive cost-cutting measures were introduced in the health care system. Total state expenditures for prescription drugs and physicians' fees have been capped. Workers' compensation payments have been reduced. Many student aid programs have been converted from stipends to loans. Child allowances (*Kindergeld*), tax-free payments by the state to parents, were cut back, especially for higher-income groups. These cutbacks, however, have been only marginal, and in 1999 the new Social Democratic–Green government of Gerhard Schröder restored some of the cuts in the child-support and pension systems.

This combination of slow economic growth, high unemployment, expensive social programs, and the costly unification process have greatly increased Germany's national debt and more importantly the costs of servicing that debt. By the end of 1998 total public debt stood at DM 2.2 trillion or DM 25,800 for every man, woman, and child in the country. From 1993 to 1998 the proportion of the budget spent on interest payments jumped from 12.4 percent to 21.7 percent. Interest payments increased from DM 56.7 billion in 1993 to DM 106.3 billion in 1998.

Critics of social programs argue that the entire structure of the welfare state must be fundamentally reformed if the spiraling costs are to be controlled.[3] Even with the recent reductions, these social programs continue to consume one-third of the gross national product. Since 1960, expenditures for the welfare state have grown at a greater rate than the economy that must finance it. Economic conservatives in the Federal Republic contend that spending for social programs is consuming capital that is badly needed to modernize the national economy and prepare Germany for the global hi-tech economy. Supporters of the welfare state respond by citing the large inequities in capital resources, the defense budget, and the numerous tax advantages and subsidies given to upper-income groups. To try to dismantle the welfare state, they warn, would endanger "social peace" and induce a "class struggle" mentality reminiscent of past periods in German history.[4]

Policy Issues: The New Poverty

The cuts in social welfare programs, slow economic growth, the influx of foreigners, and high unemployment, especially in the former East Germany, have also combined to produce a growing poverty problem. The new poverty, as Germans term it, refers especially to the condition of the long-term unemployed, single parents with children, low-income pensioners, foreign residents and refugees seeking asylum. The proportion of unemployed who have been jobless for more than one year rose from 20 percent in 1985 to over 30 percent in 1995. The longer a worker is unemployed, the lower his or her level of support. After one year (two years for older workers), unemployment compensation, which is based on employer-employee contributions and amounts to about two-thirds of the worker's prior wages, ceases and is replaced by unemployment aid. These payments are 15 to 17 percent lower than unemployment compensation and require an examination of the applicant's personal finances. Once a worker's eligibility for this support is exhausted, the only alternative is the general welfare system. These payments, however, are lower still (by about 7 percent) than the unemployment aid, and they require a needs or means test. During the past ten years, the proportion of unemployed workers in the top tier (wage-based unemployment compensation) has declined, whereas the proportion of unemployed workers dependent on either unemployment aid or welfare has increased. It is now estimated that roughly 5 percent of the population, or about 4 million people, live below the poverty line, as compared to only 2 percent in 1980.[5] Since 1990 the number of people officially on welfare has increased from 1.9 million to almost 3 million.[6]

Significantly, the proportion of East Germans on welfare is *below* the national level. About 400,000 East Germans were on the welfare rolls in 1998, or only about 8 percent of the national welfare total. The sharp increases in recent years have come largely from the West and reflect the high levels of unemployment that predate unification. However, as the retraining and public-works programs in the East are phased out, the Eastern proportion will increase; between 1996 and 1997 the number of Easterners on welfare jumped by almost 25 percent.

Increasingly, German social scientists fear the emergence of a permanent underclass of welfare recipients living in urban ghettos with few prospects for upward mobility. This phenomenon, well known in the United States and Britain, poses new challenges for a society generally considered one of the most affluent in the world.[7]

GERMANY'S NEW INTERNATIONAL ROLE

Throughout the postwar period West Germany maintained a low international profile. Securely embedded in multilateral military and economic organizations, the Federal Republic followed the lead of the United States, Britain, and France on most foreign policy and defense questions. Even as it was becoming an economic giant, it was content to remain a political dwarf. In addition to Germany's low profile, all German governments displayed a marked aversion to the use of force to resolve disputes and an even greater aversion to the projection of German military power in international conflicts. In short, the Federal Republic had little interest in world power politics. It was content to be, as one observer put it, a "sort of giant Switzerland."

German unification, the end of Soviet hegemony in Eastern Europe, and the collapse of the Soviet Union itself have changed Germany's position in the international political arena. No longer is the Federal Republic a divided nation, exposed to massive Soviet power and dependent on other nations, most notably the United States, for its security. The Germans are, once again, the most numerous people in Western Europe. United Germany's 82 million residents constitute about 22 percent of the total population of the fifteen-member European Union. Will these structural or institutional changes in the European and international environment create pressures for Germany to assume a leadership role in this region?

Since unification there have been signs of greater German independence in foreign policy. In 1991 the Federal Republic became the first European state to recognize the then-breakaway Yugoslav republics of Slovenia and Croatia. The decision was made in spite of the opposition of the United States, the United Nations, and some European Union members. Earlier international attempts to halt the civil war in the former Yugoslavia were not successful, and the Federal Republic argued that recognition of the republics would increase the prospects for a peaceful resolution of the conflict. Although the American, British, and French governments considered the Yugoslav conflict a civil war between rival ethnic groups, Germany viewed it as the result of Serbian aggression against democratically elected governments in Slovenia and Croatia that wanted to leave the Yugoslav federation. In early 1992 Germany was joined by the entire European Union in recognizing the new republics.[8]

The Croatian decision revealed an important feature of unified Germany's foreign policy: Germany is resuming its historical role as a Central European power with interests in the East that are as important as those in the West. The Federal Republic's policy towards its eastern neighbors, above all Poland, Hungary, the Czech Republic, and Russia, will seek to promote democratic institutions, human rights, environmental cleanup and protection (above all the shutdown of dangerous Chernobyl-era nuclear reactors) and German economic and financial interests.

The Federal Republic is also the primary source of economic aid for the post-communist countries of Eastern Europe and the former Soviet Union. Since 1989 almost $45 billion in grants and loans has been committed to this region. German business interests, with the support of the government, have also been prominent in establishing joint ventures with Eastern European firms.

The Federal Republic has also lobbied, discreetly but firmly, for a permanent seat on the United Nations Security Council. Within the European Union Germany in recent years has exerted pressure on both Britain and France to accept a compromise on the voting rights of individual countries. The new procedures now make it more difficult for a few countries to block decisions. Germany was also able to persuade Britain to support measures that would enable Poland, Hungary, and the Czech Republic to join the Union by the end of the century.

This increased assertiveness in international affairs is not without critics both at home and abroad. Many Germans believe that there is a residual distrust of the country among its neighbors because of the Third Reich, and they prefer that the country maintain a low international profile. They also fear that increased international leadership will eventually bring the country into a military conflict somewhere in the world. The memories of the death and destruction caused by the world wars of this century are still very much alive. Some Germans oppose, for example, any military participation even in United Nations peacekeeping operations. During the 1991 Gulf War, Germany sent no combat forces into the region. Its contributions were largely in the form of financial aid in support of the military operation. Germany thus hopes that much of its increased international responsibilities can be accommodated through its membership in the European Union; it wants to act wherever possible with and through a united Europe.[9]

Germany's neighbors are also still very mindful of what rabid German nationalism and racism did to Europe and the world in the twentieth century. While distrust and hostility to Germany among other European countries has abated over the past fifty years, especially among younger postwar generations, there remains a residual fear that Germany will once again attempt to achieve hegemony over at least the western and central parts of the continent. Indeed some Europeans see the European Union as a largely German-dominated vehicle to achieve hegemony by economic means. German economic nationalism, in other words, will succeed where military conquest failed.

In the first decade since unification, Germany has done little in the foreign arena to justify such fears. The "culture of reticence" in defense policy, the reluctance to use force for any purpose other than national defense or for NATO and UN military operations, has continued to characterize the Federal Republic's international conduct. Many Germans and some Europeans see this low-key style as a positive development. It shows, in their view, that Germany has learned the lessons from its militarist and genocidal past and is restrained and skeptical about the use of force. Others see the Germans as "free riders" in defense and security issues, letting other countries pay the price and bear the burden of military operations. During the Cold War (1948–1989) the United States spent an average of 7 percent of its Gross Domestic Product on defense and Great Britain about 5 percent; in contrast, Germany spent only about 3 percent on national defense. The "culture of reticence," in this view, "reflects a certain German selfishness and an unwillingness to live up to the meaning and obligations of collective defense . . . and a sign that Germany remains a flawed and wounded nation when it comes to questions of war and peace . . . ."[10]

While Germany is the strongest state in Europe and the only one to emerge much stronger from the Cold War, this power has been tamed. Unification has produced no changes in the Federal Republic's western ties, nor has unification affected the consensual style of politics that has characterized the last half century. Unified Germany has settled frontiers, has made no territorial claims, and faces no military threats from any direction. It has shown no interest in traditional nation-state ma-

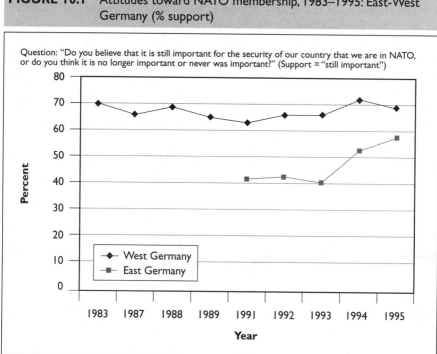

FIGURE 10.1   Attitudes toward NATO membership, 1983–1995: East-West Germany (% support)

Question: "Do you believe that it is still important for the security of our country that we are in NATO, or do you think it is no longer important or never was important?" (Support = "still important")

Source: Institut für Demoskopie, *Jahrbuch der Demoskopie, Vol. X* (1997), p. 1134.

neuvering. Germany pursues its national interests through multilateral structures like the United Nations, the European Union, and NATO.

This approach is consistent with public opinion. Germans, especially West Germans, but as Figure 10.1 shows, increasingly East Germans as well, are strong supporters of the Federal Republic's membership in NATO. About 70 percent of the adult West German population views NATO membership as important. Note that the end of the Cold War in the early 1990s did not result in any appreciable decline in support. Meanwhile, among East Germans, who were subjected to forty years of attacks on the Alliance by their communist rulers, support for NATO has grown from 42 percent in 1991 to 58 percent in 1995. Numerous public opinion surveys conducted since the end of the Cold War have also found that the great majority of Germans support a greater international role for the Federal Republic. In March 1999 almost 70 percent supported the use of German forces in the NATO operation in Serbia.

By the mid-1990s the broad contours of Germany's post-unification foreign policy were becoming apparent. First, the Federal Republic wants its Eastern European neighbors to become integrated into the major postwar international organizations of Western Europe: the European Union (EU) and NATO. At a minimum these neighbors would include the Czech Republic, Hungary, and Poland. Germany has become the leading advocate for these emerging democracies in the councils of the

EU and NATO. The great majority of Germans also believe that their country has a special responsibility to aid these nations in the transformation of their economies and political systems.[11] For German business these Eastern European societies represent new markets with a skilled, yet affordable labor force. Since 1991 German investments in these three countries have accounted for 500,000 jobs and the Federal Republic has become their largest trade and investment partner.

Second, Germany will accept a special responsibility for post-communist Russia's economic and political development. Since the end of the Cold War the Federal Republic has become Russia's chief supporter in Western Europe. This relationship will intensify in the decades ahead.

Third, Germany will become more involved in United Nations crisis management and peacekeeping operations. Since a July 1994 constitutional court decision there are no longer any legal obstacles to the deployment of German military forces in United Nations operations. Encouraged by its allies, Germany will in the future make military contributions to these activities commensurate with its resources. In 1999 the new Red-Green government of Chancellor Schröder agreed that if necessary Germany would send troops to enforce a cease-fire in Kosovo in addition to those already deployed in Bosnia and Macedonia.

The new Red-Green government, which took office in 1998, also seeks a more active foreign political role for the Federal Republic. In the councils of NATO the Schröder government, in a move that reflects Green influence, wants the Alliance to pledge a no-first-use of nuclear weapons as part of its new post–Cold War strategy. The German government would like to assume more of a leadership role in the international disarmament discussion and in Western Europe's relationship with post-communist Russia. NATO's three nuclear powers—the United States, Britain, and France—oppose the German initiative, but other NATO members such as Canada, Denmark and Norway are supportive. This proposal underscores an important characteristic of the new post-unification generation of German political leaders: they and the vast majority of Germans strongly oppose the acquisition of nuclear weapons or the deployment of the army into any country conquered by Hitler except on the rarest of occasions. When military force is used it will be in collaboration with NATO or UN security missions.

This is exactly what happened in March 1999 when Luftwaffe fighters left their base in Italy to join in the NATO attack on Serbia. It marked the first time since 1945 that German forces had been in combat. Ironically, the attack was supported by the new Social Democratic–Green government, many of whose members in the 1980s had strongly opposed the deployment of German forces overseas. Some Greens had even proposed German withdrawal from NATO. The military attack underscored the new German international role. The latent pacifism of the Cold War has been replaced by the sober realization that unified Germany, as the second largest member of NATO, cannot escape its defense and security responsibilities.

The European Union

West Germany was a charter member and enthusiastic supporter of the postwar European movement. Whether it was the Common Market, the Defense Community, or any other European organization, German participation could always be counted on. All democratic parties supported "Europe" and expressed the hope for an eventual political unification of the continent. Europe was, and to a large extent still is, an "OK" concept. Strongly supporting Europe was one way of forgetting about being German after 1945 and of reestablishing relations with neighbors. It was also highly advantageous to the German economy.

Progress toward European unification has been most apparent in the economic field. Germany had little difficulty with either the European customs union or the common external tariff policy of the Common Market. However, the efforts of French President Charles de Gaulle during the 1960s to make the internal structure and the foreign policy of the Union conform to his views did put Germany between Washington and Paris and complicated its foreign policy. The Gaullist vision of Europe also prompted a miniconflict between the Atlanticist (pro-American) and Gaullist wings of the then-ruling Christian Democratic Union.

European issues have thus far had little partisan impact. Relations with Brussels, the administrative center of the European Union, were mainly the responsibility of one department in the economics ministry and generally were treated as a technical issue. The establishment of a common agricultural price-support and marketing structure in 1967 did provoke political controversy, as farmers concerned about competition from France and other more efficient agricultural producers protested. Yet all parties made great efforts to support the farmers, so this problem did not become a partisan policy issue.

The lion's share of agricultural policymaking now takes place in Brussels. In some fields, the economics and finance ministries must work within the context of European policy. In addition, the Bundestag and the Bundesrat now examine proposed European Union regulations in their committees. Major interest groups, especially in agriculture and business, and the Länder have offices in Brussels.

In recent years the European Union has also attempted to develop common trade policies for its members. This has led to numerous European-American disputes over steel, high technology, and agriculture. As a key member of the Union, Germany plays a major role in the formulation of these policies. Yet, as Gebhard Schweigler has noted, "[Germany] is able to escape direct blame for controversial trade policies by pursuing them together with its European partners, and, if need be, by hiding, as it were, behind the decision-making process in Brussels."[12] The Union also provides the Federal Republic with a means for reducing the suspicion that a powerful Germany still evokes among some of its neighbors.

With unification the former GDR also became part of the EU. Some of the other members are concerned that the enlarged and unified Germany will turn inward and become more "German" and less "European." The Federal Republic has gone to great lengths to assure the Union that its commitment to European integration is undiminished by unification. The establishment of a single internal market in 1992, for example, was not delayed.

European Questions: Currency Union, Expansion, and Fiscal Reform

In 1999, eleven of the fifteen European Union member nations embarked on a European Currency Union. Germany and France, still the two key members of the

European Union, are the prime movers behind this historic change, which will give Europe a common currency for the first time since the Roman Empire. For the Federal Republic the Currency Union is a further expression of its commitment to a united Europe. The fabled Deutsche Mark is one of the few postwar symbols that evokes pride among most Germans. In spite of public opposition to the abandonment of the Mark, which is waning as the date for the introduction of the currency approaches, German leaders almost without exception have supported this momentous step toward political union. Germany is in effect saying to its neighbors that it is willing to sacrifice the Deutsche Mark at the altar of a united Europe. Of course, Germany has had substantial influence on the shape of the Currency Union and has insisted that the new European Central Bank pursue strong anti-inflationary monetary policies similar to those of the Bundesbank.

Germany also wants the European Union to expand into Eastern Europe, but not at the expense of sound fiscal policies. It insists that the Union's finances be reformed before the enlargement of the Union. Specifically, the addition of countries such as Poland, Hungary, and the Czech Republic, with their hundreds of thousands of small farmers selling their meat, grains, and dairy products at much lower prices than in Western Europe, would bankrupt the existing agricultural support program. As by far the largest net contributor to the Union's budget, the Federal Republic considers budget reform to be a prerequisite for expansion. Not surprisingly, the major beneficiaries of the present system, France, Italy, and Spain, are satisfied with the present subsidy program.

At the March 1999 summit meeting of European Union heads of government in Berlin, Germany was able to secure agreement on capping the Union's budget at about $95 billion, or 1.27 percent of the total Gross Domestic Product of Union members until 2006. The new arrangements will mean that Germany's net payment of about $12 billion annually to the Union will not increase, and will in fact probably decline by about 3 percent. This was far from the 20 percent reduction that Chancellor Schröder had sought, but it was a step in the right direction.

THE GERMAN EXPERIENCE AND POLITICAL DEVELOPMENT

To many Germans a good part of the twentieth century has been a traumatic *Irr-fahrt,* an error-filled journey, during which the nation has at various times experienced a variety of extremist ideologies—nationalism, fascism, communism—with disastrous consequences for itself and the world. The success of the Federal Republic represented a break from the pattern of political instability, authoritarianism, and aggressive nationalism that had characterized so much of German history. The problems currently faced by the Federal Republic still pale in comparison to this fundamental achievement of creating a genuine democratic political order.

The success of the unification process was in part a result of the Federal Republic's performance since 1949. Neither Germany's neighbors in Eastern and Western Europe nor the larger international community would have supported such a change had they not been convinced that Germany and the Germans had changed. Unification, however, also means that the question of national identity, which remained unresolved during the forty-year division of Germany and Europe, has been resolved consistent with the principles and values that have guided the Republic since 1949: political democracy, civil liberties, rule of law, social welfare, and peaceful resolution of conflict. In short, as former Chancellor Kohl stated in 1991 in his opening address to the first freely elected all-German parliament since 1932, "For the first time in Germany's history, unity, freedom, and peaceful accord with our European neighbors are inextricably linked." Unification has confirmed the validity of the postwar democratic order described in this book.

This postwar experience illustrates that a nation can overcome or change its political culture within a relatively short time. Democratic political stability does not necessarily require the centuries-long evolution characteristic of democracies such as Great Britain and the United States. Postwar Germany should also alert students of development to the importance of system performance and effectiveness, especially in the early years of a country's development. National ideologies, symbols, power, and prestige are not substitutes for meeting concrete popular demands for social change and economic stability. Finally, the German political experience, which once brought Germans the scorn and contempt of civilized societies, can also give us reason for optimism and faith in the ability of people to use democratic politics to better their lives and those of their neighbors.

NOTES

1. A 1990 survey found that 35 percent of East Germans, as opposed to only 8 percent of West Germans, wanted a "new state" to emerge from the unification process rather than an enlarged Federal Republic. Institut für Demoskopie, Surveys Nos. 4199, 5100.
2. In some fields such as banking, fringe benefits including vacations, vacation bonuses, and other benefits such as subsidized cafeterias now exceed the costs of wages and salaries.
3. Michael Jungblut, "Der Sozialstaat wird zum Moloch," *Die Zeit,* no. 49 (November 30, 1984), p. 1.
4. There is little public support for cutting back on the general pattern of welfare services. When asked in 1987 whether the social welfare program should be expanded, maintained at its present level, or cut back, only 8 percent of a national sample of voters supported a reduction in the welfare system. The argument is frequently heard among some CDU and FDP supporters that social programs restrict individual initiative and achievement. This argument was supported by only 12 percent of CDU voters and 4 percent of FDP supporters. Institut für angewandte Sozialforschung, *Politogramm, Bundestagswahl 1987* (Bonn: 1987), p. 91. Among East Germans, support for an extensive welfare state is even greater.
5. Richard Hauser, "Das empirische Bild der Armut in der Bundesrepublik Deutschland: Ein Überblick," *Aus Politik und Zeitgeschichte,* nos. 31–32 (July 28, 1995), 8. In a 1989 European Community survey, 9 percent of the German respondents stated that "in the area where they live" there were people living in poverty or extreme poverty. Commission of the European Communities, "The Perception of Poverty in Europe" (Brussels: March 1990), p. 89.
6. This figure does not include the 480,000 refugees and asylum-seekers. Federal Statistical Office, Press Release, August 19, 1998 (Internet).

7. Walter Hanesch, "Sozialpolitik und Arbeitsmarktbedingte Armut." *Aus Politik und Zeitgeschichte,* nos. 31–32 (July 28, 1995), 14–23.

8. Germany has historical ties to both Slovenia and Croatia. Slovenia was part of the Austro-Hungarian empire and was incorporated in Hitler's Greater German Reich during World War II. During the war the Nazis also set up a puppet government in Croatia, which was guilty of numerous atrocities against Serbians and Jews. Most of the 700,000 Yugoslav residents of the Federal Republic are Croatian.

9. The aid to Eastern Europe also reflects the Federal Republic's sense of responsibility for the past actions of Germany in the region.

10. Ronald D. Asmus, "German Strategy and Public Opinion After the Wall 1990–1993," Rand Corporation, February 1994, p. 47.

11. Asmus, "German Strategy and Public Opinion . . .", pp. 48ff.

12. Gebhard Schweigler, *West German Foreign Policy: The Domestic Setting* (New York: Praeger, 1984), p. 21.

Appendix: The Basic Law of the Federal Republic

This is an abridged version of the Basic Law as amended, containing only the most important provisions and including sections mentioned in the book.*

I. BASIC RIGHTS

Article 1 (Protection of human dignity)
(1) The dignity of man shall be inviolable. To respect and protect it shall be the duty of all state authority.

(2) The German people therefore acknowledge inviolable and inalienable human rights as the basis of every community, of peace, and of justice in the world.

(3) The following basic rights shall bind the legislature, the executive, and the judiciary as directly enforceable law.

Article 2 (Rights of liberty)
(1) Everyone shall have the right to the free development of his personality insofar as he does not violate the rights of others or offend against the constitutional order or the moral code.

(2) Everyone shall have the right to life and to inviolability of his person. The liberty of the individual shall be inviolable. These rights may only be encroached upon pursuant to a law.

Article 3 (Equality before the law)
(1) All persons shall be equal before the law.

---

* Based on an English translation provided by the Press and Information Office of the federal government of Germany.

(2) Men and women shall have equal rights.

(3) No one may be prejudiced or favored because of his sex, his parentage, his race, his language, his homeland and origin, his faith, or his religious or political opinions.

Article 4 (Freedom of faith and creed)
(1) Freedom of faith, of conscience, and freedom of creed, religious or ideological (*weltanschaulich*), shall be inviolable.

(2) The undisturbed practice of religion is guaranteed.

(3) No one may be compelled against his conscience to render war service involving the use of arms. Details shall be regulated by a federal law.

Article 5 (Freedom of expression)
(1) Everyone shall have the right freely to express and disseminate his opinion by speech, writing, and pictures and freely to inform himself from generally accessible sources. Freedom of the press and freedom of reporting by means of broadcasts and films are guaranteed. There shall be no censorship.

(2) These rights are limited by the provisions of the general laws, the provisions of law for the protection of youth, and by the right to inviolability of personal honor.

(3) Art and science, research and teaching, shall be free. Freedom of teaching shall not absolve from loyalty to the constitution.

Article 6 (Marriage, Family)
(1) Marriage and the family shall enjoy the special protection of the state.

(2) The care and upbringing of children are a natural right of, and a duty incumbent on the parents. The national community shall watch over their endeavors in this respect . . .

(4) Every mother shall be entitled to the protection and care of the community.

(5) Children born out of wedlock shall be provided by legislation with the same opportunities for their physical and spiritual development and their place in society as are enjoyed by other children.

Article 8 (Freedom of assembly)
(1) All Germans shall have the right to assemble peaceably and unarmed without prior notification or permission.

(2) With regard to open-air meetings this right may be restricted by or pursuant to a law.

Article 9 (Freedom of association)
(1) All Germans shall have the right to form associations and societies.

(2) Associations, the purpose or activities of which conflict with criminal laws or which are directed against the constitutional order or the concept of international understanding, are prohibited.

(3) The right to form associations to safeguard and improve working and economic conditions is guaranteed to everyone and to all trades, occupations, and professions.

Agreements which restrict or seek to impair this right shall be null and void; measures directed to this end shall be illegal.

Article 11 (Freedom of movement)

(1) All Germans shall enjoy freedom of movement throughout the federal territory.

(2) This right may be restricted only by or pursuant to a law and one in cases in which an adequate basis of existence is lacking and special burdens would arise to the community as a result thereof, or in which such restriction is necessary to avert an imminent danger to the existence of the free democratic basic order of the Federation or a Land, to combat the danger of epidemics, to deal with natural disasters or particularly grave accidents, to protect young people from neglect, or to prevent crime.

Article 12 (Right to choose trade, occupation, or profession)

(1) All Germans shall have the right freely to choose their trade, occupation, or profession, their place of work, and their place of training. The practice of trades, occupations, and professions may be regulated by or pursuant to a law.

(2) No specific occupation may be imposed on any person except within the framework of a traditional compulsory public service that applies generally and equally to all.

(3) Forced labor may be imposed only on persons deprived of their liberty by court sentence.

Article 12a (Liability to military and other service)

(1) Men who have attained the age of 18 years may be required to serve in the Armed Forces, in the Federal Border Guard, or in a Civil Defense organization.

(2) A person who refuses, on grounds of conscience, to render war service involving the use of arms may be required to render a substitute service.

The duration of such substitute service shall not exceed the duration of military service. Details shall be regulated by a law which shall not interfere with the freedom of conscience and must also provide for the possibility of a substitute service not connected with units of the Armed Forces or of the Federal Border Guard.

Article 13 (Inviolability of the home)*

(1) The home shall be inviolable.

(2) Searches may be ordered only by a judge or, in the event of danger in delay, by other organs as provided by law and may be carried out only in the form prescribed by law.

(3) If particular facts justify the suspicion that any person has committed an especially serious crime specifically defined by law, technical means of acoustical

---

* Amended March 26, 1998

surveillance of any home in which the suspect is supposedly staying may be employed pursuant to judicial order for the purpose of prosecuting the offense, provided that alternative methods of investigating the matter would be disproportionately difficult or unproductive. The authorization shall be for a limited time. The order shall be issued by a panel composed of three judges. When time is of the essence, it may also be issued by a single judge.

(4) To avert acute dangers to public safety, especially dangers to life or to the public, technical means of surveillance of the home may be employed only pursuant to judicial order. When time is of the essence, such measures may also be ordered by other authorities designated by a law; a judicial decision shall subsequently be obtained without delay.

(5) If technical means are contemplated solely for the protection of persons officially deployed in a home, the measure may be ordered by an authority designated by a law. The information thereby obtained may be otherwise used only for purposes of criminal prosecution or to avert danger and only if the legality of the measure has been previously determined by a judge; when time is of the essence, a judicial decision shall subsequently be obtained without delay.

(6) The Federal Government will report to the Bundestag annually on the use of these technical surveillance methods. On the basis of this report a parliamentary committee will exercise control over these methods. The states will assure equivalent parliamentary control.

Article 14 (Property, Right of inheritance, Expropriation)

(1) Property and the right of inheritance are guaranteed. Their content and limits shall be determined by the laws.

(2) Property imposes duties. Its use should also serve the public good.

(3) Expropriation shall be permitted only in the public weal. It may be effected only by or pursuant to a law which shall provide for the nature and extent of the compensation. Such compensation shall be determined by establishing an equitable balance between the public interest and the interests of those affected. In case of dispute regarding the amount of compensation, recourse may be had to the ordinary courts.

Article 15 (Socialization)

Land, natural resources, and means of production may for the purpose of socialization be transferred to public ownership or other forms of publicly controlled economy by a law which shall provide for the nature and extent of compensation. In respect of such compensation the third and fourth sentences of paragraph (3) of Article 14 shall apply *mutatis mutandis.*

Article 16 (Nationality, Extradition)

(1) No one may be deprived of his German citizenship. Loss of citizenship may arise only pursuant to a law, and against the will of the person affected only if such person does not thereby become stateless.

(2) No German may be extradited to a foreign country.

Article 16a (Asylum)*
(1) Anybody persecuted on political grounds has the right of asylum.

(2) This right may not be invoked by anybody who enters the country from a member state of the European Union or another third country where the application of the Convention relating to the Status of Refugees and the Convention for the Protection of Human Rights and Fundamental Freedoms is assured. Countries outside the European Communities which fulfill the conditions of the first sentence of this paragraph shall be specified by legislation requiring the consent of the Bundesrat. In cases covered by the first sentence, measures terminating a person's sojourn may be carried out irrespective of any remedy sought by that person.

(3) Legislation requiring the consent of the Bundesrat may be introduced to specify countries where the legal situation, the application of the law and the general political circumstances justify the assumption that neither political persecution nor inhumane or degrading punishment or treatment takes place there. It shall be presumed that a foreigner from such a country is not subject to persecution on political grounds so long as the person concerned does not present facts supporting the supposition that, contrary to that presumption, he or she is subject to political persecution.

Article 17 (Right of petition)
Everyone shall have the right individually or jointly with others to address written requests or complaints to the appropriate agencies and to parliamentary bodies.

Article 18 (Forfeiture of basic rights)*
Those who abuse their freedom of expression, in particular freedom of the press, freedom of teaching, freedom of assembly, freedom of association, privacy of correspondence, mail and telecommunications, property, or the right of asylum in order to undermine the free democratic basic order shall forfeit these basic rights. Such forfeiture and its extent shall be determined by the Federal Constitutional Court.

Article 19 (Restriction of basic rights)
(1) Insofar as a basic right may, under this Basic Law, be restricted by or pursuant to a law, such law must apply generally and not solely to an individual case. Furthermore, such law must name the basic right, indicating the Article concerned.

(2) In no case may the essential content of a basic right be encroached upon.

---

* Amended by federal statute of June 28, 1993

II. THE FEDERATION AND THE CONSTITUENT STATES (LÄNDER)

Article 20 (Basic principles of the constitutional right to resist)

(1) The Federal Republic of Germany is a democratic and social federal state.

(2) All state authority emanates from the people. It shall be exercised by the people by means of elections and voting and by specific legislative, executive, and judicial organs.

(3) Legislation shall be subject to the constitutional order; the executive and the judiciary shall be bound by law and justice.

(4) All Germans shall have the right to resist any person or persons seeking to abolish that constitutional order, should no other remedy be possible.

Article 21 (Political parties)

(1) The political parties shall take part in forming the political will of the people. They may be freely established. Their internal organization must conform to democratic principles. They must publicly account for the sources of their funds.

(2) Parties which, by reason of their aims or the behavior of their adherents, seek to impair or abolish the free democratic basic order or to endanger the existence of the Federal Republic of Germany, shall be unconstitutional. The Federal Constitutional Court shall decide on the question of unconstitutionality.

(3) Details shall be regulated by federal laws.

Article 23 (The European Union)*

(1) With the intention of establishing a united Europe the Federal Republic of Germany shall participate in the development of the European Union, which is committed to democratic, rule-of-law, social, and federal principles as well as the principle of subsidiarity, and ensures protection of basic rights comparable in substance to that afforded by this Basic Law. To this end the Federation may transfer sovereign powers by law with the consent of the Bundesrat.

(2) The Bundestag and, through the Bundesrat, the Länder shall be involved in matters concerning the European Union. The Federal Government shall inform the Bundestag and the Bundesrat comprehensively and as quickly as possible.

(4) The Bundesrat shall be involved in the decision-making process of the Federation insofar as it would have to be involved in a corresponding internal measure or insofar as the Länder would be internally responsible.

(5) Where essentially the exclusive legislative jurisdiction of the Länder is affected, the exercise of the rights of the Federal Republic of Germany as a member state of the European Union shall be transferred by the Federation to a representative of the Länder designated by the Bundesrat.

---

* Amended by federal statute of December 21, 1992

Those rights shall be exercised with the participation of and in agreement with the Federal Government; in this connection the responsibility of the Federation for the country as a whole shall be maintained.

Article 24 (International organizations)*

(1) The Federation may by legislation transfer sovereign powers to international institutions.

(1a) Where the Länder have the right to exercise state powers and to discharge state functions they may with the consent of the Federal Government transfer sovereign powers to transnational institutions in neighboring regions.

(2) For the maintenance of peace, the Federation may enter a system of mutual collective security; in doing so it shall consent to such limitations upon its rights of sovereignty as will bring about and secure a peaceful and lasting order in Europe and among the nations of the world.

Article 26 (Ban on war of aggression)

(1) Acts tending to and undertaken with the intent to disturb the peaceful relations between nations, especially to prepare for aggressive war, shall be unconstitutional. They shall be made a punishable offence.

(2) Weapons designed for warfare may not be manufactured, transported, or marketed except with the permission of the Federal Government. Details shall be regulated by a federal law.

Article 28 (Federal guarantee of Länder constitutions)*

(1) The constitutional order in the Länder shall conform to the principles of republican, democratic, and social government based on the rule of law, within the meaning of this Basic Law. In each of the Länder, counties (*Kreise*), and municipalities (*Gemeinden*), the people must be represented by a body chosen in general, direct, free, equal, and secret elections. In county and municipal elections persons who are nationals of member states of the European Union may also vote and shall be eligible for election in accordance with European Union law. In the municipalities the assembly of the municipality may take the place of an elected body.

(2) The communes must be guaranteed the right to regulate under their own responsibility all the affairs of the local community within the limits set by law. The associations of communes (*Gemeindeverbande*) shall also have the right of self-government in accordance with the law and within the limits of the functions assigned to them by law.

(3) The Federation shall ensure that the constitutional order of the Länder conforms to the basic rights and to the provisions of paragraphs (1) and (2) of this Article.

---

* Amended by federal statute of December 21, 1992

Article 29 (New delimitation of Länder boundaries)

(1) A new delimitation of federal territory may be made to ensure that the Länder by their size and capacity are able effectively to fulfill the functions incumbent upon them. Due regard shall be given to regional, historical, and cultural ties, economic expediency, and the requirements of regional policy and planning.

Article 30 (Functions of the Länder)

The exercise of governmental powers and the discharge of governmental functions shall be incumbent on the Länder insofar as this Basic Law does not otherwise prescribe or permit.

Article 31 (Priority of federal law)

Federal law shall override Land law.

Article 32 (Foreign relations)

(1) Relations with foreign states shall be conducted by the Federation.

(2) Before the conclusion of a treaty affecting the special circumstances of a Land, that Land must be consulted in sufficient time.

(3) Insofar as the Länder have power to legislate, they may, with the consent of the Federal Government, conclude treaties with foreign states.

Article 35 (Legal, administrative, and police assistance)

(1) All federal and Land authorities shall render each other legal and administrative assistance.

(2) In order to maintain or to restore public security or order, a Land may, in cases of particular importance, call upon forces and facilities of the Federal Border Guard to assist its police if, without this assistance, the police could not, or only with considerable difficulty, fulfill a task. In order to deal with a natural disaster or an especially grave accident, a Land may request the assistance of the police forces of other Länder or of forces and facilities of other administrative authorities or of the Federal Border Guard or the Armed Forces.

(3) If the natural disaster or the accident endangers a region larger than a Land, the Federal Government may, insofar as this is necessary, effectively to deal with such danger, instruct the Land governments to place their police forces at the disposal of other Länder, and may commit units of the Federal Border Guard or the Armed Forces to support the police forces. Measures taken by the Federal Government pursuant to the first sentence of this paragraph must be revoked at any time upon the request of the Bundesrat, and in any case without delay upon removal of the danger.

Article 36 (Staff of federal authorities)

(1) Civil servants of supreme federal authorities shall be drawn from all Länder on a proportionate basis. People employed by other federal authorities should as a rule be drawn from the Land where those authorities are located.

III. THE FEDERAL PARLIAMENT (BUNDESTAG)

Article 38 (Elections)

(1) The deputies to the German Bundestag shall be elected in general, direct, free, equal, and secret elections. They shall be representatives of the whole people, not bound by orders and instructions, and shall be subject only to their conscience.

(2) Anyone who has attained the age of 18 years shall be entitled to vote; anyone who has attained full legal age shall be eligible for election.

(3) Details shall be regulated by a federal law.

Article 39 (Assembly and legislative term)

(1) The Bundestag shall be elected for a four-year term. Its legislative term shall end with the assembly of a new Bundestag. The new election shall be held at the earliest 45, at the latest 47, months after the beginning of the legislative term. If the Bundestag is dissolved the new election shall be held within 60 days.

(2) The Bundestag shall assemble at the latest on the thirtieth day after the election.

(3) The Bundestag shall determine the termination and resumption of its meetings. The President of the Bundestag may convene it at an earlier date. He must do so if one-third of its members or the Federal President or the Federal Chancellor so demand.

Article 43 (Presence of the Federal Government)

(1) The Bundestag and its committees may demand the presence of any member of the Federal Government.

(2) The members of the Bundesrat or of the Federal Government as well as persons commissioned by them shall have access to all meetings of the Bundestag and its committees. They must be heard at any time.

Article 44 (Committees of investigation)

(1) The Bundestag shall have the right, and upon the motion of one-fourth of its members the duty, to set up a committee of investigation which shall take the requisite evidence at public hearings. The public may be excluded.

(2) The rules of criminal procedures shall apply *mutatis mutandis* to the taking of evidence. The privacy of posts and telecommunications shall remain unaffected.

(3) Courts and administrative authorities shall be bound to render legal and administrative assistance.

(4) The decisions of committees of investigation shall not be subject to judicial consideration. The courts shall be free to evaluate and judge the facts on which the investigation is based.

Article 47 (Right of deputies to refuse to give evidence)

Deputies may refuse to give evidence concerning persons who have confided facts to them in their capacity as deputies, or to whom they have confided facts in such capacity, as well as concerning these facts themselves. To the extent that this right to refuse to give evidence exists, no seizure of documents shall be permissible.

IV. THE COUNCIL OF CONSTITUENT STATES (BUNDESRAT)

Article 50 (Function)*

The Länder shall participate through the Bundesrat in the legislative process and administration of the Federation and in matters concerning the European Union.

Article 51 (Composition)

(1) The Bundesrat shall consist of members of the Land governments which appoint and recall them. Other members of such governments may act as substitutes.

(2) Each Land shall have at least three votes; Länder with more than two million inhabitants shall have four, Länder with more than six million inhabitants, five votes, Länder with more than seven million inhabitants, six votes.

(3) Each Land may delegate as many members as it has votes. The votes of each Land may be cast only as a block vote and only by members present or their substitutes.

Article 53 (Participation of the Federal Government)

The members of the Federal Government shall have the right, and on demand the duty, to attend the meetings of the Bundesrat and of its committees. They must be heard at any time. The Bundesrat must be currently kept informed by the Federal Government of the conduct of affairs.

---

* Amended by federal statute of December 21, 1992

Article 53a

(1) Two-thirds of the members of the Joint Committee shall be deputies of the Bundestag and one-third shall be members of the Bundesrat. The Bundestag shall delegate its deputies in proportion to the sizes of its parliamentary groups; such deputies must not be members of the Federal Government. Each Land shall be represented by a Bundesrat member of its choice; these members shall not be bound by instructions. The establishment of the Joint Committee and its procedures shall be regulated by rules of procedure to be adopted by the Bundestag and requiring the consent of the Bundesrat.

(2) The Federal Government must inform the Joint Committee about its plans in respect of a state of defense. The rights of the Bundestag and its committees under paragraph (1) of Article 43 shall not be affected by the provision of this paragraph.

V. THE FEDERAL PRESIDENT

Article 54 (Election by the Federal Convention)

(1) The Federal President shall be elected, without debate, by the Federal Convention (*Bundesversammlung*). Every German shall be eligible who is entitled to vote for Bundestag candidates and has attained the age of 40 years.

(2) The term of office of the Federal President shall be five years. Reelection for a consecutive term shall be permitted only once.

(3) The Federal Convention shall consist of the members of the Bundestag and an equal number of members elected by the diets of the Länder according to the principles of proportional representation.

(4) The Federal Convention shall meet not later than 30 days before the expiration of the term of office of the Federal President or, in the case of premature termination, not later than 30 days after that date. It shall be convened by the President of the Bundestag.

(5) After the expiration of a legislative term, the period specified in the first sentence of paragraph (4) of this Article shall begin with the first meeting of the Bundestag.

(6) The person receiving the votes of the majority of the members of the Federal Convention shall be elected. If such majority is not obtained by any candidate in two ballots, the candidate who receives the largest number of votes in the next ballot shall be elected.

VI. THE FEDERAL GOVERNMENT

Article 62 (Composition)

The Federal Government shall consist of the Federal Chancellor and the Federal Ministers.

Article 63 (Election of the Federal Chancellor— Dissolution of the Bundestag)

(1) The Federal Chancellor shall be elected, without debate, by the Bundestag upon the proposal of the Federal President.

(2) The person obtaining the votes of the majority of the members of the Bundestag shall be elected. The person elected must be appointed by the Federal President.

(3) If the person proposed is not elected, the Bundestag may elect within 14 days of the ballot a Federal Chancellor by more than one-half of its members.

(4) If no candidate has been elected within this period, a new ballot shall take place without delay, in which the person obtaining the largest number of votes shall be elected. If the person elected has obtained the votes of the majority of the members of the Bundestag, the Federal President must appoint him within seven days of the election. If the person elected did not obtain such a majority, the Federal President must within seven days either appoint him or dissolve the Bundestag.

Article 64 (Appointment of Federal Ministers)

(1) The Federal Ministers shall be appointed and dismissed by the Federal President upon the proposal of the Federal Chancellor.

Article 65 (Distribution of responsibility)

The Federal Chancellor shall determine, and be responsible for, the general policy guidelines. Within the limits set by these guidelines, each Federal Minister shall conduct the affairs of his department autonomously and on his own responsibility. The Federal Government shall decide on differences of opinion between affairs of the Federal Government in accordance with rules of procedure adopted by it and approved by the Federal President.

Article 65a (Power of command over Armed Forces)

Power of command in respect of the Armed Forces shall be vested in the Federal Minister of Defense.

Article 66 (No secondary occupation)

The Federal Chancellor and the Federal Ministers may not hold any other salaried office, nor engage in a trade or occupation, nor practice a profession, nor belong to the management or, without the consent of the Bundestag, to the board of directors of an enterprise carried on for profit.

Article 67 (Vote of no-confidence)

(1) The Bundestag can express its lack of confidence in the Federal Chancellor only by electing a successor with the majority of its members and by requesting the Fed-

eral President to dismiss the Federal Chancellor. The Federal President must comply with the request and appoint the person elected.

(2) Forty-eight hours must elapse between the motion and the election.

Article 68 (Vote of confidence— Dissolution of the Bundestag)

(1) If a motion of the Federal Chancellor for a vote of confidence is not assented to by the majority of the members of the Bundestag, the Federal President may, upon the proposal of the Federal Chancellor, dissolve the Bundestag within 21 days. The right to dissolve shall lapse as soon as the Bundestag with the majority of its members elects another Federal Chancellor.

(2) Forty-eight hours must elapse between the motion and the vote thereon.

Article 70 (Legislation of the Federation and the Länder)

(1) The Länder shall have the right to legislate insofar as this Basic Law does not confer legislative power on the Federation.

(2) The division of competence between the Federation and the Länder shall be determined by the provisions of this Basic Law concerning exclusive and concurrent powers.

Article 71 (Exclusive legislation of the Federation, definition)

In matters within the exclusive legislative power of the Federation, the Länder shall have power to legislate only if, and to the extent that, a federal law explicitly so authorizes them.

Article 72 (Concurrent legislation of the Federation, definition)

(1) In matters within concurrent legislative powers, the Länder shall have power to legislate as long as, and to the extent that, the Federation does not exercise its right to legislate.

(2) The Federation shall have the right to legislate in these matters to the extent that a need for regulation by federal legislation exists because:

1. a matter cannot be effectively regulated by the legislation of individual Länder, or

2. the regulation of a matter by a Land law might prejudice the interests of other Länder or of the people as a whole, or

3. the maintenance of legal or economic unity, especially the maintenance of uniformity of living conditions beyond the territory of any one Land, necessitates such regulation.

Article 76 (Bills)

(1) Bills shall be introduced in the Bundestag by the Federal Government or by members of the Bundestag or by the Bundesrat.

(2) Bills of the Federal Government shall be submitted first to the Bundesrat. The Bundesrat shall be entitled to state its position on such bills within six weeks. A bill exceptionally submitted to the Bundesrat as being particularly urgent by the Federal Government may be submitted by the latter to the Bundestag three weeks later, even though the Federal Government may not yet have received the statement of the Bundesrat's position; such statement shall be transmitted to the Bundestag by the Federal Government without delay upon its receipt.

(3) Bills of the Bundesrat shall be submitted to the Bundestag by the Federal Government within three months. In doing so, the Federal Government must state its own view.

Article 77 (Procedure concerning adopted bills—Objection of the Bundesrat)

(1) Bills intended to become federal laws shall require adoption by the Bundestag. Upon their adoption they shall, without delay, be transmitted to the Bundesrat by the President of the Bundestag.

(2) The Bundesrat may, within three weeks of the receipt of the adopted bill, demand that a committee for joint consideration of bills, composed of members of the Bundestag and members of the Bundesrat, be convened. The composition and the procedure of this committee shall be regulated by rules of procedure to be adopted by the Bundestag and requiring the consent of the Bundesrat. The members of the Bundesrat on this committee shall not be bound by instructions. If the consent of the Bundesrat is required for a bill to become a law, the convening of this committee may also be demanded by the Bundestag or the Federal Government. Should the committee propose any amendment to the adopted bill, the Bundestag must again vote on the bill.

(3) Insofar as the consent of the Bundesrat is not required for a bill to become a law, the Bundesrat may, when the proceedings under paragraph (2) of this Article are completed, enter an objection within two weeks against a bill adopted by the Bundestag. This period shall begin, in the case of the last sentence of paragraph (2) of this Article, on the receipt of the bill as readopted by the Bundestag, and in all other cases on the receipt of a communication from the chairman of the committee provided for in paragraph (2) of this Article, to the effect that the committee's proceedings have been concluded.

(4) If the objection was adopted with the majority of the votes of the Bundesrat, it can be rejected by a decision of the majority of the members of the Bundestag. If the Bundesrat adopted the objection with a majority of at least two-thirds of its votes, its rejection by the Bundestag shall require a majority of two-thirds, including at least the majority of the members of the Bundestag.

Article 78 (Conditions for passing of federal laws)

A bill adopted by the Bundestag shall become a law if the Bundesrat consents to it, or fails to make a demand pursuant to paragraph (2) of Article 77, or fails to enter an objection within the period stipulated in paragraph (3) of Article 77, or withdraws such objections, or if the objection is overridden by the Bundestag.

Article 79 (Amendment of the Basic Law)

(1) This Basic Law can be amended only by laws which expressly amend or supplement the text thereof. In respect of international treaties the subject of which is a peace settlement, the preparation of a peace settlement, or the abolition of an occupation regime, or which are designed to serve the defense of the Federal Republic, it shall be sufficient, for the purpose of clarifying that the provisions of this Basic Law do not preclude the conclusion and entry into force of such treaties, to effect a supplementation of the text of this Basic Law confined to such clarification.

(2) Any such law shall require the affirmative vote of two-thirds of the members of the Bundestag and two-thirds of the votes of the Bundesrat.

(3) Amendments of this Basic Law affecting the division of the Federation into Länder, the participation on principle of the Länder in legislation, or the basic principles laid down in Articles 1 and 20, shall be inadmissible.

Article 80 (Issue of ordinances having force of law)

(1) The Federal Government, a Federal Minister, or the Land governments may be authorized by a law to issue ordinances having the force of law (*Rechtsverordnungen*). The content, purpose, and scope of the authorization so conferred must be set forth in such law. This legal basis must be stated in the ordinance. If a law provides that such authorization may be delegated, such delegation shall require another ordinance having the force of law.

(2) The consent of the Bundesrat shall be required, unless otherwise provided by federal legislation, for ordinances having the force of law issued by the Federal Government or a Federal Minister concerning basic rules for the use of facilities of the federal railroads and of postal and telecommunications services, or charges therefor, or concerning the construction and operation of railroads, as well as for ordinances having the force of law issued pursuant to federal laws that require the consent of the Bundesrat or that are executed by the Länder as agents of the Federation or as matters of their own concern.

Article 80a (State of tension)

(1) Where this Basic Law or a federal law on defense, including the protection of the civilian population, stipulates that legal provisions may only be applied in accordance with this Article, their application shall, except when a state of defense exists, be admissible only after the Bundestag has determined that a state of tension (*Spannungsfall*) exists or if it has specifically approved such application. In respect of the

cases mentioned in the first sentence of paragraph (5) and the second sentence of paragraph (6) of Article 12a, such determination of a state of tension and such specific approval shall require a two-thirds majority of the votes cast.

(2) Any measures taken by virtue of legal provisions enacted under paragraph (1) of this Article shall be revoked whenever the Bundestag so requests.

(3) In derogation of paragraph (1) of this Article, the application of such legal provisions shall also be admissible by virtue of, and in accordance with, a decision taken with the consent of the Federal Government by an international organ within the framework of a treaty of alliance. Any measures taken pursuant to this paragraph shall be revoked whenever the Bundestag so requests with the majority of its members.

Article 81 (State of legislative emergency)

(1) Should, in the circumstances of Article 68, the Bundestag not be dissolved, the Federal President may, at the request of the Federal Government and with the consent of the Bundesrat, declare a state of legislative emergency with respect to a bill, if the Bundestag rejects the bill although the Federal Government has declared it to be urgent. The same shall apply if a bill has been rejected although the Federal Chancellor had combined with it the motion under Article 68.

(2) If, after a state of legislative emergency has been declared, the Bundestag again rejects the bill or adopts it in a version stated to be unacceptable to the Federal Government, the bill shall be deemed to have become a law to the extent that the Bundesrat consents to it. The same shall apply if the bill is not passed by the Bundestag within four weeks of its reintroduction.

(3) During the term of office of a Federal Chancellor, any other bill rejected by the Bundestag may become a law in accordance with paragraphs (1) and (2) of this Article within a period of six months after the first declaration of a state of legislative emergency. After the expiration of this period, a further declaration of a state of legislative emergency shall be inadmissible during the term of office of the same Federal Chancellor.

(4) This Basic Law may not be amended or repealed or suspended in whole or in part by a law enacted pursuant to paragraph (2) of this Article.

VIII. THE EXECUTION OF FEDERAL LAWS AND THE FEDERAL ADMINISTRATION

Article 83 (Execution of federal laws by the Länder)

The Länder shall execute federal laws as matters of their own concern insofar as this Basic Law does not otherwise provide or permit.

Article 84 (Land administration and Federal Government supervision)

(1) Where the Länder execute federal laws as matters of their own concern, they shall provide for the establishment of the requisite authorities and the regulation of administrative procedures insofar as federal laws consented to by the Bundesrat do not otherwise provide.

(2) The Federal Government may, with the consent of the Bundesrat, issue pertinent general administrative rules.

(3) The Federal Government shall exercise supervision to ensure that the Länder execute the federal laws in accordance with applicable law. For this purpose the Federal Government may send commissioners to the highest Land authorities and with their consent, or if such consent is refused, with the consent of the Bundesrat, also to subordinate authorities.

(4) Should any shortcomings which the Federal Government has found to exist in the execution of federal laws in the Länder not be corrected, the Bundesrat shall decide, on the application of the Federal Government or the Land concerned, whether such Land has violated applicable law. The decision of the Bundesrat may be challenged in the Federal Constitutional Court.

(5) With a view to the execution of federal laws, the Federal Government may be authorized by a federal law requiring the consent of the Bundesrat to issue individual instructions for particular cases. They shall be addressed to the highest Land authorities unless the Federal Government considers the matters urgent.

Article 85 (Execution by Länder as agents of the Federation)

(1) Where the Länder execute federal laws as agents of the Federation, the establishment of the requisite authorities shall remain the concern of the Länder except insofar as federal laws consented to by the Bundesrat otherwise provide.

(2) The Federal Government may, with the consent of the Bundesrat, issue pertinent general administrative rules. It may regulate the uniform training of civil servants (*Beamte*) and other salaried public employees (*Angestellte*).

The heads of authorities at the intermediate level shall be appointed with its agreement.

(3) The Land authorities shall be subject to the instructions of the appropriate highest federal authorities. Such instructions shall be addressed to the highest Land authorities unless the Federal Government considers the matter urgent. Execution of the instructions shall be ensured by the highest Land authorities.

(4) Federal supervision shall extend to conformity with law and appropriateness of execution. The Federal Government may, for this purpose, require the submission of reports and documents and send commissioners to all authorities.

Article 86 (Direct federal administration)

(1) Where the Federation executes laws by means of direct federal administration or by federal corporate bodies or institutions under public law, the Federal Government shall, insofar as the law concerned contains no special provision, issue pertinent general administrative rules. The Federal Government shall provide for the establishment of the requisite authorities insofar as the law concerned does not otherwise provide. Federal frontier protection authorities, central offices for police information and communications, for the criminal police, and for the compilation of data for the purposes of protection of the constitution and protection against efforts in the Federal territory which, by the use of force or actions in preparation for the use of force, endanger the foreign interests of the Federal Republic of Germany, may be established by federal legislation.

(2) Social insurance institutions whose sphere of competence extends beyond the territory of one Land shall be administered as federal corporate bodies under public law.

(3) In addition, autonomous federal higher authorities as well as federal corporate bodies and institutions under public law may be established by federal legislation for matters in which the Federation has the power to legislate. If new functions arise for the Federation in matters in which it has the power to legislate, federal authorities at the intermediate and lower levels may be established, in case of urgent need, with the consent of the Bundesrat and of the majority of the members of the Bundestag.

Article 87a (Build-up, strength, use, and functions of the Armed Forces)

(1) The Federation shall build up Armed Forces for defense purposes. Their numerical strength and general organizational structure shall be shown in the budget.

(2) Apart from defense, the Armed Forces may only be used to the extent explicitly permitted by this Basic Law.

(3) While a state of defense or a state of tension exists, the Armed Forces shall have the power to protect civilian property and discharge functions of traffic control insofar as this is necessary for the performance of their defense mission. Moreover, the Armed Forces may, when a state of defense or a state of tension exists, be entrusted with the protection of civilian property in support of police measures; in this event the Armed Forces shall cooperate with the competent authorities.

(4) In order to avert any imminent danger to the existence or to the free democratic basic order of the Federation or a Land, the Federal Government may, should conditions as envisaged in paragraph (2) of Article 91 obtain and the police forces and the Federal Border Guard be inadequate, use the Armed Forces to support the police and the Federal Border Guard in the protection of civilian property and in combating organized and militarily armed insurgents. Any such use of Armed Forces must be discontinued whenever the Bundestag or the Bundesrat so requests.

Article 88 (The Federal Bank)*

The federation shall establish a note-issuing and currency bank as the Federal Bank. Its responsibilities and powers may, within the framework of the European Union, be transferred to the European Central Bank, which is independent and whose primary aim is to safeguard price stability.

JOINT TASKS

Article 91a (Definition of joint tasks)

(1) The Federation shall participate in the discharge of the following responsibilities of the Länder, provided that such responsibilities are important to society as a whole and that federal participation is necessary for the improvement of living conditions (joint tasks):

1. expansion and construction of institutions of higher education including university clinics;
2. improvement of regional economic structures;
3. improvement of the agrarian structure and of coast preservation.

(2) Joint tasks shall be defined in detail by federal legislation requiring the consent of the Bundesrat. Such legislation should include general principles governing the discharge of joint tasks.

(3) Such legislation shall provide for the procedure and the institutions required for joint overall planning. The inclusion of a project in the overall planning shall require the consent of the Land in which it is to be carried out.

(4) In cases to which items 1 and 2 of paragraph (1) of this Article apply, the Federation shall meet one-half of the expenditures in each Land. In cases to which item 3 of paragraph (1) of this Article applies, the Federation shall meet at least one-half of the expenditure, and such proportion shall be the same for all the Länder. Details shall be regulated by legislation. Provision of funds shall be subject to appropriation in the budgets of the Federation and the Länder.

(5) The Federal Government and the Bundesrat shall be informed about the execution of joint tasks, should they so demand.

Article 91b (Cooperation of Federation and Länder in educational planning and in research)

The Federation and the Länder may pursuant to agreements cooperate in educational planning and in the promotion of institutions and projects of scientific research of supraregional importance. The apportionment of costs shall be regulated in the pertinent agreements.

---

* Amended by federal statute of December 21, 1992

IX. THE ADMINISTRATION OF JUSTICE

Article 92 (Court organization)

Judicial power shall be vested in the judges; it shall be exercised by the Federal Constitutional Court, by the federal courts provided for in this Basic Law, and by the courts of the Länder.

Article 93 (Federal Constitutional Court, competency)

(1) The Federal Constitutional Court shall decide:

1. on the interpretation of the Basic Law in the event of disputes concerning the extent of the rights and duties of a highest federal organ or of other parties concerned who have been vested with rights of their own by this Basic Law or by rules of procedure of a highest federal organ;

2. in case of differences of opinion or doubts on the formal and material compatibility of federal law or Land law with this Basic Law, or on the compatibility of Land law with other federal law, at the request of the Federal Government, of a Land government, or of one-third of the Bundestag members;

3. in case of differences of opinion on the rights and duties of the Federation and the Länder, particularly in the execution of federal law by the Länder and in the exercise of federal supervision;

4. on other disputes involving public law, between the Federation and the Länder, between different Länder or within a Land, unless recourse to another court exists;

   4a. on complaints of unconstitutionality, which may be entered by any person who claims that one of his basic rights or one of his rights under paragraph (4) of Article 20, under Article 33, 38, 101, 103, or 104 has been violated by public authority;

   4b. on complaints of unconstitutionality, entered by communes or associations of communes on the ground that their right to self-government under Article 28 has been violated by a law other than a Land law open to complaint to the respective Land constitutional court;

5. in other cases provided for in this Basic Law.

(2) The Federal Constitutional Court shall also act in such other cases as are assigned to it by federal legislation.

Article 94 (Federal Constitutional Court, composition)

(1) The Federal Constitutional Court shall consist of federal judges and other members. Half of the members of the Federal Constitutional Court shall be elected by the

Bundestag and half by the Bundesrat. They may not be members of the Bundestag, the Bundesrat, the Federal Government, nor of any of the corresponding organs of a Land.

(2) The constitution and procedure of the Federal Constitutional Court shall be regulated by a federal law which shall specify in what cases its decisions shall have the force of law. Such law may require that all other legal remedies must have been exhausted before any such complaint of unconstitutionality can be entered, and may make provision for a special procedure as to admissibility.

Article 97 (Independence of the judges)

(1) The judges shall be independent and subject only to the law.

(2) Judges appointed permanently on a full-time basis in established positions cannot against their will be dismissed or permanently or temporarily suspended from office or given a different function or retired before the expiration of their term of office except by virtue of a judicial decision and only on the grounds and in the form provided for by law. Legislation may set age limits for the retirement of judges appointed for life. In the event of changes in the structure of courts or in districts of jurisdiction, judges may be transferred to another court or removed from office, provided they retain their full salary.

Article 102 (Abolition of capital punishment)

Capital punishment shall be abolished.

Article 103 (Basic rights in the courts)

(1) In the courts everyone shall be entitled to a hearing in accordance with the law.

(2) An act can be punished only if it was an offense against the law before the act was committed.

(3) No one may be punished for the same act more than once under general penal legislation.

Article 104 (Legal guarantees in the event of deprivation of liberty)

(1) The liberty of the individual may be restricted only by virtue of a formal law and only with due regard to the forms prescribed therein. Detained persons may not be subjected to mental nor to physical ill-treatment.

(2) Only judges may decide on the admissibility or continuation of any deprivation of liberty. Where such deprivation is not based on the order of a judge, a judicial decision must be obtained without delay. The police may hold no one on their own authority in their own custody longer than the end of the day after the day of apprehension. Details shall be regulated by legislation.

(3) Any person provisionally detained on suspicion of having committed an offense must be brought before a judge not later than the day following the day of apprehension; the judge shall inform him of the reasons for the detention, examine him, and give him an opportunity to raise objections. The judge must, without delay,

either issue a warrant of arrest setting forth the reasons therefor or order his release from detention.

(4) A relative or person enjoying the confidence of the person detained must be notified without delay of any judicial decision ordering or continuing his deprivation of liberty.

Article 107 (Financial equalization)

(2) Federal legislation shall ensure a reasonable equalization between financially strong and financially weak Länder, due account being taken of the financial capacity and financial requirements of communes and associations of communes. Such legislation shall specify the conditions governing equalization claims of Länder entitled to equalization payments and equalization liabilities of Länder owing equalization payments as well as the criteria for determining the amounts of equalization payments. Such legislation may also provide for grants to be made by the Federation from federal funds to financially weak Länder in order to complement the coverage of their general financial requirements (complemental grants).

Article 116 (Definition of "a German," regranting of citizenship)

(1) Unless otherwise provided by statute, a German within the meaning of this Basic Law is a person who possesses German citizenship or who has been admitted to the territory of the German Reich within the frontiers of 31 December 1937 as a refugee or expellee of German ethnic origin (*Volkszugehörigkeit*) or as the spouse or descendant of such a person.

(2) Former German citizens who, between 30 January 1933 and 8 May 1945, were deprived of their citizenship on political, racial, or religious grounds, and their descendants, shall be regranted German citizenship on application. They shall be considered as not having been deprived of their German citizenship where they have established their residence (*Wohnsitz*) in Germany after 8 May 1945 and have not expressed a contrary intention.

Article 146 (Duration of validity of the Basic Law)

This Basic Law, which is valid for the entire German people following the achievement of the unity and freedom of Germany, shall cease to be in force on the day on which a constitution adopted by a free decision of the German people comes into force.

Bibliography

The following listing is selected from the English language literature on postwar German politics. Those students with a command of the German language are directed to the various endnotes in the book. The major German language surveys of the Federal Republic—Wolfgang Rudzio's *Das Politische System der Bundesrepublik Deutschland,* 3rd ed. (Opladen: Leske & Budrich Verlag, 1992), and Eckhard Jesse's *Die Demokratie der Bundesrepublik Deutschland,* 8th ed. (Berlin: Colloquium Verlag, 1997)—are important sources. For current developments, the weekly newspaper *Die Zeit* is recommended. Parliamentary proceedings are well covered in another weekly, *Das Parlament.* Many German periodicals are now available on the Internet; some of them have English language summaries. Both *Der Spiegel* (www.spiegel.de) and *Die Zeit* (www.zeit.de) have English summaries.

CHAPTER 1: THE HISTORICAL SETTING

Barraclough, Geoffrey. *The Origins of Modern Germany.* New York: Capricorn Books, 1963, reprint.

Botting, Douglas. *From the Ruins of the Reich, Germany 1945–1949.* New York: Crown Publishers, 1985.

Bracher, Karl Dietrich. *The German Dictatorship.* New York: Praeger, 1970.

Broszat, Martin. *The Hitler State.* London and White Plains, NY: Longman, 1981.

Browning, Christopher R. *Ordinary Men: Reserve Police Battalion 101 and the Final Solution in Poland.* New York and London: HarperCollins, 1992.

Calleo, David. *The German Problem Reconsidered.* Cambridge and New York: Cambridge University Press, 1978.

Childers, Thomas. *The Nazi Voter.* Chapel Hill and London: University of North Carolina Press, 1983.

Craig, Gordon. *The Germans.* New York: Putnam, 1982.

———. *Germany, 1866–1945.* New York: Oxford University Press, 1978.

Detweiler, Donald S. *Germany: A Short History.* Carbondale: Southern Illinois University Press, 1976.

Edinger, Lewis J., and Brigitte L. Nacos. *From Bonn to Berlin: German Politics in Transition.* New York: Columbia University Press, 1998.

Epstein, Klaus. *The Genesis of German Conservatism.* Princeton: Princeton University Press, 1966.

———. "The German Problem, 1945–50." *World Politics 20,* no. 2 (January 1968): 279–300.

Fest, Joachim. *Hitler.* New York: Random House, 1975.

Friedländer, Saul. *Nazi Germany and the Jews: Volume I.* (New York: HarperCollins Publishers, 1997).

Friedrich, Carl J. "The Legacies of the Occupation of Germany." In *Public Policy,* ed. John D. Montgomery and Albert O. Hirschman. Cambridge, MA: Harvard University Press, 1968, pp. 1–26.

Fulbrook, Mary. *The Divided Nation. A History of Germany, 1918–1990.* New York: Oxford University Press, 1992.

Goldhagen, Daniel Jonah. *Hitler's Willing Executioners. Ordinary Germans and the Holocaust.* New York: Alfred A. Knopf, 1996.

Gillis, John R. "Germany." In *Crisis of Political Development in Europe and the United States,* ed. Raymond Grew. Princeton: Princeton University Press, 1978, pp. 313–345.

Hamilton, Richard. *Who Voted for Hitler?* Princeton: Princeton University Press, 1982.

Holborn, Hajo. *A History of Modern Germany, 1840–1945.* New York: Knopf, 1970.

James, Harold. *The German Slump: Politics and Economics, 1924–1936.* New York: Clarendon Press Oxford, 1986.

Krieger, Leonard. "The Inter-Regnum in Germany: March–August 1945." *Political Science Quarterly* 64, no. 4 (December 1949): 507–532.

———. "The Potential for Democratization in Occupied Germany: A Problem of Historical Projection." In *Public Policy,* ed. John D. Montgomery and Albert O. Hirschman. Cambridge, MA: Harvard University Press, 1968, pp. 27–58.

Laqueur, Walter. *Weimar, A Cultural History.* New York: Putnam, 1974.

Lepsius, M. Rainer. "From Fragmented Party Democracy to Government by Emergency Decree and National Socialist Takeover: Germany." In *The Breakdown of Democratic Regimes: Europe,* ed. Juan J. Linz and Alfred Stephan. Baltimore and London: Johns Hopkins University Press, 1978, pp. 34–79.

Litchfield, Edward, ed. *Governing Postwar Germany.* Ithaca: Cornell University Press, 1953.

Luebbert, Gregory M. "Social Foundations of Political Order in Interwar Europe." *World Politics 39,* no. 4 (July 1987): 449–478.

Marsh, David. *The Germans.* London: Century Hutchinson, 1989.

Merkl, Peter H. *The Origins of the West German Republic.* New York: Oxford University Press, 1965.

Merritt, Richard L. *Democracy Imposed. U.S. Occupation Policy and the German Public.* New Haven and London: Yale University Press, 1995.

Moeller, Robert, ed. *West Germany under Construction: Politics, Society and Culture in the Adenauer Era.* Ann Arbor, MI: University of Michigan Press, 1997.

Patton, David F. *Cold War Politics in Postwar Germany.* New York: St. Martin's Press, 1999.

Peterson, Edward N. *The American Occupation of Germany: Retreat to Victory.* Detroit: Wayne State University Press, 1977.

Pulzer, Peter. *German Politics, 1945–1995.* Oxford: Oxford University Press, 1995.

Rittberger, Volker. "Revolution and Pseudo-Democratization: The Formation of the Weimar Republic." In *Crisis, Choice and Change,* ed. Gabriel A. Almond, et al. Boston: Little Brown, 1973, pp. 285–396.

Sanford, Gregory W. *From Hitler to Ulbricht: The Communist Reconstruction of East Germany 1945–1946.* Princeton: Princeton University Press, 1983.

Speer, Albert. *Inside the Third Reich.* New York: Macmillan, 1968.

Tent, James F. *Mission on the Rhine: Reeducation and Denazification in American-Occupied Germany.* Princeton: Princeton University Press, 1983.

Turner, Henry Ashby, Jr. *The Two Germanies since 1945.* New Haven: Yale University Press, 1987.

CHAPTER 2: PUTTING GERMANY BACK TOGETHER AGAIN: UNIFICATION AND ITS AFTERMATH

Adomeit, Hannes. "Gorbachev and German Unification: Revision of Thinking, Realignment of Power." *Problems of Communism* (July–August 1990), pp. 1–24.

Anderson, Christopher, et al., eds. *The Domestic Politics of German Unification.* Boulder, CO: Lynne Rienner Publishers, 1993.

Asmus, Ronald D. "A Unified Germany." *In Transition and Turmoil in the Atlantic Alliance,* ed. Robert A. Levine. New York: Crane Russak, 1992, pp. 31–109.

Burgess, John P. "Church-State Relations in East Germany: The Church as a 'Religious' and 'Political' Force." *Journal of Church and State 32,* no. 1 (Winter 1990): 17–36.

Childs, David. *The GDR: Moscow's German Ally.* London: Unwin and Hyman, 1988.

Collier, Irwin L., Jr. "The Twin Curse of the Goddess Europa and the Economic Reconstruction of Eastern Germany." *German Studies Review 20,* no. 3 (October 1997): 399–428.

Czarnowski, Gabriele. "Abortion as Political Conflict in the Unified Germany." *Parliamentary Affairs 47,* no. 2 (April 1994): 252–267.

Deeg, Richard. "Institutional Transfer, Social Learning and Economic Policy in Eastern Germany." *West European Politics 18,* no. 4 (October 1995): 38–63.

Dennis, Mike. *Social and Economic Modernization in Eastern Germany from Honecker to Kohl.* London and New York: Pinter Publishers, 1993.

Drost, Helmar. "The Great Depression in East Germany: The Effects of Unification on East Germany's Economy." *East European Politics and Societies 7,* no. 3 (Fall 1993): 452–481.

Fisher, Marc. *After the Wall: Germany, the Germans and the Burdens of History.* New York: Simon and Schuster, 1995.

Flockton, Chris, and Eva Kolinsky, eds. *Recasting East Germany.* London: Frank Cass, 1999.

Frowen, Stephen, and Jens Hoelscher, eds. *The German Currency Union: A Critical Assessment.* New York: St. Martin's Press, 1997.

Fulbrook, Mary. *Anatomy of a Dictatorship.* London and New York: Oxford University Press, 1995.

Goeckel, Robert F. *The Lutheran Church and the East German State.* Ithaca and London: Cornell University Press, 1990.

Goldberger, Paul. "Reimagining Berlin." *New York Times Magazine,* February 5, 1995, pp. 45ff.

Greenwald, G. Jonathan. *Berlin Witness.* University Park, PA.: Pennsylvania State University Press, 1993.

Hamilton, Daniel. "After the Revolution: The New Political Landscape in East Germany." *German Issues* no. 7. Washington, D.C.: American Institute for Contemporary German Studies, 1990.

Heilemann, Ullrich, and Wolfgang H. Reinicke. *Welcome to Hard Times: The Fiscal Consequences of German Unity.* Washington, D.C.: Brookings Institution, 1995.

Hirschman, Albert O. "Exit, Voice and the Fate of the German Democratic Republic: An Essay in Conceptual History." *World Politics 45,* no. 2 (January 1993): 173–202.

Huelshoff, Michael S., et al., eds. *From Bundesrepublik to Deutschland: German Politics after Unification.* Ann Arbor: University of Michigan Press, 1993.

Jarausch, Konrad H. *The Rush to German Unity.* New York: Oxford University Press, 1994.

Joppke, Christian. *East German Dissidents and the Revolution of 1989: Social Movement in a Leninist Regime.* New York: New York University Press, 1995.

———. "Intellectuals, Nationalism, and the Exit from Communism: The Case of East Germany." *Comparative Studies in Society and History 37,* no. 2 (April 1995): 213–241.

Kelleher, Catherine. "The New Germany: An Overview." In *The New Germany in the New Europe,* ed. Paul B. Stares. Washington, D.C., Brookings Institution, 1992, pp. 11–54.

Kinzer, Stephen. "East Germans Face Their Accusers." *New York Times Magazine,* April 12, 1992, pp. 24ff.

Koopmans, Ruud. "The Dynamics of Protest Waves: West Germany, 1965–1989." *American Sociological Review 58* (October 1993).

Krisch, Henry. *The Political Disintegration of a Communist State: The German Democratic Republic, 1987–1990.* Boulder, CO: Westview Press, 1992.

Kuechler, Manfred. "The Road to German Unity: Mass Sentiment in East and West Germany." *Public Opinion Quarterly 56,* no. 1 (Spring 1992): 53–76.

Lange, Thomas, and Geoffrey Pugh. *The Economics of German Unification.* Northampton, MA: Edward Elgar Publishing Inc., 1998.

Livingston, Robert Gerald. "Relinquishment of East Germany." In *East-Central Europe and the USSR,* ed. Richard F. Starr. New York: St. Martin's Press, 1991, pp. 83–101.

Lohmann, Susanne. "Dynamics of Informational Cascades: The Monday Demonstrations in Leipzig, East Germany, 1989–1991." *World Politics 47,* no. 1 (October 1994): 42–101.

Maier, Charles S. *Dissolution. The Crisis of Communism and the End of East Germany.* Princeton, NJ: Princeton University Press, 1997.

McAdams, A. James. *Germany Divided: From the Wall to Reunification.* Princeton, NJ: Princeton University Press, 1993.

———. "The Honecker Trial: The East German Past and the German Future." *The Review of Politics 58,* no. 1 (1996): 53–80.

McFalls, Laurence. *Communism's Collapse, Democracy's Demise?* New York: New York University Press, 1995.

Merkl, Peter H. *German Unification in the European Context.* University Park, PA: Pennsylvania State University Press, 1993.

Naimark, Norman M. *The Russians in East Germany: A History of the Soviet Zone of Occupation, 1945–1949.* Cambridge, MA: Harvard University Press, 1995.

Patton, David. "Social Coalitions, Political Strategies, and German Unification, 1990–1993." *West European Politics 16,* no. 4 (October 1993): 470–491.

Pickel, Andreas. "The Jump-Started Economy and the Ready-Made State: A Theoretical Reconsideration of the East German Case." *Comparative Political Studies 30,* no. 2 (April 1997): 211–241.

Quint, Peter E. *The Imperfect Union: Constitutional Structure of German Unification.* Princeton, NJ: Princeton University Press, 1997.

Razeen, Sally, and Douglas Webber. "The German Solidarity Pact: A Case Study in the Politics of the Unified Germany." *German Politics 3,* no. 1 (Winter 1994): 18–46.

Segert, Astrid. "Problematic Normalization: Eastern German Workers Eight Years after Unification." *German Politics and Society 16,* no. 3 (Fall 1998): 105–124.

Torpey, John S. *Intellectuals, Socialism and Dissent. The East German Opposition and Its Legacy.* Minneapolis: University of Minnesota Press, 1995.

Whitney, Craig R. *Spy Trader.* New York: Times Books, 1993.

Yoder, Jennifer A. *From East Germans to Germans? The New Postcommunist Elites.* Durham, NC: Duke University Press, 2000.

Zatlin, Jonathan. "Hard Marks and Soft Revolutionaries: The Economics of Entitlement and the Debate on German Monetary Union, November 9, 1989–March 18, 1990." *German Politics and Society,* Issue 33 (Fall 1994).

CHAPTER 3: THE SOCIAL AND ECONOMIC SETTING

Ardagh, John. *Germany and the Germans.* New York: Harper and Row, 1987.

Berghahn, Volker. *The Americanization of West German Industry, 1945–1973.* New York: Cambridge University Press, 1987.

Bessel, Richard. "Eastern Germany as a Structural Problem in the Weimar Republic." *Social History 3* (1978): 199–218.

Brinkmann, Christian. "Unemployment in the Federal Republic of Germany: Recent Empirical Evidence." *In Unemployment: Theory, Policy and Structure,* ed. Peder J. Pedersen and Reinhard Lund. Berlin: Walter de Gruyter, 1987, pp. 285–304.

Clement, Elizabeth. "The Abortion Debate in Unified Germany." In *Women and the Wende: Social Effects and Cultural Reflections of the German Unification Process,* ed. Elizabeth Tow and Janet Wharton. Amsterdam: Rodopi, 1994.

Conrad, Christopher, et al. "East German Fertility After Unification: Crisis or Adaptation?" *Population and Development Review 22* (June 1996): 331–358.

Dickinson, Robert E. *Germany: A General and Regional Geography,* 2nd ed. London: Methuen, 1964.

Dyson, Kenneth H.F. "The Politics of Economic Management in West Germany." *West European Politics 4,* no. 2 (May 1981): 35–55.

———. "The Politics of Corporate Crises in West Germany." *West European Politics 7,* no. 1 (January 1984): 24–46.

Esser, Josef. "Symbolic Privatisation: The Politics of Privatisation in West Germany." *West European Politics 18,* no. 4 (October 1988): 61–73.

Ferree, Myra Max. "The Rise and Fall of 'Mommy Politics': Feminism and Unification in (East) Germany." *Feminist Studies,* no. 1 (Spring 1993): 89–115.

Franz, Gerhard. "Economic Aspirations, Well-Being and Political Support in Recession and Boom Periods: The Case of West Germany." *European Journal of Political Research 14,* nos. 1 and 2 (1986): 97–112.

Frye, Charles E. "The Third Reich and the Second Republic: National Socialism's Impact upon German Democracy." *Western Political Quarterly 21,* no. 4 (December 1968): 668–681.

Grahl, John, and Paul Teague. "Labour Market Flexibility in West Germany, Britain and France." *West European Politics 12,* no. 2 (April 1989): 91–111.

Griffith, William E. "The German Democratic Republic." In *Central and Eastern Europe: The Opening Curtain?* ed. William E. Griffith. Boulder, CO: Westview Press, 1989.

Grossman, Atina. *Reforming Sex: The German Movement for Birth Control and Abortion Reform, 1920–1950.* New York and Oxford: Oxford University Press, 1995.

Heidenheimer, Arnold J. "The Politics of Educational Reform." *Comparative Education Review 18,* no. 3 (October 1974): 388–410.

Heineman, Elizabeth. "Complete Families, Half Families, No Families at All: Female-Headed Households and the Reconstruction of the Family in the Early Federal Republic." *Central European History 29,* no. 1 (1996): 19–60.

Herrigel, Gary. *Industrial Constructions: The Source of German Industrial Power.* New York, NY: 1996.

Huelshoff, Michael G. "Corporatist Bargaining and International Politics." *Comparative Political Studies 25,* no. 1 (April 1992): 3–25.

Humphreys, Peter J. *Media and Media Policy in West Germany.* London: St. Martin's Press, 1990.

Katzenstein, Peter J., ed. *Industry and Politics in West Germany.* Ithaca and New York: Cornell University Press, 1989.

Kloten, Norbert, Karl-Heinz Ketterer, and Rainer Vollmer. "West Germany's Stabilization Performance." In *The Politics of Inflation and Economic Stagnation,* ed. Leon N. Lindberg and Charles S. Maier. Washington, D.C.: Brookings Institution, 1985, pp. 353–402.

Knott, Jack H. *Managing the German Economy: Budgetary Problems in a Federal State.* Lexington, MA: Lexington Books, 1981.

Kolinsky, Eva. *Women in West Germany: Life, Work and Politics.* New York and Munich: Berg Publishers, 1989.

Kreile, Michael. "The Political Economy of the New Germany." In *The New Germany and the New Europe,* ed. Paul B. Stares. Washington, D.C.: Brookings Institution, 1992, pp. 55–92.

Maier, Frederike. "The Labour Market for Women and Employment Perspectives in the Aftermath of German Unification." *Cambridge Journal of Economics 17,* no. 4 (December 1993): 266–294.

Mintrop, Heinrich. "Teachers and Changing Authority Patterns in Eastern German Schools." *Comparative Education Review 40,* no. 4 (1996).

Mitter, Wolfgang. "Educational Reform in West and East Germany in European Perspective." *European Journal of Education 26*, no. 2 (1991): 155–165.

————. "Educational Adjustments and Perspectives in a United Germany." *Comparative Education 28*, no. 1 (1992): 45–52.

Moeller, Robert. *Protecting Motherhood: Women and the Family in the Politics of Postwar West Germany.* Berkeley: University of California Press, 1993.

Nicholls, A.J. *Freedom with Responsibility: The Social Market Economy in Germany, 1918–1963.* New York and London: Oxford University Press, 1994.

Reich, Simon. *The Fruits of Fascism.* Ithaca and London: Cornell University Press, 1990.

Roskamp, Karl W. *Capital Formation in West Germany.* Detroit: Wayne State University Press, 1965.

Scarrow, Susan E. "Party Competition and Institutional Change." *Party Politics 3*, no. 4: 451–472.

Schelsky, Helmut. "The Family in Germany." *Marriage and Family Living 16*, no. 4 (November 1954): 330–342.

Schoenbach, Klaus. "The Role of the Mass Media in West German Election Campaigns." *Legislative Studies Quarterly 12*, no. 3 (August 1987): 373–394.

Schoenbaum, David. *Hitler's Social Revolution.* New York: Doubleday, 1996.

Smyser, William R. *The German Economy.* New York: St. Martin's Press, 1993.

Turner, Lowell, ed. *Negotiating the New Germany: Can Social Partnership Survive?* Ithaca, New York: Cornell University Press, 1998.

————. *Fighting for Partnership: Labor and Politics in Unified Germany (Cornell Studies in Political Economy).* Ithaca, New York: Cornell University Press, 1998.

Webber, Douglas. "Combating and Acquiescing in Unemployment? Crisis Management in Sweden and West Germany." *West European Politics 6*, no. 1 (January 1983): 23–43.

Williams, Arthur. "Pluralism in the West German Media: The Press Broadcasting and Cable." *West European Politics 8*, no. 2 (April 1985): 84–103.

Wolter, Frank. "From Economic Miracle to Stagnation: On the German Disease." In *World Economic Growth,* ed. Arnold C. Harberger. San Francisco: Institute for Contemporary Studies, 1984, pp. 95–122.

CHAPTER 4: POLITICAL CULTURE, PARTICIPATION, AND CIVIL LIBERTIES

Aust, Stefan. *The Baader-Meinhof Group.* London: Bodley Head, 1986.

Baker, Kendall L., Russell Dalton, and Kai Hildebrandt. *Germany Transformed.* Cambridge, MA: Harvard University Press, 1981.

Banaszak, Lee Ann. "East-West Differences in German Abortion Opinion." *Public Opinion Quarterly 62*, no. 4 (Winter 1998): 545–582.

Bauer-Kaase, Petra, and Max Kaase. "Five Years of Unification: The Germans on the Path to Inner Unity?" *German Politics 5*, no. 1 (April, 1996): 1–25.

Becker, Jillian. *Hitler's Children: The Story of the Baader-Meinhof Terrorist Gang.* Philadelphia and New York: Lippincott, 1977.

Berg-Schlosser, Dirk, and Ralf Rytlewski. *Political Culture in Germany.* Providence and Oxford: Berg Publishers, 1993.

Braunthal, Gerard. *Political Loyalty and Public Service in West Germany.* Amherst, MA: University of Massachusetts Press, 1990.

Brooks, Joel E. "The Opinion-Policy Nexus in Germany." *Public Opinion Quarterly, 54* no. 3 (Fall 1990): 508–529.

Brubaker, Rogers. *Citizenship and Nationhood in France and Germany.* Cambridge, MA: Harvard University Press, 1992.

Bunn, Ronald F. *German Politics and the Spiegel Affair.* Baton Rouge: Louisiana State University Press, 1968.

Clark, John A., and Jerome S. Legge, Jr. "Economics, Racism and Attitudes toward Immigration in the New Germany." *Political Research Quarterly 50,* no. 4 (December 1997): 901–917.

Conradt, David P. "West Germany: A Remade Political Culture?" *Comparative Political Studies 7,* no. 2 (July 1974): 222–238.

———. "Changing German Political Culture." *In The Civic Culture Revisited,* ed. Gabriel A. Almond and Sidney Verba. Boston: Little, Brown, 1980, pp. 212–272. (1989 Reprint: Sage Publications.)

———. "Political Culture, Legitimacy and Participation." *West European Politics 4,* no. 2 (May 1981): 18–34.

———. "From Output Orientations to Regime Support: Changing German Political Culture." In *Social and Political Structures in West Germany,* ed. Ursula Hoffmann-Lange. Boulder, CO: Westview Press, 1991, pp. 127–142.

———. "Putting Germany Back Together Again: The Great Social Experiment of Unification." In *Germany in a New Era,* ed. Gary L. Geipel. Indianapolis: Hudson Institute, 1993, pp. 3–17.

———. "Political Culture in Unified Germany: Will the Bonn Republic Survive and Thrive in Berlin?" *German Studies Review 21,* no. 1 (February 1998): 83–104.

Cooper, Alice Holmes. "Public-Good Movements and the Dimensions of Political Process: German Peace Movements Since 1945." *Comparative Political Studies, 29,* no. 3 (June 1996): 267–289.

———. *Paradoxes of Peace: German Peace Movements Since 1945.* Ann Arbor, MI: University of Michigan Press, 1996.

Currie, David P. *The Constitution of the Federal Republic of Germany.* Chicago: University of Chicago Press, 1994.

Cusack, Thomas R. "The Shaping of Popular Satisfaction with Government and Regime Performance in Germany." *British Journal of Political Science 29,* no. 4 (October, 1999): 641–672.

Dahrendorf, Ralf. *Society and Democracy in Germany.* New York: Doubleday, 1969.

Diskant, James A. "Scarcity, Survival and Local Activism: Miners and Steelworkers, Dortmund 1945–1948." *Journal of Contemporary History 24,* no. 4 (October 1989): 547–574.

Dyson, Kenneth H.F. "Anti-Communism in the Federal Republic of Germany: The Case of the 'Berufsverbot.'" *Parliamentary Affairs 27,* no. 2 (January 1975): 51–67.

Faist, Thomas. "How to Define a Foreigner? The Symbolic Politics of Immigration in German Partisan Discourse, 1978–1992." *West European Politics 17,* no. 2 (April 1994): 50–71.

Fehrenbach, Heide. *Cinema in Democratizing Germany.* North Carolina Press: Chapel Hill, 1996.

Fetzer, Joel S. "Religious Minorities and Support for Immigrant Rights in the United States, France and Germany." *Journal for the Scientific Study of Religion 37* (1998). 41–49.

Franz, Gerhard. "Economic Aspirations, Well-Being and Political Support in Recession and Boom Periods: The Case of West Germany." *European Journal of Political Research 14,* nos. 1 and 2 (1986): 97–112.

Fulbrook, Mary. "The State and the Transformation of Political Legitimacy in East and West Germany since 1945." *Comparative Studies in Society and History 29,* no. 2 (April 1987): 211–244.

Hager, Carol J. *Technological Democracy: Bureaucracy and Citizenry in the German Energy Debate.* Ann Arbor: University of Michigan Press, 1995.

Halfmann, Jost. "Immigration and Citizenship in Germany: Contemporary Dilemmas." *Political Studies 45,* no. 2 (June 1997): 260–274.

Hartmann, Heinz. *Authority and Organization in German Management.* Princeton: Princeton University Press, 1959.

Haug, Frigga. "The Women's Movement in West Germany." *New Left Review,* no. 195 (January/February 1986): 59ff.

Helm, Jutta A. "Citizen Lobbies in West Germany." In *Western European Party Systems,* ed. Peter H. Merkl. New York: Free Press, 1980, pp. 576–596.

Herf, Jeffrey. "War, Peace and Intellectuals: The West German Peace Movement." *International Security 10,* no. 4 (Spring 1986): 172–200.

Hoffmann-Lange, Ursula, ed. *Social and Political Structures in West Germany: From Author-itarianism to Postindustrial Democracy.* Boulder, CO: Westview Press, 1991.

Hoskin, Marilyn. "Public Opinion and the Foreign Worker: Traditional and Nontraditional Bases in West Germany." *Comparative Politics 17,* no. 2 (January 1985): 193–210.

―――. "Integration or Nonintegration of Foreign Workers: Four Theories." *Political Psychology 5,* no. 4 (December 1985): 661–685.

Jennings, M. Kent. "The Variable Nature of Generational Conflict: Some Examples from West Germany." *Comparative Political Studies 9,* no. 2 (July 1976): 171–188.

Kaase, Max, and Petra Bauer-Kaase. "Five Years of Unification: The Germans on the Path to Inner Unity?" *German Politics 5,* no. 1 (April 1996): 1–25.

Karapin, Roger. "Explaining Far-Right Electoral Success in Germany: The Politicization of Immigration-Related Issues." *German Politics and Society 16,* no. 3 (Fall 1998): 24–61.

Katzenstein, Peter J. *West Germany's Internal Security Policy: State and Violence in the 1970s and 1980s.* Ithaca, NY: Cornell University Press, 1990.

Klingemann, Hans-Dieter, and Richard I. Hofferbert. "Germany: A New 'Wall in the Mind'?" *Journal of Democracy 5,* no. 1 (January 1994): 30–44.

Kolinsky, Eva. "Terrorism in West Germany." *In The Threat of Terrorism,* ed. Juliet Lodge. Boulder, CO: Westview Press, 1988.

Krieger, Leonard. *The German Idea of Freedom.* Chicago: University of Chicago Press, 1957.

Kurthen, Hermann, Werner Bergman, and Rainer Erb. *Antisemitism and Xenophobia in Germany after Unification.* London: Oxford University Press, 1997.

Kvistad, Greg. *The Rise and Demise of German Statism: Loyalty and Political Membership.* Providence and London: Berghahn Books, 1999.

Langguth, Gerd. "Origins and Aims of Terrorism in Europe." *Aussenpolitik 37,* no. 2 (1986): 163–175.

Lederer, Gerda. "Trends in Authoritarianism: A Study of Adolescents in West Germany and the United States since 1945." *Journal of Cross-Cultural Psychology 13,* no. 3 (September 1982): 299–314.

Legge, Jerome S., Jr. "An Economic Theory of Antisemitism? Exploring Attitudes in the New German State." *Political Research Quarterly 49,* no. 3 (September 1996): 617–630.

Lepsius, M. Rainer. "The Nation and Nationalism in Germany." *Social Research 52,* no. 1 (Spring 1985): 43–64.

Maier, Charles S. *The Unmasterable Past.* Cambridge, MA, and London: Harvard University Press, 1988.

Merritt, Richard L. "The Student Protest Movement in West Berlin." *Comparative Politics 1,* no. 4 (July 1969): 516–533.

―――. *Democracy Imposed: U.S. Occupation Policy and the German Public, 1945–1949.* New Haven, CT: Yale University Press, 1995.

Meulemann, Heiner. "Value Change in West Germany, 1950–1980: Integrating the Empirical Evidence." *Social Science Information 22,* nos. 4 and 5 (1983): 777–800.

―――. "Value Changes in Germany after Unification: 1990–1995." *German Politics 6,* no. 1 (April 1997): 122–139.

Minkenberg, Michael. "The Wall after the Wall: On the Continuing Division of Germany and the Remaking of Political Culture." *Comparative Politics 26,* no. 1 (October 1993): 53–68.

―――. "Context and Consequence. The Impact of the New Radical Right on the Political Process in France and Germany." *German Politics and Society 16,* no. 3 (Fall 1998): 1–23.

Moeller, Robert G. "War Stories: The Search for a Usable Past in the Federal Republic of Germany." *American Historical Review 101,* no. 4 (October 1996): 1008–1048.

Mushaben, Joyce Marie. "The Forum: New Dimensions of Youth Protest in Western Europe." *Journal of Political and Military Sociology 11,* no. 1 (Spring 1983): 123–144.

―――. "Anti-Politics and Successor Generations: The Role of Youth in the West and East German Peace Movements." *Journal of Political and Military Sociology 12,* no. 1 (Spring 1984): 171–190.

―――. *From Post-War to Post-Wall Generations: Changing Attitudes Toward the National Question and NATO in the Federal Republic of Germany.* Boulder, CO: Westview Press, 1998.

Nelkin, Dorothy, and Michael Pollak. *The Atom Besieged: Extraparliamentary Dissent in France and Germany.* Cambridge, MA: MIT Press, 1981.

Noelle-Nuemann, Elisabeth. *The Germans: Public Opinion Polls, 1967–1980.* Westport, CT: Greenwood Press, 1981.

———. "Problems with Democracy in Eastern Germany After the Downfall of the GDR." In *Research on Democracy and Society, Vol. 2,* ed. Frederick D. Weil. New York: JAI Press, Inc., 1994, pp. 213–231.

Noelle-Neumann, Erich Peter, and Elisabeth Noelle-Neumann. *The Germans, 1947–1966.* Allensbach am Bodensee: Verlag für Demoskopie, 1967.

O'Brien, Peter. *Beyond the Swastika.* London and New York: Routledge, 1996.

Olick, Jeffrey K., and Daniel Levy. "Collective Memory and Culture Constraint: Holocaust Myth and Rationality in German Politics." *American Sociological Review 62* (December 1997): 921–936.

Oppenheim, A.N. *Civic Education and Participation in Democracy.* Beverly Hills and London: Sage Publications, 1977.

Pines, Maya. "Unlearning Blind Obedience in German Schools." *Psychology Today 15,* no. 5 (May 1981): pp. 59ff.

Rabinbach, Anson, and Jack Zipes, eds. *Germans and Jews since the Holocaust.* New York: Holmes and Meier, 1986.

Rist, Ray C. *Guestworkers in Germany: The Prospects for Pluralism.* New York: Praeger, 1978.

Rohrschneider, Robert. "Report from the Laboratory: The Influence of Institutions on Political Elites' Democratic Values in Germany." *American Political Science Review 88,* no. 4 (December 1994): 927–941.

———. *Learning Democracy. Democratic and Economic Values in Unified Germany.* Oxford: Oxford University Press, 1999.

Schmidt, Rüdiger. "From 'Old Politics' to 'New Politics': Three Decades of Peace Protest in West Germany." In *Contemporary Political Culture: Politics in a Post-modern Age,* ed. John R. Gibbins. Beverly Hills and London: Sage Publications, 1989: 174–198.

Schoonmaker, Donald. "Novelist and Social Scientist: Contrasting Views of Today's West German Political System." *Polity 14,* no. 3 (Spring 1982): 414–470.

Schram, Glenn. "Ideology and Politics: The *Rechtsstaat* Idea in West Germany." *Journal of Politics 33* (February 1971): 133–157.

Schweigler, Gebhard. *National Consciousness in Divided Germany.* Beverly Hills and London: Sage Publications, 1975.

———. "Anti-Americanism in Germany." *Washington Quarterly 9,* no. 1 (Winter 1986): 67–84.

Shell, Kurt L. "Extraparliamentary Opposition in Postwar Germany." *Comparative Politics 2,* no. 4 (July 1970): 653–680.

Stern, Fritz. *The Failure of Illiberalism: Essays on the Political Culture of Modern Germany.* Chicago: University of Chicago Press, 1975.

Stoess, Richard. "The Problem of Right-Wing Extremism in West Germany." *West European Politics 11,* no. 2 (April 1988): 34–46.

Szabo, Stephen F. *The Successor Generation: International Perspectives of Postwar Europeans.* London: Butterworths, 1983.

Verba, Sidney. "Germany: The Remaking of Political Culture." In *Political Culture and Political Development,* ed. Sidney Verba and Lucien Pye. Princeton: Princeton University Press, 1965, pp. 130–170.

Watts, Meredith W. "Orientations toward Conventional and Unconventional Participation among West German Youth." *Comparative Political Studies 23,* no. 3 (October 1990): 283–313.

———. *Xenophobia in United Germany.* New York and London: St. Martin's Press, 1997.

Weil, Frederick D. "Tolerance of Free Speech in the United States and West Germany, 1970–1979: An Analysis of Public Opinion Survey Data." *Social Forces 60,* no. 4 (June 1982): 973–992.

———. "Cohorts, Regimes, and the Legitimation of Democracy: West Germany since 1945." *American Sociological Review 52,* no. 3 (June 1987): 308–324.

———. "The Sources and Structure of Legitimation in Western Democracies: A Consolidated Model Tested with Time Series Data in Six Countries since World War II." *American Sociological Review 54,* no. 5 (October 1989): 682–706.

Young, Brigitte. *Triumph of the Fatherland. German Unification and the Marginalization of Women.* Ann Arbor, MI: University of Michigan Press, 1998.

Zimmerman, Ekkart, and Thomas Saalfeld. *The Three Waves of West German Right-Wing Extremism. Encounters with the Contemporary Radical Right,* ed. Peter H. Merkl and Leonard Weinberg. Boulder, CO: Westview Press, 1993, pp. 50–74.

CHAPTER 5: THE PARTY SYSTEM AND THE REPRESENTATION OF INTERESTS

Alexis, Marion. "Neo-Corporatism and Industrial Relations: The Case of the German Trade Unions." *West European Politics 6,* no. 1 (January 1983): 75–92.

Andrlik, Erich. "The Farmers and the State: Agricultural Interests in West German Politics." *West European Politics 4,* no. 1 (January 1981): 104–119.

Betz, Hans-Georg. "Value Change and Postmaterialist Politics." *Comparative Political Studies 23,* no. 2 (July 1990): 239–256.

———. "Politics of Resentment: Right-Wing Radicalism in West Germany." *Comparative Politics 23,* no. 1 (October 1990): 45–60.

Braunthal, Gerard. *The Federation of German Industry in Politics.* Ithaca: Cornell University Press, 1965.

———. *The West German Social Democrats, 1969–1982: Profile of Party in Power.* Boulder, CO: Westview Press, 1983.

———. "The West German Social Democrats: Factionalism at the Local Level." *West European Politics 7,* no. 1 (January 1984): 47–64.

———. "Social Democratic–Green Coalitions in West Germany: Prospects for a New Alliance." *German Studies Review 9,* no. 3 (October 1986): 569–597.

Breyman, Stephen. *Why Movements Fail: The West German Peace Movement, the SPD, and the INF Negotiations.* Boulder, CO: Westview Press, 1994.

Broughton, David, and Emil Kirchner. "Germany: The FDP in Transition—Again." *Parliamentary Affairs 37,* no. 2 (Spring 1984): 183–198.

Bürklin, Wilhelm P. "The German Greens. The Post-Industrial, Non-Established and the Party System." *International Political Science Review 6,* no. 4 (October 1985): 463–481.

———. "The Split between the Established and the Non-Established Left in Germany." *European Journal of Political Research 13* (1985): 283–293.

———. "Governing Left Parties Frustrating the Radical Non-Established Left: The Rise and Inevitable Decline of the Greens." *European Journal of Political Research 3,* no. 2 (September 1987): 109–126.

Capra, Fritjof, and Charlene Spretnak. *Green Politics: The Global Promise.* New York: Dutton, 1984.

Chalmers, Douglas A. *The Social Democratic Party of Germany.* New Haven: Yale University Press, 1964.

Chandler, William M., and Alan Siaroff. "Postindustrial Politics in Germany and the Origins of the Greens." *Comparative Politics 18,* no. 3 (April 1986): 303–325.

Clemens, Clay. *Reluctant Realists: The CDU/CSU and West German Ostpolitik.* Durham, NC: Duke University Press, 1989.

Conradt, David P. *The West German Party System.* Beverly Hills and London: Sage Publications, 1972.

———. "The End of an Era in West Germany." *Current History 81* (1982): 405–408, 438.

Doering, Herbert, and Gordon Smith, eds. *Party Government and Political Culture in Western Germany.* New York: St. Martin's Press, 1982.

Edinger, Lewis J., and Kurt Schumacher: *A Study in Personality and Political Behavior.* Stanford: Stanford University Press, 1965.

Esser, Josef. "State, Business and Trade Unions in West Germany after the 'Political Wende.'" *West European Politics 9,* no. 2 (April 1986): 198–214.

Feist, Ursula, and Klaus Liepelt. "New Elites in Old Parties: Observations on a Side Effect of German Educational Reform." *International Political Science Review 4,* no. 1 (1983): 71–83.

Fichter, Michael. "From Transmission Belt to Social Partnership? The Case of Organized Labor in Eastern Germany." *German Politics and Society 23* (1991): 1–19.

Frankland, Gene E. "Green Politics and Alternative Economics." *German Studies Review 11,* no. 1 (February 1988): 111–132.

Frankland, Gene E., and Donald Schoonmaker. *Between Protest and Power: The Green Party in Germany.* Boulder, CO.: Westview Press, 1992.

Gourevitch, Peter, et al. *Unions and Economic Crisis: Britain, West Germany and Sweden.* London: Allen and Unwin, 1984.

Heidenheimer, Arnold J. *Adenauer and the CDU.* The Hague: Martinus Nijhoff, 1960.

Hofferbert, Richard I., and Hans-Dieter Klingemann. "The Policy Impact of Party Programmes and Government Declarations in the Federal Republic of Germany." *European Journal of Political Research 18,* no. 3 (May 1990): 277–304.

Joffe, Joseph. "A Peacenik Goes to War," *New York Times Magazine,* May 30, 1999.

Kaltefleiter, Werner. "Legitimacy Crisis of the German Party System?" In *Western European Party Systems,* ed. Peter H. Merkl. New York: Free Press, 1980, pp. 597–608.

Kirchheimer, Otto. "Germany: The Vanishing Opposition." In *Political Opposition in Western Democracies,* ed. Robert A. Dahl. New Haven: Yale University Press, 1966, pp. 237–259.

Koeble, Thomas A. "Trade Unionists, Party Activists, and Politicians: The Struggle for Power over Party Rules in the British Labour Party and the West German Social Democratic Party." *Comparative Politics 19,* no. 3 (April 1987): 253–266.

———. "Challenges to the Trade Unions: The British and West German Cases." *West European Politics 11,* no. 3 (July 1988): 53–67.

Linz, Juan. "Cleavage and Consensus in West German Politics: The Early Fifties." In *Party Systems and Voter Alignments: Cross-National Perspectives,* ed. S.M. Lipset and S. Rokkan. New York: Free Press, 1966, pp. 283–316.

Markovits, Andrei S. *The Politics of West German Trade Unions.* Cambridge: Cambridge University Press, 1986.

Markovits, Andrei S., and Christopher S. Allen. "Power and Dissent: The Trade Unions in the Federal Republic of Germany Re-Examined." *West European Politics 3* (1980): 68–86.

Minkenberg, Michael. "The New Right in Germany." *European Journal of Political Research 22* (1992): 55–81.

Müller-Rommel, Ferdinand. "Social Movements and the Greens: New Internal Politics in Germany." *European Journal of Political Research 13,* no. 1 (March 1985): 53–67.

Padgett, Stephen. "The West German Social Democrats in Opposition, 1982–1986." *West European Politics 10,* no. 3 (July 1987): 333–356.

———. "The German Social Democratic Party: Between Old and New Left." In *Conflict and Cohesion in Western European Social Democratic Parties,* ed. David S. Bell and Eric Shaw. London and New York: Pinter Publishers, 1994, pp. 10–30.

Poguntke, Thomas. "The Organization of a Participatory Party—the German Greens." *European Journal of Political Research 15* (1987): 609–633.

Pridham, Geoffrey. "The CDU/CSU Opposition in West Germany, 1969–1972: A Party in Search of an Organisation." *Parliamentary Affairs 26,* no. 2 (Spring 1973): 201–217.

———. *Christian Democracy in Western Germany.* New York and London: St. Martin's Press, 1977.

Pulzer, Peter G.J. "Responsible Party Government and Stable Coalition: The Case of the German Federal Republic." *Political Studies 19* (1971): 1–17.

Scarrow, Susan E. "Party Competition and Institutional Change." *Party Politics 3,* no. 4 (1997): 451–472.

Scharf, Thomas. *The German Greens: Challenging the Consensus.* Providence, RI, and Oxford: Berg Publishers, 1994.

Scharpf, Fritz. *Crisis and Choice in European Social Democracy.* Ithaca and London: Cornell University Press, 1991.

Silvia, Stephen J. "The West German Labor Law Controversy: A Struggle for the Factory of the Future." *Comparative Politics 20,* no. 2 (January 1988): 155–173.

———. "Left Behind: The Social Democratic Party in Eastern Germany." *West European Politics 16,* no. 2 (April 1993): 24–48.

Smith, Gordon. "West Germany and the Politics of Centrality." *Government and Opposition 11,* no. 4 (Autumn 1976): 387–407.

Spotts, Frederic. *The Churches and Politics in Germany.* Middletown, CT: Wesleyan University Press, 1973.

Stone, Deborah A. *The Limits of Professional Power: National Health Care in the Federal Republic of Germany.* Chicago: University of Chicago Press, 1981.

Thelen, Kathleen A. *Union of Parts.* Ithaca and London: Cornell University Press, 1992.

Webber, Douglas. "A Relationship of 'Critical Partnership'? Capital and the Social-Liberal Coalition in West Germany." *West European Politics 6,* no. 2 (April 1983): 61–86.

Westle, Bettina, and Oskar Niedermayer. "Contemporary Right-Wing Extremism in West Germany." *European Journal of Political Research 22* (1992): 83–100.

Woodall, Jean. "The Dilemma of Youth Unemployment: Trade Union Responses in the Federal Republic of Germany, the U.K. and France." *West European Politics 9,* no. 3 (July 1986): 429–447.

Yost, David, and Thomas Glad. "West German Party Politics and Theater Nuclear Modernization since 1977." *Armed Forces and Society 8* (1982): 525–560.

CHAPTER 6: ELECTIONS AND VOTING BEHAVIOR

Alexander, Herbert E., and Rei Shiratori. *Comparative Political Finance Among the Democracies.* Boulder: Westview Press, 1994.

Anderson, Christopher J., and Carsten Zelle, eds. *Stability and Change in German Elections.* Westport, CT, and London: Praeger, 1998.

Barnes, S.H., et al. "The German Party System and the 1961 Federal Election." *American Political Science Review 56* (1962): 899–914.

Cerny, Karl, ed. *West Germany at the Polls.* Washington, D.C.: American Enterprise Institute, 1978.

———. *The Bundestag Elections of the 1980s.* Durham, NC: Duke University Press, 1990.

Conradt, David P. "Unified Germany at the Polls." *German Issues* no. 9. Washington, D.C.: American Institute for Contemporary German Studies, 1990.

Conradt, David P., and Dwight Lambert. "Party System, Social Structure and Competitive Politics in West Germany." *Comparative Politics 7,* no. 1 (October 1974): 61–86.

Conradt, David P., and Russell J. Dalton. "The West German Electorate and the Party System: Continuity and Change in the 1980s." *Review of Politics 50,* no. 1 (January 1988): 3–29.

Conradt, David P., et al., eds. *Germany's New Politics.* Providence and Oxford: Berghahn Books, 1995.

———. *Power Shift in Germany: The 1998 Federal Election and the End of the Kohl Era.* New York and Providence: Berghahn Books, 2000.

Donsbach, Wolfgang. "Media Trust in the German Bundestag Election, 1994: News Values and Professional Norms in Political Communication." *Political Communication 14,* no. 2 (April–June 1997): 149–170.

Edinger, Lewis J. "Political Change in Germany: The Federal Republic after the 1969 Election." *Comparative Politics 2,* no. 4 (July 1970): 549–578.

Farrell, D.M., and M. Wortmann. "Party Strategies in the Electoral Market: Political Marketing in West Germany, Britain and Ireland." *European Journal of Political Research 15,* no. 3 (1987): 297–318.

Finkel, Steven E., and Peter R. Schrott. "Campaign Effects on Voter Choice in the German Election of 1990." *British Journal of Political Science 25,* no. 3 (July 1995): 349–377.

Fuchs, Dieter, and Rohrschneider, Robert. "Postmaterialism and Electoral Choice Before and After German Unification." *West European Politics 21,* no. 2 (April 1998): 95–116.

Hoecker, Beate. "The German Electoral System: A Barrier to Women?" In *Electoral Systems in Comparative Perspective,* ed. Wilma Rule and Joseph F. Zimmermann. Westport, CT: Greenwood Press, 1994, pp. 65–77.

Irving, R.E.M., and W.E. Paterson. "The Machtwechsel of 1982–83: A Significant Landmark in the Political and Constitutional History of West Germany." *Parliamentary Affairs 36,* no. 4 (Autumn 1983): 417–435.

Jesse, Eckhard. "The West German Electoral System: The Case for Reform, 1949–1957." *West European Politics 10,* no. 3 (July 1987): 434–448.

Kitschelt, Herbert. "The 1990 German Federal Election and the National Unification." *West European Politics 14,* no. 1 (January 1991): 121–148.

Klingemann, Hans-Dieter. "Germany." In *Electoral Change in Western Democracies,* ed. Ivor Crewe and David Denver. New York: St. Martin's Press, 1985, pp. 230–263.

Klingemann, Hans-Dieter, and Franz-Urban Pappi. "The 1969 Bundestag Election in the Federal Republic of Germany: An Analysis of Voting Behavior." *Comparative Politics 2,* no. 4 (July 1970): 523–548.

Kuechler, Manfred. "Maximizing Utility at the Polls?" *European Journal of Political Research 14,* nos. 1 and 2 (1986): 81–95.

Landfried, Christine. "Political Finance in West Germany." In *Comparative Political Finance among the Democracies,* ed. Herbert E. Alexander and Rei Shiratori. Boulder, CO: Westview Press, 1994, pp. 133–144.

Lewis-Beck, Michael. "Comparative Economic Voting: Britain, France, Germany, Italy." *American Journal of Political Science 30,* no. 2 (May 1986): 315–346.

Lohmann, Susanne, David Brady, and Douglas Rivers. "Party Identification, Retrospective Voting, and Moderating Elections in a Federal System." *Comparative Political Studies 30,* no. 4 (August 1997): 420–449.

Norpoth, Helmut. "Choosing a Coalition Partner: Mass Preference and Elite Decisions in West Germany." *Comparative Political Studies 12* (1980): 424–440.

———. "The Making of a More Partisan Electorate in West Germany." *British Journal of Political Science 14,* no. 1 (January 1984): 52–71.

Rusciano, Frank Louis. "Rethinking the Gender Gap: The Case of West German Elections, 1949–1987." *Comparative Politics 24,* no. 3 (April 1992): 335–357.

Schrott, Peter R., and David J. Lanoue. "How to Win a Televised Debate: Candidate Strategies and Voter Response in Germany, 1972–87." *British Journal of Political Science 22,* no. 4 (October 1992): 445–467.

Semetko, Holly, and Klaus Schönbach. *Germany's Unity Election, Voters, and the Media.* Cresskill, NJ: Hampton Press, 1994.

Urwin, Derek W. "Germany: Continuity and Change in Electoral Politics." In *Electoral Behavior: A Comparative Handbook,* ed. Richard Rose. New York: Free Press, pp. 109–170.

Walker, Nancy J. "What We Know about Women Voters in Britain, France, and West Germany." *Public Opinion 11,* no. 1 (May–June 1988): 49ff.

CHAPTER 7: POLICYMAKING INSTITUTIONS I: PARLIAMENT AND EXECUTIVE

Abenheim, Donald. *Reforging the Iron Cross: The Search for Tradition in the West German Armed Forces.* Princeton: Princeton University Press, 1988.

Blondel, Jean, and Ferdinand Müller-Rommel, eds. *Cabinets in Western Europe.* London: Macmillan, 1988.

Braunthal, Gerard. "The Policy Function of the German Social Democratic Party." *Comparative Politics 9,* no. 2 (January 1977): 127–146.

Burkett, Tony, and S. Schuettemeyer. *The West German Parliament*. London: Butterworths, 1982.

Clemens, Clay. "The Chancellor as Manager: Helmut Kohl, the CDU and Governance in Germany." *West European Politics 17*, no. 4 (October 1994): 28–51.

Conradt, David P. "Chancellor Kohl's Center Coalition." *Current History 85*, no. 514 (November 1986): 357–360, 389–391.

Dyson, Kenneth H.F. *Party, State and Bureaucracy in Western Germany*. Beverly Hills and London: Sage, 1978.

———. "Chancellor Kohl as Strategic Leader: The Case of Economic and Monetary Union." *German Politics 7*, no. 1 (1998): 37–63.

Grande, Edgar. "Neoconservatism and Conservative-Liberal Economic Policy in West Germany." *European Journal of Political Research 15* (1987): 281–296.

Herspring, Dale R. *Requiem for an Army*. Lanham, MD: Rowman and Littlefield Publishers, 1998.

Hoffmann-Lange, Ursula. "Positional Power and Political Influence in the Federal Republic of Germany." *European Journal of Political Research 17*, no. 1 (January 1989): 51–76.

Jelen, Ted G., and Clyde Wilcox. "Context and Conscience: The Catholic Church as an Agent of Political Socialization in Western Europe." *Journal for the Scientific Study of Religion 37* (1998): 28–48.

Johnson, Nevil. *Government in the Federal Republic of Germany: The Executive at Work*. London: Pergamon, 1973.

Kolinsky, Eva. "Political Participation and Parliamentary Careers: Women's Quotas in West Germany." *West European Politics 14*, no. 1 (January 1991): 56–72.

Korte, Karl-Rudolf. "The Art of Power: The 'Kohl System', Leadership, and *Deutschlandpolitik*." *German Politics 7*, no. 1 (April 1998): 64–90.

Lancaster, Thomas, and W. David Patterson. "Comparative Pork Barrel Politics. Perceptions from the West German Bundestag." *Comparative Political Studies 22*, no. 4 (January 1990): 458–477.

Large, David Clay. *Germans to the Front: West German Rearmament in the Adenauer Era*. Chapel Hill, NC: University of North Carolina Press, 1996.

Livingston, Robert Gerald. "Life after Kohl?" *Foreign Affairs* (November/December 1997): 1–6.

Loewenberg, Gerhard. *Parliament in the German Political System*. Ithaca and London: Cornell University Press, 1966.

———, ed. *Modern Parliaments, Change or Decline?* Chicago and New York: Aldine-Atherton, 1971.

Mayntz, Renate. "Executive Leadership in Germany: Dispersion of Power or 'Kanzler Demokratie'?" In *Presidents and Prime Ministers*, ed. Richard Rose and Ezra N. Suleiman. Washington, D.C.: American Enterprise Institute, 1980, pp. 139–170.

Messina, Anthony M. "West Germany's Grand Coalition as a Window on the Dynamics of Noncompetitive Parliamentary Government." *German Politics and Society 13*, no. 2 (Summer 1995): 60–80.

Müller-Rommel, Ferdinand. "The Centre of Government in West Germany: Changing Patterns under 14 Legislatures (1949–1987)." *European Journal of Political Research 16*, no. 2 (March 1988): 171–190.

Paterson, William. "The Chancellor and His Party: Political Leadership in the Federal Republic." *West European Politics 4*, no. 2 (May 1981): 3–17.

Rohrschneider, Robert. "Pluralism, Conflict, and Legislative Elites in United Germany." *Comparative Politics 29*, no. 1 (October 1996): 43–68.

Saalfeld, Thomas. "The West German Bundestag after 40 Years: The Role of Parliament in a 'Party Democracy.'" In *Parliaments in Western Europe*, ed. Philip Norton. London: Frank Cass, 1991, pp. 68–89.

Schmidt, Helmut. *Perspectives on Politics*. Boulder, CO: Westview Press, 1982.

Schmidt, Manfred G. "The Politics of Domestic Reform in the Federal Republic of Germany." *Politics and Society 8* (1979): 165–200.

Schüttemeyer, Suzanne S. "Hierarchy and Efficiency in the Bundestag: The German Answer for Institutionalizing Parliament." In *Parliaments in the Modern World*, ed. Gary W. Copeland and Samuel C. Patterson. Ann Arbor: University of Michigan Press, 1994, pp. 29–58.

Silvia, Stephen J. "Reform Gridlock and the Role of the Bundesrat in German Politics." *West European Politics 22*, no. 2 (April 1999): 167–181.

Smith, Gordon. "The Resources of a German Chancellor." *West European Politics 14*, no. 2 (April 1991): 48–61.

Thaysen, Uwe. *The Bundesrat, the Länder and German Federalism*. Washington, D.C.: American Institute for Contemporary German Studies, 1994.

Wehling, Hans-Georg. "The Bundesrat." *Publius 19*, no. 4 (Fall 1989): 53–64.

Wise, Michael Z. *A Capital Dilemma: Germany's Search for a New Architecture of Democracy*. New York: Princeton Architectural Press, 1998.

CHAPTER 8: POLICYMAKING INSTITUTIONS II: ADMINISTRATION, SEMIPUBLIC INSTITUTIONS, AND COURTS

Aberbach, Joel, et al. *Bureaucrats and Politicians in Western Democracies*. Cambridge, MA: Harvard University Press, 1981.

———. "American and German Federal Executives—Technocratic and Political Attitudes." *International Social Science Journal*, no. 123 (February 1990): 3–18.

Alber, Jens. "Germany." In *Growth to Limits*, ed. Peter Flora. Berlin: Walter de Gruyter, 1988 (Vol. 2), pp. 1–154.

Blair, J.M. *Federalism and Judicial Review in West Germany*. London and New York: Oxford University Press, 1981.

Blankenburg, Erhard. "Changes in Political Regimes and Continuity of the Rule of Law in Germany." In *Courts, Law and Politics in Comparative Perspective*, ed. Herbert Jacob. New Haven and London: Yale University Press, 1996.

Blum, Ulrich, and Jan Siegmund. "Politics and Economics of Privatizing State Enterprises: The Case of *Treuhandanstalt*." *Governance 6*, no. 3 (July 1993): 397–408.

Caygill, Howard, and Alan Scott. "Basic Law versus the Basic Norm? The Case of the Bavarian Crucifix Order." *Political Studies 44* (1996): 505–516.

Clemens, Clay, and William E. Paterson, eds. *German Politics: Special Issue on The Kohl Chancellorship 7*, no. 1 (April 1998): 64–90.

Derlien, Hans-Ulrich. "Repercussions of Government Change on the Career Civil Service in West Germany: The Cases of 1969 and 1982." *Governance 1*, no. 1 (1988): 50–78.

Duckenfield, Mark. "The Goldkrieg: Revaluing the Bundesbank's Reserves and the Politics of EMU." *German Politics 8*, no. 1 (April 1999): 106–130.

———. "Bundesbank-Government Relations in Germany in the 1990s: From GEMU to EMU." *West European Politics 22*, no. 3 (July 1999): 87–108.

Dyson, Kenneth H.F. "Planning and the Federal Chancellor's Office in the West German Federal Government." *Political Studies 21*, no. 3 (1973): 348–362.

———. "Improving Policy-Making in Bonn: Why the Central Planners Failed." *Journal of Management Studies 12*, no. 2 (May 1975): 157–174.

Eser, Albin. "The Politics of Criminal Law Reform: Germany." *American Journal of Comparative Law 21*, no. 2 (Spring 1973): 245–262.

Esser, Josef. "Bank Power in West Germany Revised." *West European Politics 13*, no. 4 (October 1990): 17–33.

Frowen, Stephen F., and Robert Pringle, eds. *Inside the Bundesbank*. New York: St. Martin's Press, 1998.

Gibson, James L., et al., "On the Legitimacy of National High Courts." *American Political Science Review 92*, no. 2 (June 1998): 343–358.

Goetz, Klaus. "Rebuilding Public Administration in the New German Länder: Transfer and Differentiation." *West European Politics 16,* no. 4 (October 1993): 447–469.

Goodman, John B. *Monetary Sovereignty.* Ithaca and London: Cornell University Press, 1992.

Hager, Carol J. *Technological Democracy. Bureaucracy and Citizenry in the German Energy Debate.* Ann Arbor, MI: University of Michigan Press, 1995.

Heisenberg, Dorothee. *The Mark of the Bundesbank: Germany's Role in European Monetary Cooperation.* Boulder, CO: Lynne Rienner, 1999.

Herz, John H. "Political Views of the West German Civil Service." In *West German Leadership and Foreign Policy,* ed. Hans Speier and W. Phillips Davison. Evanston, IL: Row, Peterson, 1957, pp. 96–135.

Johnson, Nevil. "The Interdependence of Law and Politics: Judges and the Constitution in West Germany." *West European Politics 5,* no. 3 (July 1982): 236–252.

Kalthenthaler, Karl. "The Restructuring of the German Bundesbank: The Politics of Institutional Change." *German Politics and Society 14,* no. 4 (1996): 23–48.

———. "Central Bank Independence and the Commitment to Monetary Stability: The Case of the German Bundesbank." *German Politics 7,* no. 2 (1998): 102–127.

———. *Germany and the Politics of Europe's Money.* Duke University Press, 1997.

Katzenstein, Peter J. *Policy and Politics in West Germany: The Growth of a Semi-Sovereign State.* Philadelphia: Temple University Press, 1987.

Kennedy, Ellen. *The Bundesbank.* New York: Council on Foreign Relations Press, 1991.

Kommers, Donald P. *Judicial Politics in West Germany: A Study of the Federal Constitutional Court.* Beverly Hills and London: Sage, 1976.

———. *The Constitutional Jurisprudence of the Federal Republic of Germany.* Durham, NC, and London: Duke University Press, 1989.

———. *The Federal Constitutional Court.* Washington, D.C.: American Institute for Contemporary German Studies, 1994.

König, Klaus. "Bureaucratic Integration by Elite Transfer: The Case of the Former GDR." *Governance 6,* no. 3 (July 1993): 386–396.

Kvistad, Gregg O. "Accommodation or 'Cleansing': Germany's State Employees from the Old Regime." *West European Politics 17,* no. 4 (October 1994): 52–73.

Landfried, Christine. "The Impact of the German Federal Constitutional Court on Politics and Policy Output." *Government and Opposition 20,* no. 4 (Autumn 1985): 522–541.

Lohmann, Susanne. "Federalism and Central Bank Independence: The Politics of German Monetary Policy, 1957–92." *World Politics 50,* no. 3 (April 1998): 401–446.

Marsh, David. *The Bundesbank: The Bank that Rules Europe.* London: Heinemann, 1992.

Mayntz, Renate. "German Federal Bureaucrats: A Functional Elite between Politics and Administration." In *Higher Civil Servants in the Policymaking Process: A Comparative Exploration,* ed. Ezra Suleiman. New York: Holmes and Meier, 1983, pp. 145–174.

———. "The Higher Civil Service of the Federal Republic of Germany." In *The Higher Civil Service in Europe and Canada,* ed. Bruce L.R. Smith. Washington, D.C.: Brookings Institution, 1984, pp. 55–68.

Mayntz, Renate, and Fritz W. Scharpf. *Policymaking in the German Federal Bureaucracy.* New York: Elsevier, 1975.

Mayntz, Renate, and Hans-Ulrich Derlien. "Party Patronage and Politicization of the West German Administrative Elite 1970–1987: Toward Hybridization?" *Governance 2,* no. 4 (October, 1989): 384–404.

Putnam, Robert D. " The Political Attitudes of Senior Civil Servants in Western Europe: A Preliminary Report." *British Journal of Political Science 3,* no. 2 (July 1973): 257–290.

Seibel, Wolfgang, G. Grabher, and D. Stark. "Privatization by Means of State Bureaucracy? The Treuhand Phenomenon in Eastern Germany." In *Restructuring Networks in Post-Socialism: Legacies, Linkages, and Localities.* ed. Seibel, et. al. Oxford: Oxford University Press, 1997, pp. 284–305.

Sturm, Roland. "The Role of the Bundesbank in German Politics." *West European Politics 12,* no. 2 (April 1989): 1–11.

Whitney, Craig R. "Blaming the Bundesbank." *New York Times Magazine,* October 17, 1993, pp. 19ff.

Woolley, John, T. "Linking Political and Monetary Union: The Maastricht Agenda and German Domestic Politics." In *The Political Economy of European Monetary Unification,* ed. Barry Eichengreen and Jeffry Frieden. Boulder CO.: Westview Press, 1994, pp. 67–86.

CHAPTER 9: SUBNATIONAL UNITS: FEDERALISM AND LOCAL GOVERNMENT

Billerbeck, Rudolf. "Socialists in Urban Politics: The German Case." *Social Research 47* (1980): 114–140.

Boehling, Rebecca. "U.S. Military Occupation, Grass Roots Democracy, and Local Government." In *American Policy and the Reconstruction of West Germany, 1945–1955,* ed. Harmut Lehmann. Cambridge and Washington: Cambridge University Press, 1993, pp. 281–306.

Fried, Robert C. "Party and Policy in West German Cities." *American Political Science Review 70,* no. 4 (March 1976): 11–24.

Gunlicks, Arthur B. "Administrative Centralization and Decentralization in the Making and Remaking of Modern Germany." *Review of Politics 46,* no. 3 (July 1984): 323–345.

———. *Local Government in the German Federal System.* Durham, NC, and London: Duke University Press, 1986.

———. "German Federalism after Unification: The Legal/Constitutional Response." *Publius 24,* no. 2 (Spring 1994): 81–98.

Häußermann, Hartmut. "Capitalist Futures and Socialist Legacies: Urban Development in East Germany Since 1990." *German Politics and Society 16,* no. 4 (Winter 1998): 87–102.

Heidenheimer, Arnold J. "Federalism and the Party System: The Case of West Germany." *American Political Science Review 52* (1958): 808–828.

Heisler, Barbara Schmitter. "Immigration and German Cities." *German Politics and Society 16,* no. 4 (Winter 1998): 18–41.

Hesse, Joachim J. "The Federal Republic of Germany: From Cooperative Federalism to Joint Policy-Making." *West European Politics 10,* no. 4 (October 1987): 70–87.

Jeffery, Charlie. "Party Politics and Territorial Representation in the Federal Republic of Germany." *West European Politics 22,* no. 2 (April 1999): 130–166.

Jeffery, Charlie, and Peter Savigear, eds. *German Federalism Today.* Leicester and London: Leicester University Press, 1991.

Klatt, Hartmut. "Forty Years of German Federalism: Past Trends and New Developments." *Publius 19,* no. 4 (Fall 1989): 185–202.

Lehmbruch, Gerhard. "Party and Federation in Germany: A Developmental Dilemma." *Government and Opposition 13* (1978): 151–177.

Lohmann, Susanne, et al. "Party Identification, Retrospective Voting, and Moderating Elections in a Federal System. West Germany, 1961–1989." *Comparative Political Studies 30,* no. 4 (August 1997): 420–449.

Pridham, Geoffrey. "A Nationalization Process? Federal Politics and State Elections in West Germany." *Government and Opposition 8,* no. 4 (Fall 1973): 455–473.

von Beyme, Klaus. "West Germany: Federalism." *International Political Science Review 5,* no. 4 (1984): 381–396.

CHAPTER 10: CONCLUSION: THE UNIFIED GERMAN POLITY FACES THE FUTURE

Anderson, Jeffrey J. *German Unification and European Union: The Domestic Politics of Integration Policy.* Cambridge and New York: Cambridge University Press, 1999.

Ash, Timothy Garton. *In Europe's Name. Germany and the Divided Continent.* New York: Random House, 1993.

———. "Germany's Choice." In *Foreign Affairs Agenda* 1995. New York: Council on Foreign Relations, 1995, pp. 68–84.

Asmus, Ronald D. "Is There a Peace Movement in the GDR?" *Orbis 27,* no. 2 (Summer 1983): 301–342.

———. *German Strategy and Opinion after the Wall, 1990–1993.* Santa Monica, CA: Rand Corporation, 1994.

Banchoff, Thomas. *The German Problem Transformed.* Ann Arbor, MI: University of Michigan Press, 1999.

Barnet, Richard J. *The Alliance: America-Europe-Japan. Makers of the Postwar World.* New York: Simon and Schuster, 1983.

Bulmer, Simon, and William Paterson. *The Federal Republic of Germany and the European Community.* London: Allen and Unwin, 1987.

Crane-Engel, Melinda. "Germany vs. Genocide." *New York Times Magazine,* October 30, 1994, pp. 56–59.

Dean, Jonathan. "Directions in Inner-German Relations." *Orbis 29,* no. 3 (Fall 1985): 609–632.

Duch, Raymond M. *Privatizing the Economy: Telecommunications Policy in Comparative Perspective.* Ann Arbor: University of Michigan Press, 1991.

Duffield, John S. *World Power Forsaken: Political Culture, International Institutions, and German Security Policy After Unification.* Stanford, CA: Stanford University Press, 1998.

Gatzke, Hans W. *Germany and the United States.* Cambridge, MA: Harvard University Press, 1980.

Geipel, Gary L. "Germany: Urgent Pressures, Quiet Change." *Current History* no. 610 (November 1994): 358–363.

Griffith, William E. "Bonn and Washington: From Deterioration to Crisis." *Orbis 26,* no. 1 (Spring 1982): 117–133.

Hacke, Christian. "The National Interests of the Federal Republic of Germany on the Threshold of the 21st Century." *Aussenpolitik 49,* no. 2 (1998): 5–25.

Hafner, Katie. "The House We Lived In." *New York Times Magazine,* (November 10, 1991), pp. 32ff.

———. "A Nation of Readers Dumps Its Writers." *New York Times Magazine,* January 10, 1993, pp. 22ff.

Hardach, Karl. *The Political Economy of Germany in the Twentieth Century.* Berkeley: University of California Press, 1980.

Hatch, Michael T. "Corporatism, Pluralism and Post-Industrial Politics: Nuclear Energy Policy in West Germany." *West European Politics 14,* no. 1 (January 1991): 73–97.

Helm Jutta. "Co-Determination in West Germany: What Differences Does It Make?" *West European Politics 9,* no. 1 (January 1986): 32–53.

Hesse, Jens J. "Germany." In *Postwar Politics in the G-7,* ed. Byron E. Shafer. Madison, WI: University of Wisconsin Press, 1996, pp. 156–182.

Joffe, Josef. "The View from Bonn: The Tacit Alliance." In *Eroding Empire: Western Relations with Eastern Europe,* ed. Lincoln Gordon, et al. Washington, D.C.: Brookings Institution, 1987, pp. 129–187.

———. "Peace and Populism: Why the European Anti-Nuclear Movement Failed." *International Security 11,* no. 4 (Spring 1987): 3–40.

Joppke, Christian. "Nuclear Power Struggles after Chernobyl: The Case of West Germany." *West European Politics 13,* no. 2 (April 1990): 178–191.

———. "Models of Statehood in the German Nuclear Energy Debate." *Comparative Political Studies 25,* no. 2 (July 1992): 251–280.

Kelleher, Catherine McArdle. "The Defense Policy of the Federal Republic of Germany." In *The Defense Policies of Nations,* ed. Douglas J. Murray and Paul R. Viotti. Baltimore and London: Johns Hopkins University Press, 1982, pp. 268–296.

Kreile, Michael. "The Political Economy of the New Germany." In *The New Germany and the New Europe,* ed. Paul B. Stares. Washington, D.C.: Brookings Institution, 1992, pp. 55–92.

Lindberg, Leon. *Politics and the Future of Industrial Society.* New York: David McKay, 1976.

Livingston, Robert Gerald. "United Germany: Bigger and Better." *Foreign Policy,* no. 87 (Summer 1992): 157–174.

McAdams, A. James. "Inter-German Detente: A New Balance." *Foreign Affairs 65,* no. 1 (Fall 1986): 136–153.

Newnham, Randall. "The Price of German Unity: The Role of Economic Aid in the German Soviet Negotiations." *German Studies Review 22,* no. 3 (October 1999): 421–446.

Rattinger, Hans. "The Federal Republic of Germany: Much Ado about (Almost) Nothing." In *The Public and Atlantic Defense,* ed. Gregory Flynn and Hans Rattinger. Totowa, NJ: Rowman and Allanheld, 1985, pp. 101–174.

Riemer, Jeremiah M. "West German Crisis Management: Stability and Change in the Post Keynesian Age." In *Political Economy in Advanced Industrial Societies,* eds. Norman J. Vig and Stephen E. Schier. New York and London: Holmes and Meier, 1985, pp. 229–254.

Schweigler, Gebhard. *West German Foreign Policy: The Domestic Setting.* New York: Praeger, 1984.

Sinn, Gerlinde, and Hans-Werner Sinn. *Jumpstart: The Economic Unification of Germany.* Cambridge, MA: MIT Press, 1993.

Sodaro, Michael J. *Moscow, Germany, and the West from Khruschev to Gorbachev.* Ithaca and London: Cornell University Press, 1991.

Stares, Paul B., ed. *The New Germany and the New Europe.* Washington, D.C.: Brookings Institution, 1992.

Stent, Angela E. *Russia and Germany Reborn: Unification, the Soviet Collapse and the New Europe.* Princeton, NJ: Princeton University Press, 1999.

Von Beyme, Klaus. "The Effects of Reunification on German Democracy: A Preliminary Evaluation of a Great Social Experiment." *Government and Opposition 27,* no. 2 (Spring 1992): 158–176.

Wallander, Celeste A. *Mortal Friends, Best Enemies: German-Russian Cooperation After the Cold War.* Ithaca, NY: Cornell University Press, 1999.

Zelikow, Philip, and Condoleezza Rice. *Germany Unified and Europe Transformed.* Cambridge, MA: Harvard University Press, 1995.

Index

Parliament: attitudes toward, 81–82, 180
  in Frankfurt, 3–4
  in Second Reich, 4–5. *See also*
    Bundesrat; Bundestag; Legislation;
    Reichstag
Parliamentary Council (1948), 15
Parliamentary investigations, 178–179
Particularism, 46–47, 246. *See also* States
Parties, political. *See also* Christian Demo-
    cratic Union; Free Democratic party;
    Green political party; Party of Demo-
    cratic Socialism; Social Democratic
    party
  attitudes toward, 82, 111–112
  in Basic Law, 110–111
  in East Germany, 18
  influence on media of, 67–68
  origins of, 109–112
Party of Democratic Socialism/Left List,
    41, 129–130, 147–148. *See also* So-
    cialist Unity Party; Radical Left
Party discipline in parliament, 175
Party preference, 161–163
Party state, 109–112
Party systems in states, 251–252
Peace movement, 27, 87–88
  Green political party and, 127
  Helmut Schmidt and, 120, 195–196
  military and, 190
  Social Democratic party and, 120
Pöhl, Karl Otto, 224–225
Poland, and East German refugees, 24–25
Police, 93, 244, 256–258
  in East Germany, 40
Political asylum, 95–96, 102
Political culture
  antisystem sentiment and, 77–80
  changes in, 74–82
  conflict and, 81
  definition of, 73
  democratic values and, 80–86
  elites and, 81–82
  founding of Federal Republic and, 15,
    74–772
  German Democratic Republic, 82–86
  leadership and, 74–75
  national division and, 75–76
  national identity and, 74–77
  occupation and, 75
  party competition and, 81
  performance of system and, 80–86
  political education and, 80
  privatization and, 14–15, 58–60
  representation and parliament, 81–82

unification and, 37–40, 82–86
  Weimar Republic and, 73
Political development, 280–281
  past political systems and, 77–80
Political participation. *See also* Citizen ini-
    tiative groups; Interest in politics; Po-
    litical culture; Voting behavior
  new forms of, 87–88
  voter involvement in campaigns,
    152–153
Political prisoners, 40
Population of Federal Republic, 43–44
  unification and, 44
Pornography laws, 140
Positive vote of no-confidence, 185–186
    See also Bundestag; Federal Chan-
    cellor
President. *See* Federal President
Press, 65–66. *See also* Television and Radio
Private Employment Agencies, 222–223
Privatization, 218–219
Proportional electoral system, 146–150. *See
    also* Electoral law; Free Democratic
    party
Prussia, rise of, 3–4. *See also* Bismarck,
    Otto von

Question hour in Bundestag, 178

Radical left, 103–105. *See also* Grand Coali-
    tion; Party of Democratic Socialism
    (PDS); Political Culture; Terrorism;
Radical right, 102–103. *See also* National
    Democratic Party (NPD); Political cul-
    ture; Republicans
Radicals. *See also* Civil service
  civil liberties and, 90–92
Rau, Johannes 120–121, 167, 203, 253
Reagan, Ronald, 76, 197
Rechtsstaat, 89. *See also* Civil liberties; Po-
    litical culture
Red Army Faction (RAF), 104–105
  Stasi and, 19
Redistribution, socioeconomic, 268–271
Refugees, 23–26, 100–101. *See also* Popu-
    lation of Federal Republic
Regional economic development, 244–245
Reichstag, 109, 173–174. *See also* Bun-
    destag; Parliament
Religion. *See also* Churches
  beliefs in, 56–58
  party preference and, 161–162, 165
Republicans (Reps), 102. *See also* Radical
    Right